Introducing the
UNIX System

Introducing the UNIX System

Henry McGilton

Rachel Morgan

McGRAW-HILL BOOK COMPANY

New York   St. Louis   San Francisco   Auckland
Bogotá   Hamburg   Johannesburg   London
Madrid   Mexico   Montreal   New Delhi
Panama   Paris   São Paulo   Singapore
Sydney   Tokyo   Toronto

Library of Congress Cataloging in Publication Data

McGilton, Henry.
  Introducing the UNIX System.

  Includes index.
  1. UNIX (Computer system)   I. Morgan, Rachel.
II. Title.
QA76.8.U65M38 1983   001.64′4   82-21640
ISBN 0-07-045001-3

UNIX is a trademark of Bell Laboratories.

Scribe is a trademark of UNI-LOGIC.

Zilog is a trademark of Zilog, Incorporated.

DEC, PDP, and VAX are trademarks of
Digital Equipment Corporation.

13 14 15 DODO 8 9 8 7 6

ISBN 0-07-045001-3

Printed and bound by R. R. Donnelley & Sons Company.

Contents

Preface

It is probably true that the UNIX* operating system has extensive documentation, since most things are written down somewhere. The problem is that an inexperienced user usually does not know where to look for a particular subject, and even when the requisite subject matter has been found, it is sometimes hard to understand.

This book sets out to lead the beginner by the hand, to show how to use the UNIX system in a simple fashion, and how to gain more information by reading the available documentation. For the user with some experience, this book shows how to use some of the more sophisticated programs provided on UNIX systems.

Caveat

This book is not a substitute for the existing UNIX system documentation, it is a supplement to it.

This book is based upon the authors' experience with a number of different UNIX systems. The bulk of this book is directed towards the UNIX system version 7. But since the Berkeley version of the UNIX system is so popular, there are frequent references to that system, in addition to a chapter describing its major features. In any case, the reader should be aware that any given UNIX system is likely to be slightly different from others, and so the UNIX Programmer's Manual should be at hand (even if it's only propping up your terminal) while using this book as a primer on the UNIX system.

Before you dip into the body of this book, you are encouraged to read through the table of contents. Although reading the table of contents is not normally the first thing you might think of doing with a book, the table of contents in this book is arranged such that it represents an overview of the topics and materials discussed herein.

---

* UNIX is a trademark of Bell Laboratories.

Who This Book is For

This book is an introductory guide for users who are new to the UNIX system. Although the UNIX operating system and its myriad utilities are comprehensively documented, that documentation is mostly in the form of reference materials, "memory joggers", and "cheat sheets".

Additionally, the commands for handling files, getting information, and processing text, tend to have short and sometimes cryptic names, such as **ls**, **grep**, **rm**, and so on. The system itself, and its many utilities, are often terse in their interactions with users.

This book provides a bridge for users who have never used the UNIX system before, to help them over the initial hurdles of learning this new and powerful computer tool.

Readers with some experience of the UNIX system can gain a better understanding of the UNIX system and its extensive but sometimes cryptic documentation. Experienced users will probably find that the logical arrangement of subject matter in this book is useful.

Educators should find this book suitable for course material, either about the UNIX system itself, or when using the UNIX operating system as a vehicle for other topics.

How This Book is Organized

Describing an operating system such as the UNIX system brings you, the reader, the problem of trying to learn everything at once; it brings us, the writers, the problem of trying to tell you everything at the same time. There is a certain core of knowledge which you must grasp, before the rest becomes clear.

For this reason, this book is really in two major parts. The essential knowledge is contained in chapters 2, 3, and 4. These chapters describe the key concepts behind the UNIX system. You should read these introductory chapters on the basics of the UNIX system, and learn how to log on (gain access to the system), learn about the directory structure and the file system, and the ideas of standard files and processes. Since there is no substitute for hands-on experience we suggest you should, if possible, follow the examples given while at a terminal connected to a real UNIX operating system.

Chapter 2 — "Getting Started on the UNIX System" introduces the basic notions of the UNIX system, such as how to gain access to the system, the notions of passwords, correcting typing errors, the format of commands, and how to find your way around the UNIX Programmer's manual.

Chapter 3—"Directories and Files" describes the file system and the directory structure. This chapter covers the way in which you can move around in the file system, get information about directories, and how to create and remove directories. It discusses the rules for assigning names to files and directories. The basic commands needed to create, copy, rename, and remove files are covered in this chapter.

Chapter 4—"Commands and Standard Files" covers the ways in which the UNIX system and its utilities communicate with your terminal and handle files. In this chapter you can learn how input to and output from a utility can be "redirected" to somewhere other than its standard places. You can also learn the way in which utilities can be hooked together, one after the other, in the form of a "pipeline".

Once you have explored the ideas presented in those three chapters, the rest is relatively easy going, for everything else in the UNIX operating system is built upon those concepts.

The remainder of the book discusses the utilities available, and the kinds of things you can do with them. We describe the UNIX system and its capabilities by means of a coherent thread of examples. The examples are introduced in a semi-tutorial fashion, starting with simple examples, and working to more complicated ones.

Chapter 5—"User to User Communication" covers the facilities by which users can communicate with each other, using the system's electronic mail utilities.

Chapter 6—"Text Manipulation" introduces some of the powerful tools for looking at files of text in various ways. In this chapter you can find out how to print a file (get a "hard copy" of a file), how to select lines from a file, and how to sort a file in any way you want, and more.

Chapter 7—"The Ed and Sed Editors" describes how to use **ed** (the basic UNIX text editor), and **sed** (the stream editor). These two editors are supplied with every UNIX system, and some knowledge of their features is a prerequisite to using many of the other tools on the system.

Chapter 8—"The Ex and Vi Editors" describes the **ex** text editor, and the **vi** display editor. These editors derive from the Berkeley version of the UNIX system, but are becoming available on many UNIX systems.

Chapter 9—"Formatting Documents" is a simple introduction to the **nroff** text formatter, which generates neatly formatted documents from unformatted text files.

Chapter 10—"More Formatting Tools" expands upon the ideas introduced in chapter 9 and introduces the way in which *macro packages* can enhance the capabilities of **nroff**. We also cover some of the other formatting tools such as **tbl** (a table layout aid).

In chapter 11 — "Programming the Shell", we describe how you can easily create your own commands, by using other commands in combination. This chapter covers the concepts of programming the Shell, to create new commands and tools.

Chapter 12 — "Tools for Software Development" provides a summary of programming tools available to the programmer, to aid the software development process.

Chapter 13 — "The UNIX System at Berkeley" gives an overview of the Berkeley version of the UNIX operating system. The Computer Science department at the University of California at Berkeley has made many modifications to the UNIX system, such that there is essentially a new genus, popularly called "Berkeley UNIX".

Chapter 14 — "UNIX System Management Guide" covers subjects of interest to anyone who might have to do the day-to-day job of caring for and feeding a UNIX system.

We have tried to show not only the facilities, commands, and utilities of the UNIX system, but what they might be used for. We use the examples to illustrate how the various utilities can be applied to transform text files in useful ways. We illustrate using the UNIX system by successively introducing more of the system's capabilities on a chapter-by-chapter basis. Each set of new capabilities uses material which has gone before. This ordering of material is part of the philosophy behind the UNIX system: to build upon what went before.

We have also tried to show areas where the misspelling of a command or a filename, or the misuse of a command, might give rise to error responses from the system. Therefore, as you read through the examples, you will find many illustrations of the form:

"If you do *this*, you will get *that* result, and here is a possible reason"

We believe that this is a positive approach to learning a new system. Many beginners get discouraged when the results of a command are not what they expected, and they have no idea why, or what to do next. In this book we have tried to remedy that situation.

There are many variations of the UNIX system out in the world. This book is based upon the authors' experiences with the UNIX system version 7, and the Berkeley version of the UNIX system. It is not our intent that you become an eclectic expert on these systems, but rather that you be aware that there are differences between versions of the UNIX system. We try to make you aware of these differences as you peruse the book.

Acknowledgments

There are many people we wish to thank for all their help.

First, thanks must go to Brian Reid for inventing **SCRIBE**, and to Mark of the Unicorn for implementing the **Scribble** subset on CP/M systems. These brilliant formatters were used to develop this book.

Aspen Software deserve thanks for manufacturing the excellent **Proofrdr** and **Grammatik** packages which eased the job of catching spelling mistakes and grammatical errors.

Most deserving of our thanks are the many friends and colleagues who encouraged us, proofread for us and corrected our blunders.

We owe special thanks to Doris Stoessel for her excellent proofreading and many suggestions for improvements.

1 Introduction

Software stands between the user and the machine.   *—HARLAN D. MILLS*

With the nicely ambiguous statement above, Doctor Harlan Mills of IBM's Federal Systems Division points out that software, like Mr. Hyde and Dr. Jekyll, can present different aspects to the users of a computer system. The software can either act as a shield against the idiosyncracies of the machine, aiding the users in their daily endeavors; or the software can stand in the way, presenting the users with Herculean labors in trying to get the job done.

This book is about the UNIX* system, a unique computer operating system in the category of help rather than hindrance. The UNIX system is "lean and clean", built around a small but powerful set of mechanisms which can be combined to provide a working environment of considerable power and effectiveness. This working environment, the UNIX operating system, has proved itself to be of great convenience to people from fields as diverse as publishing, word processing, aerospace, computer science, and software development.

The UNIX operating system developed from the Computing Science Research Group at Bell Laboratories in New Jersey. It is said that the creators of the UNIX system had this objective in mind:

---

* UNIX is a trademark of Bell Laboratories.

to create a computing environment where they themselves [the staff of the Computing Science Research Group] could comfortably and effectively pursue their own work — programming research.*

Because of the direction of the work at Bell Laboratories, the UNIX system turns out to be particularly useful both for developing computer software, and for producing documents. Both of these applications need many and varied tools for processing files of text and numbers, and the UNIX system is particularly rich in this area. The UNIX operating system comes equipped with text manipulation tools, documentation processing utilities, an electronic mail system, and a flexible file system to hold everything together.

Until 1980, the UNIX system was mostly confined to an environment consisting of university computer science departments, research laboratories connected with the Department of Defense Advanced Research Projects Agency (ARPA), and various industrial research and development organizations. With the widening of the installed base of the UNIX operating system to small machines such as those using the Motorola MC68000 and the Zilog Z8000 microprocessors, the market for this popular operating system now extends to the small business, office, and home environments.

This book is an introductory guide for users who are new to the UNIX system. The remainder of this chapter discusses the overall organization of a computer, the need for software to run that computer, and describes the way in which the UNIX operating system meets those needs.

On its own, a computer system is just a useless collection of metal, silicon, communications equipment, and magnetic media. It is the application programs which make a computer system useful to its users. Applications can range from word processing, through writing compilers, to generating new operating systems.

To exploit the communications, data storage, and information processing capabilities of the computer "hardware", the applications software requires some form of overseer, which can handle the details of managing the hardware resources, accessing the files, and interacting with the users. These supervisory functions are the job of the "operating system", which in this case, is the UNIX operating system.

Operating systems come in many shapes, sizes and guises. All operating systems have more or less the same function, namely to hold the ring between all the different hardware resources of a computer system in such a way that users can get work done. After all,

---

* Bell System Technical Journal, July-August 1978, quoted with permission from Bell Laboratories.

getting the job done faster, or easier, or cheaper, is the putative reason we use computers in the first place.

The UNIX system is a relatively "small" operating system. This is not to say that the UNIX system is poor in capability. On the contrary, it is constructed from a few basic ideas, which can be combined to form a user environment of considerable power. The UNIX operating system manages the resources of your computer system to perform useful work on your behalf. It is composed of three major parts:

the **Kernel**   is that part of the system which manages the resources of whatever computer system it lives on, to keep track of the disks, tapes, printers, terminals, communication lines, and any other devices.

the **File System**   is the organizing structure for data. The file system is perhaps the most important part of the UNIX operating system. Chapter 3 discusses the directory structure and the file system. The file system goes beyond being a simple repository for data, and provides the means of organizing the layout of the data storage in complex ways.

the **Shell**   is the command interpreter. Although the Shell is just a utility program, and is not properly a part of the system, it is the part that the user sees. The Shell listens to your terminal, and translates your requests into actions on the part of the kernel and the many utility programs.

The UNIX system is an *interactive* operating system. This means that you type commands, the system obeys the commands and displays appropriate responses, you type some more commands, the system does the work and responds, and so on.

The UNIX system is a *multi-tasking* operating system. This means that the system can perform several tasks — called *processes* — at the same time. The multi-tasking feature means that you can give the system one or more tasks to be done "in the background", and then you can get on with something else without having to wait for the task to finish.

The UNIX system is also a *multi-user* operating system. This means that more than one person can use the system at the same time. The multi-user aspect comes as a natural consequence of the multi-tasking feature just described: the system can attend to more than one user at a time just as easily as it can do more than one job at a time for one user. The multi-user facet means that groups of people can easily work together, sharing information and common utilities through the file system. Of course, if you run a UNIX operating system on a small personal computer you might be the only user, but the multi-tasking feature means that you can have more than one job going concurrently.

The UNIX system maintains a *file system* where users can store and retrieve information in named chunks called *files*. The organization of UNIX's file system is called a *hierarchical* file system, sometimes called a tree-structured file system.

A hierarchical organization means that there is a special kind of file called a *directory*. Instead of holding users' data, a directory actually contains lists of file names, and signposts to where the files can be found in the file system. On the UNIX system, this process can be carried to arbitrary limits, so that a directory can have subdirectories which in turn can have more sub-directories, and so on.

Understanding how to use the capabilities that the file system offers is perhaps the most important part of using the UNIX system effectively.

The *Shell* is a program that listens to your terminal and accepts and interprets the commands you type. The Shell interprets the commands and turns them into requests to the underlying kernel, to perform the work you want. Not all versions of the UNIX system have the same Shell. There are several popular Shells in existence. Some installations support more than one Shell, users can select which Shell they want to use.

In addition to the "core" of the UNIX operating system described above (the kernel, Shell, and file system), the UNIX system comes equipped with a large number of utilities (tools) to help users get started with useful applications right away.

A large proportion of the utilities are devoted to manipulating text files in one form or another. There are text manipulation tools such as **grep** for selecting lines from a file according to specific criteria; tools like **ed**, **sed**, **tr**, **rpl**, and **awk** for selectively changing the contents of a file; there are tools such as **sort** and **uniq** for rearranging the order of lines in a file.

Then there are utilities for formatting documents, such as **nroff** (a text formatter), **troff** (a version of **nroff** oriented towards a photo-typesetter), **eqn** (for setting mathematical equations), and **tbl** (for laying out tabular material).

There are various programming languages such as **C**, Pascal, FORTRAN, SNOBOL, BASIC and others. There are interactive arithmetic "calculators", **bc** and **dc**.

Then, as befits a system geared up for programming research, there are tools such as **make** for managing large amounts of program source-text, and advanced aids such as **lex** and **yacc** for building compilers and other language products.

The above is by no means an exhaustive list of the facilities available. There are also aids to using the UNIX system itself, such as **who**, to find out who is using the system, **mail**, for user to user communication, and lots more.

All of these utilities and tools comprise what is collectively called the UNIX operating system. In addition, by using the facilities which the Shell provides, it is very easy to tailor tools to fit your own special requirements.

1.1 UNIX System Documentation

The UNIX system is extensively documented with three (sometimes more) thick books. The physical bulk of the UNIX system manuals is not an indication of complexity. The UNIX system is in fact a fairly simple and elegant system, on which there exist many things which must be documented.

Any given user will probably only use a small fraction of the total collection of available utilities. The problem is to find the ones that will be useful to you. This can sometimes be a big job, because the utilities are documented in alphabetical order, by name rather than by function. Therefore, this book sets out to guide you through what is in the UNIX system, and show you the more useful commands.

Chapter 2 of this book — "Getting Started on the UNIX System", has some discussion on how to read the UNIX manuals, and how to get more information.

This book is not intended to replace the existing UNIX system manuals. It is a guide to the basics of the system, and how to find your way through the manuals that come with the UNIX system. Because of this, you will frequently find the phrase:

Refer to the UNIX Programmers' Manual

to remind you that this book is a supplement to the existing documentation, not a replacement for it.

1.2 Variations on the UNIX System

The UNIX operating system is an evolving system. As it was distributed into the world, various groups of people made changes. The major core is more or less the same wherever you go, but there are cultural differences.

When the DEC VAX line of computers came along, the UNIX operating was transported onto the VAX. This version is called UNIX/32V, sometimes referred to as UNIX V32.

The University of California at Berkeley has a group of programmers who have made many changes to the standard UNIX system, and so there is a popular variation called "Berkeley UNIX".

Since its inception in 1969, the UNIX System has spread to more than 3000 installations. It is now fairly evident that the UNIX system may well become the *de-facto* standard operating system for 16-bit (and possibly for 32-bit) microcomputer and minicomputer systems.

What can account for this widespread acceptance? The key elements are discussed below. They represent our observations of the UNIX operating system, as compared with some of the major time-sharing systems.

People who use time-sharing systems really want to share information, not computer time. Most time-sharing systems overlook this point, and have "security features" which make it very difficult, or sometimes impossible, for people who need to work together to share information. The UNIX operating system provides a particularly good environment for groups of people working together on the same project or related projects. Although the UNIX system has security features, they do not obtrude.

Software development is a specialized application, just like computer-aided design, or payroll processing, or accounting, or inventory control, or seismic data analysis. While there are many application packages out there for specific applications, most operating systems don't cater to the software developers at all. The UNIX operating system evolved in a Computer Science Research Environment, so it is relatively rich in programming tools.

In any cooperative venture (computer-aided design, software development), people and groups might require new tools or variations on old tools. The UNIX system file organization and the Shell make it easy to tailor tools for new applications. Such tools can then be easily made available to all users; there is no special "magic" about making and introducing new tools. By comparison, most major time-sharing systems do not cater to sharing tools. Their security features tend to get in the way of doing this, and they are not especially geared up for cooperative work.

Finding out what's going on in a time-sharing system is important. The UNIX system is open about what's happening in the system, who is using the system, and what jobs are waiting for resources such as printers. This must be viewed as a positive feature: experience shows that users can and do plan their use of the system when they can determine how heavily or lightly the system is being used.

Most operating systems are written for one specific machine or "architecture". It is a formidable undertaking to consider moving such an operating system to another computer. By contrast, the UNIX system is highly portable, because it is written in the C programming language. It has been implemented on at least ten different machine ranges, such as the DEC PDP-11 series, the DEC VAX series, on the Honeywell 6070, IBM System 370, Amdahl 470 series, on the Perkin-Elmer line, and of late, on the Zilog Z8000 and the Motorola MC68000. Because the UNIX system is not the product of a computer manufacturer, there is no axe to grind or wish to "lock in" the user community to any given hardware.

Compared with other time-sharing systems, the UNIX system is an easy one to work on, and to get work done on. Nothing is perfect, and the UNIX system has its faults, but getting in the way of the user is not one of them. Some people even think that the system takes the policy of self-effacement too far, since it does nothing to stop the user from doing stupid things. In general, though, the features that make the UNIX system unique are a help rather than a hindrance. Above all, the UNIX system provides an environment for tool-using and tool-building. No matter what the application — documentation, business, or software development — the UNIX operating system supplies an extensive set of tools to assist these processes. Just about any tool you need is there. If it isn't, you will find that it is very easy to construct the process you want by connecting together existing tools.

This, then, is the UNIX operating system. We hope that you will enjoy using the UNIX system, and gain as much from reading this book as we did from writing it.

2 Getting Started on the UNIX System

This chapter covers some of the most basic issues on how to deal with the UNIX system. First we show you how to get signed on with (gain access to) the UNIX system. This topic includes the ideas of user name and password. Then we follow with a section concerned with correcting typing mistakes. After that there are examples of some simple commands, to introduce the basic format of UNIX system commands. In this section we also introduce the idea of arguments to commands, and options which modify the behavior of commands. Finally, we give guidelines to help you find your way around in the UNIX Programmer's Manual.

It is hard for anyone to learn about a new computer system in the abstract, so the best way to learn how to use the UNIX system is to relax in front of a terminal connected to a real UNIX system, armed with a copy of this book, a glass of champagne, and the UNIX Programmer's Manuals close at hand.

2.1 User Names and Passwords

Everyone who uses the UNIX system is given a special "user name" to use when signing on to the system. A user name is also quite often called an "account", since in many installations someone is keeping an account of usage by different people and groups.

In practice, one person might have several user names; different names would be used when using the system for different purposes. For example, if Joe Mugg is responsible for payroll, he would probably use the name "joe" while developing new accounting programs; but for running the finished programs to compute people's take-home pay he would use a different user name, say "payroll".

Several people working on related things can be grouped together on the system, and the group can be allocated a group name or group identity.

One of the users on any given UNIX system is called the "super-user". This is the person who has the administrative duties of assigning new user names, and generally looking after the system. The super-user has the name "root" as the user name.

In addition to your user name, you can also have a password. This is a string of characters which you type to gain access to the system. But, whereas your user name is assigned by the super-user, your password is your own choice entirely. You can change your password at any time, and nobody, not even the super-user, can figure out what it is. These topics are expanded further in the "Sign On" section which follows.

2.2 Signing On to the UNIX System

To gain access to a UNIX system, so that you can use its facilities, you must go through a process called "signing on". This process is usually known as "logging in", or sometimes "logging on".

In the discussion to follow, we assume that the terminal which you are using is connected directly ("hard-wired") to the UNIX system in question. On some systems, you have to dial up over a telephone line, via a modem, to gain access. We ignore this aspect for the time being, and assume that the terminal is already connected and ready to go.

When you approach a terminal connected to a UNIX system, it should be displaying a message which looks something like:

```
Wonderful Widgets Co. UNIX System
;login:
```

Some UNIX systems don't have any initial display which indicates whose company it is, and some systems display "User" instead of "login". The exact details of this message differ from system to system, but they do not affect the actions you have to perform.

To log in to the system you simply type your user name, and then press the carriage-return key (labelled RETURN, or ENTER, or NEWLINE). Notice that as you type in your user name, what you type is displayed on the terminal screen. With very few exceptions, the UNIX system generally echoes (plays back to you) what you type. In all the examples in this book, what you type is shown in **bold face print**. When you have typed your user name, the system responds by asking you for your password, thus:

```
Wonderful Widgets Co. UNIX System
;login: maryann
password: wizard
```

Type in your password, then press the RETURN key. If you don't have a password, simply press the RETURN key. We show the type in of the password in shadow, because in a real system, your password is not echoed as you type it, so nothing appears on the screen. This is because your password is private and anyone who might happen to be looking over your shoulder should not be able to see it.

If you don't know, or have forgotten, your password, find a "super-user", a UNIX system administrator who can make your password anything you like. You can change your password later for privacy.

When you have typed in your user name and password, the system checks that you are indeed a known user of the system, and that you have given the correct password.

Some UNIX systems check for a known user as soon as the user name has been entered, those systems can also check whether or not that user actually has a password. If the user does not have a password, the request for "password" does not appear.

If for any reason your login is not correct, the system displays a message to that effect:

```
Wonderful Widgets Co. UNIX System
;login: maryan
password: wizard
Login incorrect
;login:
```

Getting a "Login incorrect" message can happen for a number of reasons. One way to get it wrong is to misspell either your user name or your password. In the example above, one "n" was left out of the user name.

Another possibility is that you might not even have an account on that particular UNIX system. This sometimes happens when you try to log in before the super-user has had time to assign your user name and password.

If you are at an installation where there is more than one UNIX system available, you might be trying to log in to the wrong one!

It might also happen that you log in correctly, but a different problem arises:

```
Wonderful Widgets Co. UNIX System
;login: maryann
password: wizard
No directory
;login:
```

As we shall explain in chapter 3 — "Directories and Files", there is a "home" directory associated with every user name on the system. If you get the response as above, it might be because the super-user did not assign a directory for you, or, the super-user might have misspelled the name of your login directory. In this case, you will have to go and see the super-user to have things set up correctly.

But let's be cheerful about this whole process and assume that you have logged in successfully. After you have logged in the system displays a prompt, which indicates that it is ready to do your bidding. Your terminal screen looks something like this:

```
Wonderful Widgets Co. UNIX System
;login: maryann
password: wizard
Last login: Fri Feb 12 08:05
$
```

The "Last login" message indicates the last time that your account was used. Some UNIX systems don't display this message, the presence or otherwise of the message is controlled by the System Administrator. If this is your first login session, the message displayed probably shows when the System Administrator set up your account. It is a good idea to check the message when you log in; if the date and time displayed are not in accord with your memory of when you last logged in, it could be that someone else is using your account.

Now that you've successfully logged in, you might want to know how to log out again. There is a short section, called "Signing Off", later in this chapter.

2.2.1 The UNIX System Prompt

The $ shown at the end of the above example is the system prompt. It tells you that the UNIX system is waiting for you to type a command. Every time the system has finished running a command and is listening to your terminal, it replies with the $ prompt.

Not all UNIX systems have the $ sign as the prompt. The version 7 UNIX system in general uses the dollar sign $ as the prompt. If you should happen to be using a version 6 UNIX system, or the Berkeley version of the UNIX system, the prompt is usually the % character.

On other UNIX systems, the prompt might be a whole word rather than a single character. In places where several UNIX systems form a network, the prompt often indicates which system you are using.

Most UNIX systems have the capability to let you choose your own prompt. If you have several different login-names on your system, you might want to set up your prompt so that it reminds you which user name you are currently logged in as.

In the examples we give in this book, we use the $ prompt. We generally show the prompt before what you type, and after the system's response. Also, we will show what you type in **boldface** text, and what the system types in normal type.

Remember that at the end of every line you type at the UNIX system, you have to press the RETURN key before the system sees that input. We do not explicitly show the RETURN at the end of the lines in our examples.

2.2.2 Notes and Cautions on Login

Unless you want to talk to your UNIX system entirely in upper case, LIKE THIS, do not type your user name in upper case, not even the initial letter. If you do, the system assumes that you are using a terminal that only has upper case, and henceforth talks to you only in CAPITAL LETTERS:

```
Wonderful Widgets Co. UNIX System
;login: Maryann
PASSWORD:
```

Because your password doesn't appear on the terminal as you type it, make sure that your password is easy to type. It is very frustrating to have to make several attempts at logging in, simply because you can't get your password right. You can change your password using the **passwd** command. We show you how to do this later in this chapter.

If you make any mistakes while typing your user name or password at login time, you probably use the backspace character (or possibly the # character) to erase the previous character, and the control-X character (or possibly the @ character) to kill the entire line. The general subject of correcting typing errors is covered a little later in this chapter, but we mentioned it here just to let you know that you can correct any typing errors at login time.

☞ On some UNIX systems, the # character and the @ character are used for erase and line-kill, which means that your user name and password should not contain these characters.

Some UNIX systems have a predefined limit on the number of times you can attempt to log in without getting it right. The actions taken if this limit is exceeded vary depending on the system. If you are accessing UNIX through a telephone modem, the system may well disconnect ("hang up on you"), and you have to dial again to get a connection.

2.2.3 Initial Password

Depending on the bureaucracy at your UNIX system installation, you might or might not have a password already assigned to you when you first get an account on the system.

In some installations you are not assigned a password, and you can set your own with the **passwd** command the first time you log in. Of course you can continue without a password if that suits you.

At other sites, the super-user assigns your password (sometimes of your choice, sometimes not) and it is up to you to change it if you want to.

2.2.4 Login Messages from the UNIX System

When you have typed your password, the system might well type out some messages before the $ prompt. These messages are usually information about the system: maybe some added features, or notification of planned maintenance shutdowns. Here is an example:

```
Wonderful Widgets Co. UNIX System
;login: maryann
password: wizard
Last login: Fri Feb 12 08:05
The system will be down this Saturday from 8am to 2pm
while we are doing Preventive Maintenance.
Filesystem /aa is VERY low on space ! ! !
Please inspect your files and remove moldy oldies.
$
```

This message is often called the message of the day. It appears every time you log in to the UNIX system.

Another form of initial message is concerned with the **mail** facility for inter-user communication.

```
Wonderful Widgets Co. UNIX System
;login: maryann
password: wizard
Last login: Fri Feb 12 08:05
You have mail.
$
```

This message means that someone has sent you mail through the **mail** facility. If there is a login message, it appears before any notification of mail. We cover the **mail** facility in chapter 5 — "User to User Communication".

2.3 Correcting Typing Mistakes

What do you do when you make a mistake when typing a command? For instance, suppose you wanted to use the **date** command to find the current date and time, and you typed this:

```
$ dste
```

Normally, to complete the command you would press the RETURN key, but in this case you realize that you have a spelling mistake. The easiest thing to do is to press the RETURN key anyway, and let the system try to run this mysterious **dste** command:

```
$ dste
dste: not found
$
```

on other UNIX systems, the response might be different:

```
$ dste
dste: command not found
$
```

The response to unrecognized commands is something else which varies from one UNIX system to another.

However, if there really was a **dste** command, you could be in trouble. It would be better to correct your command line, or tell the system to ignore it.

There are two characters you can use to tell the UNIX operating system you've made a mistake. The *erase* character erases the previously typed character. Erase is the backspace key on most systems. The *kill* character kills the entire line typed so far. On most systems, kill is the control-X key (but sometimes it is control-U).

But, you should be aware that on some older systems (and on those systems where the administration is not with it), the erase and kill characters are the # character and the @ character respectively. These can be changed to something sensible as we shall see.

An aside: the UNIX system began its life on systems where the terminals were Teletypes (slow hard-copy devices). Since a lot of these devices do not have a backspace key or any other form of control key, the system pre-empted some of the printing characters for control purposes. Although most UNIX systems today work on terminals with all the required controls, the legacy of the early days is still with us on some systems.

2.3.1 The Erase Character

On most UNIX systems, the character for erasing the previous character is the backspace character. This is labelled "backspace" or "BS" on some terminals, on others it is labelled as a left pointing arrow (a cursor control), and on some primitive terminals you have to type control-H.

To get a control character, you hold down the control key (marked CTRL on most terminals) while typing the character you want. For example, to get control-H, you hold down the key marked CTRL while you type "h". The control-H combination usually backspaces the cursor position on a terminal, but in general, the other control characters are non-printing characters. The control key is often marked CNTR, CNTRL, or sometimes even CONTROL. On most terminals, it is located somewhere on the left-hand side of the keyboard.

In printed documentation, it is conventional to use the "hat" (or "caret" or circumflex) character, ^ followed by a "whatever" character, to mean "control-whatever". For example ^H means you should type control-H (hold down the CONTROL key while pressing the **H** key). It doesn't mean type the separate characters ^ and **H**. In the examples in this book, we follow the convention of using the circumflex character ^ in examples, and we spell out the word "control" when talking about the examples.

Every time you type control-H the cursor moves one position to the left on the terminal screen. The erase character tells the system to ignore the last character you typed, two erases mean ignore the last two characters, and so on. So you could have corrected the misspelling:

```
$ dste^H^H^Hate
Sun Feb 14 11:35 PST 1982
$
```

The three control-H characters erase the "e", the "t", and the incorrect "s". The rest of the line is what should have been typed in the first place. As you type each control-H the cursor backspaces (moves to the left) one character on the screen. This can't be shown on a static display such as a page in a book, so the above example shows what you type, not what you see on your terminal screen.

If the erase character is a # and you need to enter a # literally, you have tell the UNIX system that this is really what you want, that you haven't made a mistake this time. This is achieved by preceding the # by a \. So to actually get # you have to type \#.

The \ is the escape character. It is used to remove any special meaning that the system might attach to the character following it.

2.3.2 The Line Kill Character

The line kill character at the end of a line means "kill", or "ignore the line typed so far". It tells the UNIX system that you didn't want it to obey the command line you have just typed.

On most UNIX systems, the line kill character is either control-X or control-U. The exact details differ from system to system. In this book, we use control-X as the line kill character. But be aware that on some older systems, the line kill character is the @ sign.

You don't have to type RETURN after the kill character. The system just ignores everything on that line so you can straight away type another command line. You do not get the $ sign prompt after typing the kill, unless you press the RETURN key. So, in our example:

```
$ dste^X
date
Sun Feb 14 11:35 PST 1982
$
```

As in the case of #, if the kill character is an @ sign and you really want a @, you have to escape it by typing \@.

2.3.3 Changing the Erase and Kill Characters with 'stty'

You can change the erase and kill characters to anything you like, using the **stty** command. This is especially valuable if you are on a system where the erase and kill characters are # and @. We are not going to go into all the details of **stty** at this point. We're just going to show you how to change erase and kill characters.

To change the erase character to control-H, you say:

```
$ stty erase ^H
$
```

If you wanted to change it back to #, you would say:

```
$ stty erase #
$
```

To change the kill character to control-U (as it is on some systems) you could say:

```
$ stty kill ^U
$
```

Now, when you type control-U, the system ignores everything on that command line.

You can change both characters in the same command:

```
$ stty erase ^H kill ^U
$
```

If you change the erase and kill characters during a login session, they only remain in effect until you log off the UNIX system. They then revert to whatever the system default is. Next time you log in you will have to give the **stty** command again. There is a way of getting commands executed automatically when you log in. This capability is exploited through a file called your "login profile", and is described in chapter 11 — "Programming the Shell".

Some versions of **stty** actually accept the literal characters " ^ " (caret), followed by "H", to mean control-H. This means that you type the **stty** command like this:

```
$ stty erase '^H'
$
```

Note that there are single quote signs around the argument. This is one of the places where you must use single quotes, and double quotes will not do. But again, the details differ from one system to another, and on some UNIX systems you don't need the quotes. These are the kinds of details which, unfortunately, you have to ferret out when you get onto a new UNIX system.

Some systems (for example, the Berkeley modified UNIX system) have a **tset** command which can be used to change the erase and kill characters. Saying:

```
% tset -e -k
%
```

sets the erase character to control-H and the kill character to control-X. Again, the changes are only effective while you are logged in. The above example shows the prompt as a percent sign, %; this is the usual system prompt on Berkeley UNIX.

If you make any mistakes while typing your user name or password at login time, you have to use whatever the system default erase and kill characters are, to correct the errors, even if your erase and kill characters are automatically set up in a login profile. This is because the system doesn't see the profile until after you have logged in.

2.4 Some Simple Commands

Let's start with a very simple command, one we have already seen, just one word to the UNIX system:

```
$ date
Sun Feb 14 11:38 PST 1982
$
```

Type the word **date**, followed by the RETURN key. All UNIX system command lines are terminated by pressing the RETURN key. The exact format of the date and time as printed by **date** varies from one system to another, but the result is the same: the system displays the current date and time (or, since the date and time can be changed by the super-user, what the UNIX operating system thinks is the current date and time).

Another simple one-word command tells you who is using the system:

```
$ who
sally     tty00   Feb 14 08:30
peter     tty02   Feb 14 08:32
henry     tty03   Feb 14 09:04
maryann   tty08   Feb 14 10:34
$
```

Again, the exact format of the system's reply varies from one UNIX system to another, but the information given is: who is logged on to the system, the system's name for the terminal they are logged on at, and the time they logged on. A variation of the **who** command is:

```
$ who am i
maryann   tty08   Feb 14 10:34
$
```

Here, we entered three words, the first word is the command **who**. The remaining words are *arguments* to that command. Arguments are separated from the command, and from each other, by one or more spaces. Arguments to commands are mostly names of files to be manipulated, but since we haven't described files yet, we are giving examples of those commands which don't use filenames.

At first sight, wanting to know who you are might seem like a dumb thing to do. But in some places, people share terminals, so if someone has not logged out, and you want to know who it is, this usage of **who** is how you find out who has abandoned the terminal.

In other cases, you may need to know your terminal identity to do other checks on the progress of jobs running on your behalf.

2.5 Format of UNIX System Commands

We have seen the general format of commands in the above example. It is a sequence of words (by which we mean non-blank characters), each word being separated from its neighbors by one or more spaces (blanks). The entire command is terminated by a newline character, which is produced when you press the RETURN key (the key marked LINEFEED or NL does it too).

The first word is the command itself, the remaining words are arguments to the command. There can be spaces before the command, and there can be spaces after the last argument, before the newline. Since spaces are used to separate the arguments, the arguments themselves must not contain spaces. If for some reason you have to give an argument containing a space, the entire argument should be surrounded with double quotes ("), or with single quotes or apostrophes ('). Do not use the grave accent (`) for this purpose. Apostrophe and grave are not the same character. Make sure that you know which is which. We show an example of this in chapter 6, when we describe the **pr** command.

Several commands can be typed on the same line by typing a semicolon (;) between them, thus:

```
$ who am i; date
maryann   tty08   Feb 14 10:34
Sun Feb 14 11:45 1982
$
```

There can be spaces on either side of the ; or not, it doesn't matter. The UNIX system obeys the **who** command first, then the **date** command. Notice that the system doesn't respond with its prompt character, $, until it has completed all the commands on that line.

2.5.1 Arguments to commands

For the most part, arguments to the UNIX system commands are one of three things:

Filename   the name of a file which the command is to manipulate in some way. Filenames can be up to fourteen characters long, and can consist of just about any characters. In practice, however, most file names are shorter and consist only of letters a-z, numbers 0-9 and some other characters such as underscore _, period . and minus sign -. On the UNIX system, uppercase letters and lowercase letters are considered different in filenames.

the system provides special "metacharacters" or "wild card characters" for filename matching, so that you can use a shorthand notation for working on groups of files at a time. The topics of filenames, file naming conventions, and wild-card matching, are covered in chapter 3 — "Directories and Files".

Option   this is a literal, usually introduced by a minus sign, for example **-al**. An option modifies the action of the command in some way, or gives details of exactly how the command is to operate. The exact effect of the option is different for each command. Some options are introduced by a plus sign rather than a minus, and some are not preceded by anything.

Expression   an expression describing a character string which is to be used as input to the command. In the simplest case the expression is the string itself. We describe string-matching expressions later, when we talk about the **grep** command.

Although we just described the types of arguments in the order: files, options, and expressions, generally the order of the arguments following the command is:

command   options   expression   filename(s)

but the exact order required for each command should be found by referring to the documentation for the specific command.

Here are some typical UNIX system commands to give you the flavors of the arguments. Don't bother about what the commands and their options actually do, just take note of the layout of the commands.

rm old.news bad.news
   a typical **rm** (remove files) command with two filename arguments. It removes the two files called 'old.news' and 'bad.news' from the file system.

rm −fr goodies.c baddies.o
   another **rm** command with two options (f and r), and two filename arguments.

grep "Sally Smith" people
   a fairly typical use of the **grep** command, (look for patterns in a file) where the first argument is an expression, and the second argument is a filename. The first argument is two words, so it is enclosed in quotes.

grep −v "Sally Smith" people
   the same **grep** command, except this time the first argument is an option.

As you read through the book, there are many examples of the different commands and their arguments.

2.5.2 Quoting Arguments to Commands

You will notice that the argument, "Sally Smith", on the **grep** command, above, was contained in quote signs, ("). Arguments to commands can be enclosed either in double quotes, or within single quote signs, ('). The single quote sign is the same character as the apostrophe.

In general, it usually doesn't matter which kinds of quotes you use. You could type the **grep** command either as:

```
$ grep "Sally Smith" people
```

with the argument in double quotes, or you could type it like this:

```
$ grep 'Sally Smith' people
```

with single quotes (apostrophes). Of course, if the argument already contains one kind of quote, (an apostrophe in the next example) you have to enclose the string in the other kind, like this:

```
$ grep "Sally Smith's Project" people
```

There are cases, however, when the Shell places some special inter-pretation on certain characters in arguments. For instance, when you get to chapter 3, you will see that the Shell uses some characters to provide the means to work with whole groups of files.

There are other cases where the Shell (the command-line inter-preter) assigns special meanings to characters even when they are enclosed in double quotes. The most likely candidate for special treatment is the dollar sign, $. If your argument contains a $ sign, it is wiser to enclose it in single quotes.

In general, the rules to follow are:

1. If a command doesn't work with an unquoted argument, enclose the argument within quote signs, (").

2. If that doesn't work either, use the single quote signs, (').

3. If that still doesn't work, "escape" any special characters by preceding them with the reverse slash character, (\ ).

4. If this still doesn't work, you should go find a UNIX system wizard who can help.

2.6 Changing Your Password
with 'passwd'

Everyone should have a password, and should change passwords at reasonably frequent intervals for security reasons. The command that changes your password (or installs one for you if you don't already have one) is **passwd**.

The **passwd** command is a little different from the ones we have been discussing, in that it is interactive. You simply type the command and **passwd** tells you what input it wants. A conversation with **passwd** goes something like this:

```
$ passwd
Changing password for maryann
Old password: wizard
New password: hazard
Retype new password: hazard
$
```

Notice that you have to type your new password twice. Because the system does not echo the passwords as you type them (illustrated by the shadowed print in the example), it asks for confirmation. If the second time you type it, it differs from the first, no action is taken. This prevents fumble-finger accidents getting into your password, which would make it difficult for you to log in next time.

Depending on which version of **passwd** is on your UNIX system, the command might or might not tell you about any rules pertaining to choice of passwords (such as restrictions on the length) before prompting for your new password. The rules are documented in the UNIX Programmer's Manual in any case.

There is a file called the password file, which contains an entry for each user of the UNIX system. Each entry consists of the user name, password and other interesting information about the user. The file can be accessed by all users, so to preserve the security of passwords, the passwords are encrypted (enciphered). This means that your password as it appears in the file looks nothing like what you type in response to the prompt "Password". The encryption of the password means that no one, not even the super-user, can figure out what it is by looking at the encrypted version, so you should not forget your password. It is recommended that you write your password on a piece of paper, then eat it with a champagne chaser: you shouldn't leave the piece of paper lying around where anyone could find it.

A description of the encryption process can be found under the command **crypt** in the UNIX Programmer's Manual.

When changing your password, there are a couple of things which can go wrong. The first is that your old password doesn't match what the system thinks it should be:

```
$ passwd
Changing password for maryann
Old password: blizzard
Sorry.
$
```

Here, Maryann typed the wrong password, and got the indicated response. It is also possible that you type a different new password on the first and second tries:

```
$ passwd
Changing password for maryann
Old password: hazard
New password: blizzard
Retype new password: blizzadr
Mismatch - password unchanged.
$
```

2.7 The Shell's Use of Special Characters

We have briefly stated that the Shell interprets some characters in special ways. Some of these characters are used for filename expansion, some are used inside the Shell itself, for substitution of arguments, and some are used to stop and start any display coming from a running program. We will just list these special characters here. The full discussions are to be found in chapters 3 and 11.

The backslash character \ is used everywhere, and is interpreted as an "escape" character. The backslash character nullifies the special meaning of any character which immediately follows it.

The Shell interprets the characters:

*, ?, [,], and −

as abbreviations for filename expansion. This subject is covered in chapter 3.

The Shell uses the dollar sign character $ for argument substitution. We discuss this in chapter 11.

The control-D character is used as a "log-out" signal to the Shell, and is an "end-of-text" signal to programs requesting input from the terminal.

The control-S and control-Q characters are used for stopping and re-starting output to the terminal. The DELETE or RUBOUT character is used for stopping a running command. These topics are discussed just below.

The moral of this section is: the special characters should be used with caution.

2.7.1 Halting Output Temporarily

The commands we have seen so far have produced very little in the way of output on the terminal, not more than a few lines. Quite frequently, the output of a command is very long, much more than will fit on a terminal screen, which holds only 24 lines. Unless you have a terminal which is slow enough for you to read things before they disappear off the top of the screen, you will want to stop the display temporarily, then continue when you've seen what you wanted.

Stopping the display temporarily is done by typing control-S (hold down the CTRL key while typing "s"). Control-S suspends the screen scrolling process. Whatever command is displaying to the screen is still running, only the display of the output to the screen is halted temporarily.

To resume displaying the command's output, you type control-Q. Output to the screen then continues until you type another control-S, or until the command is finished.

2.7.2 Stopping a Command

If the output of a command is very long, you may not want to see it all. For instance, if you simply want to check what the first few lines of a file look like, there is no need to display the entire file; and if the file is a long one it will take too much precious time to do so.

To completely stop (abandon) the command, you can hit the key marked BREAK (if there is one), or the RUBOUT key, or the DEL key. The command is interrupted and the system requests another command, so you see the system prompt $.

On some UNIX systems the character which interrupts a command can be set with **stty**, in much the same way as we could set control-H as the erase character. If you have this feature, we recommend you use it to change the interrupt character to control-C. This is particularly important if you are working over a phone line. On a bad line many spurious "delete" characters appear, each one of these causes the command you are currently running to be interrupted, so it's better to change to control-C if you can.

2.8 Signing Off

When you have finished working with the UNIX system, you can sign off ("logout", or "log off") simply by typing control-D when you see the $ sign. Control-D, at the start of a line of input, is the "end of text" character, and is used in many ways throughout the system, usually to indicate the end of something (your login session in this case). A special use of it is in response to the system prompt $.

Under those conditions, control-D has the effect of logging you off the system.

Some UNIX systems print the current time and date when you log off, but in general there is no indication that you have done so, except there is a new request for a log in:

```
$ ^D
Wonderful Widgets Co. UNIX System
;login:
```

If you are dialling into a UNIX system over a telephone line, it is possible that the logout will hang up the telephone, in which case you don't get any further requests for login.

2.9 How to Read the UNIX System Manuals

All commands are documented in a book called "UNIX Programmer's Manual". This is a large book and is usually bound in several separate volumes. The title is somewhat misleading: the book is useful to all users of the UNIX system, not just programmers.

The UNIX Programmer's Manual, Volume 1, is in eight sections:

1. Commands
2. System calls
3. Subroutines
4. Special files
5. File formats and conventions
6. Games
7. Macro packages and language conventions
8. Maintenance commands and procedures

In general, the only section needed by most users is the first one: "Commands", although the section on "Games" is interesting too. People concerned with the care and feeding of the UNIX system will need to refer to the last section: "Maintenance commands and procedures" (many commands in this section are only available to the super-user); people involved in word processing may need to refer to the penultimate section: "Macro packages and language conventions"; the remaining sections are usually used only by people involved in writing programs to run under the UNIX system.

Within each section the entries are arranged in alphabetical order. There is a table of contents which lists alphabetically the names of the commands in each section, and there is a "Permuted Index" which gives you the capability to look up commands by function rather than by name.

An example of a typical page from the UNIX Programmer's Manual is shown on the next page. It describes the **date** command, which you have already seen an example of.

Each entry for a command in the UNIX Programmer's Manual is described under these headings:

NAME   gives the name of the command and a brief description of what it does. Where there are alternative names for the command, these are listed.

SYNOPSIS   shows how the command is to be used. Possible options to the command and the type of expected argument(s) is indicated.

DESCRIPTION   gives more detail of what the command does, and how its action is modified by the options.

FILES   gives the names of any files which are important to the command.

SEE ALSO   refers to related commands or other documentation which could be useful to the reader.

DIAGNOSTICS   gives explanations of cryptic error messages which might occur if the command is misused.

BUGS   gives details of errors known to exist in the command, and sometimes tells you how to overcome these.

The NAME, SYNOPSIS and DESCRIPTION headings are present for all commands, the other headings might or might not be present, depending on whether there is any subject matter for that particular heading.

Perhaps the most important heading is SYNOPSIS, which shows how the command is to be used. Here is the synopsis for the **date** command:

```
SYNOPSIS
     date [yymmddhhmm[.ss]]
```

Under the SYNOPSIS heading, all command documentation uses these conventions:

- Words in **boldface** are considered to be literal and are typed exactly as shown. Options are usually literal. The command name is always shown as a literal.

- Square brackets around an argument indicate that it is optional and need not appear when the command is used.

- Where the word "file" appears in the SYNOPSIS, it always means a filename.

- Ellipses " .... " following an argument indicate that that type of argument may be repeated any number of times.

These conventions make it fairly easy to see the correct usage for each command. For example, if the SYNOPSIS of the **rm** (remove files) command is:

```
rm  [-fri]  file ...
```

it means that **rm** accepts three options (f, r, and i), which may be combined, and the command accepts any number of filenames. All of the following are acceptable uses of the **rm** command:

```
rm file1
rm file2 file3 file4 file5
rm -f file6 file7
rm -ri file8 file9 file10
```

An unacceptable form of the **rm** command would be

```
rm -i -i
```

where the option is specified twice, and no file names are given.

Another example of a synopsis is that for the **mail** command:

```
mail  [-r]  [-q]  [-p]  [-f file]
```

This **mail** command has four options. Each option must be given separately if used. **mail** only accepts one filename, which must be introduced with the -**f** option. So the following are all correct uses of the **mail** command:

```
mail -p
mail -r -p
mail -f file1
```

All of the above descriptions of the command documentation appears in the Introduction to the UNIX Programmer's Manual. However, experience has shown that very few people take the trouble to read that bit of the manual, so we are repeating it here for good measure.

```
date(1)                                                      date(1)
                         Version 1.1


NAME
     date - print and set the date

SYNOPSIS
     date [yymmddhhmm[.ss]]

DESCRIPTION
     If no argument is given, the current date and time are
     printed.  If an argument is given, the current date is
     set.  yy is the last two digits ˆf the year; the first
     mm is the month number; dd is the day number in the
     month; hh is the hour number (24 hour system); the
     second mm is the minute number; .ss is optional and is
     the seconds.  For example:

                date 10080045

     sets the date to Oct 8, 12:45 AM.  The year, month and
     day may be omitted, the current values being the
     defaults.  The system operates in GMT.  Date takes care
     of the conversion to and from local standard and
     daylight time.

FILES
     /usr/adm/wtmp to record time setting

SEE ALSO
     utmp(5)

DIAGNOSTICS
     `No permission' if you aren't the super-user and you try
     to change the date; `bad conversion' if the date set is
     syntactically incorrect.


7th edition                                                        1
```

Figure 2.1   Manual Page for the date Command

2.9.1 Print Manual Sections with 'man'

The UNIX Programmer's Manual itself is kept on the system. It is possible to get the documentation for any given command by using the **man** command.

The **man** command has many options to direct the results to various kinds of printers or phototypesetters. The normal action, in the absence of any option, is to display the specified page on the terminal. For example, to get the writeup for the **mesg** command, you would type the following:

```
$ man mesg
. . . . .
. . . . . writeup for the mesg command
            . . . . .
$
```

For a full-blown description of **man**, refer to the UNIX Programmer's Manual, or, alternatively, type:

```
$ man man
```

Be aware that if your UNIX system is running on a small computer system which has a limited amount of disk space, the documentation might not be on-line.

2.9.2 Table of Contents and the Permuted Index

At the front of the UNIX Programmer's Manual there is a table of contents, which shows every command and the entry under the NAME heading. An example of a table of contents entry is:

```
rm ..........................remove (unlink) files
```

The UNIX Programmer's Manual also has an index. The index is not necessarily in a form you might be familiar with. It is based upon an indexing strategy called Key-Word-In-Context, or KWIC. This index is often at the front of the UNIX Programmer's Manual, but is sometimes found at the back. The UNIX system documentation calls the KWIC index a "Permuted Index".

The Permuted Index is obtained by taking the one-line descriptions found under the NAME headings for the commands, and duplicating each line for each keyword in the line. All the lines are then sorted.

To give an example of the Permuted Index: suppose you wish to delete some files, and you need to find the name of the command to use. The way to do this is to look for a "keyword". In the Permuted Index, all the keywords appear just to the right of the centerline of the page. If you look up the keyword "files" in the Permuted Index, you will find the entry:

```
rm,rmdir - remove (unlink) files .... rm(1)
```

There will also be an entry under "remove"

```
rm,rmdir -- remove (unlink) files .... rm(1)
```

These entries tell you that the command you want to use is **rm**, and that it is documented in Section 1 of the manual. There is no entry for this command under the keyword "delete", because that word doesn't appear in the NAME entry. Sometimes you need to use a thesaurus in conjunction with the Permuted Index. The Permuted Index is constructed with the command **ptx** — if you want to know more detail, look up that command in Section 1 of the manual.

2.10 Summary

This chapter should have got you started with the basic ideas of accessing the UNIX system, how to correct typing mistakes, change your password, and the ideas of some simple commands. See if you can find out what the erase and kill characters normally are on your system. If you don't like them, see how you can get them changed. Try to find out the rules for user names and passwords on your system. See if you can get around whatever the password limitations are (you can on some versions of the UNIX system).

Now you should try exploring parts of the UNIX Programmer's Manual and any other documentation you have about your system. Look up **date**, **who**, and the other commands that we described.

Read some of the manual pages for commands other than those we described so far, and make sure you understand the conventions. Delve into the permuted index at random to see what's there. Look in the table of contents (if there is one).

The next chapter tells you about files, directories, the file system, and what you can do with it. A reasonable grasp of command syntax and the ideas of options will be helpful when you are exploring the file system.

3 Directories and Files

This chapter describes (rather than defines) the UNIX system file and directory structures, in terms of how you use it and the things you can do with it. We take the approach of first examining those files and directories already in the system before taking the step of creating new files and directories.

The UNIX system knows about three kinds of files, namely, directories, ordinary files, and special files. This chapter is concerned only with ordinary files and directories. Special files are outside the scope of this book.

In the most basic terms, a file is simply a container into which you can put data. The most important thing about a file is that it has a name by which you can refer to it. It is the container that has the name, not the data in the container. By using the container's name, commands work on the whole collection of data contained therein. The contents of a file can be displayed, files can be copied, they can be removed from file system, or they can be moved around in the file system.

A directory is a file containing information about other files and directories. It is probably easiest to think of a directory as a thing which "contains" files and other directories. A directory "contained" within another directory is called a subdirectory. The subdirectories can themselves contain files and more subdirectories. Directories in the UNIX operating system supply the glue or matrix which superimposes a structure on the file system as a whole. In this chapter we also discuss the commands that work with directories.

In everyday terms, a directory has been compared to a filing cabinet, its subdirectories to the drawers in the cabinet, and files to the actual files held in the filing drawers. This analogy is incomplete, since a filing cabinet is a much more limited filing system than the one that the UNIX operating system provides. In the UNIX system scheme of things, an index entry in a drawer of the filing cabinet could contain a reference (a pointer) to another entire filing cabinet. Nevertheless, the filing cabinet analogy is useful, as long as you realize that the UNIX system file structure can handle arbitrary depths of directories and subdirectories.

Let us start off by examining what files and directories already exist on the UNIX system. This achieves two things: it shows the overall system file structure, and introduces the commands available for using that structure.

3.1 Print Current or Working Directory with 'pwd'

When you are assigned a user name so that you can log in to a UNIX system, you are also assigned a directory. This directory is your "home" directory. Every time you log in, you will find yourself positioned in this directory.

After you have logged in and seen the system prompt $, type the command **pwd**, which is a request to print the working directory.

```
$ pwd
/aa/widget/maryann
$
```

The response from the system is the name of the directory you are working in at the moment. This directory is called the "current directory", or "working directory", or (in full) "current working directory".

This is what the example of **pwd** above shows you; since you have just logged in, it is your "home" directory. It is yours to do what you will: create files, make subdirectories, remove files, or rename files and directories.

The name of the directory, as the **pwd** command displays it, is the *full pathname* to your directory. The full pathname is a complete specification of where that directory is in relation to the total file system.

There are three directories shown in the example above, namely, 'aa', 'widget', and 'maryann'. There is in fact a fourth directory which is implicit. That directory is the "root" of the file system, and it is represented by the initial slash character in the example above. We will see this in more detail when we examine the system directories.

You can move to another directory in the system (that is the current working directory can be changed) by using the change directory command, **cd**. But, before you start using **cd** to move around to different places in the directory structure, let's see what you have in your own directory.

3.2 List Directory Contents with 'ls'

The **ls** command is a request to the system to "list the contents of a directory". If no directory is specified on the **ls** command line, you get a list of files in the current directory, which is the one you are working in:

```
$ ls
$
```

The response here is simply the prompt; this means that there are no files to list. This is hardly surprising, since you only just logged in and have not yet created any files or subdirectories. Of course if you had inherited someone else's user name, there might be some files left over, which would show up on the display.

But let's assume that this is a new user name, and there are no files or subdirectories in this directory. So, let us have a closer look at this directory, using some of the options to the **ls** command.

```
$  ls -al
drwxr-xr-x    2 maryann      32 Feb 12 20:31 .
drwxr-xr-x   12 widget      240 Jan  4 15:22 ..
$
```

The **-a** (for **a**ll) option to **ls** asks that all files and subdirectories are listed (some files are "hidden"; more on that later). The **-l** (for long) option asks for a long listing; without it only the names of the files and subdirectories are shown.

ls now shows two directories. The letter "d" in the first column indicates that they are directories. We won't bother with what the rest of the line means right now; we'll just note that the third field of the line shows the owner of the directories, and the last field shows the names of the directories, '.' and '..'.

The period character "." (usually called "dot") is ubiquitous in the UNIX operating system, and means different things in different places. In this particular case, "." means "the current directory". The two periods ".." (pronounced "dot dot") means "the parent directory", that is, the directory that this directory (".") is a subdirectory of. No matter which directory you are working in at any time, "." always stands for the current directory, and ".." is the one "above" it.

Figure 3.1 shows the relationship between the current directory and the parent directory.

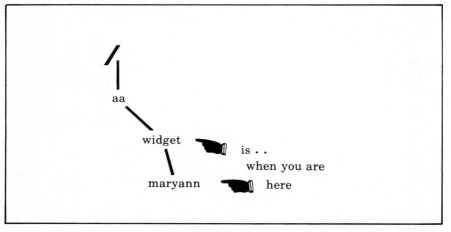

Figure 3.1   Relationship Between Current Directory and Parent Directory

Although you are the owner of your own "home" directory, you are not necessarily the owner of the parent directory. In our example, the parent directory is owned by *'widget'*.

Now let us look at some more of the file system. The full pathname to your home directory starts with the / character. In addition to separating directory names from each other when a pathname is given, the initial slash character, /, is called the *'root'* of the file system. A slash on its own means the root of the file system. Let us look at root:

```
$ ls  /
aa
ab
bin
etc
tmp
usr
$
```

In some UNIX systems, **ls** displays the filenames in multiple columns, with the filenames arranged alphabetically across the rows of the display; other versions of **ls** arrange the filenames in alphabetical order down the columns of the display. **ls** is the command that varies most between different UNIX systems. Just about the first thing that most installations seem to do is to change the **ls** command so that it displays multiple columns of filenames on the screen.

No matter what your local version of **ls** displays (names one per line, alphabetical across the rows, or alphabetical down the columns), the display from your **ls** command should at least display the names of the files and directories.

Notice that in the **ls** display above, there is no indication whether the names displayed are files or subdirectories. To discover that information, you must use the –l option to get the long list.

```
$ ls -l /
drwxr-xr-x  3 root       112 Jan 10 10:41 aa
drwxr-xr-x  3 root        96 Jan 14 08:55 ab
drwxr-xr-x  2 bin       1216 Nov 25 10:42 bin
drwxr-xr-x  2 root       960 Nov 25 10:41 dev
drwxr-xr-x  2 root       512 Nov 25 11:02 etc
drwxr-xr-x  8 root       734 Feb 14 09:02 tmp
drwxr-xr-x 19 bin        368 Nov 25 12:14 usr
$
```

The letter "d" in the very first column of each line of the display means that the entry is a directory. If an entry is a file, it is indicated by the presence of a hyphen character, "-", instead of the letter "d".

As you can see, all of the entries displayed are directories. Some of these directories might contain files, some might contain subdirectories, and some might contain both. To avoid having very long examples in future, we will only indicate some of the directory contents, and we use "<etc ... >" to mean that we have left out stuff.

Let's look at figure 3.2, to see a diagram of the root file system.

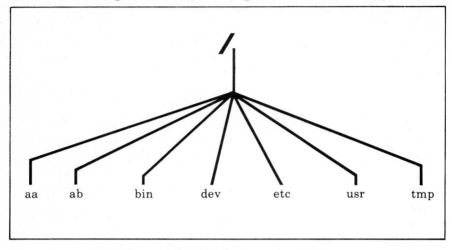

Figure 3.2   A Typical Root File System

Notice that all the directories under root / are owned either by *'root'*, or by *'bin'*; these are two special user names that are used exclusively for maintaining the UNIX system.

Now let's explore a little further and look at one of the system directories:

```
$ ls -l /bin
-r-xr-xr-x  1 bin    12986 Nov 26 12:00 ar
-r-xr-xr-x  1 bin     5604 Nov 26 11:32 as
                     <etc...>
-r-xr-xr-x  1 bin     3268 Nov 26 11:37 cp
                     <etc...>
-r-xr-xr-x  1 bin     8072 Nov 26 11:52 ls
                     <etc...>
-r-xr-xr-x  1 bin     6462 Jan  4 08:32 mv
                     <etc...>
-r-xr-xr-x  1 bin     4252 Jan  1 12:54 uniq
-r-xr-xr-x  1 bin     6348 Nov 26 10:47 who
$
```

All the entries in this display are files, indicated by the "−" in the first column of the display. There are no subdirectories in the */bin* directory. Also, don't the names look familiar? They are the names that appear on the commands documented in the UNIX Programmer's Manual. *'bin'* is short for *'binary'*, and the */bin* directory is where most (but not necessarily all) of the binary (executable) versions of the UNIX system commands are kept.

At this point, let's take time out to have a closer look at what we get when we use the −l option on **ls**. We don't have to show an entire directory with **ls**. We can see details of one file (or a group of files) by specifying the names of the files we are interested in, for example:

```
$ ls -l /bin/ls
-r-xr-xr-x  1 bin      8072 Nov 26 11:52 /bin/ls
$
```

We are now looking at details about the file *'ls'* in the */bin* directory.

The very first column tells us that we have an ordinary file, indicated by the "−" (remember that "d" in the first column means an entry is a directory). The remainder of that first field (the "r-xr-xr-x") tells us about permissions on that file, these are described later in this chapter.

The second field is the number of links. For files the number of links is usually 1. If the number of links field is more than 1, it shows that a number of identical copies of the file exist in different places on the system. For directories, the number of links is an indication of the number of subdirectories in that directory.

The next field shows the owner of the directory or file, in this case it is one of the special system users "bin".

The fourth field shows the size of the file in bytes, for text files this is the number of characters in the file.

The fifth field is a date and time entry. It is the date the file was last modified, or created. Some versions of **ls** might show two dates: the second date in this case is the date the file was last accessed or examined.

The last field on each line of the display is the actual name of the file or directory.

3.3 Changing Working Directory with 'cd'

Now let's continue looking at the other system directories. We'll look at the directory */etc,* but this time we'll do it slightly differently:

```
$ cd /etc
$ ls -l
-rw-rw-r-- 1 root          181 Feb 14 19:52 motd
                  <etc...>
-rw-r--r-- 1 root         1137 Feb 12 19:54 passwd
                  <etc...>
-rw-r--r-- 1 bin          300 Jan 14 15:36 utmp
$
```

First of all, we've used two commands instead of one. The **cd** command stands for change working directory. After the **cd**, we are "positioned" in the */etc* directory, so that it is now our working directory. Having got to the */etc* directory, which is the one we want to examine, we need not tell **ls** which directory we want. We can just let it show the current working directory.

The */etc* directory contains a mixture of files and subdirectories. The contents are probably different for each UNIX system, but just about all will have the file *'motd'* and *'passwd'*.

The file *'motd'* is the message-of-the-day file, which is displayed every time you log in.

The file *'passwd'* is the password file that we described in chapter 2 — "Getting Started with the UNIX System". The password file contains one entry for each person who can use the system. Each entry contains the user's login-name, group, encrypted password and other interesting information about the user.

Now let's look at another directory:

```
$ cd /usr; ls -l
drwxr-xr-x  3 bin         256 Jan  7 20:51 bin
drwxr-xr-x  3 bin         128 Feb 14  1981 dict
drwxr-xr-x  5 bin         432 Aug 21 15:15 games
drwxr-xr-x  3 bin         496 Feb 14  1981 include
drwxr-xr-x 13 bin         848 Dec 28 16:48 lib
drwxr-xr-x  2 root         80 Feb 14  1981 pub
$
```

Notice that this time we put our two commands on the same line, separated with the semicolon ;. There can be spaces on either or both sides of the ; command separator, it doesn't matter.

The */usr* directory has more subdirectories, so we can expand our diagram to a bigger tree as shown in figure 3.3.

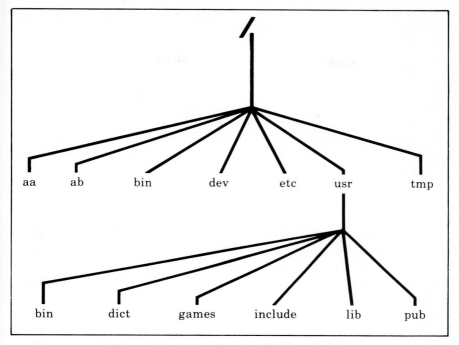

Figure 3.3 Expanding the File System Map

You can see from this diagram that there are two directories named *'bin'*. There is no confusion between them because they are on different paths; one is */bin*, the other is */usr/bin*.

The contents of */bin* we have already seen. To see the contents of */usr/bin* we can say:

```
$ ls -l bin
-r-xr-xr-x   1   bin     48110   Nov 26 12:01   adb
-r-xr-xr-x   1   bin      4072   Nov 26 12:02   cal
                        <etc...>
-r-xr-xr-x   1   bin     13914   Nov 26 12:11   write
-r-xr-xr-x   1   bin     27168   Nov 26 12:11   yacc
$
```

We saw earlier that many of the commands documented in the UNIX Programmer's Manual are to be found in the directory */bin*. This directory, */usr/bin*, is where the rest of them live. This is not always true, however. Some UNIX systems put everything in the */bin* directory, and there is no */usr/bin* directory at all.

We leave it as an exercise for the reader to examine the other system directories, using combinations of **cd** and **ls**, and checking your position in the file system hierarchy with **pwd**. Remember that if you get lost you can always return to your home directory by typing the **cd** command with no argument.

Here are some of the interesting things you will find when you look in the other system directories. If you look in the */usr/games* directory, you will see that it contains the games documented in the UNIX Programmer's Manual.

The */usr/include* directory is of interest to programmers, because it contains include files in the **C** programming language.

The */dev* directory contains the special files associated with input/output devices, such as the terminals (ttys), line printer and such.

The */etc* directory is a kind of catch-all, as its name implies. In */etc* you can find the message-of-the-day, the password file, and several programs that only the super-user can access.

The */tmp* directory is one which programmers use to create temporary or scratch files. The */tmp* directory is cleared out periodically (usually once per day), so don't try to use */tmp* to keep permanent information.

The person who owns a particular directory can set the permissions on that directory so that other users cannot use a **cd** command with that directory specified as a destination. If you try to **cd** to a directory to which you do not have access, you get an error response:

```
$ cd /aa/widget/kingsland
/aa/widget/kingsland: bad directory
$
```

This doesn't tell you much. You get the same response if you try to **cd** to a file instead of a directory, and also if you try to change to a directory that does not exist. In none of those cases is it clear why the directory or file is "bad", so you might have to look at the destination directory with the **ls** command to find out what the problem really is. You have probably misspelled the name, or got the path wrong. Check carefully what you typed to see if it is either of these problems.

3.3.1 Notes and Cautions on Changing Directory

It is a good idea to use **pwd** whenever you change directories, to verify that you are where you expect to be in the directory structure.

Of course, if the first thing you do when you arrive at the destination directory is an **ls** command, an unfamiliar list of files will alert you that you aren't where you thought you were.

However, if you were to do a **cd**, and then full of confidence in your own infallibility, immediately issue a "remove files" command, the result might be to wipe out valuable files which you (or worse, someone else) want to keep.

So get into the habit of typing a **pwd** command whenever you change directories. You will save yourself much grief in the long run.

3.4 Full Pathnames and Relative Pathnames

In our last **ls** example above, we specified simply *'bin'* as the directory we wanted to list, we didn't say */usr/bin*. This is because we were already in the directory */usr*. We just gave the *relative pathname* of the directory we wished to see. Had we been in a directory other than */usr* we would have had to specify the full pathname */usr/bin*.

Consider that our diagram is a map of the file system, and imagine an arrow with the words "you are here" pointing to the current working directory (at the moment, */usr*). To get to any other directory, or any file in any directory, you can give a command either a relative pathname (or "how to get there from here"), or a full pathname (or "how to get there from the system root"). Using the **cd** command changes the position of the "you are here" arrow.

Regardless of where you are currently positioned in the file system hierarchy, when you want to either move somewhere else, or refer to a file or directory at another place in the hierarchy, there are two basic ways of specifying the destination.

One way is to start from where you are and give a pathname corresponding to the move you want to make. This is called a "relative pathname", because it is relative to (starts from) your current directory.

Sometimes, when you are a long way down some path, an old country folks' adage applies:

If you want to get there, you shouldn't start from here!

In this case, it's best to use a full pathname, starting from the *'root'* of the file system.

Another way is to revert to your home directory, by typing a **cd** command with no pathname, and then moving on from there. A plain **cd** command with no arguments always takes you back to your home directory, which is a known place.

A pathname, whether a full pathname or a relative pathname, can be given anywhere the name of a file or directory can appear on UNIX system commands.

Let us illustrate the ways which full and relative pathnames are used with a couple of examples. Each example shows how to do the job in these different ways:

- using a relative pathname,
- using a full pathname,
- changing directory first.

In the examples we use the **cat** command to look at a file. The derivation of this odd name is given later; right now the important things are full and relative pathnames. Suppose you have the directory structure shown in figure 3.4.

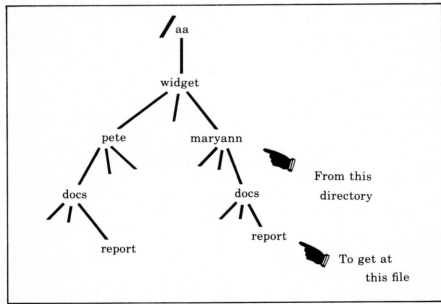

Figure 3.4   Full and Relative Pathnames

To view the *'report'* file with the **cat** command, here is how it is done with a relative pathname:

```
cat docs/report
```

and here is how to do it using the full pathname:

```
cat /aa/widget/maryann/docs/report
```

and finally, you can change directory before you do the **cat** command:

```
cd docs; cat report
```

The next example is slightly more complex, because you are looking at a file in another part of the hierarchy, as shown in figure 3.5.

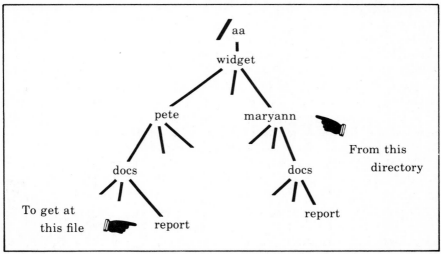

Figure 3.5   More Full and Relative Pathnames

You get at Pete's copy of *'report'* with a relative pathname like this:

```
cat ../pete/docs/report
```

with a full pathname like this:

```
cat /aa/widget/pete/docs/report
```

and then there are two ways you might use when changing directory first:

```
cd ../pete/docs; cat report
cd /aa/widget/pete/docs; cat report
```

3.5 Rules for Names of Files and Directories

So far, although we have been dealing with named files and directories, we have not specified what a filename (or a directory name) can consist of.

Filenames can be up to fourteen characters long and, at least in theory, can consist of any characters whatsoever. In practice, however, many characters in the ASCII character set can mean something special to the Shell (the part of the system that decodes your commands), and so these special characters should be avoided in filenames and directory names.

Depending on the particular UNIX system involved, filenames beginning with a period, or "dot" (.) are "hidden" and don't usually show up on an **ls** listing. It's wiser not to use " . " as the first character of a filename unless you really want to hide the file. Unfortunately, this is not a hard and fast rule. On some UNIX systems, files starting with a period do show up in the results of an **ls** command.

We already saw that the semicolon ; is a command separator. As we shall see in chapter 4, "Commands and Standard Files", the characters >, <, |, and & all mean something special to the Shell. It is best to avoid using these characters in filenames.

The Shell has certain "shorthand" notations, or character matching capabilities providing a means to refer to groups of files. For instance, it is possible to designate "all files starting with a letter", or "filenames with a single digit at the end", or "all files starting with the letters I through N", or simply, "all files in this directory". The Shell achieves this capability by pre-empting some characters as "wild-card" characters. Obviously it is a good idea to avoid using these characters when forming filenames. Wild card characters are discussed at the end of this chapter.

Here are some examples of possible filenames:

```
message            joe muggs
1982               .errors
conv.c             old-mesg
Message            %+=$!!
```

And here are filenames which could get you into BIG TROUBLE, because of the Shell's special characters:

```
>5lines            4or<lines
4|5words           ?words
?WORDS             $junk
[Aix-Ghent]        morejunk**
```

When choosing filenames, as a general rule it is best to restrict yourself to names consisting of letters, digits, the underscore character, (_), and the period character, (.). The period can be used safely in the middle of a filename, but do not use the period at the beginning of a filename unless you want the files hidden.

Uppercase letters and lowercase letters are significant in filenames on the UNIX system. The filenames:

```
POT_OF_MESSAGE          pot_of_message
Pot_of_message          Pot_Of_Message
```

all represent four entirely different files. In this respect, the UNIX system is different from most other operating systems.

3.5.1 File Naming Conventions

There are certain file naming conventions followed on the UNIX system, mostly connected with the various programming languages available. A filename ending in '.c' is usually taken to be a file containing a program written in the **C** programming language; a filename ending in '.h' is an include file (containing "header" data) for the **C** programming language.

Similarly, a filename ending in '.f' is taken to be a program written in FORTRAN, one ending in '.p' is assumed to be a Pascal program, and a filename ending in '.s' usually means a program written in assembly language.

A filename ending in '.o' is the object code produced by any of the compilers.

Some of the other conventions used are: '.y' for **yacc** source; '.r' for **ratfor** source, '.l' for **lex** source, '.e' for **efl** source, and so on.

When creating programs these conventions should be followed; your program probably won't compile if you don't. If you are not writing programs, try to name your files in such a way that there is no confusion with the conventions.

There are other conventions that are not associated with programming languages. For example, Programmers Workbench (PWB) versions of the UNIX system provide a system for maintaining source text, whether programs or documents. Source Code Control System (SCCS) files all begin with the characters 's.', and various of the SCCS commands produce files beginning with 'p.', 'g.', 'x.' and 'z.'. If you have SCCS, try to avoid using this type of name for non-SCCS files.

It should be emphasized that these are file naming conventions, not rules imposed by the UNIX system. Some commands, that deal with certain types of files, expect the names of those files to have a particular format; but the Shell, and the system in general, doesn't care.

3.6 Looking at the Contents of a File with 'cat'

One command which can be used to look at the contents of a file is the **cat** command. **cat** is so named because, if more than one file-name is specified, all files are con**cat**enated (joined end to end) and copied to the Standard Output (usually your terminal screen). You should be aware that **cat**'s main purpose is to concatenate files. It just so happens that its action of copying the result to the Standard Output is a side effect, which we can use to look at a text file. If you **cat** a non-text file to your terminal screen, the results are generally unreadable.

cat is a simple command. Suppose that you forgot to read the message of the day when you logged in; to examine the message of the day file, you just type:

```
$ cat /etc/motd
The system will be down this Saturday from 8am to 2pm
while we are doing Preventive Maintenance.

Filesystem /aa is VERY low on space ! ! !
Please inspect your files and remove moldy oldies.
$
```

Since we've mentioned the ASCII character set several times, an interesting file to look at is a chart of the ASCII character-set, which lives in */usr/pub/ascii:*

```
$   cat /usr/pub/ascii
|000 nul|001 soh|002 stx|003 etx|004 eot|005 enq|006 ack|007 bel|
|010 bs |011 ht |012 nl |013 vt |014 np |015 cr |016 so |017 si |
|020 dle|021 dc1|022 dc2|023 dc3|024 dc4|025 nak|026 syn|027 etb|
|030 can|031 em |032 sub|033 esc|034 fs |035 gs |036 rs |037 us |
|040 sp |041 !  |042 '' |043 #  |044 $  |045 %  |046 &  |047 '  |
|050 (  |051 )  |052 *  |053 +  |054 ,  |055 -  |056 .  |057 /  |
|060 0  |061 1  |062 2  |063 3  |064 4  |065 5  |066 6  |067 7  |
|070 8  |071 9  |072 :  |073 ;  |074 <  |075 =  |076 >  |077 ?  |
```

---

* /usr/pub/ascii reproduced with permission from Bell Laboratories.

¦100 →	¦101 A	¦102 B	¦103 C	¦104 D	¦105 E	¦106 F	¦107 G ¦
¦110 H	¦111 I	¦112 J	¦113 K	¦114 L	¦115 M	¦116 N	¦117 O ¦
¦120 P	¦121 Q	¦122 R	¦123 S	¦124 T	¦125 U	¦126 V	¦127 W ¦
¦130 X	¦131 Y	¦132 Z	¦133 [	¦134 \	¦135]	¦136 ^	¦137 _ ¦
¦140 `	¦141 a	¦142 b	¦143 c	¦144 d	¦145 e	¦146 f	¦147 g ¦
¦150 h	¦151 i	¦152 j	¦153 k	¦154 l	¦155 m	¦156 n	¦157 o ¦
¦160 p	¦161 q	¦162 r	¦163 s	¦164 t	¦165 u	¦166 v	¦167 w ¦
¦170 x	¦171 y	¦172 z	¦173 {	¦174 ¦	¦175 }	¦176 ~	¦177 del¦

```
$
```

This file gives the character values, in octal notation, of all the characters in the ASCII character set.

The first four lines show all the non-printing characters. Those are the characters obtained when you hold down the control key and type another character (for example, the character value 010 is control-H or backspace, abbreviated to "bs" in the table above). Although it isn't needed very often, the ASCII chart is a useful file to have on the system.

If you try to **cat** a file which doesn't exist, or a file for which you don't have read permission, **cat** displays an error response:

```
$ cat jambly
cat: can't open jambly
$
```

You usually get this message if you have misspelled the filename, or if you are not in the directory you thought you were in. It is a good idea to do an **ls** of the directory first, to make sure you get the correct filenames, or maybe a **pwd** to find out where you actually are.

If the file you are **cat**-ing is large, you might want to suspend the output so you can look at it easily. Remember you can stop and start output with the control-S and control-Q keys, as we described in chapter 2.

3.7 Looking at the End of a File with 'tail'

If what you want to see in a file is towards the end of the file, a useful command is **tail**, which simply shows the **tail**-end of the file. If you don't specify how much you want, **tail** gives you the last 10 lines of the file, but you can tell it to give more or less, for example:*

---

* /usr/pub/greek reproduced with permission from Bell Laboratories.

```
$ tail -3 /usr/pub/greek
psi        V  V  ¦  PSI       H  H  ¦  omega    C  C
OMEGA      Z  Z  ¦  nabla     [  [  ¦  not      _  _
partial    ]  ]  ¦  integral  ^  ^
$
```

This is a display of the last three lines of the file which gives information to the text formatters about how Greek symbols can be printed on certain terminals. The number we give to **tail** is preceded by a minus sign to indicate that the last 3 lines of the file are to be displayed. If you precede the number of lines with a plus sign, **tail** starts at the specified line number and displays all lines from there to the end of the file, so:

```
$ tail +6 /usr/pub/greek
xi         X  X  ¦  pi        J  J  ¦  PI       P  P
rho        K  K  ¦  sigma     Y  Y  ¦  SIGMA    R  R
tau        I  I  ¦  phi       U  U  ¦  PHI      F  F
psi        V  V  ¦  PSI       H  H  ¦  omega    C  C
OMEGA      Z  Z  ¦  nabla     [  [  ¦  not      _  _
partial    ]  ]  ¦  integral  ^  ^
$
```

displays all lines from line 6 to the end of *usr/pub/greek.*

If you use the **+** option to **tail**, and give a number greater than the number of lines in the file, **tail** does not display anything.

If you try to **tail** a file that doesn't exist, or which you don't have read permission on, you get an error message:

```
$ tail spurious
tail: Can't open spurious
$
```

3.8 Determining the Type of a File with 'file'

cat and **tail** are really only useful for displaying text files. If you try to look at something which is not a text file, they do not warn you (they don't care what is in the file), but what you see displayed will look like complete garbage.

To find out whether it makes sense to display a file on the terminal screen, using **cat** or **tail**, you can use the **file** command, which determines the type of data which is in a file. If it finds the file is ASCII, **file** even tries to identify the language (in programming terms) of the file:

```
$ file /bin/ls /usr/bin /etc/passwd /usr/include/stdio.h
/bin/ls:          pure executable
/usr/bin:         directory
/etc/passwd:      ascii text
/usr/include/stdio.h:    c program text
$
```

If you try to use **file** on a non-existent file, you will get an error message to tell you that the **file** command cannot do its thing on that file:

```
$ file illusory
illusory: cannot stat
$
```

And, if you try to use the **file** command on a file for which you don't have read permission, you'll get a different error response:

```
$ file closedown
closedown: cannot open
$
```

3.9 Creating User Directories with 'mkdir'

Having showed the simple commands for working with files, we now continue with more information on directories. Here, we describe how to make your own directories.

In the discussion and examples at the start of this chapter, we showed the layout of the directory structure for a typical file system. In those diagrams and examples, we showed two directories called /aa and /ab, that are not system directories. They are user directories, and might be called anything on your system, /u0 and /u1, for instance. We just picked some arbitrary names. The number of user directories also varies from one UNIX system to another, it depends on how big each system is, and how many people can use it.

Each person who has a user-name has a directory somewhere in the system. It could be immediately under the /aa directory, for example /aa/maryann, or there could be other directories in between. In our earlier example, we assumed that there was a group of users in the 'widget' project, and that there was a directory for the group, so pictorially, we have something like the tree shown in figure 3.6.

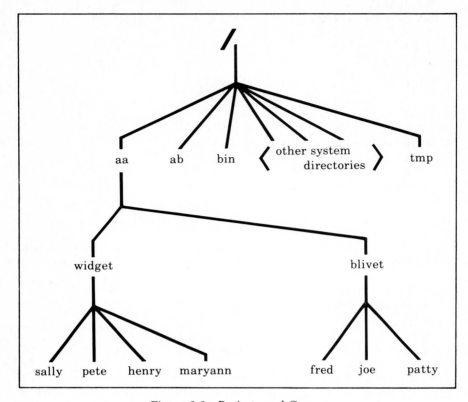

Figure 3.6   Projects and Groups

We have shown another group of people in the *'blivet'* project, who share the */aa* directory, so there are user directories under both */aa/widget* and */aa/blivet.* Each user has control over the contents of his own directory, and can create as many subdirectories and files as required.

This diagram doesn't necessarily show a typical file structure for user directories, it merely illustrates what is possible with the UNIX file system structure.

The **mkdir** command creates (or **mak**es) **dir**ectories. Suppose that you are going to write some programs, some in the C programming language and some in Pascal; and there will be documentation: specifications, memos, letters. You might want to create separate subdirectories for all these things:

```
$ cd
$ mkdir progs docs
$ cd progs
$ mkdir c pascal
$ ls -l
drwxrwxrwx  2   maryann      32 Feb 14 12:07 c
drwxrwxrwx  2   maryann      32 Feb 14 12:07 pascal
$ cd ../docs
$ mkdir memos specs letters
$ ls  -l
drwxrwxrwx  2   maryann      32 Feb 14 12:08 letters
drwxrwxrwx  2   maryann      32 Feb 14 12:08 memos
drwxrwxrwx  2   maryann      32 Feb 14 12:08 specs
$ cd
$
```

The first **cd** command is to make sure that you are positioned at your own login or "home" directory, the place where the **cd** command takes you if you don't specify anywhere.

Observe the use of "**..**" in specifying the relative pathname to *'docs'* from *'progs'*. The hierarchy of directories we have created now looks like the one shown in figure 3.7.

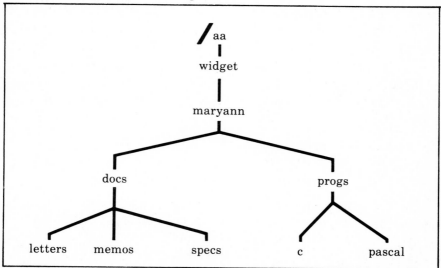

Figure 3.7 User Subdirectories

We could, in fact have created all these directories at the same time:

```
$ mkdir progs progs/c progs/pascal \
      docs docs/letters docs/memos docs/specs
$ ls -l
drwxrwxrwx  5  maryann    80 Feb 14 12:11 docs
drwxrwxrwx  4  maryann    64 Feb 14 12:11 progs
$
```

There are several points of interest in this example. First of all, we've split the command over two lines. Remember back in chapter 2 we said that the reverse slash character \ is an "escape" character, and removes any special meaning from the character immediately following it. We've used the \ character in this case to remove the special meaning of command terminator from the newline character (obtained when we typed RETURN at the end of the first line). So the Shell doesn't do anything until it sees the newline at the end of the second line.

We needn't have split the command like this in fact, because the system will accept a very long command line, much longer than will fit on a terminal screen, and we could have just kept typing. But many people find it disconcerting to do that, they prefer to split the command as we've shown.

If you split a command like this, it is important that you type the RETURN key immediately following the \; there must not be any spaces between the \ character and the RETURN.

The second noteworthy thing is the order in which we specified the directories to be created. Had we tried to make the directory *'progs/c'* before making the directory *'progs'*, the system would display:

```
$ mkdir progs/c progs
mkdir: cannot access progs/.
$
```

The directory *'progs'* must exist before the subdirectory *'c'* can be created in it. Of course, after the above command is obeyed, the *'progs'* directory will actually exist, because it was the second argument to **mkdir**. The *'progs/c'* directory will not exist.

Having tried to make the directories in the wrong order (as shown above), you might then have tried to start over, and make them in the right order. But now you are trying to make a directory *('progs')* which already exists, in which case you would get these results:

```
$ mkdir  progs  progs/c
mkdir: cannot make directory progs
$
```

By this time, things are so confused that it is better to remove the directories with the **rmdir** command described below, and start again.

The third point about the above example is that an **ls** of the current directory only shows the subdirectories *'progs'* and *'docs'*. To see the subdirectories of those directories we have to say:

```
$ ls -l docs progs

docs:
drwxrwxrwx   2   maryann      32 Feb 14 12:11 letters
drwxrwxrwx   2   maryann      32 Feb 14 12:11 memos
drwxrwxrwx   2   maryann      32 Feb 14 12:11 specs

progs:
drwxrwxrwx   2   maryann      32 Feb 14 12:11 c
drwxrwxrwx   2   maryann      32 Feb 14 12:11 pascal
$
```

The **ls** command above requests a "long" display of the two directories *'docs'* and *'progs'*. This form of **ls** places the name of each directory before the information for its subdirectories.

The entries for the subdirectories are fairly boring, being all the same except for their names. Each entry has a letter "d" in the first column to show it is a directory. Each entry has all permissions set (permissions are described later in the section entitled "Ownership and Protection"). Each directory has only two links, namely, itself and its parent; there are no files as yet.

Now that we have made some directories, we resume the discussion on working with files within those directories.

3.10 Copying Files with 'cp'

The easiest way to get a file of your own is to take a copy of someone else's. This is achieved using the copy command, **cp**:

```
$ cp /etc/motd message
$
```

copies the message of the day file into a file named *'message'* in your current working directory. You can make yet another copy of that file with another **cp** command:

```
$ cp message message_too
$
```

Assuming that you are in your login directory, an **ls** command should show a directory which looks like this.

```
$ ls -l
drwxrwxrwx  5   maryann      80 Feb 14 12:11 docs
-rw-rw-rw-  1   maryann     187 Feb 14 12:30 message
-rw-rw-rw-  1   maryann     187 Feb 14 12:31 message_too
drwxrwxrwx  4   maryann      64 Feb 14 12:39 progs
$
```

In brief, **cp** takes two arguments, the names of files, or pathnames to files. The first argument is the name of the file we want to copy from, and the second argument is the name of the file to which we want to transfer. It is important to remember this order, since every operating system seems to have its own odd ideas about file copying.

 On the UNIX system, a **cp** command which looks like this:

      cp here there

means "copy **from** *'here'* **to** *'there'*".

To get the same named file in your own directory, the filename is mentioned twice:

```
$ cp /etc/motd motd
$
```

puts a copy of the file called *'motd'* into the current directory.

However, there is another way of using **cp**. If the second argument you give it is an existing directory, **cp** copies the file named as the first argument into that directory, and retains the filename. So, we could have got our own copy of *'motd'* by saying:

```
$ cp /etc/motd .
$
```

remember that . ("dot") stands for current directory. Similarly, you could put it in one of your subdirectories:

```
$ cp /etc/motd docs/memos
$
```

When we use **cp** in this way, we are not restricted to copying one file, we can copy many files into a directory:

```
$ cp /usr/include/stdio.h /usr/include/time.h progs/c
$ ls  -l  progs/c
-r--r--r--  1  maryann  1544  Feb 14 12:40   stdio.h
-r--r--r--  1  maryann   286  Feb 14 12:40   time.h
$
```

Now the directory *'progs/c'* contains copies of the C programming language include files *'stdio.h'* and *'time.h'*.*

Here are some things which might go wrong when using **cp**, and what they mean. If a file of the name you are trying to copy *to* already exists, there is no warning unless the file is write protected; the old version of the file is simply overwritten. If you try to copy to a file which is write-protected, or if you try to copy into a directory which does not exist, you get this result:

```
$ cp goodies no_holds/barred
cp: cannot create no_holds/barred
$
```

Remember, the second argument is the destination of the copy. If you do not have read permission on the source file (the file you are trying to copy from), or if the source file or directory does not exist, **cp** gives you this answer:

```
$ cp no_such/file mine_all_mine
cp: cannot open no_such/file
$
```

In figure 3.8 we show some "before and after" pictures of a directory structure, and how it changes when you use the **cp** command to copy files. At the top is a picture of part of a simple directory structure. It shows two directories: one contains two files, the other is empty. There is an arrow pointing to the current working directory. Beneath that picture are four **cp** commands; underneath each command is a picture of the new directory structure which results from applying that **cp** command to the original structure.

---

* This example should not be interpreted as a suggestion that it is a good idea for a user to have private copies of these files. It is in fact a very bad idea; the example is purely intended to demonstrate the use of **cp**.

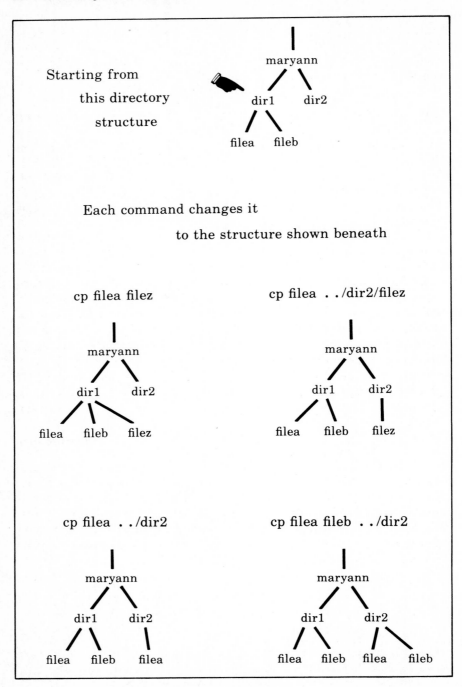

Figure 3.8   Effects of Copying Files with the cp Command

One final note on **cp**: after you have made a copy of a file, the modes for that file are the same as the original version of the file. So if you copied a read-only file from somewhere else, you have to change the mode of your copy if you want to alter the file in any way.

3.11 Moving and Renaming Files with 'mv'

The **mv** command **m**oves files and directories around in the file-system. In the process of moving a file or a directory, **mv** can rename the file or directory. The process of renaming a file or a directory is considered as a side effect of the move function.

Many people new to the UNIX system are baffled by this aspect of **mv**: "why does move rename a file?" The principal function of **mv** is to move a file or directory from one place in the file system to another. The file name in the destination directory does not have to be the same as it was in the original directory. If the starting direc-tory and the destination directory happen to be the same, the effect of specifying a different origin and destination name for the file is simply to rename the file; the file has been "moved" within the same directory.

Obviously, a move differs from a copy operation in that the original of the file disappears. For example, after we had copied the file */etc/motd* into the current directory as the file *'message'*, */etc/motd* still existed. Had we used the **mv** command, */etc/motd* would have disappeared, and would have appeared as *'message'* in the current directory.

Here is an example of renaming files, with before and after dis-plays of the filenames:

```
$ ls -l
drwxrwxrwx  5  maryann      80 Feb 14 12:11 docs
-rw-rw-rw-  1  maryann     187 Feb 14 12:30 message
-rw-rw-rw-  1  maryann     187 Feb 14 12:31 message_too
drwxrwxrwx  4  maryann      64 Feb 14 12:39 progs
$ mv message_too mesg
$ ls   -l
drwxrwxrwx  5  maryann      80 Feb 14 12:11 docs
-rw-rw-rw-  1  maryann     187 Feb 14 12:52 mesg
-rw-rw-rw-  1  maryann     187 Feb 14 12:30 message
drwxrwxrwx  4  maryann      64 Feb 14 12:39 progs
$
```

The file *'message_too'* has been renamed *'mesg'*. If a file already exists whose name is that of the second argument to **mv**, that file is removed.

```
$ ls -1
drwxrwxrwx  5  maryann     80 Feb 14 12:11 docs
-rw-rw-rw-  1  maryann    187 Feb 14 12:52 mesg
-rw-rw-rw-  1  maryann    187 Feb 14 12:30 message
drwxrwxrwx  4  maryann     64 Feb 14 12:39 progs
$ mv mesg message
$ ls  -1
drwxrwxrwx  5  maryann     80 Feb 14 12:11 docs
-rw-rw-rw-  1  maryann    187 Feb 14 12:54 message
drwxrwxrwx  4  maryann     64 Feb 14 12:39 progs
$
```

If the target file is write protected, **mv** checks with you before removing the file. **mv** prints out the mode of the target file and waits for your response. If your answer begins with the letter **y** (for yes) the move is carried out, otherwise no action is taken:

```
$ cp message mesg
$ chmod 444 message
$ ls -1
drwxrwxrwx  5  maryann     80 Feb 14 12:11 docs
-rw-rw-rw-  1  maryann    187 Feb 14 12:57 mesg
-r--r--r--  1  maryann    187 Feb 14 12:30 message
drwxrwxrwx  4  maryann     64 Feb 14 12:39 progs
$ mv  mesg   message
message: mode 444 ? y
$
```

A file can be moved from one directory to another by making the second argument to **mv** the name of the target directory:

```
$ ls -1
drwxrwxrwx  5  maryann     80 Feb 14 12:11 docs
-rw-rw-rw-  1  maryann    187 Feb 14 12:57 message
drwxrwxrwx  4  maryann     64 Feb 14 12:39 progs
$ mv message docs/memos
$ ls -1
drwxrwxrwx  5  maryann     80 Feb 14 12:11 docs
drwxrwxrwx  4  maryann     64 Feb 14 12:39 progs
$ ls -1 docs/memos
-rw-rw-rw-  1  maryann    187 Feb 14 13:02 message
-rw-rw-rw-  1  maryann    187 Feb 14 12:33 motd
$
```

As was the case for **cp**, we are not restricted to moving one file at a time, we can move several:

```
$ cd progs/c
$ ls -l
-r--r--r--  1  maryann  1544  Feb 14 12:40  stdio.h
-r--r--r--  1  maryann   286  Feb 14 12:40  time.h
$ mv stdio.h time.h ..
$ ls
$ cd ..
$ ls -l
drwxrwxrwx  5  maryann    32  Feb 14 12:39  c
-r--r--r--  1  maryann  1544  Feb 14 13:10  stdio.h
-r--r--r--  1  maryann   286  Feb 14 13:10  time.h
$
```

Remember that "**..**" ("dot dot") means the parent directory, so the include files have been moved from the directory
/aa/widget/maryann/progs/c to */aa/widget/maryann/progs*.

If you try to move or rename a file that doesn't exist, **mv** displays
an error response:

```
$ mv chimera reality
mv: cannot access chimera
$
```

Figure 3.9 shows some "before and after" pictures of a directory
structure showing what happens when you use **mv** to move files
around. These are laid out in a manner similar to those showing the
cp command. Compare the two sets of diagrams; they should give
you a clear picture of the difference between the two commands.

3.12 Removing Files with 'rm'

The **rm** command deletes or **rem**oves files from a directory. For
example, remember that we copied the message-of-the-day file into
our local directory */docs/memos*. We can now remove that file like
this:

```
$ cd
$ rm docs/memos/motd
$ ls -l docs/memos
-rw-rw-rw-  1  maryann    187 Feb 14 13:02 message
$
```

rm can remove more than one file at a time. If any file is write
protected, **rm** checks whether you really want to remove it by
informing you of the actual mode of the file, and waiting for

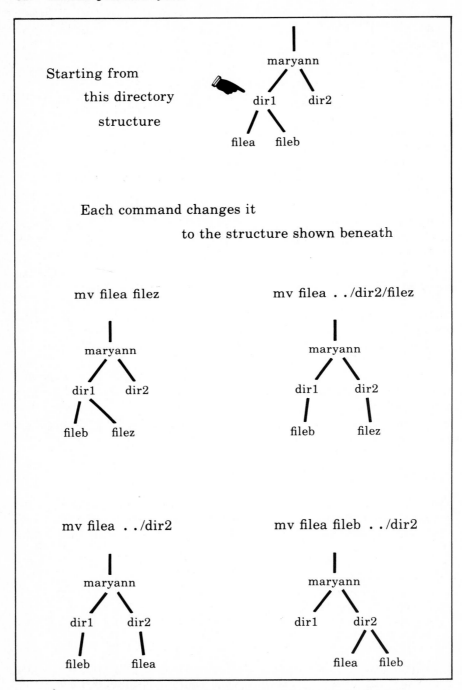

Figure 3.9   Effects of Moving Files with the mv Command

confirmation. If you type anything which begins with a **y** (for **y**es), **rm** accepts that as confirmation that the file is to be removed. If you type anything which does not start with **y**, **rm** does not remove the file:

```
$ cd progs
$ rm stdio.h time.h
rm: stdio.h 444 mode
rm: time.h 444 mode y
$ ls -l
drwxrwxrwx  5  maryann     32  Feb 14 12:39  c
-r--r--r--  1  maryann   1234  Feb 14 13:10  stdio.h
$
```

The first file, *'stdio.h'* was not removed because the reply to the check did not begin with **y**. A similar check happens when you have write permission on a directory, but try to remove a file that you don't own.

If you use the −i (for interactive) option, **rm** checks with you before removing each file, regardless of whether it is write protected. This is a very wise precaution against accidentally removing a file you really want to keep. If you use the −i option, **rm** no longer prints the mode of the file, it just prints the filename, and waits for an answer:

```
$ rm -i frammis whammo
frammis: n
whammo: y
$
```

This example succeeds in removing *'whammo'*, but leaves *'frammis'* intact.

☞ Remember that typing a **y** in answer to **rm**'s query means "Yes, go ahead and remove the file"!!

The −f (for force) option is the inverse of the −i option; it forces removal of the files without question, even if they are write protected:

```
$ rm -f c stdio.h
c: directory
$ ls -l
drwxrwxrwx  5  maryann     32  Feb 14 12:39  c
$
```

This example also shows what happens if you try to remove a directory: you get a message to tell you that it is a directory, and the directory is left alone.

The −i option and the −f option are mutually exclusive. If you use both of them, the −i option takes precedence, and the −f option is ignored.

Normally, **rm** is for removing files rather than directories, as illustrated in the example above. But **rm** can be made to remove directories and, recursively, files and subdirectories by giving the −r (for recursive) option:

```
$ rm -r progs docs
$ ls
$
```

When used with the −r option, **rm** searches down the directory tree, removing all files it finds. When a subdirectory is empty, **rm** then removes that subdirectory. The command does this for every file in every subdirectory (and so on) that it finds in the specified directory. As we shall show in the discussion on wild-card characters which follows, the * character means "everything"; so, if you were to type the command:

```
$ rm -r *
```

every file and subdirectory (and all their subdirectories) from the current directory on down, would get removed. You had better be sure that this is what you really wanted. When used with the recursive option, **rm** is a very powerful command; use it with care and caution, and much trepidation.

If you try to remove a file which does not exist, **rm** informs you in no uncertain terms:

```
$ rm nonesuch
rm: nonesuch non-existent
$
```

3.13 Deleting Directories with 'rmdir'

The command to delete (or **rem**ove) a **dir**ectory is **rmdir**. To remove a directory with **rmdir**, the directory must be empty, that is it must not contain any files or subdirectories. So if you decided you weren't going to write any programs and tried to use the **rmdir** command get rid of the *'progs'* directory, you would get this result:

```
$ rmdir progs
rmdir: progs not empty
$
```

You get this response because *'progs'* still contains two subdirectories, even though there are no files. You have to get rid of the subdirectories first:

```
$ rmdir progs/pascal progs/c progs
$
```

Had there been any files in any of the directories, you would have to remove them before you could remove the directories. Alternatively, you could use **rm** with the **–r** option.

If you try to remove a directory that does not exist, the system responds with an error message:

```
$ rmdir nonesuch
rmdir: nonesuch non-existent
$
```

3.14 Wild-card Characters or Metacharacters

You have seen some of the commands for working with files and directories in the UNIX system. Now we describe one of the most powerful features of the Shell, the capability to use a "shorthand" notation for operating upon whole aggregates of files and directories in a single command. Using the Shell's shorthand notation, you can refer to filenames such as "all files consisting of the letter 'c' followed by a digit", or "all four letter filenames", or "all filenames containing the letters 'a' through 'g'", or "every file in this directory", and so on.

The Shell achieves this capability by using some characters to represent things other than themselves. These special characters are often called "wild-card" characters, taken from the analogy with card games, where (for instance) a Joker can be any card. In the Shell, the wild-card characters are called metacharacters. These special characters are used to "match" filenames or parts of filenames. They ease the job of specifying particular files or whole groups of files.

The asterisk character * represents any arbitrary character string, including an empty (null) string.

The question-mark character **?** represents any single character.

Brackets, [and] enclose a list of characters where the match is on "any single character enclosed in the brackets". The hyphen character - used inside the brackets indicates a range of characters, for instance

```
[a-z]
```

is a shorthand notation for every lowercase letter in the alphabet.

To illustrate the use of these characters, let's assume we have a directory containing files relating to some document. There are chapters (abbreviated to "c"), appendices (abbreviated to "a"), some figures and some tables (abbreviations "f" and "t"). Then there are some miscellaneous files. Let us say here that these are very bad file names. It would be much better to call the files *'chapter1'*, or at least *'chap1'*, *'fig1'* and so on. The names have been chosen with a view to illustrating the use of wild-card characters, rather than making them decently mnemonic. To keep the size of the following examples to a reasonable length, we assume a version of the **ls** command which can display multiple columns of filenames:

```
$ ls
a           aA          aB          aC          c1
c10         c11         c12         c13         c2
c3          c4          c5          c6          c7
c8          c9          contents    f1-1        f10-1
f11-1       f11-2       f2-1        f2-2        f2-3
f7-1        f8-1        f8-2        t3-1        t3-2
t6-1        t8-1        temp        zonk8
$
```

We use **ls** to show the Shell's file matching capabilities because **ls** simply prints the names of the files matched, but the special characters can be used to specify filenames in *any* command.

3.14.1 Match any Single Character with ?

The question-mark character **?** matches any single character:

```
$ ls c?
c1          c2          c3          c4          c5
c6          c7          c8          c9
$
```

This command finds all files that have names consisting of the letter "c" followed by a single character, which in this case happens to be numbers.

```
$ ls a?
aA          aB          aC
$
```

Similarly, this command finds all files whose names start with "a" and are followed by one other character (here, they are uppercase letters). Notice that the file 'a' was not found because the "a" isn't followed by any other character.

```
$ ls ?
a
$
```

However, this command does find 'a', and only 'a' — it is the only single-character filename.

```
$ ls f?
ls: no match
$
```

There are no filenames which consist of "f" followed by a single character; all the files beginning with the letter "f" are four or more characters long. This is shown by the "no match" message.

```
$ ls c??
c10         c11         c12         c13
$
```

This last command prints the names of all files which consist of a "c" followed by two more characters.

3.14.2 How the Shell Interprets Metacharacters

We pause here for a brief discussion on how the Shell interprets the wild-card characters when matching filenames. The important thing here is the difference between what you actually type on the command line and what the command eventually sees when the Shell passes it the argument list.

What happens is that, for every file which matches the selection criteria, the Shell creates a filename argument for the command, then builds a command line, exactly as if you had typed everything out in full. So, when you say

```
ls c?
```

the Shell expands this to:

```
ls c1 c2 c3 c4 c5 c6 c7 c8 c9
```

and then runs that **ls** command.

It is the Shell that interprets the wild-card characters. Any program the Shell then subsequently calls upon has no clue that the user actually typed some shorthand.

There is a limit to the length of a command that the system can handle. The length varies from one system to another, but on most systems the limit seems to be around 250 characters. It may be more or less, depending upon your particular system, but all UNIX systems have some limit. If there are a large number of files that match your wild-cards, and/or all the filenames are long, the command that is built up may well be too large for the Shell to digest at one sitting. If this happens, you will get a message that might read:

```
too many args
```

or maybe:

```
arg list too long
```

or something similar, depending upon which Shell you are using.

This may mean that your wild-cards are matching more than you think, but it may also mean that you can't do what you want, with all the files you want, in one fell swoop. In that case you might have to process the files in smaller groups, or find another way of doing things. Maybe the answer is to write a shell procedure, or script, to achieve what you want.

3.14.3 Match String of Characters with *

The asterisk character * matches any string of characters, including a string of zero length (also called a null string):

```
$ ls c*
c1        c10       c11       c12       c13
c2        c3        c4        c5        c6
c7        c8        c9        contents
$
```

This command finds all filenames that begin with "c", regardless of
how long the filename is.

```
$ ls f*
f1-1       f10-1      f11-1      f11-2      f2-1
f2-2       f2-3       f7-1       f8-1       f8-2
$
```

Here we find all filenames that begin with "f". The next example
finds all those files that begin with "a":

```
$ ls a*
a          aA         aB         aC
$
```

The string "a*" finds the file 'a' even though there are no following
characters in the name. This is because the * matches a null string
as well as any other string.

The * can be used in conjunction with ?, for example:

```
$ ls ?8*
c8         f8-1       f8-2       t8-1
$ ls ?11*
c11        f11-1      f11-2
$ ls ?1*
c1         c10        c11        c12        c13
f1-1       f10-1      f11-1      f11-2
$ ls *8*
c8         f8-1       f8-2       t8-1       zonk8
$
```

The first **ls** in the above example finds all files relating to chapter
8, including figures and tables; the second does the same thing for
chapter 11. The third **ls** attempts to do the same for chapter 1, but
this time we have also found files pertaining to chapters 10 through
13 too, because they all contain "1" as the second character.

The character * on its own matches *all* filenames, so be wary of it.
Also be careful when typing commands containing *, since an extraneous space can do much harm. For example, supposing we had
mistyped the

```
$ ls c*
```

command from the example above, and inadvertently placed a space
between the letter "c" and the * character:

```
$ ls c *
c: no such file or directory
a            aA           aB           aC           c1
c10          c11          c12          c13          c2
c3           c4           c5           c6           c7
c8           c9           contents f1-1            f10-1
f11-1        f11-2        f2-1         f2-2         f2-3
f7-1         f8-1         f8-2         t3-1         t3-2
t6-1         t8-1         temp         zonk8
$
```

Given such a command, **ls** first tries to list the file "c" (which doesn't exist, hence the error message), then proceeds to list everything else.

Since we are using **ls**, no harm is done, but,

☞ If the command had been the **rem**ove files command, **rm**, we would have just wiped out our entire directory!!

Here are some simple rules to follow to avoid this type of accident:

1. Always use **ls** before **rm** with wild-cards. Then you can check that what you are actually going to remove is what you really want to remove.

2. After you have typed the **rm** command line, study it and make sure there are no mistakes BEFORE you hit RETURN.

3. Get into the habit of using the –i (interactive) option on **rm**.

4. Always keep your important files write-protected (mode 444 or r--r--r--). This way, **rm** checks with you before it destroys them. You are also protecting them from being overwritten by **cp** and **mv**. This can be a bit of a nuisance, because now you have to change the mode of a file to make it writeable before you can alter it, and then change the mode back again. However, in the long run this can be less work than having to recreate a file (even from a backup tape) because you accidentally destroyed it.

3.14.4 Classes of Characters with [and] and –

A string of characters enclosed in the [and] brackets is known as a "character-class". The meaning of this construct is "match any single character which appears within the brackets". For example:

```
$ ls c[12684xyz]
c1           c2           c4           c6           c8
$
```

This command lists all filenames which begin with "c" and are followed by one of "1" or "2" or "6" or "8" or "4" or "x" or "y" or "z". As it happens, we don't have files "cx", "cy" or "cz", but the system is happy as long as it can find some files that match the wild-cards. However, if the system can't find any files:

```
$ ls c[xyz]
ls: no match
$
```

you get a message as shown above.

```
$ ls c1[0123]
c10        c11        c12        c13
$
```

Here we find files starting with "c1" and followed by a digit in the range 0 through 3.

```
$ ls [tf]*
f1-1       f10-1      f11-1      f11-2      f2-1
f2-2       f2-3       f7-1       f8-1       f8-2
t3-1       t3-2       t6-1       t8-1       temp
$
```

This last example finds all files which begin with the letter "t" or the letter "f". The filenames are still shown in alphabetical order, even though you didn't specify your character class in that order.

Within brackets, the minus sign – can be used to denote a range of characters:

```
$ ls c1[0-3]
c10        c11        c12        c13
$
```

This **ls** command reproduces the third example in the previous set of examples. It finds all files starting with "c1" and followed by a digit in the range 0 through 3.

```
$ ls a[A-Z]
aA         aB         aC
$
```

This command finds all filenames consisting of "a" followed by an uppercase letter.

It should be emphasized that the ends of the range are actually the values of the characters as they are represented in the ASCII character code. So the range

    [A-z]

(capital "A" through lowercase "z") not only gets all lower and upper case letters, but all other characters whose values fall in the range between. You can see what those are by looking at the **cat** example earlier in this chapter, where the file */usr/pub/ascii* appears.

This aspect of character classes can be particularly confusing when dealing with filenames with digits in them. For instance:

    $ ls c[10-13]
    c1   c3
    $

This **ls** command does *not* find files beginning with "c" and followed by a number 10 through 13. It finds files beginning with "c" and followed by a character which is either "1", or lies in the range "0" through "1", or is a "3".

The same is true of this next example. In fact here, since "6" is greater in the ASCII ordering than "1" it doesn't recognize a range at all:

    $ ls c[6-12]
    c1   c2   c6
    $

In all the above, notice that "hidden" files (those whose names start with a **.**) don't get found by the wild-cards. For example, if we had had a file called *'.trouble'*, it would not show up in any of the examples, not even in

    ls *

It could have been explicitly found by using

    ls .*

but that expands up to the command line:

    ls .trouble . ..

so, as well as seeing the file *'.trouble'*, you also get an **ls** of both the current directory and its parent directory. In general, these hidden files are not much used. To see them it is best to use the –**a** option of **ls** to find the proper names, then use the full names, rather than trying to short-cut using the wild-card characters.

One easy way to see the effects of the Shell's filename expansion is to use the **echo** command, which simply plays back its argument list to the terminal. So, to determine the effect of a command such as **rm**, type:

```
$ echo rm [ca]*
rm a aA aB aC c1 c10 .... c5 c6 c7 c8 c9 contents
$
```

Using **echo** in this way is a good way to learn the effects of the wild card matching without affecting any files or directories.

3.15 Non-Printing Characters in Filenames

Because a filename in the UNIX system can consist of *any* characters, it sometimes happens that you accidentally create a file whose name contains a non-printing character, or a control character. Control-A seems to be a common culprit, and so is ESCAPE (control-[ ). These characters are almost always inserted by "fat-fingering" two keys at a time when typing a filename. The CONTROL key is often just to the left of the "a" on most terminal keyboards, and you often hit the two keys together when you are typing the "a".

This can lead to the anomalous situation where **ls** shows a file exists, but some other commands such as **cat** or **rm** give "no such file" type of error messages.

There are various ways of coping with this situation. In the following example, we assume we want to get rid of file *'square'*, but fail because it has a non-printing character in it. It is quite often possible to isolate the file by using one of the wild-card characters:

```
$ ls
arrow     circle    square    triangle
$ rm square
rm: square non-existent
$ ls s*
square
$ rm s*
$
```

However, you might not be able to isolate the file in this way. Another approach is to make all the files read-only, and then try to remove them all. When **rm** asks whether you want to remove the files reply "yes" only to the troublesome file. Then you can change the mode of the other files back to what they were. The following example shows this process:

```
$ ls
cosine    sine       square    squareroot  tangent
$ rm square
rm: square non-existent
$ ls -l
-rw-rw-r--  1   maryann      123 Jan 29 08:23 cosine
-rw-rw-r--  1   maryann       45 Jan 29 08:23 sine
-rw-rw-r--  1   maryann      167 Jan 29 08:25 square
-rw-rw-r--  1   maryann      251 Jan 29 08:25 squareroot
-rw-rw-r--  1   maryann      189 Jan 29 08:21 tangent
$ chmod 444 *
$ rm *
rm: cosine 444 mode
rm: sine 444 mode
rm: square 444 mode y
rm: squareroot 444 mode
rm: tangent  444 mode
$ ls
cosine    sine        squareroot  tangent
$ chmod 664 *
$
```

Similar things can be done when you want to keep the file, but just get rid of the funny characters in the name:

```
$ ls
arrow    circle    square    triangle
$ rm square
rm: square non-existent
$ ls s*
square
$ mv s* square
$ ls square
square
$
```

Again, if you cannot isolate the file simply, you have to do more work. For example, you could move all the other files out of the directory into some temporary directory, then rename the file, then move all the other files back again.

Of course you wouldn't have to go through all this palaver if you knew exactly what the funny character was. There are some versions of **ls** which display non-printing characters in filenames. Some display the actual character (such as **^A**; others just display a **?** in the filename, but don't actually indicate what the dud character is. If you don't have an **ls** which has the ability to display non-printing characters, do not despair, all is not lost. You can put the output of the **ls** command in a file. We show you how to do that in chapter 4 — "Commands and Standard Files". Then you can use a text editor to examine the file and show any funny characters it might contain, we show you that in chapter 7.

3.16 Ownership and Protection

In common with other time-sharing systems, the UNIX operating system provides a means to assign permissions for files and directories, such that the range of users who can access those files and directories is constrained. Here, we discuss the ideas behind access rights to files and directories.

Every file or directory anyone creates on a UNIX system has an owner, usually the person who created the file or directory in the first place. The owner of a file or directory can then assign various permissions (or protections), allowing or prohibiting access to that directory or file.

For every file and every directory in the file system, there are three classes of users who may have access:

Owner   The owner is the user who initially created it. In some UNIX systems it is possible for the creator of a file to give it to somebody else (the **chown** command changes ownership of a file), but in general, the super-user is the only person who can use the **chown** command. For this reason, we do not discuss **chown** here; **chown** is covered in chapter 14 — "UNIX System Management Guide".

Group   Since a bunch of users can be combined into a user group, there is a group ownership associated with each file and directory. There is an option to **ls** that can show you information about group ownership.

Public   All other users of the UNIX system. That is, anyone who has a user-name and can gain access to the system.

Every file and every directory on the UNIX system has three types of permission, which describe what kinds of things can be done with the directory or file. Because directories and files are slightly different entities, the interpretation of the permissions also differs slightly. The meanings assigned to the permissions are:

Read   A user who has read permission for a file can look at the
                             contents of that file.

                             A user who has read permission for a directory can find
                             out what files there are in that directory. If detailed
                             information about the files in the directory is required
                             (the −l option to **ls**), the directory must have execute per-
                             mission for that user. Whether the user can see the con-
                             tents of the files in the directory, depends on the read
                             permissions for the files themselves.

Write   A user who has write permission for a file can change
                             the contents of that file.

                             A user who has write permission for a directory can
                             change the contents of the directory: she can create new
                             files and remove existing files. Whether she can change
                             existing files in the directory depends on the write per-
                             mission for the files themselves.

Execute   A user who has execute permission for a file can use that
                             filename as a UNIX system command.

                             A user who has execute permission for a directory can
                             change directory to that directory, and can copy files
                             from that directory, providing she also has read permis-
                             sion for the directory. The **x** permission for a directory is
                             often called a "search" permission.

By combining the three types of permissions and the three types of
user, we can come up with a total of nine sets of permissions:

read   permission for the owner (user)
write   permission for the owner (user)
execute permission for the owner (user)

                    read   permission for the group
                    write   permission for the group
                    execute permission for the group

                                read   permission for the public (others)
                                write   permission for the public (others)
                                execute permission for the public (others)

These nine permissions are usually written:

    rwxrwxrwx

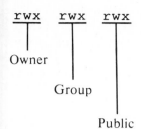

As we show in the sketch, the leftmost three letters refer to the permission that the owner (user) has; the middle three refer to the group permissions; the rightmost three letters refer to the permissions that other users of the system (the public) have. These permissions appear on the long directory listing (**ls –l**) in the first field, adjacent to the directory or file indication ("d" or "–").

A missing permission is indicated by a "–" and is called a "protection" (hence the title of this section). The nine permissions, or protections, are collectively known as the "mode" of the file or directory, and can be changed with the **chmod** command, which is described below. A "read-only mode" file has these permissions:

```
r--r--r--
```

A file with this mode can be read by the owner, the group, and the public. It is protected from being written (modified) or executed by anybody: the public, the group, or the owner.

When we were exploring the system directories we looked at the contents of */bin* and */usr/bin,* where the system commands are held. Files in those directories usually have entries that should look like this:

```
$ ls -l /bin
-r-xr-xr-x  1 bin     12986 Nov 26 12:00 ar
-r-xr-xr-x  1 bin      5604 Nov 26 11:32 as
                      <etc...>
-r-xr-xr-x  1 bin      3268 Nov 26 11:37 cp
                      <etc...>
-r-xr-xr-x  1 bin      8972 Nov 26 11:52 ls
                      <etc...>
-r-xr-xr-x  1 bin      6462 Jan  4 08:32 mv
                      <etc...>
-r-xr-xr-x  1 bin      4252 Jan  1 12:54 uniq
-r-xr-xr-x  1 bin      6348 Nov 26 10:47 who
$
```

The important thing about these files is that the mode is (or should be):

```
r-xr-xr-x
```

That is, they can be read and executed by everybody, but cannot be written over by anybody. Some installations make the modes of the files in */bin* and */usr/bin* such that the owners (super-user, or "bin") have write permission as well, but it is better to set the modes so that there is little chance of accidentally removing the files. Even the super-user can make mistakes.

For any important files, it is a good idea to make them read-only mode to prevent accidental loss of the files.

If you have any files you want to keep private, you should make them mode:

```
rw-------
```

so that only you can read them or write them, and the group and all others are excluded.

3.17 Changing Permissions with 'chmod'

The command **chmod** changes the **mode** of a file or directory. The mode can only be changed by the owner (that is the user who first created the file or directory), or by the super-user.

Newcomers to the UNIX operating system are sometimes confused about the directory/file indication, and the directory or file modes, in the display from **ls**. Although the permissions appear on the output of **ls –l** next to the directory indication, these two things have nothing to do with each other. In other words:

> you cannot convert a file into a directory, or change a directory into a file, by changing its mode!!

There are various versions of **chmod**, and they accept specifications of the required mode in different ways:

• As an absolute value given as an octal number

• As what is termed a "symbolic mode", described below.

The format of the command is:

```
chmod mode file  ....
```

The different versions of **chmod** accept different combinations of the "mode" (new mode or changes to mode) specifications. Some will only accept the first format: the absolute octal number. Others accept the second format, the symbolic mode, as well as the first format. Refer to your UNIX Programmer's Manual to find which version you have on your system.

Since the numerical specification of mode is common to both versions of **chmod**, let's deal with that first, although it is not the easiest to use unless you are familiar with binary arithmetic. For users who know binary arithmetic it's easy — each permission in the group of nine is represented by a one, each protection (lack of permission) is represented by a zero. So "rw-r--r--" translates to "110100100", or "644" in octal notation.

Users not familiar with binary notation can use the translation diagram shown in figure 3.10.

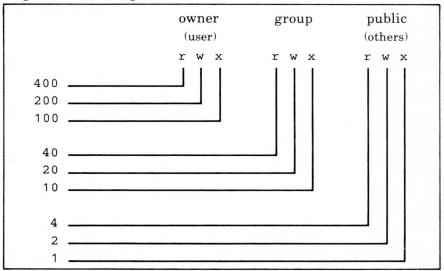

Figure 3.10   Translation Diagram for Permissions

In order to translate the mode you require to a number, simply add up the numbers corresponding to the individual permissions you want. So, if you want the files to be readable and writeable by the owner (that is, you), readable by the group, and readable by all the other users of the system, you perform the addition:

```
400
200
 40
  4
---
644
```

So your **chmod** command will look like:

```
$ chmod 644 thisfile thatfile theotherfile
$
```

If you try to change the mode of a file or directory that doesn't exist, you will get an error message:

```
$ chmod 444 nonesuch
chmod: can't access nonesuch
$
```

If you should get this response, check that you have spelled the filename correctly.

If you try to change the mode of a file or directory that you don't own, you will get the message:

```
$ chmod 644 notmine
chmod: can't change notmine
$
```

In this case, use **ls –l** to check ownership of the file.

Remember that the mode must be the first argument to **chmod**:

```
$ chmod filefirst 644
chmod: invalid mode
$
```

will not work because *'filefirst'* was taken to be the mode.

Using octal numbers to specify the mode may seem cumbersome at first, but you soon get to know the numbers corresponding to the most common permissions attached to files, when you have reached this stage this is the easiest method to use. For instance, here are a few of the common ones:

`644 is rw-r--r--`
> the owner can read and write the file or directory, everybody else can only read it.

`755 is rwxr-xr-x`
> the owner can read, write, and execute the file, everybody else can read or execute it. For a directory, this mode is equivalent to 644.

`711 is rwx--x--x`
> the owner can read, write, and execute the file, everybody else can only execute it.

`444 is r--r--r--`
> this permission implies read-only for everybody.

The second method of specifying the modes is the "symbolic mode", and is rather more complex. You have the choice of saying what you want the mode to be, or of saying how you want the existing

permissions to be modified. To do this, the following abbreviations
are used:

```
u    user (owner) permissions
g    group permissions
o    others (public) permissions
a    all of user, group and others permissions
=    assign a permission absolutely
+    add a permission
-    take away a permission
```

the types of permission are, as usual **r**, **w** and **x**.

Let us look at a few examples of this method of changing mode,
with "before and after" directory listings. Here is how to assign
read/write permission for user, read for group, and read for others:

```
$ ls -l
-r--------  2  maryann    48 Feb 14 12:07 thatfile
-r--------  2  maryann    48 Feb 14 12:07 theotherfile
-r--------  2  maryann    48 Feb 14 12:07 thisfile
$ chmod a=r,u+w thisfile thatfile theotherfile
$ ls -l
-rw-r--r--  2  maryann    48 Feb 14 12:07 thatfile
-rw-r--r--  2  maryann    48 Feb 14 12:07 theotherfile
-rw-r--r--  2  maryann    48 Feb 14 12:07 thisfile
$
```

The first symbolic mode allocates read permission for everybody,
the second adds write permission for the user. If we had said "u=w"
instead of "u+w", we would have allocated write permission but
removed the read permission for the user.

The new mode you require must form a single argument to
chmod. That means there must not be any spaces in it. So if
there is more than one change to be specified, they are separated
by commas but no spaces — though that is unusual in the UNIX
system way of things.

Another way of achieving the required permissions would be:

```
$ chmod u=rw,go=r thisfile thatfile theotherfile
$
```

If the directory was already readable and writeable by everybody:

```
$ ls -l
-rwxrwxrwx   2   maryann    48 Feb 14 12:07 thatfile
-rwxrwxrwx   2   maryann    48 Feb 14 12:07 theotherfile
-rwxrwxrwx   2   maryann    48 Feb 14 12:07 thisfile
$
```

we could have simply removed the write permissions for group and others:

```
$ chmod go-w thisfile thatfile theotherfile
$ ls -l
-rwxr-xr-x   2   maryann    48 Feb 14 12:07 thatfile
-rwxr-xr-x   2   maryann    48 Feb 14 12:07 theotherfile
-rwxr-xr-x   2   maryann    48 Feb 14 12:07 thisfile
$
```

As another example, if you want a file to be executable by everybody, but you want to leave the read/write permissions as they are:

```
$ chmod a+x file
$
```

If you don't specify any of user, group or others, it is taken to be everybody. So:

```
$ chmod +x file
$
```

does exactly the same thing as the previous example.

There are other protections described under **chmod** in the UNIX Programmer's Manual. These additional protections are not used by most users; they are primarily used by the system administrator or super-user. Some of them are concerned with making a file accessible only via a command or program. Another gets the system to treat an executable program file in a special way, this can only be set by the super-user. If these additional protections apply to a file, you see the letter "s" or the letter "t" in the place where you normally see the letter "x".

The permissions assigned when a file or directory is created are different in different UNIX systems. They are under the control of something called the "user mask", or **umask** for short.

The most common default modes you find in any system are:

```
666 or 644 for files,
777 or 755 for directories.
```

3.18 Summary

By now, you should be comfortable with the commands for displaying the contents of a directory (**ls**), for moving around in the directory structure (**cd**), for making and removing directories (**mkdir** and **rmdir**), those for copying and renaming files (**cp** and **mv**, for removing files (**rm**), and some of the commands (such as **cat** and **file**) for examining what is in a file.

Once you are at ease with the notions of directories and files in the UNIX system, you are in a position to use the system effectively. Experiment with making your own directories and creating files in those directories. Play with full pathnames and relative pathnames to gain facility in their use.

Also try using **chmod** to change permissions on your own files and directories. See what happens when you can write files but not directories, and vice versa. It is important to explore the different effects of permissions for files and directories, and their interactions.

Used effectively, the UNIX system file structure is a powerful tool in its own right; experienced users can exploit the capabilities of the file system to organize their data in efficient structures.

4 Commands and Standard Files

When a program runs on the UNIX system, it usually expects some input (data) and it usually produces some output (results). With very few exceptions, most UNIX programs have three "standard" files. One of these files is the "Standard Input", and is the place from which a program expects to read its input. Another is called the "Standard Output", and is the file to which the program writes its results. The third file is the "Diagnostic Output", and it is a file to which the program writes any error responses.

In general, if a command expects input, and no file is specified, the Standard Input for that command is taken to be the user's terminal keyboard. Most commands are geared up to display their results on the Standard Output, which is usually the user's terminal screen. Lastly, the diagnostic output is also usually sent to the terminal screen.

The UNIX operating system provides a simple but very powerful capability to change the default cases listed above. It is possible to tell the Shell that the Standard Input for a command is to be taken from a file. It is also possible to have the Standard Output of a command written to a file. This process is called "redirection of Input and Output".

The Diagnostic Output can be redirected just as can the Standard Output. You can arrange that any error messages from a command go to a file other than the one where the Standard Output is going, so that error messages do not clutter up the results.

It is also possible to take the Standard Input of a command directly from the Standard Output of another command, and similarly to direct the Standard Output of one command straight to the Standard Input of the next command. This feature is called "piping", and a string of commands hooked together in this way is called a "pipeline".

There are a few minor exceptions to these rules. These exceptions constitute end cases, where reading input from the terminal, and writing output to the terminal, do not make sense. For instance: the **ls** command takes its "input" as the name of a directory whose contents are to be displayed; the **lpr** command sends its output to a line printer; the **rm** command has no output.

4.1 Redirecting the Standard Output

If a filename argument to a command is prefixed by the **>** character, the Standard Output of that command is **redirected** so that it is placed in that file instead of going to the terminal screen. For example, the straight **ls** command displays a list of the contents of a directory on your terminal screen:

```
$ ls -l
drwxrwxrwx   5   maryann      96 Feb 14 12:11 docs
-rw-rw-rw-   1   maryann     181 Feb 14 12:30 message
-rw-rw-rw-   1   maryann     181 Feb 14 12:31 message_too
drwxrwxrwx   4   maryann      80 Feb 14 12:39 progs
$
```

But if we use the **>** sign as a redirection indicator, the command line:

```
$ ls -l > dirconts
```

puts the contents listing of the current working directory into a file called 'dirconts', which is placed into the current directory. You can now view the file at your leisure, or change it around for any useful purposes of your own.

It is not necessary to surround the **>** character with spaces, so the commands:

```
$ date > today
$ date >today
$ date>today
```

are all correct and all do the same thing, namely direct the output of the **date** command into a file called *'today'*.

If the named file to which output is redirected doesn't already exist, it is created.

☞ If the file to which the Standard Output is redirected *does* already exist, the previous contents of the file are lost!! This is because the first thing the Shell does when it sees the redirection mark, >, is to create an empty file to hold the results of the command.

On the Berkeley version of the UNIX system, setting the Shell variable called "noclobber" inhibits the Shell from clobbering the file.

Now, if you look in the *'dirconts'* file with the **cat** command, you should see a regular directory listing:

```
$ cat dirconts
-rw-rw-rw-   1   maryann      0 Feb 14 12:42 dirconts
drwxrwxrwx   5   maryann     96 Feb 14 12:11 docs
-rw-rw-rw-   1   maryann    181 Feb 14 12:30 message
-rw-rw-rw-   1   maryann    181 Feb 14 12:31 message_too
drwxrwxrwx   4   maryann     80 Feb 14 12:39 progs
$
```

You see that *'dirconts'* itself appears in the directory listing as a zero-length file. The reason for this is that it is the Shell which creates the file to receive the command's output, and it does this before the command runs. So, at the instant the **ls** command starts, there is an empty file, called *'dirconts'*, in the directory. Here is a case where you might want to use one of those "hidden" files whose names start with a period:

```
$ ls -l > .dirconts
$
```

4.1.1 Redirecting and Appending the Standard Output

If you don't want to lose the contents of an existing file, but want the output of a command appended to the end of it, you can do this by prefixing the file name with two right chevron signs **>>**. For example:

```
$ pwd >> dirconts
$
```

prints the name of the current working directory at the end of the contents listing of the directory that we obtained above.

If the file to which the Standard Output is being redirected via the >> sign doesn't exist, it is created. So if we hadn't done the previous **ls –l > dirconts** the *'dirconts'* file would contain only the name of the current working directory. In many ways >> is safer to use than >, because it doesn't destroy previous information.

4.2 Redirecting the Standard Input

Just as the > character or the >> sign redirects the Standard Output of a command to a file, so we can redirect the Standard Input for a command to come from a file, instead of the terminal keyboard, by prefixing the file name with a left chevron sign <.

An example of the use of this redirection is with the **mail** facility:

```
$ mail
```

enters the **mail** utility, and expects mail messages from the terminal keyboard, while:

```
$ mail <message
$
```

enters **mail**, and takes mail messages from the file *'messages'*, created previously by means of (say) an editor.

In general, redirection of Input is not used as often as redirection of Output, because a lot of commands are designed to take their input from files anyway. The exceptional cases are like those mentioned just above, namely when a UNIX program generates a file of commands for another UNIX program.

If no files are specified, commands use the Standard Input. Let us show this with an example of using the **cat** command:

```
$ cat
So the IRS said to us:
hold out your wallets and repeat after me:
Help yourself.
^D
So the IRS said to us:
hold out your wallets and repeat after me:
Help yourself.
$
```

Having typed the **cat** command as shown above, the system responds with a glassy-eyed stare. There is no indication that **cat** wants anything. Even when you type some lines, you see nothing. **cat** holds a certain amount of data before playing it back. The exact amount varies, but it is usually 512 characters. We indicated the end of the data by typing a control-D character (**^D**) in the example. Here, we had typed less than 512 characters before the control-D, so at that point, **cat** replayed what we had typed. We can get **cat** to echo on a line by line basis by giving it the **–u** (for **u**nbuffered) option.

Now talking to yourself with the **cat** command is an exercise in futility. The really useful aspect of **cat** is to con**cat**enate files, and copy the result onto the Standard Output. So, the more appropriate use of **cat** is like this:

```
$ cat < thisfile
```

which con**cat**enates the contents of the file called *'thisfile'* to the Standard Output. As it happens, **cat** is one of the many commands which accept filenames as arguments, and as such, **cat** does not actually need the redirection marker:

```
$ cat thisfile
```

has just the same effect as does the example above.

However, there are many commands which only act on the Standard Input. If you want these to work on a file you have to redirect the input to be from that file. An example of this is the command **tr** (**tr**anslate characters) which we show you how to use in chapter 6.

4.3 Notes and Cautions on Redirection

You must take special care if you are redirecting both Standard Input and Standard Output, for example:

```
$ cat < left > right
$
```

Don't use the same filename in both places. A **cat** command which looks like this:

```
$ cat < thisfile > thisfile
$
```

is a sure way to lose *'thisfile'*. This is because, when the Shell sees the redirection character >, it creates an empty file ready to hold your output. If the output file happens to be the same name as the input file, the command just empties your input file!!

By the same token:

```
$ cat thisfile > thisfile
$
```

is no good either, but:

```
$ cat thatfile >> thatfile
$
```

is OK — you just copy *'thatfile'* onto the end of itself. This might not be what you want, but at least you haven't lost anything.

4.4 Creating a File the Easy Way with 'cat'

We have said that commands which are not given a file name take the Standard Input, which is usually the terminal keyboard. Thus if you simply say:

```
$ cat
```

everything you type is transferred to the Standard Output. Under normal circumstances this means that whatever you type is echoed on the screen. But, supposing you redirect the Standard Output, like this:

```
$ cat > newfile
```

everything you type (including your mistakes) gets put in the file called *'newfile'*. As we said earlier, **cat** holds a certain amount of data (usually 512 characters) before producing any output. So nothing appears in the file until you have typed that amount. If you accidentally interrupted the process, or if the system crashed while you were typing, you would lose a lot of work. It is best to use the −u (for unbuffered) option:

```
$ cat -u > newfile
```

so that each line goes into *'newfile'* as it is typed.

To stop input and revert to the Shell, you type the "end of text" character (control-D) after your last line. At that point you will again see the system prompt $. So, using **cat** is a way to create files without having to learn how to use the text editor. Of course, if you make mistakes you will have to use the editor, or some other means, to correct them.

For instance, suppose you want to make a list of the people in your project, with their phone numbers:

```
$ cat -u >people
Maryann Clark     101
Sally Smith       113
Jane Bailey       121
Jack Austen       120
Steve Daniels     111
Sylvia Dawson     110
Henry Morgan      112
^D
$
```

You can also use **cat** to modify the file by adding things to the end of it:

```
$ cat -u >>people
Hank Parker       114
Charlie Smith     122
Bill Williams     100
^D
$
```

Remember to type the end-of-file character, control-D, to terminate input to the **cat** command, as we have shown in the examples.

Now, of course, we can use **cat** to play back what we just created:

```
$ cat people
Maryann Clark     101
Sally Smith       113
<and so on and so on>
Charlie Smith     122
Bill Williams     100
$
```

4.5 Connecting Commands with Pipelines

We have said that the Standard Output of one process (or program) can be the Standard Input of another process. When this is done a "pipeline" is formed.

We already showed the **who** command back in chapter 2. **who** displays a list of users on the system. There is another command called **wc**, which counts things. Using these two utilities, we can find out how many people are logged in:

```
$ who | wc -l
19
$
```

This simple example shows the Standard Output of the **who** command feeding to the Standard Input of the **wc** command (which we told to count lines with the –l option). The result is a count of the number of users on the system.

Pipelines provide a flexible and powerful mechanism for doing jobs easily and quickly, without the need to construct special purpose tools. Existing tools can be combined, to do those one-off jobs that crop up so often.

To explain pipelines it is often easier to think of this as a flow of data which is operated on by several programs (or processes) in turn. Consider a number of operations being performed on a set of data, as shown in the diagram in figure 4.1.

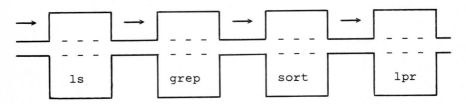

Figure 4.1   A Pipeline of UNIX System Commands

We could write this sequence:

```
$ ls -1 /tmp | grep maryann | sort +3nr | lpr
```

The symbol | (vertical bar) is known as the "pipe" symbol. The Standard Output of the command to the left of the | becomes the Standard Input to the command on the right of |.

The output of the above **ls** command is a "long" listing of all files and subdirectories in the system directory */tmp*. Instead of being written to the terminal (the default Standard Output), it is passed to the **grep** command.

grep and **sort** are two of the utility programs which find all kinds of uses. In this particular example, **grep** is selecting all lines containing the string "maryann" from its Standard Input, and **sort** is sorting the fourth field of all those selected lines in reverse numerical order. We explain **grep** and **sort** in some detail in chapter 6 — "Text Manipulation". What is important is to understand the concept of taking the results of one command, and passing it through various operations which modify it in some way, before the final result is seen. This string of connected commands is a pipeline.

The final stage of our pipeline is the command **lpr**, which routes its input to a printer, so we get a print-out instead of seeing the results on the terminal screen. This, in fact, is the most common use of **piping**. Since all commands except **lpr** provide output to the Standard Output (normally the terminal screen), the only way to get a hard copy (print-out) of anything is to pipe it to **lpr** (covered in chapter 6).

The effect of the above pipeline could be achieved by typing the commands one at a time and using temporary files, in a sequence like this:

```
$ ls -l /tmp >temp1
$ grep maryann temp1 >temp2
$ sort +3nr temp2 >temp3
$ lpr temp3
$ rm temp[123]
$
```

Note the use of temporary files. Although we used three, we could have got away with two by re-using *'temp1'* for the output of **sort**. For tidiness, and to avoid eating up space, these files should be removed. *But*, we must be careful not to remove *'temp3'* before it has finished printing.

This is one of the major advantages of pipes: the system does all the intermediate work for you. Were you to use temporary files instead of pipelines, you burden yourself with unnecessary work; you have to keep track of which temporary files you use; then you must ensure they get removed when you have finished with them. All this adds up to boring busy-work that a computer is better fitted to take care of.

Another point to note is that piping is quicker. With redirection of output, each command must be completed before the next one begins to work on the data. In a pipeline, each process starts executing as soon as there is some data for it to work on.

4.6 Filters

A command which accepts its input from the Standard Input, and produces its output on the Standard Output, is known as a "filter". The word "filter" is derived from the analogy with the kinds of filters used in plumbing or electronics. A command which is a filter takes some input, performs some filtering action (weeding out blank lines, for instance), and finally generates some output.

There are some commands (**tr** for example) which can *only* be used as filters. If you want to apply them to files you have to **redirect** the Standard Input.

Most commands on the UNIX system can be used as filters. Commands which are filters can be used as intermediate operations in a pipeline (between two | symbols). In our examples above, **grep** and **sort** are filters, and can be used at intermediate places in the pipe.

Some commands are not filters because either their input does not come from the Standard Input, or they do not produce their output on the Standard Output.

The **ls** command is not a filter since it does not accept the Standard Input — its "input" is a directory whose contents are to be listed. **ls** can only be the first command in a pipeline.

Similarly, the **lpr** command cannot be used as a filter because it does not write to the Standard Output — its "output" is to a printer somewhere. **lpr** can only be used as the last command in a pipeline.

Redirection of input and output can be used in conjunction with pipelines, but:

- It makes no sense to redirect input in any of the commands in the pipeline other than the first.

- It is nonsense to redirect output on any command in a pipeline except the last.

4.7 To See and to Save with 'tee'

Sometimes, although you want to save the output of a command in a file, you would also like to see it on the terminal as it is being produced. Then, if you see that the output looks wrong, you can stop the command. A useful command which helps you achieve this is

tee, which acts like a T-junction, as shown in figure 4.2.

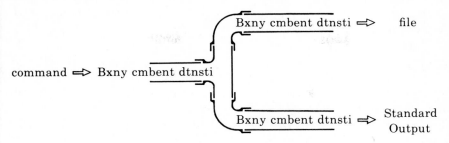

Figure 4.2   Effects of the tee Command

The command:

```
$ ls -l ¦ tee dirconts
```

shows a full listing of the contents of the current directory on the terminal screen, and also puts it in the file *'dirconts'.*

4.8 Diagnostic Output

The output from most commands is written to the Standard Output, but if errors occur when the command is executed, the error messages produced are not necessarily written to the Standard Output. There is another type of output that commands can generate: this is called the Diagnostic Output.

Like the Standard Output, the Diagnostic Output is the user's terminal screen by default. Also like the Standard Output, the Diagnostic Output may be redirected to a file. Redirection of the Diagnostic Output is not quite such a straightforward matter as redirecting the Standard Output, before we can do it we must know about File Descriptors.

A File Descriptor is simply a number associated with a file of data. Three such numbers are assigned by default on UNIX systems:

0 is the file descriptor for the Standard Input,

1 is the file descriptor for the Standard Output,

2 is the file descriptor for the Diagnostic Output.

When you redirect the Standard Output to a file by using the notation

```
> outfile
```

the Diagnostic Output is not redirected. So error messages still appear on the terminal screen. In order to put the error messages into a file it is also necessary to redirect the Diagnostic Output.

It is the Shell that redirects Input and Output. An individual command does not know that its Standard Input and Output have been redirected.

There are many different versions of the Shell. Although the method of redirecting Standard Input and Output is the same in all versions, the method of redirecting the Diagnostic Output differs from one version of the Shell to another. In this book, we are mostly concerned with two versions of the Shell: the UNIX system version 7 Shell, and the C-shell which is available on the Berkeley UNIX system.

The following paragraphs describe the different ways of redirecting the Diagnostic Output in these Shells.

In the version 7 Shell, the Diagnostic Output can be redirected by preceding the usual redirection sign > with the file descriptor number associated with the Diagnostic Output:

```
$ cat somefile nofile 2> errfile
```

redirects the error messages to the file *'errfile'.* The normal output of the command still appears on the terminal screen. If you wish to redirect both Standard and Diagnostic Outputs, you have to give two redirection signs:

```
$ cat somefile nofile > outfile 2> errfile
$
```

The simple > sign, which redirects the Standard Output, is merely the default case of the more general:

```
file_descriptor_number> filename
```

so that the command:

```
$ cat somefile nofile 1> outfile 2> errfile
$
```

has exactly the same effect as the previous example.

If you want to redirect both the Standard Output and the Diagnostic Output to the same place, the format of the command is like this:

```
$ cat firsthalf secondhalf 1> composite 2>&1
```

If you don't want to see error messages appearing anywhere, they can be effectively thrown away by redirecting the Diagnostic Output to the device called */dev/null*

```
$ cat somefile nofile > outfile 2> /dev/null
$
```

/dev/null is a special file which acts just like an end-of-file when a program tries to read it, and is an infinite sink when a command writes to it.

In the C-Shell, the Diagnostic Output can be redirected along with the Standard Output by using the notation >&. For example:

```
% cat thisfile nofile >& output
%
```

redirects both the normal output of the **cat** command, and the error messages to the file *'output'*. In a similar manner, the Diagnostic Output can be piped to another process along with the Standard Output by using the notation ¦&:

```
% cat thisfile nofile ¦& lpr
%
```

means that both error messages and the normal output of the **cat** command are routed to the line printer.

4.9 Background Processing

In the introduction, we said that the UNIX operating system is a multi-tasking system. This means that the system can attend to more than one job at a time, for any given user. In UNIX system terminology, each one of these multiple tasks is called a "process". A process is a running program with some specific job to do. For example, there is a process, which happens to be the Shell, doing the job of listening to your terminal. Every time you ask the Shell to run a command, the Shell runs that command as a separate process. For historical reasons, the process which converses with your terminal is called a "foreground" process, so called because it is in the foreground of your attention. Normally, each command you type, or each pipeline of commands, is a foreground process, and as such they run "while you wait", at the terminal.

It is possible, however, to run commands in the "background". This means that the system prompt re-appears immediately after you type the command. The command has not completed: it is still running, but you can use the system to do other things while the background command proceeds. If you want to run a command which takes a long time to complete, you can run that command in the background.

The way in which you ask the UNIX system to run a command in the background, is by ending the command with the ampersand character **&**, for example:

```
$ nroff doc &
2042
$
```

The command **nroff** is the text formatting command described in chapter 9 — "Formatting Documents". Text formatting is a time-consuming process, so it is a good candidate for background processing. We put a space between the last argument and the **&**, but a space is not necessary,

```
nroff doc&
```

would do just as well.

When you ask the UNIX operating system to run a command in the background, it replies with a number ("2042" in our example above). This is the process number (or process identity, abbreviated PID) which the operating system associates with the command you typed. Sometimes the command (process) you put in the background calls up other commands (processes) which you don't know about, but only the number for the primary (parent) process is shown when you type the command.

When you put a command in the background, make a note of the process number which the UNIX system displays: it is useful when you want to see what's going on, or if you decide to stop the background process.

After displaying the process number associated with the background task, the system displays its prompt sign. You can then type another command, so you are actually having the UNIX system doing two things for you at the same time. Alternatively, you can log off. The background command continues running, even while you are not using the system.

In fact, you can have several commands running in the background if you want to. But avoid having too many things going on at the same time: it slows the system down considerably, and you might end up taking just as long to complete all your tasks as if you had done them one by one at the terminal keyboard waiting for the prompt each time (in the foreground). The definition of "too many things going on" depends on the size of the machine and the number of other users. You have to guess at it.

☞ One word of caution: if your background process is taking input from a file, don't start another command, either in the background or in the foreground, which will modify the contents of that file. If, in our example

> **nroff doc&**

we had immediately called up a text editor and used it to modify the file *'doc'*, the results of the text formatting operation would be unpredictable.

What happens to the output from a background task? The answer is, nothing out of the ordinary. The output of the command: **nroff doc&** goes to the Standard Output as usual. So, if the text formatting process finishes while you are in the middle of an **ls –l** command, the results of both commands will be mixed up together on the screen. Even worse, if you have logged off, the output of the formatter will be completely lost. Perhaps the very worst is when someone has put a process in the background, then logged off, then you log on at the same terminal: you get the output of someone else's command on your screen!

Obviously, the thing to do is to redirect the output of the background command to a file:

```
$ nroff doc > doc.format &
2042
$
```

Now the output of your background command will not disturb you, or anyone else, who is executing commands in the foreground.

Alternatively, you could pipe the results to the printer:

```
$ nroff doc ¦ lpr &
2042
$
```

In practice, you may want to redirect the Diagnostic Output as well as the Standard Output. This is especially true if you are going to log off: if your command fails for some reason, you still want to see what error messages were produced.

4.9.1 Finding Out What Is Going On with 'ps'

When you are executing commands in the background, how can you check whether they are still running or have finished?

There is a command called **ps** which displays the status of active processes. If you simply type the **ps** command on its own, you will see something like this:

```
$ ps
PID TTY TIME CMD
2036 02  0:05 -sh
2037 02  0:01 ps
$
```

These are the processes belonging to (activated by) the user who typed the **ps** command. As you can see, there are two — the login process shown by "−sh" (the Shell), and the **ps** process itself.

The information given is the process identification number (PID), the terminal that the process was started from (TTY), the amount of time (computer time, not wall-clock time) that the process has taken to execute so far (TIME), and the command line that was typed to initiate the process (CMD). The CMD information is not always exact. **ps** comes up with the nearest approximation it can to the typed command line.

If you type a **ps** command, and you see something like this:

```
$ ps
PID TTY TIME CMD
1098 08  0:20 -sh
2036 02  0:05 -sh
2038 02  0:01 ps
$
```

it means you are logged on twice, once on tty02 and once on tty08. This illustrates that **ps** displays all processes associated with the user, not those associated with a particular terminal.

Now suppose you put a command to be processed in the background:

```
$ nroff doc &
2042
$ ps
PID TTY TIME CMD
2036 02  0:05 -sh
2042 02  0:02 nroff doc
2043 02  0:01 ps
$
```

You can see that the **nroff** command is running. If a **ps** sometime after this doesn't show **nroff** running, it means that formatting is complete, or has failed for some reason.

Here is a general rule on how to misuse the UNIX operating system:

If you put a command to be executed in the background, then do nothing but sit at your terminal typing **ps** commands until you see that it is complete — there was no point in putting it in the background in the first place!!

You might just as well have run the command in the foreground, and waited for the system prompt to tell you it was finished. This may seem obvious, but it quite commonly happens with fairly new users of the system when they first "discover" background processing.

Nevertheless there are still a couple of advantages to using background processing. One is that you can decide to do something else at any time while background job is running. The other advantage is that you are not likely to interrupt the job accidentally by hitting the interrupt key on the keyboard.

There are various options to the **ps** command, one is the l option, which gives a "long" listing of the processes statuses.

ps is one command that does not care whether you use a − sign to introduce its options. Because **ps** doesn't take any filenames, there is no chance of confusing an option with a filename, as on many other commands.

```
$ ps l
F S UID  PID PPID CPU PRI NICE ADDR SZ WCHAN TTY TIME CMD
1 S  99 2036    1   3  30   20 5512 12 50602 02  0:02 -sh
1 R  99 2058 2036  52  53   20 6021 20       02  0:02 ps l
$
```

Much of the information here is concerned with details of what the operating system does when it is processing your commands. We refer you to the description of **ps** in the UNIX Programmer's Manual if you want to know about this. However, some of the columns are of interest:

- The column headed S displays the state of the process. There are many different values that can appear in this place, the interesting ones are R, which means that the process is running; S, which means that the process is sleeping (while the system is doing something else); W, which means that the process is waiting for some other process to finish before it can proceed.

- UID is the user identity number of the user who started the process. Some versions of **ps** are kind enough to print the user-name in this column.

- PPID is the name of the parent process, in our example the PID of the login process (–sh) is the PPID of the other commands.

- PRI shows the priority allocated to the process, the user has no control over this. However, one of the factors that the UNIX system uses to compute the priority of a process is the figure given under the next column, NICE, and the user can control this to some extent by using the **nice** command. In both the PRI and NICE columns, a high number means a low priority.

Another option to **ps** is **a** (for **all**). Normally **ps** only displays the processes activated by the user who types the **ps** command. When the **a** option is given, the processes activated by all users are displayed. Both the **a** and **l** options can be given together:

```
$ ps al
F S UID   PID PPID CPU PRI NICE ADDR SZ WCHAN TTY TIME CMD
1 S 45 1317    1    0  30   20  6203 12 50762 03  0.15 -sh
1 S 83 1514    1    0  30   20  4732 12 51266 06  0.03 -sh
1 S 45 1491 1317    0  29   20  4454 13 51356 03  0.10 ed conv.c
1 S 83 1615 1514    0  28   20 10244 12  7102 06  0.03 nroff spec
1 S 99 2036    1    3  30   20  5512 12 50602 02  0:02 -sh
1 S 83 1621 1514    2  29   20  7756 02  2722 06  0.01 ls
1 R 99 2058 2036   52  53   20  6021 20       02  0:02 ps l
$
```

We can see that users number 45 and 83 are logged on, as well as number 99. Number 45 is using the editor **ed** and number 83 is formatting a file called *'spec'* (probably in the background) and using **ls**.

4.9.2 Running Low Priority
Commands with 'nice'

If you are not in a hurry for the results of the command you put in the background, you can tell the operating system that this is not of high priority by using the **nice** command:

```
$ nice nroff doc > doc.fmat &
2099
$
```

This is a nice thing to do, because then the UNIX system can give more attention to things that require quick response (an **ls** command typed at a terminal, for instance). Here are some illustrations of the effects of using **nice**. First, we simply put a **nroff** command in the background:

```
$ nroff doc > doc.fmat &
2151
$ ps l
F S UID  PID PPID CPU PRI NICE ADDR SZ WCHAN TTY TIME CMD
1 S  99 2036    1   3  30  20  5512 12 50602 02 0:02 -sh
1 R  99 2151 2036 111  56  20 10244 34       02 0.15 nroff doc
1 R  99 2152 2036  39  52  20  6021 20       02 0:02 ps l
$
```

You can see that all the processes have the same value of 20 in the column headed NICE. The system uses this value to calculate the priority it attaches to each process; the priority value is shown in the column headed PRI. As you can see, the **nroff** command and the **ps** command have very similar priority values. This means that the system is giving more or less equal time to both commands, with the foreground **ps** getting slightly more than the background **nroff**. Highest priority is given to the **sh** command which is watching what you type at your terminal, indicated by its having the lowest number under PRI.

Now we will put the same command "nicely" in the background.

```
$ nice nroff doc > doc.fmat &
2154
$ ps l
F S UID  PID PPID CPU PRI NICE ADDR SZ WCHAN TTY TIME CMD
1 S  99 2036    1   3  30  20  5512 12 50602 02 0:02 -sh
1 R  99 2154 2036 160  70  30 10244 34       02 0.03 nroff doc
1 R  99 2155 2036  36  52  20  6021 20       02 0:02 ps l
$
```

You can see that the NICE value is now 30, and the priority value is up to 70. Now the **nroff** command will take longer to complete, but you are not hogging the system to the possible detriment of the other users, or your own foreground processes.

You can control the amount of "niceness" by giving a number:

```
$ nice -5 nroff doc > doc.fmat &
2160
$ ps 1
F S UID  PID PPID CPU PRI NICE ADDR SZ WCHAN TTY TIME CMD
1 S  99 2036    1   3  30   20 5512 12 50602 02  0:02 -sh
1 R  99 2160 2036 148  64   25 10244 34       02  0.03 nroff doc
1 R  99 2164 2036  33  52   20 6021 20        02  0:02 ps 1
$
```

As you can see from the above **ps**, this adds a "niceness" value of 5 to the "not nice" number of 20. The **nroff** command runs at a higher priority than it would with a straight **nice**, but not so high as it would without any **nice** command at all. The highest niceness (lowest priority) that can be called for is 39, this is achieved by putting a value of 20, or higher, on the **nice** command.

The super-user can use **nice** to execute high priority commands by giving a negative niceness, for example, –10 runs a command at a very high priority.

4.9.3 Immunity from Disconnects with 'nohup'

Another command which can be used in connection with background processes is **nohup**. The name of this command is derived from **no hang-up**, and has nothing to do with the state of one's psyche.

nohup makes a command immune from a telephone line connection getting disconnected. However it can be interrupted by the DEL key, so the command should be put in the background:

```
$ nohup nroff doc&
2176
$ Sending output to 'nohup.out'
```

The output of the command is automatically re-directed to a file called *'nohup.out'*, as indicated by the message in the example above.

The priority is equivalent to using the **nice** command with **–5**; that is to say, the niceness value is 25. If you want to alter this value, you can use both **nohup** and **nice** together. For example:

```
$ nice -5 nohup nroff doc > doc.fmat&
2180
$
```

allocates a total niceness value of 30: the "not nice" 20, plus 5 for the
nohup, plus another 5 for the **nice**.

4.9.4 Stopping Background
Processes with 'kill'

If you start a command running in the background, and then change
your mind for some reason, you can stop the process with the **kill**
command. To do this you need to know the process identification
number (PID). For instance, in the very first example we gave of a
command put in the background, we showed a process identification
number of 2042. To stop that command running, we say:

```
$ kill 2042
$
```

If the process you put in the background started lots of other sub-
processes (called children), they will all eventually die. However,
this may take some time. You might want to find the PID numbers
of these child processes using **ps**, then kill them all with the same
kill command. You can put more than one process identification
number on the **kill**.

Processes are usually stopped when the UNIX system sends them a
certain signal. Signals are numbered 1 through 15, signal number 15
being the usual termination signal that the **kill** command sends.
However, some processes are clever enough to be able to ignore that
signal, so they cannot be stopped in this fashion. You can send a different signal if you wish, by specifying the signal number as an
option to the **kill** command. Signal number 9 is a sure kill signal, so
if your process refuses to die in the normal manner, you can zap it
with:

```
$ kill -9 2042
$
```

A final word of caution. We saw in **ps** that your login is a process
and has a process identification number. If you **kill** that process, you
will log yourself off of the UNIX system. Luckily, the login process
avoids a normal **kill**, but **kill –9** is a sure way to suicide.

4.10 Summary

If you have made it this far, you have covered the essential core ideas behind the UNIX operating system. Now is probably a good time to take a rest, lay back with a glass of champagne, and mull over what you have learned so far.

The power of the UNIX system derives from the synergism of the concepts we have discussed: the hierarchical directory and file system; redirection of input and output; pipes, and filters. The combinations of all these facilities is what makes the UNIX operating system a benign environment for the software developer, and for the serious technical writer.

The remainder of this book describes individual utilities in some detail, and illustrates their use in processing textual data.

5 User to User Communications

Part of the philosophy behind the UNIX operating system is that of cooperation between the people who are using it for their day to day work. Cooperation and working together imply good facilities for communications.

This chapter covers those facilities whereby users can communicate via the computer system, without the need to telephone each other, or walk around to find each other.

The UNIX system features which facilitate communication are: the **write** command, which enables a message to be sent directly to another user; and the **mail** facility, for "electronic mail". There is also a "timed delivery" command called **at**, which has many applications when combined with the electronic mail facilities.

5.1 Sending Messages with 'write'

The **write** command sends a message to a specified user, right at the time when you type the message, provided that the recipient is logged in to the system. **write** should really only be used when you are in a real panic and wish to talk at somebody right away. Some people get very distracted and annoyed when messages start appearing at random intervals while they're trying to type at the terminal. For this reason, you should be circumspect in your use of **write**.

If someone is logged in over a phone line, their phone will be continuously busy, and **write** is the handiest way to get in touch with them.

Here is a typical example of how to use the **write** command:

```
$ write henry
Flee, all is discovered!!!!!!
^D
$
```

Since **write** takes the message from the Standard Input, there is nothing to indicate that the command is waiting for input after you have typed **write** and the login name. You simply type in the message you want to send, as many lines as you like, and you terminate the message with the end-of-text character, control-D. You don't get any indication that your message has actually been received anywhere.

What the recipient, in our case the user "henry", sees is:

```
Message from maryann tty08...
Flee, all is discovered!!!!!!
EOF
```

The EOF indicates the the message is finished, and Maryann has quit writing.

In this example we have shown a simple one-line message. If the message is more than one line, the recipient doesn't receive it all in one fell swoop. Rather, he sees each line as it is typed, so he has no indication that the message is complete other than the EOF. When conducting a two-way "conversation" this can be a problem, as we discuss below.

Considering the content of the message in the above example, the one-way nature of the communication may be justified. But under normal circumstances, you would expect the "conversation" to be two-sided. For example, suppose Maryann tries to get in touch with Steve:

```
$ write steve
```

she doesn't immediately enter the message, but waits to see if Steve responds. Steve receives a message that says:

```
Message from maryann tty08...
```

At this point Steve gives his own **write** command:

```
$ write maryann
Hi.   What?
```

Steve doesn't type control-D, so now we have two people "talking" to each other, until one of them types control-D to drop out of the conversation.

At the end of the conversation, Maryann's screen might look like this:

```
$ write steve
Message from steve tty04...
Hi. What?
How about dinner tonight?
I have to wash my socks, how about tomorrow?
I must take the cat to the vet. Friday?
chess club.   Next week?
^D
$
```

What Maryann has typed is shown boldface, Steve's replies are in normal type. Steve's side of the conversation would leave his screen looking like:

```
$ Message from maryann tty08...
write maryann
Hi. What?
How about dinner tonight?
I have to wash my socks, how about tomorrow?
I must take the cat to the vet. Friday?
chess club.   Next week?
EOF
^D
$
```

Here we have shown what Steve typed boldface, and Maryann's contributions in normal type.

There are two points to notice about this conversation. One is that Maryann "hung up" on Steve — that is, she terminated her part of the conversation without warning, which is rather rude. Another point is that on either side, the dialogue consisted of one-line questions. But this is not always going to be the case, you are often going to convey information rather than ask questions, and the information may well take more than one line. How does each party know when the other has finished and is waiting for a reply? There is no easy way, the people concerned must set up some protocol so that they understand each other.

The protocol suggested in the Unix Programmers Manual is that each message is terminated by the character "o", for "over", and when one party is about to quit the conversation they type "oo", for "over and out". Another way is to set up the signals when you first invoke the **write** command, for instance:

```
$ write henry
I will signal the end of each message with "->" are you
receiving me ? ->
Message from henry tty03...
receiving you loud and clear ->
  .
  .
                    <etc...>
  .
  .
That's all. Bye
^D
$
```

If you try to write to someone who is not logged in, you get a message:

```
$ write sylvia
sylvia not logged in.
$
```

and the **write** command terminates. If you try to write to someone who is not a user,

```
$ write percival
percival not logged in.
$
```

you get the same message, because **write** doesn't check for known system users, only for users logged in. Before writing, you could check to see who is logged in with:

```
$ who
sally     tty00    08:30
henry     tty03    08:31
steve     tty04    09:05
sally     tty06    09:15
hank      tty07    09:15
maryann   tty08    09:10
$
```

It takes the UNIX system a while to check if the user you wish to communicate with is logged in. You may have already started typing your message before the system finds the user is not logged in, and decides to ignore your command. If this happens, it is a good idea to cancel what you have typed using your line kill character. If you don't, next time you type RETURN, the system will try and interpret your partial message as a command. This is unlikely to do any damage, but can be disconcerting.

There are some UNIX system commands that "lock out" the **write** command for potential recipients. These are commands designed to produce a nicely formatted output, which would be really messed up if messages were received in the middle of it. If you try to **write** to someone who is using one of these commands, you get a message:

```
$ write hank
Permission denied.
$
```

and the command terminates. You also get this message if you try to write to a user who has used **mesg** to prevent you writing to his terminal.

Although we have been talking about writing messages to a user, we are really writing to that user's terminal. When we say

```
write henry
```

we are really writing to the terminal tty03, where our **who** example shows Henry logged in.

The example of the **who** command shows that the user "sally" is logged in to the system twice, once on tty00, and again on tty06. You cannot write to both terminals, you have to choose one. If you get no response, you can quit that **write** command, and try to get the user on the other terminal:

```
$ write sally tty06
Are you there?
^D
$ write sally tty00
Are you there?
Message from sally tty00...
yup. que pasa?
tennis saturday 10am - OK?
ok. bye
EOF
^D
$
```

If you don't specify a terminal, **write** chooses one for you:

```
$ write sally
sally logged more than once
writing to tty00
```

The **write** command always chooses the lowest number terminal that the user is logged in at. If you get no response there, you will have to specify the tty number to get messages sent to the other terminal.

In all the examples so far, the messages have been short. If you have a long message to communicate, you may wish to use a text editor to prepare the message in a file, so that you can correct any mistakes you make before anyone else sees them. You can then send this message by redirecting the Standard Input:

```
$ write steve < message
$
```

The recipient receives the message all at once. There is no waiting between lines, as there is when the message is typed following the **write** command. To send a long message with **write** is not a very polite thing to do. It is better to use **mail** for long messages. That means the recipient can choose his own time to read the message.

Another feature of **write** is that lines starting with the exclamation mark character ! are interpreted as UNIX system commands, and are obeyed. As an instance of how this can be useful, let's suppose you have had a query as to the location of some files. You roam around the system using **cd** and **ls** commands until you find them, and now you want to answer the inquirer. However, half way through your message, you realize that you've forgotten the pathname to the current directory. You can find out in the middle of writing by saying **!pwd**, thus:

```
$ write hank
The files you want are in the directory:
!pwd
/aa/widget/maryann/docs/specs/thing
!
/aa/widget/maryann/docs/specs/thing
^D
$
```

The output of the command called up via ! does not form part of the message being sent. You still have to type the information. Of course, the command you give following ! may have nothing to do with the message you are sending. You may even redirect the Standard Output of the command, so that you see no output on the screen. That is why, when the command has terminated, **write** signals that termination by the second ! sign.

This use of ! to access UNIX system commands from within another command is quite common in those commands which are interactive in nature.

5.2 Controlling Messages with 'mesg'

When you are working at your terminal, it can be very annoying to be interrupted with messages. This is especially true when you are using an editor to enter text to create new files. Novice users have been known to re-do hours of work, because they mistakenly thought a received message had destroyed their text input.

You can stop these rude interruptions by using the **mesg** command to prevent other users writing to your terminal.

```
$ mesg n
$
```

The "**n**" (for **no**) tells the system that if anyone tries to **write** to you, they will get the message

    Permission denied

The argument to **mesg** can be a full word if you like. So long as it begins with the letter "n", the write permission is denied. So **mesg** followed by any of "no", "none" or "nyet" will do just as well.

If you decide to **write** to somebody, and expect to get a reply, you must allow (permit) messages again by typing:

```
$ mesg y
$
```

The "**y**" means "yes", which allows messages to come through again. Again, you can give a whole word, like "yes", or "yeah", or "yoiks". Provided that it starts with the letter "y", you will be able to receive messages.

If you just type the **mesg** command on its own, it tells you the current state of things:

```
$ mesg
is y
$
```

As you can see, the **mesg** command confirmed that messages are enabled. This is not surprising, since we just turned them on.

The default state of the write permission to your terminal is "y". If you use **mesg** to deny access to your terminal, that denial only lasts for your current login session. After you have logged out, it reverts to "y".

5.3 The Electronic Mail
System Using 'mail'

mail is the UNIX facility where users can send messages to each other, such that the messages pile up in a "mailbox" somewhere in the system.

If the user you are mailing to is logged in to the system, they are notified of the arrival of mail when they have completed whatever command they are using at the time. If the user is not currently logged in, the mail remains in the mailbox file, and they are notified of its delivery next time they log in:

```
Wonderful Widgets Co. UNIX System
;login: maryann
password: wizard

You have mail.
$
```

Unlike the **write** command, which interrupts whatever you are doing to display the message on your screen, **mail** waits until you have finished what you are doing before telling you there is mail waiting.

The system informs you of waiting mail at two different times: one time is just after you log in, as shown in the example above; the other time is when mail arrives while you are using some UNIX command. After you have finished whatever you are doing, you get the message that says

```
you have mail
```

You do not have to look at your mail immediately. You can simply ignore the messages and carry on with whatever you are doing. However, it is easy to get engrossed in the job at hand, so that you forget all about your pending mail, and eventually log out and head home. The UNIX system does not remind you that there are messages waiting. The next time you log in, the "You have mail" message will appear again. By this time, the mail might have gone stale, and be of little use. For this reason, it usually pays to inspect your mail as soon as possible after you get it.

5.3.1 Sending Mail

To send mail to somebody, you simply type the **mail** command, followed by the user-name of the person you want to send the mail to:

```
$ mail henry
```

Like **write**, **mail** takes the message from the Standard Input, so at this point you see nothing — **mail** is waiting for you to type in your message. The full process of sending mail looks like this:

```
$ mail henry
It's our turn to play tennis for the league.
I've booked a court for 4:30 on Saturday afternoon.
Maybe we could have dinner together afterward?
^D
$
```

As usual, **^D** means that you type control-D at the end of your message. The **mail** command will also take the period character **.** on a line by itself, as a signal meaning end of the message. We show this in some of the following examples.

You can send mail to several people by giving more than one user name on the command line:

```
$ mail maryann sylvia jack bill
There will be a meeting at 3:30 Friday, to
discuss staff relocation to our new offices.
The meeting will be held in my office.
Bill.
.
$
```

In this case, Bill sent notification of a meeting to Maryann, Sylvia and Jack. He also sent a copy to himself — this is a good idea, especially if you are expecting an answer to your mail and want to remember exactly what you said.

If you have a long message to send, you might wish to prepare it before-hand using a text editor, so that you can correct any mistakes before anyone else sees them. In this case, you can send the message by redirecting the Standard Input:

```
$ mail bill sylvia jack < memo
$
```

The **mail** command does not check that the recipient is a known user of the system until it tries to deliver your message. If you try to send mail to someone who is not a user of the system (for example, you might misspell the name), you see something like this:

```
$ mail sulvia
The files you are interested in are in the
directory /aa/widget/maryann/docs/specs/thing.
^D
mail: can't send to sulvia
Mail saved in dead.letter
$
```

So that you won't have to type your message all over again, the **mail** command saves it in a file called *'dead.letter'*, in the current directory. So you can send it to the correct recipient by:

```
$ mail sylvia < dead.letter
$ rm dead.letter
$
```

When sending mail to more than one person, if any one of them is not a known user, the message is saved as shown in the above example. However, if you don't have write permission on the current working directory at the time you send the mail, the mail is not saved. The messages you see are:

```
$ mail sulvia
The files you are interested in are in the
directory /aa/widget/maryann/docs/specs/thing.
^D
mail: can't send to sulvia
mail: cannot open dead.letter
$
```

It is a good idea to make sure that you are in your own user directories, rather than in the system directories, when you send mail.

5.3.2 Reading Your Mail

When you get the message:

```
You have mail
```

it indicates that there is a new message in your "mailbox" since you last looked there. In order to read it, you simply type the command **mail**, on its own. The command does have some options, which we describe later. For the moment we won't bother with them.

If you only have one message, it is printed out. If you have several messages, the last one that was received is printed. Your other messages are not lost, but will be printed later. **mail** just happens to show you your mail in the order last delivered, first "opened".

After showing you one message, **mail** waits for you to type in something to say what shall be done with the message. **mail** prompts you for input with the **?** character. If you respond with another **?**, **mail** shows you what choices you have:

```
$ You have mail.
$ mail
From henry Wed Jun 9 17:58:23 1982
Saturday at 4:30 is fine for tennis.
Dinner sounds good, too.  Where?
? ?
q         quit
x         exit without changing mail
p         print
s[file]   save (default mbox)
w[file]   same without header
-         print previous
d         delete
+         next (no delete)
m user    mail to user
! cmd     execute cmd
?
```

There are ten actions you can take listed above. There are also two other responses that are not listed, you can type RETURN, or you can type control-D. For the most part, these responses achieve some combination of four basic operations:

> print (show, display) a message
>
> save the message
>
> delete the message
>
> get out of the **mail** command

As we saw in the last example, simply invoking the **mail** command causes the first of your messages to be displayed. If you wanted to save that message you could respond as follows:

```
$ mail
From henry Wed Jun 9 17:58:23 1982
Saturday at 4:30 is fine for tennis.
Dinner sounds good, too.  Where?
? s from_henry
From steve Wed Jun 9 16:29:02 1982
A gang of us are going for Sunday brunch
would you like to join us?
? w from_steve
From bill Wed Jun 9 13:54:32 1982
There will be a meeting at 3:30 Friday, to
discuss staff relocation to our new offices.
The meeting will be held in my office.
Bill
?
```

We saved the mail from Henry with the command

```
s from_henry
```

This does three things. If the file *'from_henry'* does not exist, it is created and the entire message, including the header line "From henry ...." is placed in it. If the file already exists, the message is appended to the end of the file. The message is then deleted from the mail, and the next message in the mail is displayed. If there are no other messages, the **mail** command quits and you see the UNIX system prompt $.

In our example, we saved the mail from Steve too, but we did it with the **w** operation instead of **s**. The only difference is that, with **w**, the header line "From steve ...." does not get saved in the file. The message is deleted and the next message, if any, is displayed.

If you don't give any filename to the **s** and **w** operations, they create, or append to, a file called *'mbox'* in the current directory. If you are going to use this default filename for saving your mail, it is a good idea to make sure you are always in the same directory when you read your mail, otherwise you will have mail saved all over the place. You could always use your "home" directory, or you could create a special *'mail'* directory.

If you don't have write permission on the current directory when you save your mail, or if you try to save mail in a file which is write protected, the **mail** command displays an error response:

```
? s some_mail
mail: cannot append to some_mail
?
```

You can repeat the **s** or **w** operation and give a pathname to a file that is in a directory you do have write permission on. Alternatively, you could

```
!chmod 644 some_mail
```

and then repeat the **s** command. This is another good reason for being in your own home directory when you read your mail.

The above example illustrates a feature of the **mail** command which can be useful when saving messages. Everything following **!** on the line is passed to the Shell and executed. So you could use it to check which directory you are in before saving any mail:

```
? !pwd
/aa/widget/maryann/mail
!
?
```

This example shows that we are in an appropriate directory. Had we not been, we could have exited from **mail** without disturbing anything, as we describe later. Then we could have changed directory to a good one, and re-entered the **mail** command. You cannot change directory from within the mail command. Another good use, is to type **!ls** to check the spelling of a file for appending saved mail to.

You can also use **!** to answer messages as you read them, without exiting from the **mail** command:

```
From bill Wed Jun 9 13:54:32 1982
There will be a meeting at 3:30 Friday, to
discuss staff relocation to our new offices.
The meeting will be held in my office.
Bill
? !mail bill
I'm sorry, I can't make it to Friday's meeting,
I have a dental appointment at 3.
^D
!
?
```

If you want to get rid of a message when you have seen it, you must give the **d** operation to delete it. If you don't do this, the message will appear again next time you read your mail. Messages are not deleted immediately. They are only removed when you exit from the **mail** command.

If you just want to leave a message in your mail file, you can display the next message by typing the **+** operation, or simply by typing RETURN. If there is no other message, the **mail** command is terminated.

If your message is a very long one, by the time you get to the end, the first part of it might have scrolled off the top of the screen. If you want to see the first part a second time, you can display the same message again by typing "p" for print. When you have seen enough, you can stop the rest of that message printing by pressing the "Interrupt" key. This is usually the BREAK key, or the key marked DEL or RUBOUT, unless you have changed it as we described in chapter 2.

If you want to go back and re-examine a previous message, you type a minus sign − in response to the **?** prompt. This will show you the message immediately before the one you've just seen. If you want to see the message before that, you can type − again when you get the prompt. You cannot go directly back to any specific previous message; you have to examine each message in between, but you can always interrupt the messages that you are not interested in.

5.3.3 Forwarding Mail to Other Users

In the above paragraphs, we didn't cover the **m** operator. **m** stands for "mail", and it can be used to forward mail you have received on to other users. For instance:

```
$ mail
From sally Tue Jun 8 10:24:16 1982
We're having a party Friday night, pass this
invite on to anyone else you'd like to be there.
Show up around 8.
? m henry steve
?
```

The message is deleted from your mail file, after it has been sent to the named users. When they receive the mail, they can see that it is forwarded mail, and also they can see the name of the original sender. For example, Steve will get mail:

```
You have mail.
$ mail
From maryann Tue Jun 8 12:38:01 1982
>From sally Tue Jun 8 10:24:16 1982 forwarded
We're having a party Friday night, pass this
invite on to anyone else you'd like to be there.
Show up around 8.
? m jane
?
```

Steve can forward the mail again, and what Jane will see is:

```
$ mail
From steve Wed Jun 9 07:15:23
>From maryann Tue Jun 8 12:38:01 1982 forwarded
>From sally Tue Jun 8 10:24:16 1982 forwarded
We're having a party Friday night, pass this
invite on to anyone else you'd like to be there.
Show up around 8.
?
```

If you type **m** on its own, without any following user name, the message is left alone.

5.3.4 Exiting from 'mail'

You will exit from the **mail** command automatically after you have responded to the prompt **?** following the last message. Deleted messages are removed from the mail file, and the rest are put back. You see the UNIX system prompt $.

However, you can quit reading your mail at any time, in one of three ways:

by typing control-D

by typing the **q** for quit operation

by typing the **x** for exit operation

The **q** operation and control-D do the same thing. Deleted messages are removed from the mail file; undeleted and unread messages are put back. You see the UNIX system prompt $.

If you use **x** to exit from **mail**, the mail file is left unchanged. That is, messages are not deleted, even though you did something that would normally delete them. So if you delete a message, then change your mind, you can exit safely with **x**. As usual, you then see the $ system prompt.

When you quit reading your mail, you might get the message:

```
? q
you have mail
$
```

This doesn't necessarily mean that you have any new mail that you haven't seen. If you exit from **mail** with some, but not all, messages deleted, the system can get confused. Because your mail file is not empty (there are some messages you didn't delete), but has changed since you last looked at it (because some messages got deleted), the system reminds you that you still have mail.

If new mail arrives while you are reading existing mail, then you see:

```
? q
new mail arrived
you have mail
$
```

when you try to get out of the **mail** command.

5.3.5 Options to the 'mail' Command

We have seen that when you read your mail, the latest received message is shown to you first. For instance, suppose someone has sent you two messages on the same subject, and has referenced the first message in the second. It can be confusing to find a reference to an as yet unread message.

You might prefer to read your mail in the order it was delivered. You can call up the **mail** command with the **–r** (for **r**everse) option:

```
$ mail -r
From bill ....
<etc>
?
```

We have also seen that **mail** pauses after each message, and asks you what action to take. If you don't want **mail** to ask you what to do, but simply to print all your messages in turn, you should use the **–p** (for **p**rint) option.

If you give the **–q** (for **q**uit) option to **mail**, and happen to interrupt the printing of any of the messages, **mail** exits without updating the mail file (that is, as if you had done a **x** operation).

The **–f** (for file) option tells **mail** to look at a file other than the mail file. For example, to look at all the mail saved in the file *'from_henry':*

```
$ mail -f from_henry
```

When you look at a file of saved mail, what you see depends on how the messages were written onto the file. If they were saved using **s**, which saves the message headers too, you see the messages one at a time, just as if you were reading your mail file. However, if the messages were written onto the file with **w**, the headers are not in the file, and the messages are displayed one after the other without pause. If you have a mixture of "saved" and "written" messages, the output could be very confusing.

If you give more than one option to **mail**, all the options must be given separately:

```
$ mail -r -p -q -f from_steve
```

5.4 Keeping an Engagement Diary with 'calendar'

The **calendar** command is not concerned with communicating with other users, but is more a means of reminding yourself of things to do. In order to use this facility, you must set up a file, called *'calendar'*, in one of your directories. It is best if this is set up in your home (or login) directory, for reasons which we'll explain later.

Let's look at an example of a calendar file:

```
$ cat calendar
June 14th - Dad's birthday (Monday)
Thurs Jun. 10 - shop for present for Dad
6/10 classes start, 7-10pm.
Friday 6/11 - dentist 3pm
Saturday at 4:30 is fine for tennis.  henry, jun 12
Dinner sounds good, too.  Where ?
A gang of us are going for Sunday brunch -steve, Jun 13
would you like to join us?
There will be a meeting at 3:30 Friday, to -bill, June 11
discuss staff relocation to our new offices.
The meeting will be held in my office.
Bill
Mon june 14 lunch Jane
We're having a party Friday night, pass this -sally, 6/11
invite on to anyone else you'd like to be there.
Show up around 8.
14th June, collect cleaning.
$
```

The first few entries in the file are simple enough, they are just one-line reminders of what's happening, or what has to be done, on a particular date. The next entry is a bit more subtle: it is what you would get if you saved your mail with

```
w calendar
```

Unfortunately, that isn't quite good enough. For the **calendar** command to be of any use, it must contain dates, so we have added the date on the end of the first line of the message from Henry, and the following messages from Steve, Bill, and Sally. We used a text editor to do this — text editors are explained in chapters 7 and 8. If people put the date in the mail they send you, you won't have to add it yourself.

Notice that the dates are given in a variety of styles: some are in number only form, some give the month in words. When the month is given as a word, it is sometimes given in full, sometimes abbreviated, sometimes it has a capital initial letter, and sometimes not.

If we run the **calendar** command on a particular date, we get:

```
$ date
Thu Jun 10 08:29:32 1982
$ calendar
Thurs Jun. 10 - shop for present for Dad
6/10 classes start, 7-10pm.
Friday 6/11 - dentist 3pm
There will be a meeting at 3:30 Friday, to -bill, June 11
We're having a party Friday night, pass this -sally, 6/11
$
```

The **date** command is not necessary here, we have only given it to show that we gave the command on a Thursday, and that the date was June 10th. The output of the **calendar** command consists of selected lines from the *'calendar'* file. The lines selected are those which contain dates representing today (June 10th), and tomorrow (June 11th). Lines which contain other dates, and lines which do not contain dates, are not shown.

On a weekend, **calendar**'s idea of "tomorrow" covers the whole weekend through to Monday. So if we give the command on Friday, June 11th:

```
$ calendar
June 14th - Dad's birthday (Monday)
Friday 6/11 - dentist 3pm
Saturday at 4:30 is fine for tennis.   henry, jun 12
```

```
A gang of us are going for Sunday brunch -steve, Jun 13
There will be a meeting at 3:30 Friday, to -bill, June 11
Mon june 14 lunch Jane
We're having a party Friday night, pass this -sally, 6/11
$
```

we see all the engagements for the weekend, and the following Monday.

There was one reminder in the *'calendar'* file that did not get shown. This is the reminder to collect cleaning on Monday. **calendar** doesn't show this entry because the date is given as "14th June". **calendar** only recognizes dates in the form month followed by day, although it is pretty elastic about how you specify the month. If you give the date entirely in numbers, it must be in the form "6/11", **calendar** will not recognize "6-11", for example.

The *'calendar'* file can be in any of your directories; as long as you are in that directory when you give the **calendar** command, you will see your daily engagements. However, many systems have an automatic reminder service. What happens is that sometime during the night, the **calendar** command is run on every user's *'calendar'* file, and the results are mailed to each user. In order to get this reminder service, your *'calendar'* file must be in your login or home directory.

If your system doesn't have a reminder service, you can set the command running in the middle of the night, and get the results mailed to you, by using the **at** command.

5.5 Timed Delivery Messages with 'at'

The **at** command is not specifically concerned with communication. It provides the facility to perform UNIX commands at some time in the future. One of its applications, however, is to arrange for messages to be delivered at a specific time, which is the reason it is discussed here.

Suppose that you wanted to run the **calendar** program at sometime during the night. You could say:

```
$ at 0130
calendar
^D
$
```

As usual, **^D** indicates that you should type control-D. This command says "run the **calendar** command at 1:30 in the morning".

Unfortunately, this won't do you much good. The output of the **calendar** command goes to the Standard Output, and it just gets lost unless you do something to save it. So you need to redirect the output of **calendar**:

```
$ at 0130
calendar > do_today
^D
$
```

or, better still, pipe it to the **mail** command:

```
$ at 0130
calendar | mail maryann
^D
$
```

When you log in, you will get the "you have mail" message, and when you read your mail you will find the output of the **calendar** command.

There are various ways of specifying the time at which you want your commands to run. You can give the time in terms of the 24-hour clock, where 0130 is 1:30am, and 1330 is 1:30pm. If you are only interested in the hour, you can simply leave out the minutes, 8 is 8 o'clock in the morning, and 20 is 8 o'clock in the evening. Alternatively, you can specify the time as being "am" or "pm", by following the time by the letter "a", or "p" respectively. 12 o'clock noon and midnight are distinguished by following the figure by "n" or "m". We show some of these different time specifications in the following examples.

The way we called the **at** command in the previous example shows that it takes the Standard Input, up until a control-D, and executes that command at the specified time. You are not limited to one command, for example:

```
$ at 10p
nroff -ms doc1 >doc1.fmt
nroff -ms doc2 >doc2.fmt
nroff -ms doc3 >doc3.fmt
^D
$
```

We have used the **nroff** command, which formats documents (see chapter 9). Because formatting is a lengthy process, it is a good candidate for execution late at night, when you don't expect the system to be busy.

Another way of using **at** is to create a file containing the commands that you want executed, then tell **at** the name of the file:

```
$ cat > format
nroff -ms doc1 >>doc.fmt
nroff -ms doc2 >>doc.fmt
nroff -ms doc3 >>doc.fmt
^D
$ at 1130p format
$
```

The advantage of doing this is, if you think of something else to be
done at the same time, you only have to add the additional commands to the "format" file.

You can use **at** to send yourself a reminder:

```
$ cat > reminder
time to go to dentist
^D
$ at 230p
mail maryann < reminder
^D
$
```

Now, if you are logged on to the system at 2:30 in the afternoon,
you will get mail reminding yourself that it's time to leave for your
dental appointment.

You could keep a general purpose "reminder" file for occasions like
this, but if you don't want to have such a file, you can use the **echo**
command. The **echo** command simply echoes its arguments on the
Standard Output:

```
$ echo time to go
time to go
$
```

you can pipe the Standard Output to the **mail** command:

```
$ at 1430
echo time to go ¦ mail maryann
^D
$
```

With **at** you are not restricted to scheduling things by time alone.
You can give a day of the week, or a date. The day of the week can
be abbreviated. For example, to remind Jane about a lunch date,

```
$ at 11a Mon
echo lunch in 30 mins ¦ mail jane
^D
$
```

Jane will get the message at 11 o'clock on the Monday following the day on which you gave the **at** command. If you give a day of the week, followed by the word "week", the execution of the commands are postponed one week. For example, if on Thursday June 10th, you give the command:

```
$ at 4a Fri week
echo happy birthday ¦ mail steve
^D
$
```

the message will be delivered, not on the following day, but on Friday June 18th. In this case, we were not especially interested in what time the message was delivered, only in the day, but we always have to specify a time.

We can also give **at** a date, in the form month-name followed by day of the month. The month name can be abbreviated. For instance, we could send Steve birthday greetings by:

```
$ at 4 jun 18
echo happy birthday ¦ mail steve
^D
$
```

When you give **at** a date, it is always "this year". If today is June 10th, and you give the command:

```
$ at 12n jan 1 format
$
```

the commands will be executed almost immediately. This is because **at** thinks they were scheduled for the beginning of the year, and they are about six months late, so it does them straight away. **at** works on day number, so it doesn't check for correct dates. You can say:

```
$ at 2300 jun 31 format
$
```

The commands in the "format" file will run at 11pm on July 1st. So you can fool **at** into scheduling something for next year by giving a date like "Dec 32", which becomes the first day of next year. To get

January 13, for example, you have to tell **at** that you want December 44th.

You should be aware that when you schedule something with **at**, the commands are not necessarily run at the exact time you specify. Work scheduled with **at** is actually done by a system program called **atrun**. This program runs at periodic intervals, the size of the intervals depends on how the System Administrator set various parameters in the system. If **atrun** runs every minute, your commands will run on time. However, it is far more likely that **atrun** only runs every five minutes. In that case, something scheduled for 10:32, say, will not be run until 10:35. If it turns out that **atrun** only goes every 30 minutes, there is no point in trying to schedule something closer than half-hourly intervals.

5.6 Summary

We have showed you here that the UNIX operating system has facilities for users to communicate with each other electronically, either directly using **write**, or indirectly via **mail**. You should try using these facilities initially to write messages to yourself, and to send mail to yourself. When you think you understand these things, find a kindred spirit (another UNIX system user), and write messages to each other, and send mail to each other.

In addition, the UNIX system provides convenient mechanisms to keep an electronic datebook, via **calendar**, and also to perform prescheduled tasks by the **at** command. Try out these capabilities: set up an engagement diary, send yourself reminders of things to do.

In this chapter we have outlined the facilities provided on UNIX Version 7. As always, you should be aware that your own particular version of the UNIX system may be different. Experiment to find out just what facilities you have.

At many sites, there are multiple systems connected via networks, so users at remote locations can communicate easily, avoiding the hazards of human-carried mail.

We now leave the communication capabilities, and go on to describe some of the power tools available on the UNIX operating system for manipulating text files.

6 Text Manipulation

An amazing amount of the day-to-day work on a computer system is concerned with very simple processing of text in some form or another. The job of computer programming might seem to involve analysis, design, verification, redesign, and so on, but if you actually analyze the situation, you will find that computer programmers also spend a major portion of their time editing and re-arranging text in various forms. This is especially true now that computers are used to support the entire design and documentation process, as well as the programming. As the customer base and applications areas for the UNIX system move into the office environment, the requirements for text processing will expand.

There are many utilities on the UNIX system which provide ways of manipulating files of text. We cover some of the more useful commands in this chapter. The contents of a file can be printed using the **pr** and **lpr** commands; lines in a file can be sorted into alphabetic or numeric order, using the **sort** utility; you can count the lines, words, and characters in a file with the **wc** command; lines from a file can be selected for inspection or further processing according to quite complex criteria with the **grep** and **awk** facilities; individual characters can be changed selectively with the **tr** command; character strings (parts of lines) can be replaced by using **rpl**; it is possible

131

to track differences or commonality of files using the **diff** and **comm** programs.

These text processing utilities, in conjunction with redirection of Standard Output and/or piping, make it possible to select parts of files for display, or make selective changes to text files, without having recourse to a text editor, and indeed, can sometimes perform jobs that are difficult or impossible with a text editor.

One of the first questions most newcomers to any system have is:

> How do I print a file?

So before we get into any other form of text manipulation, let's see how to get a hard-copy of a file.

6.1 Printing a File

One easy way of getting a hard-copy of a file is to log in on a hard-copy terminal, then **cat** the file. However, many installations have very few such terminals, and sometimes there are none. Where there are few hard-copy terminals, a method that could be used is to **cat** the file, and redirect the output to the hard-copy device, for example:

```
$ cat file >/dev/tty10
$
```

Problems arise if someone is already using the hard-copy device when the output of **cat** is redirected there, or when more than one user tries to redirect output to that device at the same time.

For this reason, most installations have a "spooled" printing device. The term "spool" is an acronym for simultaneous peripheral output on-line, and it provides a mechanism whereby several people can apparently use an output device, such as a printer, without conflict.

The printing device driven by such a spooling mechanism is most often a line printer (which prints an entire line in one fell swoop, rather than typing each character separately). For this reason, the spooler on most UNIX systems is called the "line printer" spooler, and the command to use it is **lpr**. If printout is requested while the printer is in use, the request is queued. Queued requests are usually serviced on a first in, first out basis. Depending on the installation, there may be several printers of different types and capabilities.

6.1.1 The Line Printer Spooler — 'lpr'

The command to route files to the printer is used this way:

```
$ lpr thisfile thatfile theotherfile
$
```

There is no output to the terminal screen, unless there are error messages. The exact workings of this command and its options vary from one installation to another, since they largely depend on the number and the types of printers available. For this reason we cannot give details of the operation of **lpr** in this book. We refer you to your UNIX Programmer's Manual, or your local UNIX wizard. We can state that your system will have variations of the **lpr** command, or options to the command, which give you the capability of displaying the printer queue (usually the command variation **lpq**) and removing requests from the queue (usually the command variation **lprm**).

All that **lpr** does is route the named file(s), or the Standard Input if there are no named files, to the printer. It does nothing else, so your file is printed beginning at the very top of the page. Also, if your file takes more than one page, the printing carries over the perforations (assuming you are using fan-fold paper) without a break. This isn't very readable — it is usual to have a few blank lines at the top and bottom of each page. The program which achieves this is **pr**, the next command we describe.

We can point out a few of the useful options to **lpr**. The −c (for copy) option makes a copy of the file, so that you are sheltered from any changes that might get made before the file is actually printed.

The −m (for mail) option indicates that **lpr** should notify you by mail when the file has been printed. This, and the −c option, are useful on busy systems, where files might lie in the printer queue for ages before printing.

The −r (for remove) option tells **lpr** to remove the file after it is transferred to the print queue. This is useful when the file to be printed is a temporary file, such as the listing from a compiler. In such cases, the −r option obviates your having to remember to get rid of the file later.

6.1.2 Preparing a File for Printing with 'pr'

The description of **pr** in the UNIX Programmers Manual is "print file", but this is misleading since the "printing" is done to the Standard Output, which is normally your terminal screen. Really what **pr** does is **pr**epare a file for printing, or, make a file **pr**etty for printing. Mostly you will use **pr** in conjunction with the **lpr** command, thus:

```
$ pr myfile ¦ lpr
$
```

The output of **pr** is separated into pages and normally each page has a five-line header at the top and a five-line trailer at the foot. The trailer at the foot of the page consists of blank lines. In the header, one of the lines forms a title consisting of a date, the file name and a page number. The date shown in the header is the date the file was last modified. The header can be changed by various options to the **pr** command. Here is an example of the results of running a **pr** command on the *'people'* file which we created in chapter 4:

```
$ pr people

Feb 14 13:33 1982 people Page 1

Maryann Clark      101
Sally Smith        113
Jane Bailey        121
Jack Austen        120
Steve Daniels      111
Sylvia Dawson      110
Henry Morgan       112
Hank Parker        114
Charlie Smith      122
Bill Williams      100

$
```

There are more blank lines at the end of the printout than we have shown. There are enough to make the entire output fill an 11-inch long page. The value of the page-length can be adjusted by the –l option, as we describe in a little while.

The –t option suppresses both the header and the trailer, so if you simply wish to get a readable printout of a file you say:

```
$ pr -t myfile ¦ lpr
$
```

If you want the title line in the header to contain something other than the file name, you can use the **–h** (for **header**) option:

```
$ pr -h Distribution people | lpr
$
```

Now the printout, instead of having the file name *'people'* in the page header, has the word "Distribution". The **–h** option tells **pr** to take the very next argument as the required header. If the header you want has spaces in it, you must put quotes (**"**) around it:

```
$ pr -h "Distribution List" people | lpr
$
```

otherwise **pr** tries to interpret everything except the first word as a file name.

If you want to retain the page numbers, but without any title in the header, you can give a blank string on the **–h** option:

```
$ pr -h "" myfile | lpr
$
```

Even so, when using a blank header field, you still get the date printed on the output.

pr assumes that the page you are printing on has enough room for 72 characters across the page and 66 lines down the page. This is normal U.S.A. letter size pages (8 ½ inches by 11 inches).

If you are using a wide printer which has 132 characters across the page, and assuming the file you wish to print uses all or most of these, you use the **–w** (for **w**idth) option to adjust the width of **pr**'s output:

```
$ pr -w132 -h "Conversion Program" conv.c | lpr
$
```

Some versions of **pr** assume that the "normal" page size is 132 columns wide. If you have such a version on your system, you have to use the **–w** option when you want a narrower page.

Similarly, if the length of the page you are using is not 66 lines, use the **–l** (for **l**ength) option to adjust it:

```
$ pr -l25 -t addresses | lpr
$
```

Be careful when adjusting the page length — if the number of lines you give to **pr** doesn't match the physical size of the paper you are printing on, the results are probably not going to be what you expect.

6.1.2.1 Multi-Column Printing with 'pr' Another capability of **pr** which is sometimes useful is multi-column output. Suppose that your list of people contains 70 or 80 names, obviously when this is printed it will take more than one page. Apart from wasting paper, this is awkward to handle. It would be better if there were only one page with several columns of names on it. To achieve this, we tell **pr** how many columns we want by preceding the number of columns with the − character which usually introduces options:

```
$ pr -3 -h "Distribution List" lotsofpeople ¦ lpr
$
```

to produce three columns of names.

We haven't shown all the things you can do with **pr**, but we hope we have shown enough to give you the feeling for the command. For the other available options refer to the **pr** description in the UNIX Programmer's Manual.

6.2 Splitting a File Apart with 'split'

Many commands are limited in the size of file which they can digest. For example, the text editor, **ed**, reads the text file to be edited into an internal "buffer", and works on that, rather than the actual contents of the file itself. This means that there are times when a file is too large, and in these cases we use the "divide and conquer" principle, and split the file into smaller and more manageable chunks. The **split** utility performs this task. Having **split** a file into smaller pieces, the pieces can be edited singly, then the pieces can be concatenated into one whole file again with the **cat** command.

You can split a mammoth-sized file into smaller pieces with a **split** command, like this:

```
$ split mammoth
$
```

The file *'mammoth'* is **split** into 1000-line pieces. Each piece gets put into a different file in the current directory. The names of the output files are generated by using the letter "x", followed by two letters.

The first output filename in this example is called *'xaa'*, the second is called *'xab'*, the third, *'xac'*, and so on through *'xaz'* and then *'xba'*, and so on right through *'xzz'*.

The number of lines in each output file can be controlled via an option to **split**, so this version of the command:

```
$ split -500 mammoth
$
```

carves our *'mammoth'* file into 500-line pieces.

☞ Note that the number given is the number of lines per chunk, not the number of separate chunks.

split can also take a second, optional, filename on the command line:

```
$ split mammoth ribs
$
```

Now the output files are named *'ribsaa'*, *'ribsab'*, and so on.

Having done whatever you want to do with the smaller files, you can put the whole lot back together again, using a **cat** command that looks like this:

```
$ cat ribs?? >mammoth.new
$
```

And having done that, you get rid of all the *'ribs'* files, using an **rm** command like this:

```
$ rm ribs??
$
```

One very useful application of **split** is to print individual pages of a file. Suppose you had obtained a printout of a large file, say 100 pages or so, then discovered some minor errors in the sixth and tenth pages. After correcting the file, you don't necessarily want to print the whole thing again, just the pages with errors. You can achieve this with **split**:

```
$ pr infile >outfile
$ split -66 outfile
$ lpr xaf xaj
$
```

The sixth page is the file *'xaf'*, and the tenth page is the file *'xaj'*. You might try using the UNIX system commands to draw up a correspondence chart of the numbers versus the filenames that **split** generates.

Remember to remove the 'x' files when they have finished printing, *'outfile'* can be removed immediately following the **split**.

6.3 Sorting Text Files with 'sort'

sort is a utility program which sorts the contents of a file into alphabetic or numeric order. There are many options which control the sort order. We make no attempt to cover all the intricacies of **sort**, but in the next few paragraphs we show some of the more useful options and suggest ways in which you might want to use the program. For more detail refer to the description of the **sort** utility in the UNIX Programmer's Manual.

We must point out here that the **sort** utility on the UNIX system is quite different from the sort/merge utilities found on other systems. In common with the majority of the UNIX system's text-processing software, **sort** does not expect fields on a line to appear in a fixed columnar layout. The **sort** utility just works on *fields*, which are normally separated by spaces or tabs (you can specify any field-separator you want). If you come from the punched card orientation which most of the computer industry forces on its users, you might at first find **sort** odd, but after a while, the typewriter oriented approach becomes much more natural.

6.3.1 Sorting into Alphabetical Order

Let's take our *'people'* file and see what happens when we sort it.

```
$ sort people
Bill Williams     100
Charlie Smith     122
Hank Parker       114
Henry Morgan      112
Jack Austen       120
Jane Bailey       121
Maryann Clark     101
Sally Smith       113
Steve Daniels     111
Sylvia Dawson     110
$
```

The output of **sort** is a list of people sorted into alphabetical order by their first names. This is unusual, since it's more common to find lists of people sorted on last name. We could have entered the names in the form "Smith, Sally", then the result would have been in order of last name. But we can tell **sort** to sort on last name. Each line in the file is considered to consist of fields, the fields being separated by spaces. To get our file in order of last name, we tell the program to skip one field (the first names) before it starts the sorting process, thus:

```
$ sort +1 people
Jack Austen      120
Jane Bailey      121
Maryann Clark    101
Steve Daniels    111
Sylvia Dawson    110
Henry Morgan     112
Hank Parker      114
Sally Smith      113
Charlie Smith    122
Bill Williams    100
$
```

Of course this method breaks down if someone has a middle initial which they insist on using, because that would give an extra field on that line. So you might find that you have to hold people as "Parker, Hank J." after all.

However, if everybody had a middle initial, and only one, that would be OK. In that case, you just ask **sort** to skip two fields before starting the sort process.

Notice that Sally Smith comes before Charlie Smith, which is not in the true spirit of alphabetical order. This is because, once you have told **sort** which field to start on, it sorts from that field on to the end of the line. In order to get true alphabetical order you have to say:

```
$ sort +1 -2 people
```

that is, skip one field before you start sorting (first names), then stop sorting after the second field (last names). When **sort** stops sorting after the second field, it then resumes sorting from the beginning of the line again, so it will sort on first names. This gives us the result we want.

6.3.2 Sorting into Numerical Order

Suppose we wanted to show our list of people in order of phone numbers, we want to skip 2 fields before we start sorting:

```
$ sort +2 people
Sally Smith      113
Hank Parker      114
Jack Austen      120
Jane Bailey      121
Henry Morgan     112
Bill Williams    100
Maryann Clark    101
Sylvia Dawson    110
Steve Daniels    111
Charlie Smith    122
$
```

This is obviously not correct. Notice that all the shorter names appear first, followed by the longer ones. This is because of two things: firstly, each field is considered to start immediately after the end of the previous field, so the spaces between the last name and the phone number count as part of the phone number; secondly, **sort** is really sorting on ASCII characters, and the character for space has a lower value than any of the characters for the digits 0 through 9.

We can tell **sort** to ignore leading spaces (blanks) in the fields by using the **–b** (for **blank**) option:

```
$ sort -b +2 people
Bill Williams    100
Maryann Clark    101
Sylvia Dawson    110
Steve Daniels    111
Henry Morgan     112
Sally Smith      113
Hank Parker      114
Jack Austen      120
Jane Bailey      121
Charlie Smith    122
$
```

Using the **–b** option in this way, tells **sort** to ignore blanks in *all* fields on the line. If we want to restrict the effect of ignoring blanks to *only* the numeric field, we can use the **b** option in this way:

```
$ sort +2b people
Bill Williams    100
Maryann Clark    101
        <etc...>
Charlie Smith    122
$
```

When you attach the **b** to one of the fields like this, it is called a "flag", rather than an option. In our example we get the same results either way, but there will be cases where the different ways of specifying that blanks are to ignored, will produce different results.

We have got what we wanted, but this is not *really* numeric sorting. We got there more or less by accident. The ASCII characters for the digits 0 through 9 are in ascending order, and because all our numbers have exactly the same number of digits, we have the appearance of numerical order.

But suppose our file holds, not phone numbers, but some other numbers which don't all have the same number of digits. Take the example of a tennis league, where we want to keep track of the number of games that each person has won. The file we create in this case looks something like:

```
$ cat tennis
Maryann Clark    18
Sally Smith      14
Jane Bailey       2
Jack Austen       3
Steve Daniels    11
Sylvia Dawson     7
Henry Morgan      5
Hank Parker      18
Charlie Smith     9
Bill Williams     2
$
```

If we merely sort the file by skipping 2 fields, and ignoring blanks in the third, we get:

```
$ sort +2b tennis
Steve Daniels    11
Sally Smith      14
Hank Parker      18
Maryann Clark    18
Bill Williams     2
        ...
```

```
Jane Bailey      2
Jack Austen      3
Henry Morgan     5
Sylvia Dawson    7
Charlie Smith    9
$
```

This is obviously not the right order. We have to tell **sort** that the
characters in the field we are sorting are to be treated as numbers,
and to sort according to the arithmetic values of those numbers. We
do this by adding the letter **n** (for **n**umeric) after the number of the
fields skipped before the field that is to be treated in this way:

```
$ sort +2n +1 tennis
Jane Bailey      2
Bill Williams    2
Jack Austen      3
Henry Morgan     5
Sylvia Dawson    7
Charlie Smith    9
Steve Daniels    11
Sally Smith      14
Maryann Clark    18
Hank Parker      18
$
```

We don't have to use the **b** option in this case, because using the **n**
for numeric sorting implies that spaces are ignored. People having
the same scores should be shown in alphabetical order, so we need to
specify the ordering of that field (by **+1**) too.

We could specify that we want numerical order like this:

```
$ sort -n +2 +1 tennis
Bill Williams    2
Jane Bailey      2
Jack Austen      3
      <etc...>
Hank Parker      18
Maryann Clark    18
$
```

Specifying **–n** in this way tells **sort** to treat *all* fields as numeric. As
you can see, this doesn't give quite the right answer, because people
with the same scores are no longer in alphabetical order.

In a list of scores like this, it is more usual to see the winners listed first. We can tell **sort** to reverse the order of sorting by adding the letter **r** (for reverse) after the field that we want reversed:

```
$ sort +2nr +1 tennis
Maryann Clark     18
Hank Parker       18
Sally Smith       14
Steve Daniels     11
Charlie Smith      9
Sylvia Dawson      7
Henry Morgan       5
Jack Austen        3
Jane Bailey        2
Bill Williams      2
$
```

The use of **r** to reverse the order of the sort is not restricted to numeric sorting, although that is where it is most commonly found. We could, for example, have used **+1r** and **+0r** to produce the names in reverse alphabetic order.

Again, we could have used **−r** to tell **sort** to reverse the sort order on all fields. Interestingly, in our particular example, using both options **−nr** will produce the results we want. The wrongness introduced by trying to numerically sort non-numeric fields, is cancelled by the wrongness of reversing the order of all fields. However, be aware that this is just a lucky coincidence, don't rely on it happening in your files.

6.3.3 Saving Sorted Output

So far, the output of **sort** has been displayed on the terminal screen. You might want to save the output in a file — you can do this with the **−o** (for output) option. When you give the **−o** option, the very next argument to **sort** must be the name of a file that is to contain the output. For example:

```
$ sort -o speople +1 -2 people
$ cat speople
Jack Austen      120
Jane Bailey      121
        <etc...>
$
```

Because **sort** normally sends its results to the Standard Output you can achieve the same effect by redirecting the Standard Output to a file:

```
$ sort +1 -2 people >speople
$
```

6.3.4 Merging Already Sorted Files

So far we have only shown **sort** operating on one file. If we give
more than one filename, the contents of all the files named are considered to be joined together, end to end, and the composite is then
sorted.

Suppose that instead of one file of people we had several. Perhaps
your project has two types of people, those concerned with designing
hardware, and those involved with software development. Then
there will be some administrative people like the manager and the
secretary. So maybe we want to keep these people in separate files:

```
$ cat adminpeople
Bill Williams   100
Maryann Clark   101
$ cat hardpeople
Jack Austen     120
Charlie Smith   122
Jane Bailey     121
$ cat softpeople
Sylvia Dawson   110
Sally Smith     113
Steve Daniels   111
Henry Morgan    112
Hank Parker     114
$
```

We can produce a distribution list of software developers by **sort**ing
'*softpeople*', and one for hardware designers by **sort**ing '*hardpeople*',
but what about a distribution list that includes everybody? We simply give *all* the filenames to the **sort** command:

```
$ sort +1 -2 adminpeople hardpeople softpeople >everybody
$
```

or we could make use of the Shell's file matching capabilities and
say:

```
$ sort +1 -2 *people >everybody
$
```

If your input files are already sorted you can simply merge them
by using the **–m** (for **m**erge) option:

```
$ sort +1 -2 adminpeople >sadmin
$ sort +1 -2 hardpeople >shard
$ sort +1 -2 softpeople >ssoft
$ sort -m +1 -2 sadmin shard ssoft >everybody
$
```

The **−m** option tells **sort** that the files are already sorted, and need only be merged, thereby saving **sort** some work.

Note that the final **sort** can NOT be replaced by a simple **cat** command — that wouldn't give a fully sorted output. What you would get with **cat** would be 'adminpeople' sorted into order, followed by 'hardpeople' sorted into order, followed by 'softpeople' sorted into order. With **sort** you get 'adminpeople', 'hardpeople', and 'softpeople' all together sorted into order.

If you use the **−m** option to **sort**, your input files had really better be sorted. If they are not already sorted, the final result is not properly sorted:

```
$ sort -m +1 -2 *people
Jack Austen      120
Jane Bailey      121
Sylvia Dawson    110
Charlie Smith    122
Sally Smith      113
Steve Daniels    111
Henry Morgan     112
Hank Parker      114
Bill Williams    100
Maryann Clark    101
$
```

6.3.5 Duplicated Lines in Sorted Files

Suppose that instead of having a separate file for the administrative people, we had put them in both the files 'hardpeople' and 'softpeople'. And further suppose that we had a file which contained only the managers. For this example we're going to forget about phone numbers, we assume our three files look like:

```
$ cat hardpeople
Bill Williams
Maryann Clark
Jane Bailey
Jack Austen
Charlie Smith
        . . .
```

```
$ cat softpeople
Bill Williams
Maryann Clark
Sylvia Dawson
Sally Smith
Steve Daniels
Henry Morgan
Hank Parker
$ cat managers
Bill Williams
Jack Austen
Sylvia Dawson
$
```

Now if we sort and merge the files, what we'll get is:

```
$ sort +1 managers hardpeople softpeople
Jack Austen
Jack Austen
Jane Bailey
Maryann Clark
Maryann Clark
Steve Daniels
Sylvia Dawson
Sylvia Dawson
Henry Morgan
Hank Parker
Charlie Smith
Sally Smith
Bill Williams
Bill Williams
Bill Williams
$
```

which won't do at all. To get rid of the duplications we use the **–u** (for **u**nique) option, thus:

```
$ sort -u +1 managers hardpeople softpeople >everybody
$
```

We could also do it by using another utility program called **uniq**, whose purpose is to remove adjacent duplicate lines from a sorted file. We take the output of **sort** and pipe it to **uniq**:

```
$ sort +1 managers hardpeople softpeople | uniq >everybody
$
```

Some versions of the **sort** utility don't have the –**u** option, and so you have to use **uniq** to remove duplicate lines.

Duplicate lines must be adjacent to one another for **uniq** to find them, so you must use **sort**, then **uniq**, not the other way around.

6.3.6 Field Separators for Sorting

Normally **sort** assumes fields are separated by spaces or tabs. However some files may have a format where the fields are separated by something else. To tell **sort** this, we use the –**t** option.

A file that does not use spaces as field separators is the password file */etc/passwd*. This file uses the colon character : as its field separator. We can sort on the sixth field of each line (the users' home directory names) by typing this command:

```
$ sort -t: +5 /etc/passwd
```

It is unfortunate that many of the characters that are most likely to be used as field separators mean something special to the Shell. For example, if you have a file with the fields separated by |, and you try:

```
$ sort -t| myfile
```

you will have problems, because the system will try to take the output of the (incomplete) **sort** command on the left of the | and pipe it to the (unknown) command 'myfile'. In this situation you have to remove the special meaning of | by preceding it with the Shell "escape" character \, thus:

```
$ sort -t\| myfile
```

6.4 Counting Things in a File with 'wc'

The **wc** command counts the number of lines, words, and characters in a file. It is used heavily for things such as counting the number of lines of source code in a program, the number of words in a document, and other (ostensibly useful) statistics so dear to the hearts of project management.

We can count what is in our *'people'* file with a **wc** command like this:

```
$ wc people
   10      30      200 people
$
```

The first number is the number of lines in the file. The second number is the number of words in the file. The third number is the number of characters (including newlines) in the file. Finally, **wc** displays the name of the file it counted.

A "word" in the context of **wc** is a string of characters delimited by spaces, tabs, or newlines.

wc can accept any combination of three options. The options restrict the counting process to the indicated object. The **–l** (lines) option means that only lines are to be counted. The **–w** (words) option indicates that **wc** should only count words. The **–c** (characters) option implies that characters are the only thing to be counted.

We can just count the number of lines in the *'people'* file with a **wc** command line like this:

```
$ wc -l people
   10 people
$
```

The options can be combined, so the number of lines and characters in *'people'* can be counted this way:

```
$ wc -lc people
   10      200 people
$
```

Of course, using all three options together is a complicated way to get **wc**'s normal behavior, namely, count everything.

If **wc** counts its Standard Input, it does not, obviously, display the name of the file which was counted. This is what happens when you count lines in the Standard Input, redirected from the *'people'* file:

```
$ wc -l < people
   10
$
```

Here, there is no filename to display, and all we get is the count of the number of lines in the Standard Input.

You can count more than one file at a time with **wc**. In this case, you get the counts for the individual files, and, as a bonus, **wc** prints the total for all the files. So suppose we had three small files of people, instead of one big *'people'* file:

```
$ wc *people
    2        6         40 adminpeople
    3        9         60 hardpeople
    5       15        100 softpeople
   10       30        200 total
$
```

Do not confuse the last line designated "total" with a file called *'total'*. It really is the totals of the previous files. This can be done in a different way, using the **cat** command piped to the **wc** utility:

```
$ cat *people ¦ wc
   10       30        200
$
```

Although the **wc** command seems trivial, it finds application in literally scores of mundane tasks in the system every day. Perhaps the canonical example of **wc** is finding out how many users are logged on to the system:

```
$ who ¦ wc
   17       34        510
$
```

This display tells us that there are 17 users on the system. With that many people sharing a $1,000 central processing unit, it is time to have lunch.

6.5 Finding Text Patterns in a File with 'grep'

grep is a utility program which searches a file, or more than one file, for lines which contain strings of a certain pattern. Such lines are said to match the pattern. Lines which match the specified pattern are printed on the Standard Output.

In its simplest use, **grep** just looks for a pattern which consists of a fixed character string. It is possible, however, to describe more complex patterns, called "regular expressions". We start off the examples showing simple fixed strings, then later we move on to regular expressions.

6.5.1 Searching for Character Strings

The simplest pattern to give to **grep** is a fixed character string. For example, suppose we want to find the phone number of Sally Smith. We simply use **grep** to find the string "Sally" in the file *'people'*, which contains the phone numbers:

```
$ grep Sally people
Sally Smith     113
$
```

With the people arranged in three files, as we used in examples for **sort**, we can tell **grep** to scan all three files at the same time:

```
$ grep Sally adminpeople hardpeople softpeople
softpeople: Sally Smith    113
$
```

Now we have the name of the file in which Sally was found — this could be useful, depending on how well we had named our files. If we don't want to see the filename, we can suppress it with the **–h** (omit file **header**) option. Assuming a judicious choice of filenames in the first place, the above example could also be written as:

```
$ grep Sally *people
softpeople: Sally Smith    113
$
```

We used the word "Sally" to search for the phone number, but we could equally well have used "Smith":

```
$ grep Smith people
Sally Smith     113
Charlie Smith   122
$
```

There are two lines containing "Smith" in the file *'people'*, and both are printed. If we are interested only in Sally Smith, and don't want to see anything about any other Smith, or any other Sally, we have to give the full name as a search string:

```
$ grep "Sally Smith" people
Sally Smith     113
$
```

Note that the name is surrounded by quote signs ("). This is because the pattern you're looking for must form one argument to **grep**. Since a space is used to separate arguments, a pattern which also contains spaces must be enclosed in quotes. If we leave out the quotes and say:

```
$ grep Sally Smith people
grep: can't open Smith
$
```

we get an error message as you can see, because the program is trying to look for Sally in the files *'Smith'* and *'people'*. Since the first of the files it's looking for doesn't exist, **grep** gives up the search after printing the message.

6.5.2 Inverting the Search with the 'v' Option

So far we have seen how **grep** prints all lines which contain the given character string. The −v (for invert) option instructs **grep** to print all lines *except* those which match the string.

As an example of how this can be useful, suppose Henry Morgan leaves the group and his place is taken by James Walker. We now have to update our list of people. James Walker can easily be added to the file using **cat**, as we showed in the last chapter, but to eliminate Henry we will have to use **grep** with the −v option.

Since our *'people'* file is out of date, let's start by renaming it. The entire sequence of commands to do the update job is:

```
$ grep Henry softpeople
Henry Morgan      112
$ mv softpeople softpeople.old
$ grep -v "Henry Morgan" softpeople.old >softpeople
$ cat >>softpeople
James Walker      112
^D
$ rm softpeople.old
$ chmod 444 softpeople
$
```

The first **grep** of the sequence is simply to find Henry's phone number so that we can allocate it to James. Note that we did NOT say:

```
grep -v "Henry Morgan" people >people
```

That would destroy our original *'people'* file (unless we had protected it by making it read-only mode). The final stage in the process is to use the **chmod** command to make the new *'softpeople'* file read-only mode as a protection against accidental loss.

6.5.3 Regular Expressions in Text Patterns

So far we have only given **grep** a fixed character string to look for, but it is capable of more complex searches. We can give **grep** a pattern (or template) of the text we want to search for. We can ask for things like

find all four-letter words beginning with d,

or

all words ending in able,

or

all 6-digit numbers appearing at the end of a line

Such a pattern or template is called a "regular expression" and the name of the command derives from that. **grep** stands for "**g**lobal **r**egular **e**xpression **p**rinter". When we get to chapter 7 on the UNIX text editor **ed**, the derivation of this apparently odd name will be made clear.

Regular expressions work in a way similar to the Shell's file-matching capability that we discussed in chapter 3 — "Directories and Files". Certain characters have a special meaning. These special characters are called "metacharacters" because they represent something other than themselves.

Unfortunately, the metacharacters used in **grep** (and incidentally, in the editor **ed** and many other utilities) are not quite the same as those that the Shell uses for matching filenames. This can cause confusion, especially if you are using both in the same command, so be careful about how you specify your text-patterns.

Because many of the characters which have special meanings in regular expressions also have special meaning to the UNIX Shell, it is best to enclose the regular expression in quotes. Single quotes (') are safest, but often double quotes (") are sufficient.

6.5.3.1 Match Beginning and End of Line with ^, and $ Two of the simplest metacharacters to use are the circumflex ^ and the dollar sign $, which match the beginning of a line and the end of a line, respectively.

A ^ appearing at the beginning of a string matches the beginning of a line. So, whereas the string:

    "Genesis"

finds any line containing the word "Genesis", preceding it with the
^ character like this:

    "^Genesis"

only finds lines starting with the word "Genesis".

Similarly $ appearing at the end of a string matches the end of a line, so:

    "eschatus$"

selects only those lines ending with the word "eschatus".

An expression preceded by ^ and followed with $, for instance:

    "^Out in the cold$"

selects only those lines consisting of the phrase "Out in the cold", and nothing else.

A text pattern which matches at a specific place on a line is called an "anchored match", because it is "anchored" to a particular position.

The ^ and $ characters lose their special meaning if they appear in places other than the beginning of the pattern, or the end of the pattern, respectively.

Blank lines in a file can be found with the expression ^$. This pattern finds lines which have only a newline, and no other text. If there are spaces or tabs or other non-printing characters on the line, the pattern ^$ will not find them.

6.5.3.2 Match Any Character with . The period (or "dot" as it's usually known in the UNIX system) is a metacharacter which matches any character at all.

So the string

    " d... "

selects all words starting with the letter "d", and having three more characters, provided they are preceded and followed by a space. To find such words at the beginning of a line we need to use

```
"^d... "
```

To find such words at the end of a line we would use the expression

```
" d...$"
```

However, following the word with a period

```
" d...."
```

won't only find four-letter "d"-words at the end of a sentence: it will find all sequences of five characters starting with the letter "d". To tell **grep** that you want that final dot to really be a period character, you have to remove its special significance by preceding it with the escape character \, and use the expression

```
" d...\."
```

We said that **grep** will find words starting with "d" with this expression, but we lied a little. What **grep** actually finds is any string of four characters starting with the letter "d". So

```
" d... "
```

finds any of the patterns:

```
dc13            drat
dr-x   as well as   dumb
dry!            dogs
```

To specify that we only want letters in the "word", we have to give a different expression, and this is discussed below.

The period metacharacter never matches the newline at the end of a line. A consequence of this is that text patterns never match across lines, they only match within a line. There is a good practical reason for this apparently antisocial behavior.

6.5.3.3 Character Classes with [and] and – Characters enclosed in brackets, [ ], specify a set of characters that are to be searched for. The match is on any one of the characters inside the brackets. For example, the expression:

```
[Gg]enesis
```

finds both "genesis" and "Genesis". The expression:

```
^[abcxyz]
```

finds all lines beginning with "a" or "b" or "c" or "x" or "y" or "z".

Inside [ ], the hyphen character – specifies a range of characters, so

```
^[abcxyz]
```

can also be expressed in the shorthand notation as:

```
^[a-cx-z]
```

The patterns:

```
[a-z]  all lowercase letters
[A-Z]  all uppercase letters
[0-9]  all digits
```

are very common regular expressions. So, for our previous example of "d"-words, to really limit it to letters only, we should use the pattern:

```
"  [Dd][a-z][a-z][a-z]  "
```

assuming that only the initial letter can be in uppercase.

In the example

```
^[a-cx-z]
```

you should note that the ^ metacharacter (match the beginning of the line) is outside the brackets. When it appears inside the brackets it has a different meaning. If the character ^ is the first character inside [ ] it doesn't mean "beginning of line". Instead it inverts the selection process. So the expression:

```
"  [^Dd][a-z][a-z][a-z]  "
```

specifies all four letter words that begin with something other than "D" or "d", and the pattern:

```
^[^a-z]
```

finds all lines except those that begin with lowercase letters.

It should be emphasized that ranges of characters pertain to the ASCII character set, so that the pattern:

```
[A-z]
```

not only gets you all upper and lowercase letters, but all the other characters that fall in that range of ASCII character values, namely:

    [\   ]   ^   _   '

This sort of confusion occurs most often when dealing with digits. The pattern:

    [1-30]

does NOT mean "numbers in the range one through 30", it means "digits in the range 1 through 3, or 0". It is the same as a pattern that looks like:

    [1230] or [0-3]

If you really wish to include – in the class of characters, it isn't necessary to escape it so long as it is positioned such that it won't be confused with a range specification. For example, a hyphen at the beginning of the pattern stands for itself:

    [-ab]

means the pattern – or "a" or "b". The same is true for the characters [and] themselves.

6.5.3.4 Closures — Repeated Pattern Matches

A number enclosed in braces { } following an expression specifies the number of times that the preceding expression is to be repeated. So our search for four letter words could be expressed:

    " [Dd][a-z]{3} "

This repeat number specification is known as a "closure".

The general format of the closure is {n,m}, where n is the minimum number of repeats and m is the maximum number of repeats. A missing n is assumed to be one, and a missing m is assumed to be infinity (or at least huge).

There are shorthand ways of expressing some closures:

An asterisk *   is equivalent to {0,}, meaning that the preceding pattern is to be repeated zero or more times.

A plus sign **+**   is equivalent to {1,}, it means that the preceding pattern is to be repeated one or more times.

The character **?**   is the same as {0,1}, which means that the preceding pattern can be repeated zero or once only.

Closures are the reason why text patterns do not span across lines. If you just type a **grep** command like this:

```
$ grep '.*' people
```

you are using a pattern which says:

"match zero to infinity amounts of any character"

If patterns could span lines, this would (try to) eat up an entire file. Like any other utility, **grep** has some limit to the size of the pattern which it can hold internally, and a whole file probably is too big for it to digest.

Since there is a restriction which says that patterns do not match a line boundary, the command:

```
$ grep '.*' people
```

simply finds (and displays) every line in the *'people'* file. This is the same as saying:

```
$ cat people
```

but **cat** is a lot easier and faster.

6.5.4 Subsets of Regular Expressions

There are different versions of the **grep** utility on various UNIX systems. Many of the versions do not support all the metacharacters as described above. Some of the things that are most often missing are:

- the use of ^ inside [ ] to invert the class of characters.
- the full format of closures {**n,m** }
- both of the closures **+** and **?** are not always available, though one of them usually is. ∗ is always there.

Regular expressions are used by many other commands in the system, most notably the text editors. The range of metacharacters available varies from one UNIX system to the next, and varies between commands, and different versions of the same command. Always consult your UNIX Programmer's Manual to find out what you have available.

6.5.5 Examples of Regular Expressions

Regular expressions are a powerful tool, but they can be very complex and they need practice in using them. To an inexperienced user, it often seems that figuring out a regular expression to find a number of character strings takes longer than doing things the hard way and finding each string one at a time.

It is difficult to give examples covering all possible combinations of metacharacters, but here are some situations where you will find regular expressions useful. More examples are given under the other commands that use regular expressions.

You can delete all blank lines from a file by:

```
$ grep -v "^$" file > newfile
$
```

The regular expression   ^$ finds all the blank lines, and the −v option tells **grep** to save all the other lines and ignore the blank lines. This only gets rid of lines that are really blank. Lines that only appear blank, but actually contain spaces, will remain in *'newfile'.* To delete the apparently blank lines as well, we should say:

```
$ grep -v "^ *$" file > newfile
$
```

The regular expression says, in effect, "look for a beginning of line, followed by any number of spaces (including no spaces), followed by an end of line". But what if the apparently empty line contains tabs as well as spaces? You must replace the simple space in the above regular expression with an expression that says "space or tab":

```
$ grep "^[ ^I]*$" file > newfile
$
```

The ^I in the above example doesn't mean the characters ^ and I. It indicates that you should type control-I, which is the tab character. When you type the tab character the cursor will move to the next tab position, so what you will see on the screen is:

```
"^[         ]*$"
```

Many keyboards have a separate "tab" key, marked TAB, so you don't actually have to type control-I.

Suppose we want to find the person or persons having the initials "SD", we can use **grep** for this:

```
$ grep "S.* D.*" people
Steve Daniels    111
Sylvia Dawson    110
$
```

The regular expression looks for an initial "S" followed by some characters, followed by a space, followed by a "D" followed by some more characters. This is a fairly sloppy pattern, we could have made it tighter by introducing beginning of line and lowercase letters:

```
"^S[a-z]* D[a-z]* "
```

but we are relying on our knowledge of the format of the file.

There is no point in making a regular expression more complex than it need be. However, be aware that a regular expression will find the longest string of characters which matches the pattern — this often causes grief. We show an example of this in **rpl**, below.

6.5.6 Other Options to 'grep'

Earlier we showed the use of the −**v** option to **grep**, to invert the search. There are other options which can be given to the command.

The −**n** (number) option asks **grep** to show the line numbers of lines that match the string or pattern, for example:

```
$ grep -n Smith *people
hardpeople:3:Charlie Smith    122
softpeople:2:Sally Smith      113
$
```

This can be sometimes be useful when you intend to use an editor, or some other command, to process the file using line numbers.

When you give the −**c** (count) option, lines that match the pattern are not displayed. Instead, a count of the number of lines that match the pattern in each file is shown:

```
$ grep -c "S.* D.*" *people
adminpeople:0
hardpeople:0
softpeople:2
$
```

This is useful when you want to see the distribution of a string throughout a set of files.

The **–l** (list) option is usually only used when you give multiple filenames to the **grep** command. Instead of showing every line in every file that matches the pattern, **grep** simply displays the name of each file that contains at least one line that does match the pattern:

```
$ grep -l Smith *people
hardpeople
softpeople
$
```

This is used when you are only interested in which of a set of files contains a particular string.

There is a **–y** (why? — not mnemonic) option on some versions of the **grep** command. This saves you the trouble of typing uppercase characters, since it tells the program that uppercase patterns in the file match lowercase characters in the pattern specification. So, for example:

```
$ grep -y -n smith *people
hardpeople:3:Charlie Smith    122
softpeople:2:Sally Smith      113
$
```

This can be useful when you are not sure whether the string you want to find contains uppercase letters or not. For instance, the pattern " the " will find the word "the", except when it starts with a capital "T" (such as at the beginning of a sentence). To make sure you get them all, you would normally need to give the string " [Tt]he ". The **–y** option means you don't have to do that; when using it " the " will find both strings. Be aware that the process is one-way:

```
$ grep -y MITH *people
$
```

Upper-case letters specified on the command line are not matched by lowercase letters in the file.

6.6 Fast Searching for Fixed Strings with 'fgrep'

The **fgrep** utility is another text processing utility in the same family as **grep** (described above), and **egrep** (described below). The **fgrep** command only handles fixed character strings as text patterns. **fgrep** stands for "fast **grep**", or maybe, "fixed **grep**". The **fgrep** command cannot process wild-card matches, character classes, anchored matches, or closures. For these reasons, **fgrep** is considerably faster than **grep**, when all you want to look for is a fixed text string.

fgrep is typically used as in our **grep** examples above:

```
$ fgrep Sylvia *people
softpeople: Sylvia Dawson    110
$
```

You can also feed **fgrep** a file of fixed strings. Each string appears on a line by itself, but the newline characters have to be escaped with the \ character.

6.7 Finding Full Regular Expressions with 'egrep'

Another variation on the basic **grep** utility is **egrep**. **egrep** stands for "extended **grep**". The **egrep** command is an extension to the basic **grep**, such that it can handle full regular expressions.

egrep can handle more complex regular expressions, of the form:

"find a pattern, followed by a this or a that or one of those, followed by something else".

Alternative patterns are specified by separating the alternative patterns with the | (vertical bar) character. This form of regular expression is technically called "alternation".

Alternate patterns within regular expressions can be grouped by enclosing the patterns within parentheses ( ).

To give a simple example, let us revert to our original *'people'* file. Let's assume that Sally Smith married someone called White, but we are unsure whether she changed her name, or whether the file has been updated to reflect such a change. To find her in the *'people'* file we can use **egrep** like this:

```
$ egrep 'Sally (White|Smith)' *people
Sally Smith      113
$
```

What we are searching for here is an occurrence of either "Sally White", or "Sally Smith". Using the alternation capability of full regular expressions makes this easy to express. The regular expression above asks to match a line containing the string "Sally", followed by either of the strings "White" or "Smith".

Notice that the alternatives are in parentheses. If we had typed it as:

```
$ egrep 'Sally White¦Smith' *people
```

the results would be to look for a line containing "Sally White", or a line containing "Smith", which is not what we wanted.

6.8 Replacing Character Strings with 'rpl'

On some UNIX systems there is a utility called **rpl** (it stands for **rpl**ace) which gives you the capability to change character strings in a file. **rpl** has the same pattern matching capabilities as does **grep** and its variants, but in addition, **rpl** supplies the means to make changes to the matched lines, once they are found. Unfortunately this useful command doesn't exist on most UNIX systems.

Everything that can be done with **rpl** can be achieved with the stream editor **sed** (described in chapter 7), but **rpl** is somewhat easier to use.

rpl uses regular expressions, so the examples we give should be of interest even if your UNIX system does not have the utility. The examples are repeated in the description of **sed**.

To continue our **egrep** example, let's assume that when Sally Smith married she changed her name. We can modify our *'people'* file:

```
$ mv people people.old
$ rpl Smith White < people.old > people
$
```

rpl only works on the Standard Input, so to operate on a file we must redirect the Standard Input from that file. The first argument to **rpl** is a regular expression to find a string, and the second argument is a string to substitute for the matched pattern. The substitution takes place for every instance of the string found in the file.

In our example, this is unfortunate because we have also changed Charlie Smith's name to Charlie White. To change Sally Smith's name without affecting any other Smith, we must say:

```
$ rpl "Sally Smith" "Sally White" <people.old >people
$
```

We could have replaced Henry Morgan with James Walker (from one of our **grep** examples) with a similar command.

We said that regular expressions always find the longest string that fits the pattern. Let us see an example of this feature. Suppose we decide to remove the phone numbers from the list of people. We can do this by finding the numbers at the end of the line and replacing them with a null string:

```
$ rpl " [0-9]*$" "" <people
Maryann Clark
Sally Smith
Jane Bailey
     <etc...>
Bill Williams
$
```

But, had we used the notation "any character", instead of rigidly specifying "digits 0 through 9", we would get quite a different result:

```
$ rpl " .*$" "" <people
Maryann
Sally
Jane
     <etc...>
Bill
$
```

The phone numbers fit the specified pattern of "space, followed by any number of any characters followed by end of line", but so does the last name followed by phone number, and it is the longer string that the regular expression selects. So, although you don't have to make your regular expressions more complex than necessary, you should make sure that they are precise enough to get exactly what you want, no more and no less.

We can use **rpl** to compress a file by replacing all occurrences of eight consecutive spaces with a tab character:

```
$ rpl "        " "^I" <file >newfile
$
```

As usual the ^I indicates where you should type control-I, or TAB. In this case we have spelled out the eight spaces, we could equally well have said:

```
$ rpl " {8}" "^I" <file >newfile
$
```

This is not necessarily the best way to insert tabs instead of spaces, for there is no guarantee that the alignment of fields in your file will be preserved.

Many UNIX systems have a command designed to perform this function of collapsing spaces to tabs. This function is sometimes called **tab** (not to be confused with the command **tabs**), or **unexpand**. You can use the **tab** command to do this job more easily than by typing **rpl** commands.

You can use **rpl** to give a left margin like this:

```
$ rpl "^" "        " < people
        Maryann Clark    101
        Sally Smith      113
        Jane Bailey      121
            (etc...)
        Bill Williams    100
$
```

We have replaced each beginning of line with eight spaces, we could also have used the TAB character, control-I.

An interesting use of **rpl** is to create double-spaced output from a single-spaced file by inserting a blank line after every line in the file:

```
$ rpl "$" "\012" <people
Maryann Clark    101

Sally Smith      113

Jane Bailey      121

    (etc...)

Bill Williams    100
$
```

In this case, the second argument is the octal value of the ASCII character for newline preceded by a \ to tell **rpl** that you are giving a character value rather than the string "012". There are other commands that will accept this type of argument, for example **tr** which we describe below.

6.9 Translating Characters with 'tr'

The utility program **tr** translates (or transliterates) characters in a file. **tr** works on the Standard Input. If you want to take input from a file, you have to redirect the Standard Input so that it comes from that file.

tr can take two arguments which specify character sets. Each member of the first set is replaced by the equivalent member of the second set. To give a crazy example:

```
$ tr abcdefghijklmnopqrstuvwxyz   \
      zyxwvutsrqponmlkjihgfedcba   <people
Mzibzmm Cozip    101
Szoob Snrgs      113
Jzmv Bzrovb      121
      <etc...>
Broo Wroorznh    100
$
```

We have reversed the alphabet for lowercase letters, uppercase letters are not affected because we didn't include them in our character set.

We could have stated the first character set by giving a range "a-z", but not the second since it is not in ascending order of ASCII character values.

If the second character set doesn't contain as many characters as the first, it is extended to be the same length as the first by repeating the last character. Had we left out the "ba" at the end of the second argument in the above example, all of "x", "y" and "z" would have been transliterated to "c". Some versions of **tr** don't do this "collapsing" function — they simply don't transliterate the missing characters.

Suppose we want our file of *'people'* to be printed all in capital letters. For instance, there are still some installations with uppercase only line printers. We can get our file ready for such a printer like this:

```
$ tr a-z A-Z <people
MARYANN CLARK    101
SALLY SMITH      113
JANE BAILEY      120
      <etc...>
BILL WILLIAMS    100
$
```

All characters in the range "a" through "z" are replaced by the corresponding character in the range "A" through "Z". Everything can be turned into lower case by reversing the strings "a-z" and "A-Z".

Some versions of **tr** do not recognize "a-z" as a range of characters unless the range is enclosed in brackets [ ], as in the regular expressions described in the **grep** command. So, if you run **tr**, and get:

```
$ tr a-z A-Z <people
MAryAnn ClArk    101
SAlly Smith      113
JAne BAiley      121
     <etc...>
Bill WilliAms    100
$
```

it means that **tr** is seeing "a-z" as a set of the three characters "a", "-" and "z". In this case you must enclose the range in [ ], and to stop the Shell trying to do special things with the brackets you must either escape them or put the argument in quotes:

```
$ tr \[a-z\] \[A-Z\] <people >u-people
$ tr "[a-z]" "[A-Z]" <people >u-people
$
```

Both of the above commands do the same thing.

We can get rid of the phone numbers in our *'people'* file by using the **–d** (for delete) option of **tr**:

```
$ tr -d 0-9 <people
Maryann Clark
Sally Smith
Jane Bailey
     <etc...>
Bill Williams
$
```

In this case we only give **tr** one set of characters, the **–d** option tells **tr** to delete all characters in that set. Since the only digits we have are those in the phone numbers, **tr** has the effect of removing the phone numbers. There are still spaces at the end of the line. It would be dangerous to use this technique to remove numbers from the end of a line if the file might contain digits elsewhere. It is really better to use something like **rpl** for this purpose.

The **–s** (for squeeze) option has the effect of squeezing, or collapsing, multiple consecutive occurrences of a character in the set into a single occurrence. For example, to replace lots of spaces by one space:

```
$ tr -s " " <people
Maryann Clark 101
Sally Smith 113
Jane Bailey 121
     <etc...>
Bill Williams 100
$
```

The —s option can also be used to get rid of blank lines in a file:

```
$ tr -s "\012" <file >newfile
$
```

"\012" is the value of the ASCII character for newline. This will only get rid of really blank lines. Lines that are apparently blank, but contain spaces and tabs, are still around.

The —c option complements (inverts) the set of characters given in the first string. For example, to delete everything except digits from the *'people'* file:

```
$ tr -cd 0-9
10111312112011111101121141 22100$
```

Notice that even newline characters have been deleted. The UNIX system prompt appears at the end of the output line. To preserve the newlines we need to say:

```
$ tr -cd "\012[0-9]" <people
101
113
<etc...>
100
$
```

6.10 Tracking Differences between Files with 'diff'

A fairly common state of affairs is that there are several different versions of a file around, at various stages of development. When that situation arises, it is important to be able, at any time, to get an answer to the question: "How does the latest version of this file differ from the previous version of the file?" The **diff** utility is intended to answer just that question. **diff** can display the **diff**erences between two text files. The name **diff** comes from "**diff**erential file comparator".

To illustrate **diff**'s usage, let us revisit our *'people'* file. We did various changes to that file, and we kept our original version in *'people.old'*. So now we have two files:

```
$ cat people.old
Maryann Clark      101
Sally Smith        113
Jane Bailey        121
Jack Austen        120
Steve Daniels      111
Sylvia Dawson      110
Henry Morgan       112
Hank Parker        114
Charlie Smith      122
Bill Williams      100
$ cat people
Maryann Clark      101
Sally White        113
Jane Bailey        121
Jack Austen        120
Steve Daniels      111
Sylvia Dawson      110
Hank Parker        114
Charlie Smith      122
Bill Williams      100
James Walker       112
$
```

You can see by visual inspection that there are a few changes between these two files. But using a computer utility to track the changes gives us a mechanical and more reliable indication. You can run the **diff** utility to tell what lines are different in the two files:

```
$ diff people.old people
2c2
< Sally Smith        113
---
> Sally White        113
7d6
< Henry Morgan       112
10a10
> James Walker       112
$
```

This tells us that there are three changes to the file. To start with, the second line of the file has changed, but it is still line number two (indicated by "2c2"). We then see the old version of the line, preceded by " < ", and the new version of the line, preceded by " > ".

The next change to the file is that line 7 of the original file has been deleted. This is indicated by the "7d6".

The third and last change is that a new line has been added after line 10 of the original file. The new line is still line 10 in the new file, because we deleted the original line 7.

Of course, if we specify the files the other way round on the command line, the results from **diff** will look different:

```
$ diff people people.old
2c2
< Sally White      113
---
> Sally Smith      113
6a7
> Henry Morgan     112
10d10
< James Walker     112
$
```

When looking at **diff** output, be sure you know which way round you specified the filenames, or you could misinterpret it. Lines starting with " < " show lines which are in the first file, but do not appear in the second of the two files you specify. Lines starting with " > " show new lines that appear in the second file you specify. Lines changed between the two files show as both " < " and " > ".

The order of filename arguments on the **diff** command line is important. The **diff** command line is like:

```
$ diff old_file new_file
$
```

Here is a short summary of the meaning of **diff**'s results. There are only three ways in which **diff** indicates changes to a file:

a means that lines are added, or appended, to the first file, in order to obtain the result shown in the second file.

d means that lines have been deleted from the second file.

c means that lines have been changed between the first file and the second file.

diff finds *all* differences, so if you change the spacing on a line, or remove spaces from the end of a line, these will show up as differences:

```
$ diff oldfile newfile
4,5c4,5
< There once was a lady from Maine
< Whose name was thought to be Jane,
---
> There  once  was  a  lady  from  Maine
> Whose name was thought to be Jane,
$
```

You can see that the difference in line 4 is that there are two spaces between each word in *'newfile'*. It is not so obvious that there are spaces at the end of line 5 in one of the files. Much of the time you are not really interested in a difference in spacing. You can suppress these differences with the **–b** (for blanks) option. The **–b** option tells **diff** to ignore trailing space and tab characters, and differences in spacing between words:

```
$ diff -b oldfile newfile
$
```

This time there are no apparent differences between the two files, as shown by the fact that there is no output from **diff**.

The **–b** option does not ignore spaces appearing at the beginning of a line. If you use the **–b** option and a line has leading spaces in one file but not in the other file, it will still show as a difference.

There is a **–e** (for ed) option to **diff**, which makes it display the differences between the files in a different way:

```
$ diff -e people.old people
10a
James Walker    112
.
7d
2c
Sally White     113
.
$
```

This format represents the editor commands we would have to give if we were using the **ed** text editor to change *'people.old'* to look like *'people'*.

You will learn just what these commands do when you get to chapter 7 but here is a brief rundown: first we add a new line after the line number 10 in the old file; then we delete line 7 of the old file; lastly we change line 2 of the old file to be the new line given.

You will notice that the differences are shown starting at the end of the file and working backwards towards the beginning. This is necessary when using line numbers in the editor. The **ed** text editor numbers its lines relative to the start of the file. So if you add or delete lines at the beginning of the file, the location of the rest of the lines in the file changes. For this reason, **diff** generates its **ed** commands to start editing at the end of the file, and work towards the start of the file.

You can keep a permanent record of the differences between two files by redirecting the output from **diff** into a file:

```
$ diff -e people.old people > changes
$
```

Now, to change the old version of the file into the new version, you simply run the **ed** text editor, with the *'changes'* file as input:

```
$ ed - people.old < changes
$
```

This tells **ed** to edit the file called *'people.old'*, using the editing commands contained in the file called *'changes'*. The "−" option on the **ed** command line suppresses messages which **ed** usually prints when used interactively. We end up with a file which looks just like the new file *'people'*.

```
$ cat people.old
Maryann Clark      101
Sally White        113
Jane Bailey        121
Jack Austen        120
Steve Daniels      111
Sylvia Dawson      110
Hank Parker        114
Charlie Smith      122
Bill Williams      100
James Walker       112
$
```

In practice, things aren't quite this easy. Before you can edit the file in this way you have to add two lines to the end of the *'changes'* file. One contains the letter "w", which tells the editor to write away the changed file; the other says "q" which tells the editor to quit the editing job. These are described in more detail in Chapter 7.

The burning question is: why would you want to do this? Consider the following scenario. You start off with a program (or it could be a document, but we're going to talk about a program) which initially exists as Version 0, say. Then it gets changed and becomes Version 1, then it gets changed again to be Version 2, and so on, until it's changed so many times that it's at Version 10.

Now suppose you want to be able to get at any one of these versions. When a bug* is found in the program, it's sometimes nice to know if it was always there, or if it was introduced by some other change made during the program's history.

One way to achieve this is to keep every version of the program, so you have all these files:

```
prog.v0 prog.v1 prog.v2 ..... prog.v9 prog.v10
```

Unless you have a very small program, keeping multiple versions is going to consume massive amounts of space. Also, if you want to know just what changes were introduced in each different version, you have to run **diff** on each pair:

```
$ diff prog.v0 prog.v1 > changes1
$ diff prog.v1 prog.v2 > changes2
              <etc...>
$ diff prog.v8 prog.v9 > changes9
$ diff prog.v9 prog.v10> changes10
$
```

A different way to achieve the objective is to keep only the first version of the program, but keep all the changes files too:

```
prog.v0 changes1 changes2 ..... changes9 changes10
```

Now you can see what changes were made for each new version of the program just by looking at the changes files. To get any version of the program, you simply apply all the changes in turn. For example, to get 'prog.v3', you use this sequence of commands:

---

* a euphemism for mistake.

```
$ cp prog.v0 prog.v3
$ ed prog.v3 < changes1
$ ed prog.v3 < changes2
$ ed prog.v3 < changes3
$
```

In practice, the process may be a bit more awkward than shown above, but this is enough to give you the idea. As we said, this method can be applied to documents too.

The size of file that **diff** can handle is limited, and so is the number of differences that it can cope with. Should you get a message indicating that **diff** is out of space, you can try using the **–h** option:

```
$ diff –h oldfile newfile > changes
$
```

This tells **diff** to do a half-hearted job, and it only works when the changed portions of the file are short and far apart. You can't use the **–e** option when you use the **–h** option.

Another solution to lack of space is to do a judicious **split** on your files, then apply **diff** to the pieces. This is not always satisfactory, because if the changed portions of the file cross the boundary of the **split** files it can be difficult to see the exact differences.

Some versions of the UNIX system also have a command called **bdiff** (for big **diff**) which can handle larger files than **diff**. However, **bdiff** works by **split**ting the files and then finding the differences in the pieces, so it's better to use **diff** if you can.

6.11 Comparing Files with 'cmp'

Another utility program which can be used to find differences between two files is **cmp**, for **comp**are. While **diff** looks for lines that are different, **cmp** just does a byte-by-byte (character-by-character for text files) comparison of the two files you specify:

```
$ cmp people.old people
people.old, people differ: char 26, line 2
$
```

As soon as **cmp** finds one byte that is different between the two files, it prints out a message as shown in the example, and stops. If you want to see all the differences in the files, you need to use the **–l** (for long) option:

```
$ cmp -l people.old people
 26  123  127
 27  155  150
 30  150  155
121  145  141
123  162  153
   <etc>
192  163   40
197   60   61
198   60   62
$
```

cmp now prints out every byte that is different in the two files. For each difference, it prints the position of the byte in the file (in decimal), the octal value of the byte in the first file, and the octal value of the byte in the second file. For text files, these values are the octal values of the characters as they are represented by the ASCII character set.

In our example, bytes 26, 27 and 30 are different because we changed "Smith" to "White". The line containing "Henry", that we deleted from *'people.old'*, causes all the remaining bytes in the file to be different, except when both files coincidentally contain the same character.

As you can see, **cmp** is not very usable for showing the differences between text files, it is more suited for program object and data files. However, it does provide a quick way to find out whether files are different or not. If the files are different, you can then use **diff** to get details of the differences.

6.12 Finding Commonality between Files with 'comm'

The **diff** and **cmp** commands answer the question "what is different about these two files?". We now discuss a command that answers the question "what is the same about these two files?".

The **comm** command prints lines that are **comm**on to two files. To give an example of this command, we are going to revert to the files we used in some of the **sort** examples. Instead of having everybody in the group in one *'people'* file, suppose you have one file for software development people, one for hardware designers, and the administrative people appear in both; furthermore, you have a file containing only the managers. Two of the files look like this:

```
$ cat managers
Bill Williams
Jack Austen
Sylvia Dawson
$ cat softpeople
Bill Williams
Maryann Clark
Sylvia Dawson
Sally Smith
Steve Daniels
Henry Morgan
Hank Parker
$
```

In this example we leave out the phone numbers, just as we did in **sort**. Now we run the **comm** command on these two files:

```
$ comm managers softpeople
                Bill Williams
Jack Austen
            Maryann Clark
                Sylvia Dawson
            Sally Smith
            Steve Daniels
            Henry Morgan
            Hank Parker
    $
```

The **comm** utility produces three columns. Unfortunately they overlap, so they aren't too easy to read.

The first column shows lines that are in the first of the files you specified, but not in the second.

The second column shows lines that are in the second file, but not in the first.

The third column shows lines that appear in both files. So, Jack Austen is a manager but not a software person. Hank, Henry, Steve *et al.*, are software people, but not managers. Sylvia and Bill are both software people and managers.

If you don't want to see all this information, some of it can be suppressed by giving **comm** an option which states which column or columns you don't want to see. To see columns 1 and 3 only, and suppress column 2, you use **comm** like this:

```
$ comm -2 managers softpeople
        Bill Williams
Jack Austen
        Sylvia Dawson
$
```

Just to confuse you, column 3 has shifted over to the left, so that it occupies the space normally taken by column 2.

To see only those lines which appear in both files, that is column 3, you need to suppress both columns 1 and 2:

```
$ comm -12 managers softpeople
Bill Williams
Sylvia Dawson
$
```

For **comm** to be really useful, lines in the two files being compared should be in the same order. Notice that in our example, Bill appeared before Sylvia in both files. To show what happens if lines in the files are not in the same order, let's take our original *'people'* file and sort it two different ways, then compare the results:

```
$ sort people > people1
$ sort +1 people > people2
$ comm people1 people2
Bill Williams    100
Charlie Smith    122
Hank Parker      114
Henry Morgan     112
                 Jack Austen       120
                 Jane Bailey       121
                 Maryann Clark     101
Sally Smith      113
                 Steve Daniels     111
                 Sylvia Dawson     110
        Henry Morgan     112
        Hank Parker      114
        Sally Smith      113
        Charlie Smith    122
        Bill Williams    100
$
```

After the two **sort** commands, *'people1'* contains lines sorted by first-name order, and *'people2'* contains lines sorted by second-name order. The result of trying to find the common lines is hopelessly confused. First we see that Bill is in *'people1'*, but not *'people2'*. But then the last line of the results show that Bill is in *'people2'*, but not in *'people1'*. In fact **comm** only recognizes five lines as being common to the two files. The moral is: make sure that lines in your files are in the same order, before you try to use **comm**.

6.13 Programmable Text Manipulation with 'awk'

awk is another text selection and alteration tool in the same family as **grep** (already described), and **sed** (described in chapter 7).

In addition to providing a means to search for text patterns, **awk** extends the capabilities to selecting specific fields from lines and testing relationships between those fields. **awk** can be thought of as a "programmable report-generator".

A full writeup on **awk** can be found in the paper called:

Awk — A Pattern Scanning and Text Processing Language (Second Edition), by A. V. Aho, B. W. Kernighan, and P. J. Weinberger

By the way, **awk** is not an acronym for anything. As far as we can see, it is the initials of the three authors listed in the reference above. They are all members of the Computing Science Research Group at Bell Laboratories.

At its simplest, what **awk** does is to select a line (from a file) according to some *selection criteria*. The selection criteria can be text patterns (regular expressions) as in **grep** and **egrep** and other utilities. Having found lines of interest, **awk** can then perform some actions on the line, or portions of the line.

This selection-action process is represented in **awk** notation by:

    pattern {action}

and means, for every record (line) which matches the specified *pattern*, perform the specified *action*.

Both the pattern and the action are optional. A pattern with no corresponding action simply selects the matched record for display on the Standard Output. An action with no associated pattern is performed on all records in the file. In other words, a missing pattern matches all lines in the file.

An **awk** pattern is specified by enclosing it in slashes:

    /pattern/

The pattern can be regular expressions as described in **grep** and others. **awk** has the extended pattern matching capabilities, such as alternation, described in **egrep**.

6.13.1 Referencing Fields in a Line

Let us demonstrate a very simple **awk** example. Recall our *'people'* file from before:

```
$ cat people
Maryann Clark     101
Sally White       113
Jane Bailey       121
Jack Austen       120
Steve Daniels     111
Sylvia Dawson     110
Hank Parker       114
Charlie Smith     122
Bill Williams     100
James Walker      112
$
```

We assume that the bureaucracy has finally dictated that the people must appear in the file in order of last name, followed by first name. This is easy to achieve with **awk**:

```
$ awk '{print $2 ", " $1 "^I" $3}' people
Clark, Maryann    101
White, Sally      113
Bailey, Jane      121
Austen, Jack      120
Daniels, Steve    111
Dawson, Sylvia    110
Parker, Hank      114
Smith, Charlie    122
Williams, Bill    100
Walker, James     112
$
```

This is a very simple **awk** program, with an action but no pattern. In this case, the missing pattern selects every record in the file. For the time being, we consider records and lines as equivalent, but they need not be.

The action part (enclosed in the braces) specifies that **awk** is to print the fields in the order indicated. **awk** considers every record in a file to be composed of *fields*. Fields are separated by *field separators*, which are normally spaces or tabs, but can be changed to whatever you like. As we showed in the above example, fields are accessed by the notation **$n** where "n" is the number of the field you want. The field reference **$0** is special: it refers to the whole record (line). The only result in the above example is a rearrangement of the fields in a line. It is possible, however, to use **awk** to perform complex selection and computations on the elements of lines.

Notice that we had to specifically insert spaces or tab characters in the example, by enclosing them in quoted strings. If you just typed the field references one after the other (even with spaces between them) the resultant output would appear all scrunched together. The print statement in the above example could be written like this:

```
print $2, $1, $3
```

in which case the fields appear on the output with a single space between them.

In the example above, we illustrated the **awk** program, enclosed in single quotes (apostrophes) on the command line. It is unfortunate that most of **awk**'s special characters duplicate those of the Shell, so it is a good idea to get into the habit of always enclosing the **awk** command-line program in single quotes.

The normal mode for **awk** is to take its program as the first argument on the command line. If we wish **awk** to take its program from a file, we must precede the file name with the **–f** (for file) option, as in the example below. Instead of placing the name swapping program on the **awk** command line, we can create a file called *'swap'*, containing the **awk** program. Here is the contents of the *'swap'* file:

```
$ cat swap
{print $2 ", " $1 "^I" $3}
$
```

The **awk** program is now simply a line in a file. The apostrophes have gone away. To run **awk** with this program, simply use the command with the **–f** option like this:

```
$ awk -f swap people
```

to achieve the same results as in the example before. When using **awk** in this way, you can think of *'swap'* as being a program file, and *'people'* as being a data file. If the program is specified wrongly, the program file can be modified using a text editor, then **awk** can be rerun. For complex manipulations, this is much easier than having to type the program on the **awk** command line each time.

6.13.2 Built-In Patterns and Variables

awk has two special "built-in" patterns, called BEGIN and END. If BEGIN appears as a pattern, it matches the beginning of file, so that you can gain control before any other processing is done. Similarly, the pattern END matches the end of the file so you can gain control when you get to the end of the file.

The next example shows how END is used to calculate the average score in our tennis league. First of all, we create an **awk** program in a file called *'average'*:

```
$ cat >average
{total = total + $3}
END {print "Average score is ", total / NR}
^D
$
```

Then we compute the average with **awk**, like this:

```
$ awk -f average tennis
Average score is 8.9
$
```

In this simple **awk** program we have introduced quite a few new features. The first line of the program adds the value of the third field of each record (line) of the data file to the variable called "total". When a variable (such as "total" in the example) is first mentioned, **awk** creates it and sets its initial value to zero.

The second line in our **awk** program indicates what has to be done when the end of the data file is reached (specified by the pattern "END"). First we print a message "Average score is", then on the same line we print the value of "total" divided by "NR". The variable "NR" is built in to **awk**. Its value is always equal to the Number of Records (lines) in the file.

6.13.3 Conditional Pattern Selection

An **awk** pattern can in fact be a *conditional expression*, not just a simple character string. We illustrate this by selecting, from our list of tennis players, those whose scores are 10 or more. We can achieve this by the following **awk** program:

```
$ awk '$3 >= 10 {print $0}' tennis
Maryann Clark    18
Sally Smith      14
Steve Daniels    11
Hank Parker      18
$
```

This **awk** program introduces the idea of conditional selection based on properties of the individual fields in the record. In this case, the pattern part is the conditional expression which selects all records whose third field is 10 or more. The action part is simply to print the entire line.

The symbol **>=** means "greater than or equal to". The construct:

```
$3 >= 10
```

is a conditional expression.

awk has a complete set of facilities for testing conditions and performing actions depending on the truth or falsity of those tests.

The next example shows how we use **awk** to select wines from a list of wines, vineyards, years, and prices. We have a directory called *'wine'*, in which there live files called *'chardonnay'*, *'cabernet'*, *'pinotnoir'*, and so on.

Then we can use **awk** to ask questions like: "find me a Chardonnay, somewhere in the years 1976 to 1980 at less than $5.50 per bottle".*

Here we change directory to the *'wine'* directory, show the files there, and then show the contents of the *'chardonnay'* file:**

```
$ cd wine
$ ls
cabernet chardonnay pinotnoir
$ cat chardonnay
1976    12.00    Caymus Vineyards
1976    18.00    Mount Veeder
1976    11.50    Chateau St. Jean
1977     9.00    Robert Mondavi
1976     7.75    Chateau St. Jean
1976    10.00    Spring Mountain
              . . .
```

---

* If you find one, please write to the authors.

** From: "A Consumer's Guide to 114 California Chardonnays". Printed with permission from the Wine Appreciation Guild of San Francisco.

```
1977    6.99   Franciscan
1976    7.50   Chateau St. Jean
1976   10.00   Sterling Vineyards
1977    8.50   Chaparral
1977    6.75   Alexander Valley Vineyards
1977    8.00   Dry Creek Winery
1977   10.00   St. Clements
1975   10.00   Chateau Montelena
1976   11.00   Mayacamas Vineyards
1977    7.50   Raymond Vineyards
1977    8.00   Conn Creek Vineyards
1977    7.50   Chalone
1977    9.00   Carneros Creek Winery
1977    5.99   Charles Krug
1977   10.00   Sonoma Vineyards
$
```

The first field in the file is the year, the second field is the price, and the third field is the vineyard which produced the wine.

Now let us use **awk** to select something good to go with our veal piccata:

```
$ awk '$1 ~ /197[5678]/ && $2 <= 8.00' chardonnay
1976    7.75   Chateau St. Jean
1977    6.99   Franciscan
1976    7.50   Chateau St. Jean
1977    6.75   Alexander Valley Vineyards
1977    8.00   Dry Creek Winery
1977    7.50   Raymond Vineyards
1977    8.00   Conn Creek Vineyards
1977    7.50   Chalone
1977    5.99   Charles Krug
$
```

This **awk** pattern selects only those entries whose first field lies in the years 1975 through 1978 (using the character class text pattern), *and* whose second field (the price) is $8.00 or under. The tilde ~ means "match", that is, if field 1 matches the pattern shown enclosed in slashes.

The double ampersand **&&** is used to indicate that both conditions must be met for the action to be taken. The operators used in **awk** programs are similar to those of the C programming language. A detailed list of these operators can be found in the document referred to at the start of this section.

The result is a reasonably short list of Chardonnays for our enjoyment. It would be nice if **awk** could then advise as to the quality, but there are some things we must do for ourselves.

Note that the second field in each line (the price) has a decimal point. **awk** performs all its computations in floating point notation, so it doesn't matter whether numbers are entered as integers or fractions.

There are many ways to use **awk**'s capabilities. It is a matter of personal choice and experience whether to use string matching, relational expressions, or other forms.

For instance, the **awk** command in the example above could have been written in two other and equally good ways:

```
awk '/^197[5678]/ {if ($2 <= 8.00) print $0}' chardonnay
awk '$1 >= 1974 && $1 <= 1978 && $2 <= 8.00' chardonnay
```

The first selects lines beginning with the selected pattern (note the ^ sign to indicate a match anchored to the start of the line), then performs a conditional statement to print all lines whose second field is in the price range.

The second example uses a relational expression to isolate the range of years that were required.

6.13.4 Pattern Ranges

An **awk** pattern can reference a range of lines, for example:

```
/1976/, /1977/
```

is a pattern range. There are two patterns here, separated by a comma. **awk** selects all lines (inclusive) starting at the first line in which the first field is 1976 or more, and ending the first time a line is found where the first field is 1977.

We would like to apply this to our *'chardonnay'* file, but that file is not sorted properly for the job, since the years are all out of order. First we sort the file so that it ends up with the lines in order by year:

```
$ sort -n -o chard.s chardonnay
$ awk '/1976/,/1977/ {if ($2 <= 8.00) print $0}' chard.s
1976    7.50    Chateau St. Jean
1976    7.75    Chateau St. Jean
1977    5.99    Charles Krug
$
```

Note that the pattern range as we gave it above stops at the first occurrence of 1977, not the last.

The complete range of applications of **awk** are far beyond the scope of this book. We have tried to give you some of the flavor of **awk** so that you can explore further. For further exploration, read the paper referred to at the start of this section:

Awk — A Pattern Scanning and Text Processing Language (Second Edition), by A. V. Aho, B. W. Kernighan, and P. J. Weinberger

6.14 Summary

We have covered a lot in this chapter. The text processing utilities are some of the things which make the UNIX system such a powerful tool.

You should use **grep** and its variations to study and thoroughly understand the ideas of regular expressions, since many of the UNIX system utilities revolve around their use.

Try playing with options to **pr** so that you can get multiple columns of stuff on a terminal screen, with no headers, trailers, or any extraneous data.

Experiment with **sort**, to determine the kinds of things you can do with it. Although most UNIX systems already have a spelling checker, you can construct your own, using **tr**, **sort**, **uniq**, and **comm**, in a pipeline. See if you can do this, or find out how to do it.

Experiment using **awk** to do the same things as **grep**, **sort**, or **comm**, and see if the jobs are easier with **awk**. One of the claims made for **awk** is that someone programmed it to find "All Chinese restaurants within walking distance of Lower Manhattan". See if you can figure out how to do that job or one similar.

The next two chapters describe text editors. The concepts of regular expressions are deeply entwined in the capabilities of those editors, so it is essential that you are comfortable with regular expressions and their use.

7 The Ed and Sed Editors

An **editor** is a utility program which you use to make modifications to the contents of a file. When we talk about an editor, we usually mean a **text** editor. That is, an editor designed to deal with files containing strings of characters in a particular character set. Additionally, an editor usually means an *interactive* utility, where you can view what you have already, before deciding to make changes. There are exceptions to the interactive editors, such as the **sed** stream editor, discussed in the latter half of this chapter.

Utilities such as **grep**, **tr**, **rpl**, **awk**, and others, have two characteristics which differentiate them from text editors. First, they do not change the original file in any way. They simply modify the data contained in the file, on its way from one place (the original file) to another (another file, the line-printer, or the terminal screen). Second, those commands select and alter things on a global basis. That means that the things to be selected or altered must conform to regular patterns.

But there are times when you want to make selective and detailed changes to specific lines, or parts of lines, and also make those changes permanent. With a text editor, you can interactively browse through a file, inspecting things and deciding if you want to change them. When you have finished the process of inspection and modification, you can instruct the text editor to make the changes permanent. The **sed** stream editor is an exception, since it is more often used for making transient changes.

In general, editors fall into two categories, namely, *line* editors, and *screen* editors. By a *line* editor, we mean one in which the basic unit for change is a line (a string of characters terminated by a newline character). You can give commands to the editor to perform various operations on the lines: lines can be printed (displayed); lines can be changed; new lines can be inserted; existing lines can be deleted; lines can be moved or copied to a different place within the file; substitutions of character strings can be made within a line or group of lines.

A *screen* editor is one where a portion of the file is displayed on the terminal screen, and the cursor can be moved around the screen to indicate where you want to make changes. You can select which part of the file you want to have displayed. Screen editors are also called *display* editors, or *visual* editors. In chapter 8, we describe **vi**, one of the more popular screen editors that run on the UNIX system.

Most available editors, both line editors and screen editors, have one thing in common, namely that they do not change the file in situ. The file is first copied into a temporary scratch-pad area, called a "buffer", and changes are made in that buffer. When the changes are complete (or at some convenient point in the editing session), the file must be "saved" (or "written" — the terminology used depends on the editor). Any changes you have made during the editing session do not appear in the original file until you have done this save operation.

In some ways this is a good thing. If you really make a mess of things, as you are apt to do when you're just learning, you can easily get back to square one.

However, there is a disadvantage, in that should your UNIX system "crash" before you have saved your file, you have lost all your changes. So if you have a fragile system, we recommend that you save your file often during a heavy editing session. It's a good idea even if your system seems fairly robust — disease can strike rapidly at times. This is particularly important when using the editor to create a new file, and is a reason for using **cat** (as we showed earlier) to create a new file by entering text directly, without an editor. If the system goes down while you're using **cat**, you still have all lines that you have typed so far.*

---

* Provided that you use the -**u** option to **cat**, as we described in chapter 4 — Commands and Standard Files.

Another possible disadvantage to the use of an editor which uses a buffer, is that the buffer might not be big enough to hold the file you wish to modify. Depending on the particular system you are using, the buffer limit varies from about 64,000 characters to about 128,000 characters. In normal text, this represents somewhere between 1,000 to 3,000 lines. Sometimes, the file you want to edit might be bigger than the limit. If this is the case you must **split** the file into pieces. We described the **split** command in chapter 6. Having **split** the file, you can then edit the pieces one at a time using the editor of your choice, then use **cat** to put them back together again.

The UNIX system has two basic editors. **ed** is the interactive text editor which forms part of the basic UNIX system. **ed** is a line editor, and is in some ways considered rather primitive, which is the reason that there are screen editors around.

The other basic text editor on the UNIX system is the "stream editor", called **sed**. It similar to **ed** in the operations it can perform, but it is not interactive, and cannot move backwards in the edit file. **sed** is not normally used to make permanent changes to a file. Rather, it is used more like the filter utilities which we described in earlier chapters. **sed** is somewhat reminiscent of the kinds of editors used in the dark ages for editing files on magnetic tape.

Because the basic UNIX system editors are primitive, other editors (mostly screen-oriented) have become available. On any given UNIX system, there might or might not be a choice of editors other than **ed**, but if there are, you will probably find one of **ex** and **vi**, which come with the Berkeley version of the UNIX system; **emacs**, from MIT; **edit**, a cut-down version of **ex** from Berkeley; the **rand** editor, developed at the Rand Corporation. There are many more editors around. They all have more or less the same sets of features. The **ex** and **vi** editors are described in chapter 8. Consult your local systems wizard to find out what's available.

7.1 'ed' — The Basic UNIX System Editor

ed is the basic editor in the UNIX system. That is to say, every UNIX system has **ed** available. The presence of other editors is not guaranteed.

ed is a line editor — whatever operation you want to perform, you must specify what line or lines on which to perform that operation.

Lines can be accessed (addressed, in **ed** terminology) in several ways, but the most easily understood way of addressing lines is by line number. In practice, addressing lines by number proves to be the most awkward to use, and editors such as **ed** provide other mechanisms (by the line's textual contents, for instance) for addressing lines.

This description of **ed** is not to be considered as a full **ed** tutorial. We try here to give you a quick tour through the main features of **ed**. We introduce **ed**'s capabilities by showing how to add some new text to the edit buffer, and then change that text around in various ways, using different **ed** commands. The examples of **ed** are given in terms of some of the examples introduced in the chapter on "Text Manipulation". We show you how similar manipulations can be achieved with **ed**.

If you want more detail on **ed**, refer to the description of **ed** in the UNIX System Manuals, or to "A Tutorial Introduction to the UNIX Text Editor", or to "Advanced Editing on UNIX", both by Brian W. Kernighan.

7.1.1 Starting the 'ed' Text Editor

Depending on the particular UNIX system you have, your version of **ed** might or might not have a prompt. If **ed** has a prompt, it displays a character which indicates that it is waiting for you to type commands. Those versions which do not have a prompt are not nearly so easy to use as those which do. *

In all our examples we show the **ed** prompt as the asterisk character * since this makes the examples easier to follow.

To look at or make changes to a file called *'nonesuch'*, you start **ed** like this:

```
$ ed nonesuch
?nonesuch
*
```

ed is not exactly the most talkative text editor in this world. Whenever **ed** doesn't understand something, it responds with a **?**. Here, we asked **ed** to **ed**it a file called *'nonesuch'*. **ed**'s response is just a question mark **?** followed by the file name. This we take to mean that the file called *'nonesuch'* doesn't exist.

---

* Some versions of **ed**, which do not normally display a prompt, have a command-line option which requests **ed** to provide a prompt during the editing session.

Other versions of **ed**, which do have a prompt, have a command-line option to turn the prompt off, for use in those cases where you are driving **ed** from a pre-prepared script of editing commands.

Some versions of **ed** are more polite than that, they might respond something like this:

```
$ ed nonesuch
<*** New File ***>
*
```

If you get the "New File" message, or the "?filename" message, when you are not expecting it, it is a good indication that you have either misspelled the filename, or you are probably in the wrong directory.

Having told you that something was amiss, **ed** then prints the asterisk character * which we are using as the prompt in our examples.

Now let us try editing a file which does exist:

```
$ ed myfile
1083
*
```

This time, the file is there, and **ed** didn't start with just a query. The number "1083" (or whatever the number is) is a count of the number of characters in the file you are editing.

You get out of **ed**, and back to the UNIX system Shell, by typing a **q** (for **q**uit) command:

```
* q
$
```

There is more information on the **q**uit command later, and a discussion on **q**uit's interactions with the **w**rite command.

In common with many of the UNIX system utilities, you can give **ed** a Shell command preceded with an exclamation mark ! When **ed** sees a line beginning with ! it passes the whole line to the Shell. The Shell runs that command, and then returns to the editor. For instance, suppose you get the "?myfile" message when you weren't expecting it, but you think you have spelled the filename correctly. By typing

```
!pwd
```

you could check that you were in the correct directory, and

```
!ls
```

would give you a list of the files in that directory to check that your spelling was indeed correct.

7.1.2 The Current Line in the Buffer

While **ed** is working on the buffer, it keeps track of which line is the one on which you last performed some operation. This line is called the "current line". You can indicate the current line by typing a period character **.** (it's that "dot" again), so **ed** aficionados (and **ed** documentation) use the word **dot** to mean the current line. We follow this convention of using the word **dot** to represent the current line in the buffer.

If you don't specify a line for a command to operate on, most **ed** operations work on the line-addressed by **dot**.

When **ed** starts working on a file, **dot** is positioned at the last line in the buffer. Thereafter, **dot** usually changes when any operation is performed. In general, **dot** sits at the last line affected by whatever **ed** command you used. For instance, if you print lines 1 through 10 of the buffer, after the lines are displayed, **dot** will be positioned at line 10.

7.1.3 Enter a New File with 'e'

The **e** (for **e**nter) command enters (starts editing) a completely new file into the buffer, discarding the previous contents of the buffer. The command:

    e filename

reads the contents of *'filename'* into the buffer. The original contents of the buffer are discarded. The remembered file name (see the file command) is set to the filename given on the **e**nter command. **Dot** is set to the last line in the buffer.

You use the **e**nter command in situations such as getting a "?filename" response from **ed**, indicating that you probably misspelled the filename. In this case, you simply use the **e** command to start on the correct file.

The **e** command can also be used as a quick way to edit a new file after you have saved the changes to another file, or as a way to abandon one file and start work on a new one.

7.1.4 Adding New Text with 'a'

You add new text to the buffer with the **a**ppend or insert commands. To illustrate the append command, we start an editing session with a completely blank file, and add text into it.

We use our file of people from earlier chapters, but this time we use **ed** to create the file, and change it around.

Let us start a new file called *'people'*:

```
$ ed people
?people
*
```

Here, we asked **ed** to **ed**it a file called *'people'*. That file doesn't exist, so **ed**'s response is just a query of the filename.

Since there is nothing in the buffer (because this is a new file), we don't have to bother with line-addressing. We can just type an append command. Whenever you use any of the commands where **ed** wants you to type new text, **ed** waits silently (no prompts) for the new input, and is said to be in "text input mode":

```
$ ed people
?people
* a
Maryann Clark     101
Sally Smith       113
Jane Bailey       121
Jack Austen       120
Steve Daniels     111
Sylvia Dawson     110
Henry Morgan      112
.
* p
Henry Morgan      112
* w
140
* q
$
```

Having added the new text into the buffer, we terminate the text insertion by typing a period character **.** (the good old "dot" again), at the beginning of a line, immediately followed by a carriage-return. This gets you back to the "command mode", where you can type **ed** commands again. In our example, this is indicated by the prompt *****.

Commands that place new text into the buffer are the **a** (for append, or maybe **a**fter) command, the **i** (for insert, or maybe in front of) command, and the **c** (for **c**hange) command (described later). All three of these commands have the same properties: firstly that they place you in "text input mode", where you are entering text instead of editor commands; and secondly that a period on a line of its own tells **ed** that you have stopped typing new text, and wish to get back to typing **ed** commands.

After an **a**, **i**, or **c** command, **dot** stands at the last line of text typed into the buffer.

Remember that the text we inserted only goes into the edit buffer at this time. It does not appear in the original file until the buffer is saved away with a **w**rite command.

After we got back to command-mode, we gave **ed** a **p** (for **p**rint) command, and **ed**'s answer is to print the last line we typed. This verifies that we are actually not inserting text any more, but are back at the **ed** command level.

Then we issued a **w** (for **w**rite) command to tell **ed** to write the edit buffer away in the file called *'people'*. When you do a **w**rite, **ed** responds with the number of characters in the file. Newlines and spaces are counted in the total number of characters.

The **i** (for insert) command functions just the same as the **a**ppend command, except that insert places the new text before the specified line.

As in our examples in the earlier chapters, we now wish to complete the *'people'* file by adding more names and telephone numbers to the list. To do this, simply edit the *'people'* file again. When **ed** reads the file into the edit buffer, **dot** is left standing at the last line read in. So you can add new text by just typing an **a**ppend command right away:

```
$ ed people
140
* a
Hank Parker       114
Charlie Smith     122
Bill Williams     100
.
* w
200
*
```

When we start **ed** working on an existing file, **ed** displays a count of the number of characters in the file.

Since **dot** is positioned at the end of the buffer when **ed** reads the file, we don't have to specify a line number for the **a**ppend command. The new text is automatically placed at the end of the buffer. Had we wanted to place the new text somewhere else in the buffer, we would have had to supply a line address on the command.

7.1.4.1 Possible Problems when Inserting New Text   Text input mode is the one that causes most problems, especially when using a version of **ed** that does not provide a prompt. It is not always easy to tell when you have really ended text input mode and are back at the stage of typing **ed** commands. The trouble is that text input must be terminated by a dot **.** at the very beginning of a line, and immediately followed by a carriage-return. It is important that there be no spaces or any other characters on the line, either before or after the period. If you accidentally get some non-printing characters in the line because of "fat-fingering" (control-A is a common offender), you do not terminate text input mode. Yet there is nothing to indicate that on your terminal.

If you have a version of **ed** which displays a prompt when it is ready to accept commands, the matter is straightforward. If you don't see a ✱ (or whatever), you are still in text insertion mode. In this case, type, very carefully, a period character **.** followed by RETURN. You should now see the **ed** prompt. At this point it is a good idea to check that what you have **a**ppended (or inserted or changed) is what you thought it was. You may find that you have some garbage lines which need to be deleted.

When using a version of **ed** that doesn't provide a prompt, things are not so easy. One way of finding whether you are still in text input mode is to type a **p**rint command, followed by RETURN. It might be better to type **1,$p** (print every line in the buffer), in case the last line you appended was a blank line. Whichever method you choose, if you are not in text input mode, **ed** will print whatever it was you asked for.

If **ed**'s response is still a glassy-eyed stare, not even a blank line, you are still in text input mode. To get out of text input mode, carefully type the period character **.** followed by RETURN. Then type a **p** command again. This time **ed** should reply with the last line you **a**ppended (or inserted or changed), which should be the letter "p". Now you should check what you actually did. You will have at least one garbage line (the "p" you used to determine whether you were still in text input mode) to delete.

Here are some examples: let's assume you are using a version of **ed** that doesn't give a prompt, and you want to add some lines to the end of a file:

```
$ ed derangement
a
Whom God would destroy He first makes mad
Quos Deus vult pedere, prius dementat
He whom Fortune would ruin she robs of his wits
Stultum facit fortuna quem vult pedere
.
p
Stultum facit fortuna quem vult pedere
w
q
$
```

Because **ed**'s response to your **p** command was the last line you appended, you know that you have finished text insertion mode correctly. However, here is an example where it goes wrong:

```
$ ed derangement
a
Whom God would destroy He first makes mad
Quos Deus vult pedere, prius dementat
He whom Fortune would ruin she robs of his wits
Stultum facit fortuna quem vult pedere
.
p
.
p
p
d
p
.
d
p
Stultum facit fortuna quem vult pedere
w
q
$
```

The first time you typed **p**, there was no response. This indicates that you goofed when you typed the period character. You got some undesirable character in there. So now you type the period character **.** more carefully this time, and test by typing another **p** command. This time **ed** replies with the last line that you typed. It happens to be the "p" which you typed when you thought you were back in command mode, but weren't.

Having verified that, you just type the **d** (for **d**elete) command to get rid of that line, and then another **p** command. This time the line that is displayed is the period character that you thought was going to terminate text input mode, but didn't. So you have to type another **d** to delete that, then yet another **p** command to verify that there is no other bad line in there. This is OK, so you can save the file in the usual way.*

You can see that leaving **dot** standing at the last line entered is reasonable behavior on **ed**'s part. If the last line you type is not what you want, you just exit from text input mode, then delete or change that line in any way you want.

7.1.5 Displaying the Contents of the Buffer

The next thing to try is the all important business of looking at what is in the buffer. There are two different **ed** commands to do this. The most widely used is the **p** (for **p**rint) command. The **l** (for list, or maybe **l**ook) command functions just like print, but displays non-printing characters as well.

The usual way of displaying lines from the buffer is to use the **p** (for **p**rint) command. Just typing a plain **p** displays the current line:

```
* p
Bill Williams     100
*
```

Remember that the **a** command leaves **dot** standing at the last line which was appended. The third line in the buffer can be printed with this command:

```
* 3p
Jane Bailey       121
*
```

The first three lines can be displayed by typing:

---

* The *exact* sequence of **ed** commands shown in the example only works if you add text *at the end* of the buffer. If you enter text somewhere in the middle of the buffer, you have to back up one line after each delete operation, before printing it.

```
* 1,3p
Maryann Clark    101
Sally Smith      113
Jane Bailey      121
*
```

and the contents of the entire buffer can be displayed by typing the command:

```
* 1,$p
Maryann Clark    101
Sally Smith      113
Jane Bailey      121
Jack Austen      120
Steve Daniels    111
Sylvia Dawson    110
Henry Morgan     112
Hank Parker      114
Charlie Smith    122
Bill Williams    100
*
```

Here is some notation that **ed** uses: the dollar sign, $, is the address of the last line in the buffer.

The l (for list) command displays non-printing characters as well as the printable characters. For example, if there are tabs, bell characters, and other control characters in the buffer, list displays them in a special form. Some of the special characters are displayed this way:

>   tab character,

<   backspace character,

$ newline character.

Other "funny" characters show up as the octal value of their ASCII representation, preceded by the backslash character \. For example, control-A appears as \001, the "bell" character shows as \007.

7.1.6 Format of ed Commands

You have seen some of the operations that **ed** can perform. The format of a command to **ed**, using the convention followed by the UNIX system manuals, is:

```
[line[,line]]operation[parameter]
```

In words: an **ed** command consists of an optional line-address, or two optional line-addresses separated by a comma, then a single letter operation, optionally followed by some other parameter.

The form of this mysterious "other" parameter varies for each operation, it is mostly obvious what it should be. For the move and transpose operations it is the line that the addressed lines are to be moved or transposed after. These operations actually have three line-addresses.

For the read operation, the extra parameter specifies the name of the file that is to be read.

For many **ed** operations, there is no extra parameter. Supplying one on a command is invalid and results in an error message.

The substitute operation is an exception, because between the operation and the optional parameter you also have to specify the string you want to have substituted, and what you want in its place. Substitution is the most powerful feature of **ed**, and we cover it in detail later in this section.

7.1.7 Line Addressing

The format of commands above showed that a command can be preceded by one or two line-addresses. Both of the line-addresses are optional.

In general, if no line-addresses are supplied, **ed** performs the indicated command on the line addressed by **dot**. There are exceptions to this rule. For instance, the **write** command takes as its default a range which is the entire buffer **1,$**. The **read** command always reads lines in after **$** (the end of the buffer) by default.

If only one line-address is specified, the command is performed on that specific line. If two line-addresses are supplied, the command is done on all lines in the range between them.

The simplest form of line-address is a line number. For example, a straight **4** means line 4 in the buffer. The range **1,10** means lines 1 through 10 in the buffer.

It should be clearly understood that, unlike some other editors, the line numbers that **ed** knows about are not physically a part of the text in the lines.

Also, it is important to understand that the line numbers in the **ed** buffer are relative to the start of the buffer. This means that if you delete line 1, the line which was line 2 now becomes the new line 1, and all the other lines move up by one. Similarly, if you append two new lines after line 3, the two new lines become the new lines 4 and 5, and all the other lines move down by two.

If you are doing changes and deletes by line number, it is wise to start at the end of the buffer. That way, you don't have to recompute all the line numbers on the fly. The **diff** program which we saw back in chapter 6 generates its **ed** commands in this back to front manner.

7.1.7.1 Line Zero in the Buffer

One important thing to remember is that there is a zero'th line in the **ed** buffer. Line 0 never has any text associated with it. It is an "imaginary" line which is useful when you want to put stuff before the first real line in the buffer. Line 0 is used solely as a crutch to enable operations that are clumsy or impossible in other editors.

For example, some editors make it extremely hard, if not impossible, to add text before the first line in the buffer. With **ed**, simply use the **append** command to append text after line 0.

```
* 0a
This is how the world began
Not with any whimper, but with
a great big bang!
.
*
```

Of course, **ed** has the **insert** command, which inserts things before a specified lines, so that the same effect can be achieved by inserting before line 1.

```
* 1i
Tell me, how did the world begin?
.
*
```

You can see the effects of those insertions with the **print** command:

```
* 1,4p
Tell me, how did the world begin?
This is how the world began
Not with any whimper, but with
a great big bang!
*
```

Because **ed** gives you the capability to add text either before or after a given line, the imaginary line zero is not too important for inserting new lines of text into a file. There are, however, other commands such as move, transpose and read, where line 0 is crucial to convenient editing.

7.1.7.2 Stepping Forward and Backward in the Buffer Just entering a plain RETURN is an **ed** command. A RETURN advances **dot** to the next line in the buffer, then prints that line. This is a convenient way to "step" through the buffer, printing lines one at a time.

Typing a plus sign **+** is the same as a single RETURN. The plus sign advances **dot** to the next line in the buffer, then prints that line. Plus signs are cumulative, so typing five of them in a row:

+++++

advances **dot** by five lines, then prints that line.

It is not possible to step past the end of the buffer. When the end of the buffer is reached, **ed** displays its usual question mark for a response.

It is also possible to step backwards through the buffer one line at a time in the same way that a RETURN steps forwards through the buffer. Typing a minus sign − moves **dot** to the previous line and then displays that line. Minus signs are cumulative, so typing several in a row moves **dot** back that number of lines. When stepping backwards through the buffer, it is not possible to step before line 1 in the buffer. An attempt to do so results in a question mark response from **ed**.

Both the plus signs and the minus signs may be followed by a decimal number. Typing

+7

moves **dot** ahead seven lines, then displays that line. Similarly, typing

−19

moves **dot** back by 19 lines, then displays the addressed line.

7.1.7.3 Text Patterns as Line Addresses Lines can be addressed by their textual contents as well as by line numbers. Line numbers are convenient, but it is even more convenient to be able to locate an arbitrary line in the buffer, based on the actual text in the line. **ed**'s pattern-matching facility makes this easy. For example, to tell **ed** to find the line containing the string "Steve", we type this line address:

```
*   /Steve/
Steve Daniels    111
*
```

ed starts at the line after **dot** and searches *forward* in the buffer, looking for the string "Steve". The search continues to the end of the buffer, then starts again at the beginning of the buffer. This behavior is called "wraparound". If the search ends up back at **dot**, without finding the requested pattern, **ed** prints a **?** to indicate that the search failed.

If the search succeeds, **dot** is set to the line containing the string.

Some older versions of **ed** don't print the line automatically when it has been found, so you have to place a **p** command after the search pattern:

```
*   /ark/p
Hank Parker    114
*
```

To search *backwards* in the buffer, simply enclose the string in question mark characters:

```
*   ?ley?
Jane Bailey    121
*
```

Some of the examples of contextual line-addressing just shown demonstrate an important feature, namely that you can look for a part of a word.

The examples above use fixed character strings as the search pattern, but you are not restricted to this. Line-addresses in **ed** can be specified as regular expressions, just like those we described in the **grep** command in chapter 6.

7.1.7.4 The Remembered Pattern When a text-pattern is used to specify a forward or backward search, **ed** stores the pattern away as the "remembered pattern". This means that having found a particular line, the next line containing that pattern can be found just by typing two slashes **//** or two question marks **??**.

For example, to find Sally Smith's telephone number in the file, we use her name as a search pattern:

```
*   /Smith/
Sally Smith    113
*
```

Although there are two Smith's in the buffer, we only found the first one. To find the next Smith in the buffer, we use the remembered pattern:

```
* //
Charlie Smith    122
*
```

If we now type the remembered pattern again, we will get back to Sally Smith:

```
* //
Sally Smith      113
*
```

because there are only two Smith's in the buffer, and the search wraps around.

The remembered pattern saves much tiresome and possibly error-prone typing. The remembered pattern is also used in the substitute command, described later in this chapter.

7.1.7.5 Marking Lines Another way of specifying the line you want, is by addressing a marked line. This is useful when you have large amounts of text to delete, or move around in a file. It mostly finds use in cut-and-paste editing, which we describe later, but here is a simple example which illustrates the mechanism:

```
* /Steve/p
Steve Daniels    111
* ka
* /ark/p
Hank Parker      114
* 'a,.p
Steve Daniels    111
Sylvia Dawson    110
Henry Morgan     112
Hank Parker      114
*
```

Two steps are involved. First a line is marked; line marks are single letters, so 26 lines can be marked at any time. Lines marked in this way can then be accessed at some later stage in the edit session.

The **k** (for mark) command is used to mark (or label) a line with a single letter. At this point the mnemonics are becoming somewhat strained: since the letter **m** is used for the move command, **ed** uses the last letter of mar**k** for the command.

In the example above, we first positioned to the line containing the string "Steve", then used **k** to attach the mark **a** to that line. Like most **ed** commands, **k** defaults to the current line.

Lines that have been marked with the **k** command can subsequently be accessed by typing an ' (apostrophe), followed by the marking letter. In the example above, we repositioned to the line containing the string "ark", then **printed** all lines from the line marked **a** through the current line.

In practice, the **ed** commands that are most likely to be used in conjunction with marking lines, are **d**elete, **m**ove, and **t**ranspose. There is further discussion on this subject under the heading "Cut and Paste".

7.1.7.6 Line Addressing Expressions
It is also possible to combine patterns with numbers to form line-addressing expressions. The following are examples of valid expressions:

`$-1`	addresses the penultimate line of the buffer.
`$-10`	addresses the line 10 lines before the end of the buffer.
`/blurb/+`	addresses the line after the one containing "blurb".
`?burble?-2`	addresses the line that is 2 lines before the one containing "burble".
`'a+5`	addresses the 5th line after the one marked **a**

If you use a range of line-addresses in a command, the two parts of the range do not have to be the same. One could be formed as a simple line number, and the other could well be formed as a text pattern. For instance

       `1,/Char/p`

addresses all lines from line 1 through to the line containing the character string "Char".

7.1.8 Saving the Buffer with 'w'

At the end of an edit session (see the **q**uit command below), **ed** does not automatically write the buffer onto the original disk file. An explicit **w** (for **w**rite) command must be used to write out the contents of the buffer.

If you just type a plain **w** command, the entire contents of the buffer are written onto the file specified on the **ed** command line. That is, if a filename is not explicitly stated in the **w**rite command, the buffer contents are written to the original edit file.

The **w** command can be prefixed with a line-address range, to write selected portions of the buffer to the file. It is also possible to specify the name of the file onto which the contents of the buffer are to be written:

```
*  100,200w wurzel
4538
*
```

writes a copy of lines 100 through 200 (inclusive) onto a file called *'wurzel'*. Lines 100 through 200 remain in the buffer — the **w**rite command does not delete them.

When a write command is performed, **ed** displays a message stating the number of characters written to the file.

7.1.9 Quitting the Edit Session with 'q'

Another important command is the means of ending ("quitting") the edit session. To quit the edit session, just type a **q** command:

```
*  q
$
```

You can see that we got out of **ed** and reverted to the Shell, where we once more got the $ sign system prompt.

Note that the **q**uit command does not automatically write the edited buffer onto the file. To capture any changes made during the editing session, an explicit **w**rite command (described above) must be given.

ed makes a note of whether the editing session to date has changed the buffer in any way. If a **q**uit command is given without having previously written the buffer to a disk file, and the buffer has been changed, **ed** responds with its usual question mark:

```
*  q
?
*
```

as a reminder that the buffer has been changed but not written to any file. A second **q**uit command forces an exit back to the Shell with no further comment.

If the buffer has not been changed during the edit session, one **q**uit command is enough to get back to the Shell.

ed's memory of the buffer contents is fallible. If you change a line, then change it back to what it was originally, there is no change as far as you are concerned, but **ed** really has no way to know what you actually did, so the buffer is marked as changed.

7.1.10 Deleting Lines with 'd'

The **d** (for **d**elete) command removes selected lines from the buffer. A plain:

    d

deletes the current line,

    10,20d

deletes lines 10 through 20 inclusive,

    .,$d

deletes all lines from the current line through to the end of the buffer and:

    ?Clark?,/Austen/d

deletes all lines between the lines that contain "Clark" and "Austen".

In the description of **grep** in chapter 6, we showed the way to remove Henry Morgan from the *'people'* file, and replace him with James Walker. You can do this with the **delete** and **append** command of **ed**:

```
*  /Henry/
Henry Morgan     112
*  dp
Hank Parker      114
*  $a
James Walker     112
.
*  p
James Walker     112
*
```

The **delete** command leaves **dot** standing at the first undeleted line. It is possible to append a **p** (for **p**rint) suffix after the **delete** command, as we showed in the example above.

The above example is an exact repetition of the example we gave in chapter 6, where we deleted a line from the middle of the file, then added another line to the end of it. In practice, when using **ed**, it is simpler to replace the line containing Henry with one containing James, in the same place in the file.

7.1.11 Changing Whole Lines with 'c'

Strictly speaking, the change command is redundant. If you want to change some lines in the buffer, you can first delete the lines, then append the replacement text, as we showed in the previous example. The change command is simply an extra convenience.

The change command changes entire lines in the buffer. Changed lines are deleted from the buffer, and new lines typed in to replace them.

We can apply the change command to the same example as before, that is, removing Henry Morgan from the *'people'* file, and adding James Walker instead. Here is how to do the job using change:

```
$ ed people
200
* /Henry/
Henry Morgan    112
* c
James Walker    112
.
* p
James Walker    112
*
```

A period at the beginning of the line, followed by a RETURN, terminates the insertion of new text, just as it does for the append and insert commands.

Dot is left standing at the last line of inserted text, as it is for the append and insert commands.

7.1.12 Global Commands

A text-pattern can be used with a *global prefix*, to perform an operation on all lines that contain, or do not contain, a specified pattern. There are two global prefixes, **g** and **v**. The **g** prefix operates on all lines that contain the specific pattern. The **v** prefix inverts the search, just as the −**v** option did on **grep**, so commands preceded with the **v** prefix operate on all lines that do not contain the pattern.

The basic form of the **g**lobal prefixes in **ed** command lines is like this:

```
line_1,line_2g/text_pattern/command parameters
```

where **text_pattern** is the text-pattern to search for in the buffer.

command is the command to be performed on all lines that match the pattern (in the case of the **g** prefix), or on all lines that do not match the pattern (in the case of the **v** prefix).

The text-pattern matching is attempted on all lines between **line_1** and **line_2** inclusive. If you don't specify any line numbers before the **g** or **v**, the pattern match is attempted on all lines in the edit buffer.

Referring to our *'people'* example from above, we can find all the Smith's in the buffer in one go with a **g**lobal command like this:

```
* g/Smith/p
Sally Smith       113
Charlie Smith     122
*
```

The command says to **p**rint every line containing the word "Smith". The pattern that you give to the global commands can be a regular expression, for example

```
v/^$/p
```

displays all non-blank lines in the edit buffer.

As we promised back in chapter 6 — "Text Manipulation", here is the derivation of the **grep** command name. **grep** simply stands for:

```
g/re/p
```

which is to say: **g**lobally search for a **r**egular **e**xpression and **p**rint every line which contains it. In other words, **grep** is a **g**lobal **r**egular **e**xpression **p**rinter.

The global prefixes usually find most use in connection with the substitute command, but any command can be done globally. For instance, to delete all blank lines, whether really blank or only apparently blank, we can use the global prefix with the **de**lete operation:

```
$ ed file
* 1234
* g/^[ ^I]*$/d
* w newfile
* 1221
* q
$
```

As usual ^I indicates control-I or TAB. The **g** prefix finds only lines consisting of nothing or spaces or tabs, the **d** operation gets applied only to those lines found by the **g**lobal prefix.

We can make the file double spaced by using the **v** operation in combination with the transpose command:

```
$ ed file
* 200
* 1i

.
* v/^$/1t.
* 1d
* w newfile
* 210
* q
$
```

First we inserted a blank line at the beginning of the file, then we used the **v** operation to find all non-blank lines. Details of the transpose (or copy) command are given later under the heading "Cut and Paste". In this example, the **t** operation copies line 1 (our blank line) after each line found by **v**. Finally we removed our blank line.

We could achieve the same thing by using the **a**ppend command instead of **t**ransposing a blank line:

```
$ ed file
* 200
* g/^.*$/a\
* w newfile
* 210
* q
$
```

We leave it as an exercise for the reader to look up the **ed** write-up in the UNIX Programmer's Manual and figure this one out.

7.1.13 Text Substitution with 's'

The substitute command, **s**, is probably the most useful command in **ed**. Substitution works on character strings within individual lines, instead of entire lines. This obviates re-typing entire lines of text when you only want to change a small part of the line.

A substitution command looks like this:

```
* /bread/s/wheat/rye/
```

which means: in the next line containing "bread" replace "wheat" with "rye".

The remembered pattern applies in the **s** command as well as everywhere else. So if your search string and the string you want to substitute for are the same, the above **s** command can be shortened:

```
* /wheat/s//rye/
```

means: in the next line containing "wheat", replace that string with "rye".

The use of the remembered pattern works even if the searching and substitution are done separately:

```
* /wheat/
* s//rye/
*
```

The substitution only affects the first occurrence of the string on the line. Suppose we print the current line of this imaginary buffer:

```
* p
wheat bread is my favorite, make my sandwich on wheat
* .
```

we can substitute the first occurrence of the word "wheat", like this:

```
* s/wheat/rye/
* p
rye bread is my favorite, make my sandwich on wheat
*
```

To change the second occurrence of "wheat" we would have to repeat the substitute command.

However, there is a way to change *all* occurrences of a string on any one line in one fell swoop, by adding the **g**lobal flag at the end of the substitute command. To illustrate this, let us go back to the original example:

```
* p
wheat bread is my favorite, make my sandwich on wheat
* s/wheat/rye/g
* p
rye bread is my favorite, make my sandwich on rye
*
```

You can see that this time, the substitute command got them all at the same time.

The other optional extra parameter on the substitute command is the **p** (for **p**rint) flag. This can be combined with the **g** flag if needed, so our previous example could be done like this:

```
* p
wheat bread is my favorite, make my sandwich on wheat
* s/wheat/rye/gp
rye bread is my favorite, make my sandwich on rye
*
```

Now you can see that the substitute command is considerably more compact than some of the earlier examples.

To make substitutions on more than on line, the **s** can be preceded by a range of lines, for example:

```
1,10s/water/wine/
```

changes "water" into "wine" in the first 10 lines of the buffer, and the command:

```
1,$s/water/wine/
```

does that change in all lines in the buffer.

If either of the above substitute commands were to be typed with the **p** option after it:

```
1,$s/water/wine/p
```

the last line affected by the substitute is the one that is printed.

In all cases, if substitution is done on more than one line, **dot** is left standing at the last line on which a substitute took place.

7.1.13.1 Global Substitution Substitution on a range of lines can also be achieved by using the **g**lobal prefix:

```
* g/water/s//wine/
*
```

finds all lines containing "water" and changes it to "wine". This still only changes the first occurrence of "water" on each line, to change "water" to "wine" *everywhere* we have to use both the **g**lobal prefix (to find all lines containing the pattern), and the **g**lobal suffix (to do the substitute on all occurrences in each line).

```
* g/water/s//wine/g
*
```

There is an important distinction between the **g** at the beginning of the above command, and the **g** at the end of it. The initial **g** is the global command prefix, and can be applied to any command. The final **g** is the global flag suffix, and only applies to the substitute command.

The examples which follow repeat some of the examples of chapter 6, to illustrate how to achieve the same results with **ed**'s global substitution feature.

We can compress a file by changing all sequences of 8 spaces to tabs by using the following global command:

```
$ ed file
* 769
* g/        /s//^I/g
* w newfile
* 629
* q
$
```

ed does not support the "{8}" type of closure, so we have to spell out the 8 spaces. As we cautioned for **rpl**, this doesn't necessarily achieve what you want because the alignment of words in the file may be altered.

We can also use the **g** and **s** operations to remove the phone numbers from our *'people'* file:

```
$ ed people
* 200
* g/[0-9]*$/s///
* w nophone
* 170
* q
$
```

We still have some spaces at the end of each line, to remove those too we should have used the regular expression

```
*[0-9]*$
```

7.1.13.2 The Remembered Text A special character which is used in the substitution string is the ampersand character, **&**. It stands for "whatever text you are replacing". For example, to replace "bread" by "wheat bread", we can say:

```
* /bread/s//wheat &/
```

Here, the **&** simply serves as a shorthand notation, because we searched for a fixed string and could have said:

```
* s/bread//wheat bread/
```

But when the search pattern is a regular expression we don't know exactly what we're going to find, so it is important to have a way of referring to the string that matched the expression on the left hand side.

7.1.13.3 Undoing Damaged Substitutions with 'u' We can apply the substitute command to our file of people, to do the same job as in the delete and change commands, namely to replace Henry Morgan with James Walker:

```
* /Henry Morgan/s//James Walker/p
James Walker   112
*
```

We are lucky that the name "James Walker" has the same number of characters as does "Henry Morgan". If this was not the case, we would have to put extra spaces in one place or the other to preserve the alignment of the telephone numbers.

In the above example, we just did the substitution on the addressed line. In practice, we would be wise to display the line we are about to operate on. Our next example illustrates this.

We want to change Sally's last name from Smith to White. Again, we use the substitute command:

```
* /Smith/s//White/p
Charlie White   122
*
```

Unfortunately, we changed the wrong Smith. This is because, after we had changed Henry to James, **dot** was left standing at that line. The next occurrence of Smith in the buffer is Charlie Smith. This demonstrates that it is safer to display the line before you change it. Having botched the substitute, however, we can retrieve the original line with the undo command.

The undo command "undoes" the last substitute command. In our example from above, we can use the undo command to change Charlie's last name back to Smith, then we can then carry on as before:

```
* u
Charlie Smith    122
* //
Sally Smith      113
* s//White/p
Sally White      113
* w
* 200
*
```

7.1.13.4 Grouping Regular Expressions in the 's' Command
Within the left-hand side of a substitute command, it is possible to delineate parts of the regular expression, in such a way that they can be referred to in the right-hand side.

On the left-hand side, a part of a regular expression can be marked by enclosing it between \(and \). You can mark up to nine chunks of a pattern in this way.

Then, on the right-hand side, the delimited groups can be retrieved by using the notation \n, where n is the n'th group, numbered from 1 to 9, left to right.

We can illustrate this process by using our 'people' file again. If you remember from chapter 6, we used the **awk** utility to reverse the first and last names in the 'people' file as a sop to a bureaucracy which cannot handle peoples' names in the right order. Here is how we do the same job using **ed**:

```
$ ed people
200
* 1,$/s/\([A-Za-z]*\) \([A-Za-z]*\)/\2, \1/
* 1,$p
Clark, Maryann    101
Smith, Sally      113
Bailey, Jane      121
Austen, Jack      120
Daniels, Steve    111
Dawson, Sylvia    110
Morgan, Henry     112
Parker, Hank      114
Smith, Charlie    122
Williams, Bill    100
*
```

This is not the world's most readable edit command. But take it one thing at a time. We want to operate on every line in the file, so the **1,$** addresses every line.

On every line, we look for two groups of alphabetic characters (either uppercase or lowercase), separated by a space. Each group is represented by the pattern

```
[A-Za-z]*
```

and each group is then enclosed in the **\(** and **\)** delimiters.

On the right hand side of the substitute, those groups are simply accessed by the **\2** and the **\1** markers. The effect is to reverse the names on each line.

7.1.14 Some Notes on Searching and Substitution

We have seen that when searching for a string it is not always necessary to give an entire word that you really want to find, but be careful how you abbreviate. For example, suppose you wanted to find the word "mankind". If you specify:

```
/man/
```

as your search string, not only will you find "mankind", but also "womankind" (which may be OK) and "manumission" (which probably isn't OK) plus a lot of other words like "man", "manual", "emancipate", and so on. In this case,

```
/mank/
```

is probably a good abbreviation, or

```
/anki/
```

though that's not so easy to think of.

Another thing to beware of is a whole word which can also form part of another, longer, word. For example, suppose you want to find all instances of the word "his", maybe because you want to replace it by "her". Using

```
/his/
```

may also get you "history", "histogram" and "this". So if you tried to do your change by the command:

```
g/his/s//her/g
```

you would end up with words like "hertory" and "ther", which is not what you want.

Using

```
/his /
```

avoids "history", "histogram", and "antihistamine", but you still find "this". Using

```
/ his /
```

solves that one, but now we can think of another problem. What happens if "his" is at the start of a sentence and therefore is actually "His"?

This is where regular expressions can help us out:

```
/ [Hh]is /
```

finds the word starting with either an uppercase or a lowercase letter, as long as it has a space before it and a space after it. Fine, what about "his" (or "His") at the beginning of a line?

```
/^[Hh]is /
```

takes care of that, and likewise:

```
/ [Hh]is$/
```

looks after the case where the word is at the end of a line. In fact, all these can be combined and we can use the search string

```
/[ ^][Hh]is[ $]/
```

We still haven't accounted for the case where the word may be at the end of a sentence, and therefore is followed, not by a space or newline, but by a period. If the text in the file you are editing is grammatically correct, the chances of that happening are low, but what if the file contains " his,"?

The moral is: if you are doing extensive changes by search and substitution, be careful how you specify your strings. A good practice is to display what the search finds, before actually making any substitutions, otherwise the results can be disastrous (though sometimes hilarious).

7.1.15 Cut and Paste with 'm', 't', 'k', and 'r'

The **m** (for **m**ove) and **t** (for **t**ranspose) commands are handy for moving blocks of text from one place to another in the buffer, thus providing a means for "cut and paste" editing. The basic form of move is:

```
line_1,line_2mline_3
```

This means: "move all lines between **line_1** and **line_2** inclusive, and place them after **line_3**".

It doesn't make much sense to use an editor to arrange a file into alphabetical order. Either you are going to **sort** the file, or you are going to keep the file in order, in which case you would have created it that way in the first place. However, rearranging the buffer can be done, albeit somewhat laboriously, using the **m**ove operation:

```
$ ed people
* 200
* /Austen/m0
* /Bailey/m/Austen/
* /Clark/m/Bailey/
      <etc...>
```

```
*  1,$p
Jack Austen        120
Jane Bailey        121
Maryann Clark      101
Steve Daniels      111
Sylvia Dawson      110
Henry Morgan       112
Hank Parker        114
Charlie Smith      122
Sally Smith        113
Bill Williams      100
*  w
*  200
*  q
$
```

The **transpose** command works exactly like the **move** command except that the original lines in the buffer also stay where they are. The **transpose** command is thus a good way to duplicate blocks of text within the buffer.

The **r** (for **read**) command reads the contents of a specified file into the buffer after a specified line. The basic form of the **read** command is:

```
liner   filename
```

where "line" is the number of the line after which to read the file contents, and "filename" is the name of the file whose contents are to be read. Here is an example of where line zero is useful for editing. The command:

0r /aa/widget/steve/old.mail

reads the contents of the *'old.mail'* file from the */aa/widget/steve* directory, and places it before the first line in the buffer.

The **k** (for **mark**) command is also useful for cut-and-paste editing. It finds most use when you have large chunks of text, more than can be displayed on the screen at one time, to move or copy to another place. There are of course other ways of doing the job, but it is safest to use the **k** command in conjunction with one of the other commands. Let us see how to move the lines between "Maryann" and "Steve" in our *'people'* file after Bill Williams:

```
$ ed   people
200
* 1,$p
Maryann Clark    101
Sally Smith      113
Jane Bailey      121
Jack Austen      120
Steve Daniels    111
Sylvia Dawson    110
Henry Morgan     112
Hank Parker      114
Charlie Smith    122
Bill Williams    100
* /Maryann/ka
* /Steve/kb
* 'a,'bm/Bill  Williams/
* 1,$p
Sylvia Dawson    110
Henry Morgan     112
Hank Parker      114
Charlie Smith    122
Bill Williams    100
Maryann Clark    101
Sally Smith      113
Jane Bailey      121
Jack Austen      120
Steve Daniels    111
*
```

Another marked advantage of the **k** command is that the marks stay with the lines if you move them.

If you transpose a block of marked lines, the marks stay with the last copy that was made. The marks on the originals go away.

If you delete or change a marked line, the mark also goes away, but if you substitute within a marked line, the mark stays with the line.

7.1.16 Miscellaneous 'ed' Commands

An equals sign = as a command simply prints the line number of the addressed line. This can be used when you want to find the line number of a line containing a particular character string, for instance:

```
* /Maryann/=
6
*
```

This is especially useful when you have been moving text around in the buffer, thereby altering line numbers from their original values. The = command defaults to the last line in the buffer, so you can see how many lines you have in total by typing = on its own.

When an editing session is started on an already existing file with a command of the form:

```
$ ed garfield
```

ed "remembers" the name of the file that was originally entered. Thus, a subsequent write command to write out the buffer contents will write to the remembered file.

The **f** (for file) command has two flavors. Just typing a plain **f** displays the current file name:

```
* f
garfield
*
```

The current file name can be set to something else by supplying a parameter to the file command:

```
* f something.else
* f
something.else
*
```

From here on, the remembered file name is *'something.else'*, and if a write command is issued at this time, the buffer is written to that file.

7.1.17 Final Notes on 'ed'

Be aware that all changes permanently affect the file once we have done the write operation. Many of the modifications we made to the files in our earlier examples of text manipulation were of a transient nature. They didn't affect the file itself, they merely modified it some way as it was being transferred to another file, or to some subsequent command. This is important, since some changes should NOT be made permanently.

Consider the case of our file of people. It is easier to maintain this file in any order, then sort it according to what we need as output. If we want the output to be double-spaced, this should be a transient change applied to the output of **sort**. If we put blank lines in the file *'people'* the output of **sort** will be incorrect, as all the blank lines will appear at the beginning.

If the results of the editing session are to be routed to another file we can use **ed**. We simply give the new filename when we do the write operation, as we have shown in some of the examples in this section. But if the output is to be piped to another command, such as **lpr**, we must use the stream editor **sed**, which is described in the second half of this chapter.

7.2 The Stream Editor 'sed'

The stream editor, **sed**, is a non-interactive text editor. Whereas **ed** copies your original file into a buffer, and lets you explore the text in whatever order you want, **sed** works on your file from beginning to end, and allows you no choice of edit commands once you have invoked it.

If you think of **ed** as performing some changes on a set of data, you should think of **sed** as passing some data through a set of transformations. This concept is similar to the idea of pipelines that was described in chapter 4 — "Commands and Standard Files", in that a stream of data is passed through some processes which modify it in some way. In this case, the "processes" are editor commands.

Because **sed** does not read the file to be edited into a buffer, it can be used to edit files that are too big for **ed**.

Because the "default" mode of **sed** is to apply edit commands globally on the file, and also because its output is to the Standard Output, **sed** is ideal for changes which are of a transient nature, rather than permanent modifications to a file.

In particular, **sed** can be used in place of the **rpl** command which we described earlier, and which is not available on many UNIX systems. However, **sed** can also be used to simulate the **grep** and **tr** commands, as we will show in the examples which follow.

On the face of things, **sed** is a relatively simple command, having only three options. However, because **sed** has regular expression capabilities, and also most of the editing operations provided by **ed**, using it can be a fairly complicated affair. We make no attempt to explain all the intricacies of the stream editor. Rather, we show you how to perform some useful operations, which will give you sufficient insight to be able to work out more complex operations for yourself. Mostly, we repeat the by now familiar examples introduced in chapter 6 — "Text Manipulation".

7.2.1 Taking Edit Script from a File

If **sed** is invoked with the **–f** (for file) option, the edit commands are taken from a named file:

```
$ sed -f edcomds oldfile > newfile
$
```

The name of the file containing the edit commands must be the very next argument after the **–f** option. The above example shows a command which applies the edit commands contained in *'edcomds'* to the file *'oldfile'*. The Standard Output of **sed** is redirected to *'newfile'*.

The edit commands which can be contained in *'edcomds'* are similar to the edit commands available in the interactive text editor **ed**, but the format of them is slightly different in some cases.

The general format of the commands is the same as **ed** commands:

```
[line[,line]]operation[parameter]
```

that is: an optional line-address, or two line addresses separated by a comma, then a single letter edit operation, optionally followed by another parameter. However there are some important differences from **ed**:

- The only operation which can take the optional final parameter is the **s** (substitute) operation.

- If no line numbers are specified, the operation is performed on *all* lines. This is quite different from **ed**, where the default line is usually **dot**.

- Lines can be addressed by number, or by text pattern using fixed character strings, or by regular expressions. Because the default mode of operation is global, there is no concept of "current line", nor of relative line addresses. Line numbers are absolute in the file.

- Operations that require text input (**a**, **i** and **c**) have a different format from the same operations in **ed**.

- Many **ed** operations have no counterpart in **sed**. In particular, the **m** (move) and **t** (transpose, copy) operations do not exist.

- Contrariwise, there are some operations that are available in **sed** that do not exist in **ed**. One of these is **y** (for transform, or maybe translyterate — not too mnemonic).

Let's take a concrete example, using our old friend the *'people'* file. Among the many changes we did to this file in our text manipulation examples were:

- delete the line containing Henry Morgan
- add a line containing James Walker at the end of the file
- change Sally Smith's name to Sally White

To make these changes using **sed**, we first create a file containing the edit commands:

```
$ cat > changes
/Sally/s/Smith/White/
/Henry/d
$a\
James Walker      112
^D
$
```

These commands tell **sed** to change Smith to White on the line containing Sally, to delete the line containing Henry, and to add the line James Walker   112 at the end of the file. The dollar sign $ stands for "last line" just as it did in **ed**.

The form of the **a**ppend operation differs from that of **ed**. In **ed**, text input is terminated by a period character **.** on a line of its own, after the last line of text to be input. In **sed**, you place a reverse slash character \ on the end of every line of text, *except* the last one. Note that there is a \ character even on the end of the **a** command line.

We can now execute **sed** to do the changes:

```
$ sed -f changes  people
Maryann Clark   101
Sally White     113
Jane Bailey     121
       <etc...>
Bill Williams   100
James Walker    112
$
```

sed sends its results to the Standard Output. To capture the changes permanently we have to use redirection:

```
$ mv people people.old
$ sed -f changes people.old > people
$
```

In our *'changes'* file we gave the edit commands in the order that they would be applied to the file. **sed** actually goes through a pre-processing stage, where it sorts the commands into an order which it thinks is logical.

For example, deletions take precedence over substitutions. After all, there is no point in doing substitutions on a line which is later deleted.

So, we could specify the commands in a different order:

```
$ cat > changes
$a\
James Walker      112
/Henry/d
/Sally/s/Smith/White/
^D
$ sed -f changes people
Maryann Clark    101
Sally White      113
       <etc...>
Bill Williams    100
James Walker     112
$
```

Either way gives the same results.

To show the global nature of **sed**, here is an example of how to make a file double-spaced by adding a blank line after each line in the file:

```
$ cat > putblank
a\

^D
$ sed -f putblank people
Maryann Clark    101

Sally Smith      113

Jane Bailey      121

       <etc...>

Charlie Smith    122

Bill Williams    100

$
```

Because we didn't specify any line address for the **a** (add text) operation, the text (our blank line) is added after every line.

We could put a box around our file like this:

```
$ cat > dobox
s/^/¦ /
s/ [1-9]/¦&/
s/$/ ¦/
1i\
\ _____
a\
¦_____¦_____¦\
^D
$ sed  -f dobox  people
 _____
¦ Maryann Clark  ¦ 101 ¦
¦_____¦_____¦
¦ Sally Smith    ¦ 113 ¦
¦_____¦_____¦
        <etc...>
¦                ¦     ¦
¦_____¦_____¦
¦ Hank Parker    ¦ 114 ¦
¦_____¦_____¦
¦ Charlie Smith  ¦ 122 ¦
¦_____¦_____¦
¦ Bill Williams  ¦ 100 ¦
¦_____¦_____¦
$
```

The three substitute commands draw the vertical lines. The insert command draws the top line of the box, and the append command draws all the other lines. To get a space in the first column of the line forming the top of the box, we had to escape that space with the reverse slash character, \. **sed** strips leading spaces and tabs from the beginning of edit commands, so to insert text with leading spaces and tabs we have to escape them in this way.

7.2.2 Putting Edit Operations on the Command Line

It is not always necessary to make a file containing edit commands. If the commands are few and simple, you can put them on the **sed** command line. For example, the command:

```
$ sed /Henry/d people > newpeople
$
```

deletes the line containing Henry from *'people'*.

You use the **-e** (for **edit**) option to place editing commands right there on the **sed** command line. In addition, you can use both the **-e** and the **-f** options at the same time.

In our example above, however, we didn't use any option at all. If you are only putting one edit command on the **sed** command line, you can omit the **-e**. If we want to be formal about it, we should say:

```
$ sed -e /Henry/d people > newpeople
$
```

If you put more than one edit command on the **sed** line, each one must be preceded by **-e**, thus:

```
$ sed -e /Henry/d -e /Sally/s/Smith/White/ people
Maryann Clark    101
Sally White      113
Jane Bailey      121
Jack Austen      120
Steve Daniels    111
Sylvia Dawson    110
Hank Parker      114
Charlie Smith    122
Bill Williams    100
$
```

If your edit command contains spaces, you must surround it with quotes:

```
$ sed -e "s/Henry Morgan/James Walker/" people
Maryann Clark    101
Sally Smith      113
Jane Bailey      121
Jack Austen      120
Steve Daniels    111
Sylvia Dawson    110
James Walker     112
Hank Parker      114
Charlie Smith    122
Bill Williams    100
$
```

If you don't put quotes around commands containing spaces, you will get an error message:

```
$ sed -e s/Henry Morgan/James Walker/ people
command garbled: s/Henry
$
```

You should also use quotes if your edit command contains characters which the Shell treats specially. This will happen when you are using regular expressions. The command:

```
$ sed -e "/^[ ^I]*$/d" somefile > noblanks
$
```

can be used to get rid of blank lines, or apparently blank lines, from a file. As usual, ^I stands for control-I, or TAB.

You can use both –e and –f options together. To make the required changes to our *'people'* file, and draw a box round the result:

```
$ sed -e /Sally/s/Smith/White/  \
      -e "s/Henry Morgan/James Walker/" -f dobox people
```

```
 ---------------------
| Maryann Clark | 101 |
|---------------|-----|
| Sally White   | 113 |
|---------------|-----|
      <etc...>
|---------------|-----|
| James Walker  | 112 |
|---------------|-----|
| Hank Parker   | 114 |
|---------------|-----|
| Charlie Smith | 122 |
|---------------|-----|
| Bill Williams | 100 |
 ---------------------
$
```

7.2.3 Suppressing Normal Output

As you can see in the above examples, **sed** normally copies all input lines to the output, transformed by the edit operations performed on them. The –n option suppresses this normal output, and only lines specially requested with the **p** (print) edit operation appear on the output. For example, the command:

```
$ sed -n /Smith/p people
Sally Smith     113
Charlie Smith   122
$
```

gives output similar to **grep**. Only those lines containing the string "Smith" appear. Because we only have one edit command on the line, we didn't bother to use the **-e** option. If we had used the edit command "/Smith/p" without giving the **-n** option, we would have got the result:

```
$ sed /Smith/p people
Maryann Clark    101
Sally Smith      113
Sally Smith      113
Jane Bailey      121
Jack Austen      120
Steve Daniels    111
Sylvia Dawson    110
James Walker     112
Hank Parker      114
Charlie Smith    122
Charlie Smith    122
Bill Williams    100
$
```

The Smiths appear twice, because we see the normal output as well as the specially requested output.

The **-n** option is useful for selectively displaying parts of a file. For example, to display only the first 4 lines of a file:

```
$ sed -n 1,4p people
Maryann Clark    101
Sally Smith      113
Jane Bailey      121
Jack Austen      120
$
```

So if you don't have the **head** command on your system, you can use **sed** instead. You can also use it for context displays:

```
$ sed -n 1,/Smith/p people
Maryann Clark    101
Sally Smith      113
$ sed -n /Sally/,/Steve/p people
Sally Smith      113
Jane Bailey      121
Jack Austen      120
Steve Daniels    111
$
```

Displaying only the first part of a file can also be achieved by using the **q** (quit) operation, described in "Examples" below.

7.2.4 Multiple Filenames

sed can be given more than one file to edit at a time. The edit commands are applied to all files. Line numbers increment through all files, and $ means the last line of the last file. So if we had people in 3 separate files, as we did in some text manipulation examples:

```
$ cat adminpeople
Maryann Clark    101
Bill Williams    100
$ cat hardpeople
Jane Bailey      121
Jack Austen      120
Charlie Smith    122
$ cat softpeople
Sally Smith      113
Steve Daniels    111
Sylvia Dawson    110
Henry Morgan     112
Hank Parker      114
$ sed -n 4,7p adminpeople hardpeople softpeople
Jack Austen      120
Charlie Smith    122
Sally Smith      113
Steve Daniels    111
$
```

You can see that as far as **sed** is concerned, line 4 is the second line of the second file, because the first file contained only two lines.

If no file is specified to **sed**, the Standard Input is used. **sed** is a popular filter used in pipelines. For example, to apply a command to every file in a directory:

```
$ ls ¦ sed "s/^/command /" ¦ sh
$
```

The output of **sed** is a series of lines of the form

```
command file
```

These command lines are then executed by piping them to the Shell command **sh**.* Using **sed** in this manner is a useful technique when there are too many files, or their names are too long, for the Shell's * pattern matching character to find them all.

7.2.5 Examples of 'sed'

In this section we give examples of ways in which some of the edit operations can be used, where they haven't already been covered in the previous paragraphs.

We have already seen examples of the **s** (substitute) operation. The general format is the same as the **ed** substitute command:

```
s/string1/string2/
```

The first occurrence of "string1" is replaced by "string2" on each of the addressed lines (remember that in **sed** the default is every line). "string1" need not be a fixed character string, it can be a regular expression. In all our previous examples, we have shown the strings separated by the slash character /, but in fact we can use any character that doesn't form part of either the search string or the replacement string. So we can change Sally's name from Smith to White by:

```
$ sed /Sally/s-Smith-White- people > newpeople
$
```

You can use any character to surround the arguments to the substitute command (here we used −). But the string which actually addresses the line you want must be surrounded by / characters, no other character will do.

As in **ed**, if we want to substitute all occurrences of the string on the same line, we have to append **g** (for **g**lobal) to the end of the substitute command.

```
$ sed "s,[0-9],,g" people
Maryann Clark
Sally Smith
     <etc...>
Bill Williams
$
```

---

* This pipeline assumes a version of **ls** that produces filenames one per line; it will not work if **ls** produces multi-column output. However, even if your version of **ls** normally produces its output in several columns, there is most certainly an option to produce single columns, so that you can use this technique. Check your UNIX Programmers Manual for such an option.

The above example deletes the phone numbers from the file, but there are still spaces at the end of the line. To get rid of the spaces as well, we need to use a more precise regular expression:

```
$ sed "s, *[0-9]*$,," people
Maryann Clark
     <etc...>
Charlie Smith
Bill Williams
$
```

A **sed** operation which has no counterpart in **ed** is **y** (transform). This works in a way similar to the **tr** command. Two strings are given, each character in the first string is replaced by the equivalent character in the second string. So we can reverse the alphabet for lowercase characters by:

```
$ sed y/abcdefghijklmnopqrstuvwxyz\
>    /zyxwvutsrqponmlkjihgfedcba/ people
Mzibzmm Cozip     101
Szoob Snrgs       113
     <etc...>
Hzmp Pzipvi       114
Csziorv Snrgs     122
Broo Wroorznh     100
$
```

The two strings must be of the same length, there is no padding out as there is in the **tr** command. Neither can you use ranges, so if you try to shorten the first string, you get an error message:

```
$ sed   y/[a-z]/zyxwvutsrqponmlkjihgfedcba/   people
command garbled: y/[a-z]/zyxwvutsrqponmlkjihgfedcba/
$
```

The message arises because the first string "[a-z]" is taken to be 5 characters long, whereas the second string "zyxw...dcba" is 26 characters long. Both strings must be the same length.

However, you can use a character other than **/** to separate the strings, so long as the character you use is not contained in the strings:

```
$ sed y,0123456789,9876543210, people
Maryann Clark    898
Sally Smith      886
    <etc...>
Charlie Smith    877
Bill Williams    899
$
```

We can add blank lines to a file by using a combination of **sed** and **tr**:

```
$ sed "s:$:#:" people ¦ tr # "\012"
Maryann Clark    101

Sally Smith      113

        <etc...>

Bill Williams    100

$
```

First we add some character, that isn't normally found in the file, to the end of every line. Here we have used the hash, or octothorpe, character #.

Then we use **tr** to replace # with the newline character, which is the value 012 in octal notation. We have to use **tr** to do this. We can't use the **y** edit operation because none of the **sed** operations will accept characters by their octal values.

If the file you want to be double spaced could contain any characters, you can use a non-printing character, say control-A:

```
$ sed "s:$:^A:" file ¦ tr "\001" "\012" > newfile
$
```

The **^A** indicates where you type control-A in **sed**; 001 is the octal value of control-A, we use this in **tr**.

Another way to get double spacing is to use the **r** (read) command, to read a file containing only a blank line into the text you want spaced out:

```
$ cat > blankline

^D
        . . .
```

```
$ sed "r blankline" people
Maryann Clark    101

Sally Smith      113

      <etc...>

Bill Williams    100

$
```

If there is no file of the specified name you give on the **r** command, you don't get an error message. **sed** just carries on, and nothing gets read into your file.

The **w** (for **write**) operation can be used to selectively extract lines from the original file and write them into another file. For example:

```
$ sed "/Smith/w smiths" people
Maryann Clark    100
Sally Smith      113
      <etc...>
Charlie Smith    122
Bill Williams    100
$ cat smiths
Sally Smith      113
Charlie Smith    122
$
```

The **w** operation can be appended to an **s** operation. Then the substitutions are done before the lines are written to the file:

```
$ sed "s/Smith/White/w smiths" people
Maryann Clark    100
Sally White      113
      <etc...>
Charlie White    122
Bill Williams    100
$ cat    smiths
Sally White      113
Charlie White    122
$
```

The next example shows how we can split up our *'people'* file into the three separate files we showed in an earlier example. To do this, we use the knowledge that all administrative people have phone numbers 10-something, software people have 11-something and hardware people have 12-something.

```
$ sed -n -e "/10.$/w adminpeople" \
         -e "/12.$/w hardpeople" \
         -e "/11.$/w softpeople" people
$ cat adminpeople
Maryann Clark    101
Bill Williams    100
$ cat hardpeople
Jane Bailey      121
Jack Austen      120
Charlie Smith    122
$ cat softpeople
Sally Smith      113
Steve Daniels    111
Sylvia Dawson    110
Henry Morgan     112
Hank Parker      114
$
```

We still have our original *'people'* file, besides the new ones we have created.

As we said earlier, the **q** (quit) operator can be used to display the head of a file. The command:

```
$ sed 4q people
Maryann Clark    100
Sally Smith      113
Jane Bailey      121
Jack Austen      120
$
```

stops producing output (quits) after line number 4. When given a search pattern, **sed** quits after the first occurrence of a line containing that pattern, for instance:

```
$ sed /Steve/q people
Maryann Clark    100
Sally Smith      113
Jane Bailey      121
Jack Austen      120
Steve Daniels    111
$
```

stops after the line containing Steve.

7.3 Summary

That is all we have to say about **ed** and **sed**. As we indicated earlier, many people now consider **ed** a fairly primitive editor, and the world is moving towards the type of editor which can display the file on a screen, and provide for on-screen editing. A popular screen editor is **vi**. It, and its companion line-editor, **ex**, are the subject of the next chapter.

But, many UNIX system tools use **ed** as a basic tool for keeping track of differences between files. For example, the **diff** utility can generate the differences between two files in terms of **ed** commands. There are other packages which use **ed** as a vehicle to tracking differences. It is also worthwhile understanding how to use **sed**, since it is of great value in making transformations to data files.

8 The EX and VI Editors

Some UNIX systems support the text editors called **ex** and **vi**. The **ex** editor is based on **ed**, but has many extensions and additional features. The **vi** editor is a "display" editor, or "screen" editor. In actual fact, **ex** and **vi** are just two different facades of the same editor. They were developed by William Joy of the University of California at Berkeley, and for details of using them you should refer to his papers "Ex Reference Manual", and "An Introduction to Display Editing with Vi".

More and more UNIX systems are supporting display editors, and the **ex/vi** combination seems to be one of the more widely available ones. This chapter describes the **ex** and **vi** text editors. Because many of the more useful operations that can be performed in **vi** simply call upon **ex** functions, the first section of the chapter is devoted to **ex** — the second part of the chapter covers **vi**.

8.1 The 'ex' Text Editor

The **ex** text editor is based on **ed**, but has many extensions and improvements to that editor. The experienced **ed** user can use **ex** quite happily. However, unless the additional features provided are used, using **ex** like **ed** is not going to be as efficient as it could be. In general, **ex** is somewhat easier to use than **ed**. This is mostly because **ex** is more communicative; it tells you what you've done wrong, rather than simply displaying "?".

In this section, we assume that the reader is familiar with **ed**, we only talk about the things that are additional, or different, in **ex**. So if you skipped the chapter on **ed**, we suggest you refer to the **ed** chapter whenever you find anything confusing in this section.

The features of **ex** which are expansions and improvements to **ed** are:

- Operations are not restricted to a single character, so they can be remembered more easily — for example, "co" for copy instead of "t" for transpose. However the single-letter operations used in **ed** are retained, so the experienced **ed** user will not have to remember the new ones.

- Introduction of additional operations not found in **ed**.

- Variants of some editor operations, which modify the way in which those operations are performed under certain conditions. Operation variants are invoked by placing a ! character following the normal operation, for example **a!**.

- Improved messages for error conditions, with instructions as to how to override the error condition.

- Editor "options" which modify the overall behavior of **ex**.

- Provision of a means of recovery if the system crashes during an editing session

- Introduction of a "visual" mode which turns the editor into a screen editor. In this mode, **ex** is identical with the **vi** editor described in the latter part of this chapter. There is also an "open" mode, which provides intraline editing.

- The **ex** and **vi** editors react to different terminal types, this is necessary because of the screen editing capability.

Be aware that there are many different versions of **ex** around, at various stages of its development. Not all the features we mention below may be available in the version you have.

8.1.1 Getting Started with 'ex'

To use **ex** to edit a text file, you just give the UNIX system command:

```
$ ex myfile
"myfile" 698 lines, 24113 characters
:
```

Just as in the **ed** text editor, **ex** reads your file into a scratchpad area which it calls a "buffer". All changes are now made in the buffer, and the original version of your file is unaltered until you specifically write the contents of the buffer over it, using the **w** command, described later.

As **ex** reads your file into the editing buffer, it tells you how long the file is, both in lines and characters.

The **ex** prompt is the colon character, ":".

Again, just as with **ed**, there is a limit to the size of the editing buffer, and hence a limit to the size of file that you can edit with **ex**. What this limit actually is, depends on which version of **ex** you have. In some older versions, the size limitation is the same as for **ed**. Later versions of **ex** have a much larger buffer.

One of the first differences to notice about **ex** is that you can give more than one filename when invoking it:

```
$ ex thisfile thatfile theotherfile
3 files to edit
"thisfile" 280 lines, 10994 characters
:
```

ex first tells you how many files you are going to edit (this is useful if you've used a command line like **ex c∗**), then reads the first of the files into the editing buffer. It tells you how long the file is, in lines and characters, then responds with its prompt character, ":". The next file on the command line can be accessed from within the editor by using the **n** (for **n**ext) command, described in more detail later.

8.1.1.1 Specifying Your Terminal Type   A major feature of **ex** and **vi** is their ability to respond to different types of terminals. This is necessary when you are using the "visual" mode of **ex**, or the **vi** variation of the editor. When you are using **ex** in line addressing mode, it shouldn't in theory care what type of terminal you are using, but in practice it likes to know.

In some installations, **ex** seems to be able to divine the terminal type automatically. In others, you have to tell it. When you start **ex**, if you see some odd characters on the display which you are sure are not in your file, the chances are that **ex** needs to be told what type of terminal you are using.

You can do this from within **ex** by using the **set** command, which is used to set **ex** "options". For example, if you are using a Lear-Siegler ADM-3a terminal, you should type the **ex** command:

```
: set term=adm3a
:
```

If, like most people, you usually use the same terminal, you won't want to do this every time you call up **ex**. There is a file called an "**ex** profile", in which you can put this command.

Depending on what version of the Shell your installation has, there may be a command called **setenv**. This is used to tell the Shell various things about your working environment. One of the things you can tell it is the terminal type you use. The Shell passes this information on to **ex** (or **vi**) when you call up the editor. So, if you are using a Lear-Siegler ADM-3a terminal, type this **setenv** command before entering the editor:

```
$ setenv TERM adm3a
$
```

setenv is not an editor command, but a UNIX system command which you have to give before calling up **ex**. You only have to give this command once, before you enter the editor the first time. Each subsequent call on **ex** will receive the information about your terminal type from the Shell. However, if you log out, you will need to give the **setenv** command again next time you log in. If you find you have to use this command, you should consider putting it in your login profile.

A full description of the ways you can tell different Shells the type of your terminal is given in the paper "Ex Reference Manual", by William Joy. A list of the terminal types supported, and the corresponding codes to be used with **set** (or **setenv**) can be found at the front of the paper "An Introduction to display Editing with Vi" by William Joy. The list will possibly not be complete for terminals at your installation. Details of the terminal types known to your system can be found in the file */etc/termcap*. If all else fails, consult your local **ex**pert.

If you set your terminal type to "unknown" or "dumb", **ex** will work in line addressing mode, but you won't be able to use visual mode. For instance, you could set up for a dumb terminal like this:

```
: set term=dumb
:
```

In the absence of any **set term** command during an **ex** edit session, the default terminal setting is taken from the environment.

8.1.1.2 'ex' Editor Profile   Just as you can have a login profile, into which you put commands which the Shell obeys at login time, so you can have an **ex** profile, which contains editor commands that are obeyed each time **ex** is invoked.

Each time you use **ex**, it looks in your home directory for a file called '*.exrc*'. If there is such a file, the **ex** commands in it are executed, before you are prompted for the usual interactive edit commands.

If there are any **ex** options which you wish to use on a regular basis, the **set** operations for these can be placed in that **ex** profile, '*.exrc*'. An example of an **ex** profile is:

```
$ cat .exrc
set ai nomagic sw=4 term=adm3a
$
```

which sets the 'autoindent' option, makes the shiftwidth 4 spaces, unsets the 'magic' option, and sets the terminal type for an ADM-3a.

The **ex** commands that can be put in the editor profile are not limited to **set**ting options, but these are the most likely candidates for inclusion.

8.1.2 Setting 'ex' Options

Options can be set or unset to affect the overall operation of **ex**. Each option usually has an abbreviation which is used with the **set** command. For instance, the 'autoindent' option, which requests automatic indentation of lines during text entry, is abbreviated to 'ai'. To set it you use the **ex** command:

```
: set ai
:
```

The meaning of automatic indentation is described in the paragraphs below.

Options are unset, or nullified, by preceding the abbreviation by the letters 'no'. For example, to request "no automatic indentation" you say:

```
: set noai
:
```

Some options have values or strings associated with them. In this case they follow the option name, separated by an equals sign:

```
: set sw=4
:
```

Another example is the 'term' option which sets your terminal type, as we showed above.

More than one option can be set or unset by the same "set" operation, the different options are separated by spaces. Setting and unsetting can be mixed, for example:

```
: set ai noopen sw=8 nowarn
:
```

All options have some default setting. The **set** command on its own displays the current state of those options that have been changed from the default. To examine the state of any one option, you follow **set** with a question mark:

```
: set magic ?
nomagic
:
```

The command "**set all**" displays the settings of all the possible options that can be set or unset.

Some of the options are only applicable when using the visual mode. We talk about those when we describe the **vi** screen editor. Many other options are associated with features of **ex** that are additional to the features of **ed**. Those options are discussed along with the additional feature.

The **ex** options discussed in the paragraphs below are concerned with communicating with the user.

The 'terse' option is concerned with reducing the length of messages from **ex**. The messages produced by **ex** are fairly lengthy. In many instances error messages include statements as to how to override the error condition The experienced user might grow impatient with all this verbiage, and the person using a slow terminal will probably be upset by it. The messages can be shortened by **set**ting the 'terse' option. For instance, the statement about the file length, which normally looks something like:

```
"thisfile" 280 lines, 10994 characters
```

is shortened to:

```
"thisfile" 280/10994
```

when the 'terse' option is set. The default setting is **noterse**.

When a command changes a large number of lines, **ex** reports this fact. The value of the 'report' number determines what **ex** considers a "large" change to the buffer. The default definition of "large" is 5. When you are doing an extensive "cut-and-paste" operation on a file, you will probably consider 5 lines a small change rather than a large one. The command:

```
:  set report=20
:
```

changes things so that **ex** only reports when 20 lines or more are affected by an edit command.

The 'beautify' option ('bf'), when set, instructs **ex** to clean up any text that you input, by discarding all unimportant control characters. Significant control characters, such as control-I (tab), control-L (form feed) and newline (which happens to be control-J), are not discarded. Also, control characters don't get discarded from **ex** command lines. This is a useful option, because some programs (like the **nroff** text formatter) don't behave properly if their input text contains funny characters like control-A. The default setting for this option is **nobf**, which puts everything you type (including the garbage) into the edit buffer.

When the 'autoprint' option ('ap') is set, **ex** automatically prints the current line after each editor command. In the case of global commands, the last line changed is printed. The default state is **ap**. However, if you don't want this useful feature, you can set **noap**.

If the 'number' option ('nu') is set, **ex** prints (displays) lines with numbers prepended. This is useful if you are giving **ex** commands in terms of line numbers. The default setting is **nonu**.

8.1.3 Printing or Displaying Lines of Text

The 'autoprint' option ensures that lines are always printed after they have addressed or changed, so you don't specifically have to use the **p** command:

```
:  1,5
Bacchus must now his power resign -
I am the only God of Wine!
It is not fit the wretch should be
In competition set with me,
Who can drink ten times more than he.
:
```

However, the **p** command still exists, and must be used if you have **noap** (no automatic printing of lines) set.

There is also an l command, which shows you all the control characters, which are normally non-printing. In **ed**, l indicates control characters by their octal ASCII values. In **ex** they are displayed using the abbreviation "^" for control. So a tab appears as "^I" and control-A appears as "^A". This is great improvement, since you can see what crazy key you typed, without having to look it up in the */usr/pub/ascii* file.

You can see line numbers by displaying lines with the command #, for example:

```
: 6,$#
6      Make a new world, ye powers divine!
7      Stock'd with nothing else but Wine:
8      Let Wine its only product be,
9      Let Wine be earth, and air, and sea -
10     And let that Wine be all for me!
:
```

If you have the 'number' option set, lines are always displayed with numbers prepended, even with the **p** and l commands.

A very useful feature of **ex** is the context display. A screenful adjacent to the specified line is displayed. If you are using a terminal which doesn't have a screen, the display is 8 lines. The display may be specified in different ways. The **z** command displays the addressed line at the top of the screen, z– shows the addressed line at the bottom of the screen, and **z.** puts the addressed line in the middle of the screen. In any case, **dot** is set to the last line displayed, that is, the last line displayed becomes the new current line.

Another variation of the context display is z=, which is like z., in that the current line is at the center of the display. But the current line is marked on the display:

```
: 6z=
In competition set with me,
Who can drink ten times more than he.
-----------------------------------------
Make a new world, ye powers divine!
-----------------------------------------
Stock'd with nothing else but Wine:
Let Wine its only product be,
:
```

and **dot** is not changed, the current line is still the one marked by the ---'s on the display.

If the 'number' option is set, the lines are displayed with line numbers prepended. If the 'number' option is not set (the default), you can combine the **z** and **#** commands, and say something like "**z.#**". The **z** and **l** commands can be combined in a similar way.

8.1.4 Insertion of New Text

ex has commands to append text after a given line, to insert text before a given line, and to change the text of a given line, or group of lines. Just as in **ed** these commands are **a**, **i**, and **c**, and text insertion is terminated by a "dot", or period character, on a line by itself.

There are also variants of these commands, **a!**, **i!**, and **c!**. The action of these variants is tied in with the idea of automatic indentation of lines. This feature of **ex** is handy when the text you are entering is program source, although it is not very useful for documentation text. Automatic indentation of lines is governed by the options 'autoindent' and 'shiftwidth'.

8.1.4.1 Program Text Options 'autoindent', 'shiftwidth' A useful option when you are typing programs is 'autoindent', abbreviated to 'ai'. The 'ai' option can be set with the command:

```
: set ai
```

Because the feature is not generally useful for text other than program source, the default case is no auto-indentation, (**noai**).

When **ai** is set, each new line of text inserted is automatically started at the same indentation depth as the previous line. So for example, if you start your second line of text spaced in 4 spaces from the first, then when you type the RETURN for that line, the cursor will not appear in column 1 of the screen, but directly in line with the start of the second line. Thus, once you have indented one line, all succeeding lines are indented by the same amount. This continues until you either cancel the indentation, or change the indentation by putting spaces or tabs at the beginning of the next line.

To back up (outdent, if you like) you type control-D. The number of columns that control-D backs up is controlled by the shiftwidth option, so it pays to use a uniform depth of indentation and to set the shiftwidth to that number.

'shiftwidth' is another option, it has a value associated with it. If you are using auto-indent, and not using shiftwidth, you are going to experience problems unless you always have your indentation depths at TAB (control-I) positions. The auto-indentation, as far as positioning the cursor for indents (that is, to the right) is concerned, always works. But the outdent function of control-D always moves leftwards by 'shiftwidth' spaces.

By default, 'shiftwidth' is set to 8 spaces, the same as the system tab stops as produced by control-I or the TAB key. So if you always indent 8 spaces, everything goes smoothly. However, 8 spaces is a lot of indent on a program, 4 is more reasonable, and even 2 is enough for program readability. If you try to do this without adjusting your shiftwidth, what will happen is that all your indents will be OK, but your outdents won't take you to the right place; you will have to indent again in most cases.

If you want to use an indentation depth of 4 spaces, the correct thing to do is set the shiftwidth option:

```
: set shiftwidth=4
```

or it can be abbreviated:

```
: set sw=4
```

Now the control-D will only take you 4 spaces back to the left.

There are two other commands associated with auto-indent and shiftwidth. These are > and <. They have the effect of shifting the addressed lines 'shiftwidth' spaces to the right or left. They are cumulative, so if 'shiftwidth' is set to 4 spaces, the command >>> will shift the current line 12 spaces to the right; −<< will shift the previous line 8 spaces to the left.

8.1.4.2 Variations on Text Insertion Commands The variants of the text insertion commands have the effect of toggling the auto-indentation feature. So if **ai** is set, the **a** operator will give you automatic indentation, but if you use **a!**, you will not get automatic indentation. However, if you have set **noai**, **a** will not give you automatic indentation, but **a!** will. The effect of **i!** and **c!** is similar.

The default setting for the automatic indentation feature is **noai**. So if you don't change the option, and don't use the command variants, you will not get automatic indentation.

8.1.5 Changing and Deleting Lines of Text

Lines of text can be changed using the **c** command. The rules for text insertion described above apply. When you want to change several lines of text, there are two ways that you can express this. For example, suppose you wish to change the four lines starting at line number 9 to something different. You can use the **c** command in the same way that you would use it in **ed**:

```
:  9,12c
something different
.
:
```

In **ex** there is another, slightly easier, way of specifying the **change** command. You can give an initial line address, then give **c** a trailing count, thus:

```
:  9c  4
something different
.
:
```

The space following the command is not significant. A **change** command of the form **9c4** will do the job just as well.

The same format, using a trailing count, can also be applied to the **delete** command. For instance, to delete 5 lines starting at the next line containing the string "God", you can say:

```
:  /God/d  5
:
```

which is easier to type, and less prone to error, than the old-fashioned **ed** way:

```
:  /God/,/God/+4d
:
```

8.1.6 Searching and Regular Expressions

Searching for character strings is similar to **ed**, but in **ex** you can be lazy: you don't have to put the final / or ? at the end of your character string or regular expression.

ex provides some additional metacharacters that are not found in other UNIX system commands that use regular expressions:

\\< The two characters mean beginning of word, in the same way as ^ means beginning of line. So the string "\\<d" would only find lines containing a word, or some words, beginning with "d". A "word" is a string consisting of letters, numbers or underscore "_", surrounded by characters which are not letters, numbers or "_".

\>   These two characters mean end of word, so "y\>" will find lines that contain words ending in "y".

~   The tilde character ~ used in a regular expression matches the replacement text specified in the last substitute command.

Let's show some examples of these in action, using the verse of Henry Carey's drinking song:

```
: g/\<m
Bacchus must now his power resign -
In competition set with me,
Who can drink ten times more than he.
And let that Wine be all for me!
: g/s\>
Bacchus must now his power resign -
It is not fit the wretch should be
Who can drink ten times more than he.
Make a new world, ye powers divine!
Let Wine its only product be,
:
```

The first global search finds all lines that contain words starting with "m"; The second finds all lines containing words that have "s" at the end.

```
: /Bacch/s/must/should
Bacchus should now his power resign -
:/~
It is not fit the wretch should be
:
```

In this example, we first substitute "should" for "must"; the metacharacter ~ then searches for "should".

In some of the above examples we used the global command **g**. The **g!** variant of the **g** command inverts the meaning of the search, for example:

```
: g!/Wine
Bacchus must now his power resign -
It is not fit the wretch should be
In competition set with me,
Who can drink ten times more than he.
Make a new world, ye powers divine!
:
```

finds all lines that do NOT contain the word "Wine". The **g!** variant is exactly the same as the **v** command.

In **ex** there is a useful flag that can be put at the end of a global substitution command. This is the **c** (for confirmation) flag. When the **c** flag is used, substitution does not happen automatically. Instead, each time the search string is found, **ex** prints it out and waits for input, which must be terminated by a carriage return. If the input begins with 'y', the substitution occurs, otherwise the string is left as it is. Here is an example:

```
: g/ine/s//ater/gc
I am the only God of Wine!
                    ^^^y
Make a new world, ye powers divine!
                          ^^^
Stock'd with nothing else but Wine:
                              ^^^y
Let Wine its only product be,
     ^^^y
Let Wine be earth, and air, and sea -
     ^^^y
And let that Wine be all for me!
              ^^^y
:
```

Each time **ex** found the string "ine" as part of the word "Wine", we typed **y** for "yes"; but when the word "divine" was selected, we didn't respond with anything other than carriage return. The result is that "Wine" is changed to "Water" everywhere, but "divine" is left intact, it doesn't get changed into "divater". If you are not sure how good your search string or regular expression is, this is a good flag to use for safety. However, if you have a big file, giving all the responses can be a tedious business.

There are several **ex** options which are connected with searching, these are 'ignorecase', 'magic', and 'wrapscan'.

8.1.6.1 The 'ignorecase' Option When the 'ignorecase' option is set, uppercase letters and lowercase letters are considered to be the same for string searching operations. If the option is not set, uppercase letters are distinct from lowercase letters in a regular expression. The option is abbreviated **ic**; the default setting is **noic**.

Let's set the option, and repeat one of our searches from the previous examples:

```
: set ic
: g/\<m
Bacchus must now his power resign -
In competition set with me,
Who can drink ten times more than he.
Make a new world, ye powers divine!
And let that Wine be all for me!
:
```

this time the search has found one more line, that containing "Make".

The 'ignorecase' option is useful, because you don't have to use regular expressions like

```
"[Hh]is "
```

to ensure you find words at the start of sentences as well as elsewhere.

8.1.6.2 The 'magic' Option

The 'magic' option is concerned with the metacharacters used in regular expressions. When **magic** is set, you have the full range of metacharacters in regular expressions used for searching and substitution. This means that if you really want to search for a character which acts as a metacharacter (for example "."), you need to escape it by preceding it with a reverse slash \. The default in **ex** is for magic to be set.

If you do not, as a general rule, use regular expressions very often, you may wish to set **nomagic**. This removes the special meaning from all characters except ^ and $, which still mean beginning and end of line respectively.

If you find that you need a regular expression now and again, you can still use them without turning 'magic' on again. This is done by preceding the metacharacters you want to use with a \. The \ character "toggles" the effect of the metacharacters. When magic is set, \ removes the special meaning from the following character. When magic is not set, \ makes the following character behave magically, if it can.

8.1.6.3 The 'wrapscan' Option

The 'wrapscan' option controls the extent of a search. The 'wrapscan' option is abbreviated 'ws'. Normally, when searching for a string with

```
/string/
```

ex searches forward from the current line to the end of the buffer, and if the string hasn't been found, proceeds to search from the beginning of the buffer to the current line. A similar action occurs when searching backwards with "?string?".

If you want **ex** to stop searching when it hits the end (or beginning) of the buffer, you can set 'no wrapscan' option:

```
: .p
Make a new world, ye powers divine!
: /power
Bacchus must now his power resign -
: /
Make a new world, ye powers divine!
: set nows
: /
Address search hit BOTTOM without matching pattern
:
```

The search no longer wraps round the buffer, and you get a message if the pattern is not found before the end of the buffer is reached. If you have the 'terse' option set, the message is shorter:

```
No match to BOTTOM
```

The default setting is **ws**, or 'wrapscan' on.

8.1.7 Substitution

The editor **ed** attaches special meaning to the ampersand character **&** when it is used in the replacement text in a substitute operation. **ex** has this feature, and in addition has special character sequences which can be used in the replacement text.

~	has a similar meaning as when it is used in a regular expression: the string found is replaced with the replacement text specified in the last substitute command.
\u and \l	the first character of the replacement string (which immediately follows \u or \l) is converted to upper or lower case respectively.
\U and \L	are similar, but all characters are converted to upper or lower case until the end of the replacement string or \e or \E is reached. If there is no \e or \E, all characters of the replacement text are made upper (or lower) case.

These last two can be used to change the case of individual characters, or whole words, or groups of words. For example, let's assume we are editing our *'people'* file:

```
: /Jane
Jane Bailey    121
: s/Jane/\U&
JANE Bailey    121
:
```

We used the special character sequence U to change "Jane" to uppercase. There is obviously some interaction between using these character sequences and using the 'ignorecase' option. If we try to change the word back:

```
: s//\L&
Substitute pattern match failed
:
```

we get an error message, because we are still trying to substitute for "Jane", and that string no longer exists. However, if we set the 'ic' option and try again:

```
: set  ic
: s//\L&
jane Bailey    121
:
```

the substitute operation is successful. The initial capital "J" can be restored using the character sequence **\u**:

```
: s//\u&
Jane Bailey    121
:
```

All the above examples assume that 'magic' is set.

An entire file can be made uppercase by the **ex** command:

```
: g/./s//\u&/g
```

Again, this assumes that **.** has its magic meaning of "match any character". If 'nomagic' is set, the above command has a very different effect — all period characters are changed to ampersands! We can restore the magical effects to both **.** and **&** by preceding them with a reverse slash:

```
: g/\./s//\u\&/g
```

This temporary restoration of metacharacters is often quicker than setting **magic** and then unsetting it again.

ex also has two shorthand forms of substitute operation, namely **&** and **~**. The ampersand operation **&** repeats the last substitute operation exactly. The tilde **~** replaces the last search or substitute regular expression with the replacement string specified in the last substitute operation. The difference is illustrated by the following examples:

```
: /power
Bacchus must now his power resign -
: s//crown
Bacchus must now his crown resign -
: /world
Make a new world, ye powers divine!
: &
Make a new world, ye crowns divine!
:
```

Although we have changed our search string from "power" to "world", the **&** still substitutes for "power" — it repeats the last substitute command. However, if at that point we had used **~** instead, the result would be different:

```
: /world
Make a new world, ye powers divine!
: ~
Make a new crown, ye powers divine!
:
```

In this case, the last replacement string "crown" is put in place of the last search string "world".

Although these two shorthand forms are useful, it is easy to confuse them and use the wrong one. In this case, it is tempting to use **u** to undo the substitution, then use the other. Unfortunately, this doesn't work, because the first use of **&** changes the effect of a following **~**. Similarly, if you use **~** first, a following **&** only repeats what you did with the original **~**. This is because **&** and **~** are expanded to full **ex** commands at the time they are typed, and the patterns remembered. The **u** command only undoes the *effect* of the command, it doesn't undo the remembrance of patterns.

8.1.8 The 'undo' Command

In **ed**, the command **u** has the effect of 'undoing' the last substitute command. The 'undo' command in **ex** has a much broader impact. It undoes the last change made to the edit buffer, and repositions the current line to where it was before the undone change was made.

If the last command was a global operation, all changes made by that command are reversed. The "visual" and "open" modes are considered to be global. If you enter visual mode, do a lot of changes, exit from visual mode back to line-address mode, then a **u** command will undo *all* the changes you made while you were in visual mode.

As in **ed**, **u** toggles — a second **u** undoes the first undo, thereby applying the undone changes again.

8.1.9 Reading, Writing, and Editing Files

The **r**ead, **w**rite, and **e**dit commands interact with the file system so that the contents of files can be read into the edit buffer, and the buffer contents can be written to a file. Also, as we have seen, you can specify multiple filenames on the **ex** command line; there are commands to deal with these files too.

8.1.9.1 Reading Files into the Buffer The **r** command reads the contents of a file into the edit buffer after the specified line. If no line is specified, the file is read in after the current line.

This is an important difference from **ed**, where the default is to read in the file at the end of the edit buffer.

Line 0 is a valid line number for the read operation:

```
: 0r preface
```

reads the contents of the file *'preface'* and places them at the beginning of the edit buffer. The last line of the file read in to the buffer becomes the current line.

The **r**ead command can also be used to get the results of a UNIX system command entered into the edit buffer. This is done by giving the command to be executed, preceded by a ! character, in place of the file name. For instance, supposing you are composing a memo, and you want to be sure you get today's date on it. You can use the **date** command:

```
$ ex memo
"memo" [New file]
: a
From: Bill Williams

To: Fred Bloggs

 .
: r !date
!
Wed Mar 17 09:33 PST 1982
: 1,$p
From: Bill Williams

To: Fred Bloggs

Wed Mar 17 09:33 PST 1982
:
```

Unfortunately, the date produced by the **date** command is not in the format that you usually see it written in memos, but a small editing change will fix that.

ex displays a ! character to indicate that it is executing the UNIX system command that you have specified. This is displayed on the screen only, it does not get entered into the buffer. When the command has finished running, the last line brought into the buffer is printed. In the example above, only one line was brought into the buffer, and that line was printed. The last line brought into the buffer becomes the current line.

8.1.9.2 Writing the Buffer to a File The **w** command writes the buffer, or part of the buffer, to a file. This works the same as for **ed**. A plain **w** on its own writes the buffer back onto the file you asked to edit, which is the most common use of the write command. In **ex** the write and quit operations can be combined, and you can save your file and exit from the editor by typing **wq**.

w followed by a filename writes the contents of the buffer to that specified file. If the file exists already, you get a message:

```
: w oldfile
"oldfile" File exists - use "w! oldfile" to overwrite
:
```

If the 'terse' option is set, the message is simply "File exists", and the conditions for overriding the situation are not detailed.

If the **w** operation is preceded by line address, or range of lines, only those lines are written to the specified file.

As indicated in the example above, the **w!** variant of the **w** command forces a write over an existing file.

Another thing which affects overwriting of existing files is the 'writeany' option, which is abbreviated 'wa'. If this option is set, **ex** does not check to see if the file already exists when you type a **w** command.

All **write** operations to existing files are dependent on the mode of the file. If you don't have write permission, you will get a "Permission denied" message.

The edit buffer can be appended to the end of an existing file using the notation:

```
: w >>oldfile
```

The edit buffer, or a part of it, can be made the input to a UNIX system command. This is achieved by specifying the command, preceded by a ! character, in place of the filename. For instance, if you want to print the first 100 lines of the buffer on the line printer:

```
: 1,100w !lpr
!
:
```

ex tells you when it's finished by repeating the ! character.

Beware of confusion between **w! filename** and **w !command**, spacing is very important.

8.1.9.3 Editing a New File When you call up **ex** with a specified filename, you usually get a message telling you how long the file is, in lines and characters:

```
$ ex song
: "song" 10 lines, 337 characters
:
```

If the file you specify doesn't exist, the message is:

```
: "sing" [New File]
:
```

If you see this message when you are not expecting it, you have probably spelled the filename wrongly.* You can get at the correct file using the **e** command:

```
: e song
```

When you have finished editing a file, you can bring another file into the edit buffer with the **e** command. If you haven't written away the first file, **ex** warns you in no uncertain terms:

```
: e another
No write since last change (edit! overrides)
:
```

If you have the 'terse' option set, the message is simply "No write".

As the non-terse message implies, you can use a variant of the command to force the new file to be brought into the buffer. However, you don't have to spell out in full **edit!**, **e!** is sufficient. All changes made to the file currently in the buffer are lost.

8.1.9.4 Multiple Filenames on the Command Line　We showed earlier that you can give several files as arguments when calling up **ex**, for example:

```
$ ex thisfile thatfile theotherfile
3 files to edit
"thisfile" 280 lines, 10994 characters
:
```

There are editor commands to access these files. The **n** (for next) command brings in the next file specified in the argument list when **ex** was invoked:

```
: n
"thatfile"  120 lines, 7156 characters
:
```

If the current file has been modified but not written, you get a message:

```
: n
No write since last change (next! overrides)
:
```

---

* On some older versions of **ex** the message is "No such file or directory", but it means the same thing.

The **n!** command variant forces the next file into the buffer, and changes made to the current file are lost. If the current file you are editing is the last file in the argument list, so that there are no more files left to edit, you get a message to that effect.

The **args** (for **arg**uments) command displays the argument list and indicates the file currently being edited:

```
: args
thisfile [thatfile] theotherfile
:
```

By using the **rew** (for **rew**ind) command, the argument list is "rewound" and **ex** starts editing the first file all over again. You get the "N files to edit" message, then the first file in the list is read into the buffer. If the current file has been modified but not written, you get the usual error message, and there is the usual command variant (**rew!**) that overrides it.

8.1.9.5 The Remembered File and the Alternate File   In the previous chapter, we described how **ed** remembers the name of the file you are editing, so that when you issue a **w**rite command you don't have to specify the filename. **ex** does the same thing, and the remembered file name can be accessed using the percent sign % as a shorthand notation. So, if you want to create a backup file before you make any changes, you can make your first command inside the editor a **w**rite operation:

```
$ ex myfile
"myfile" 698 lines, 24113 characters
: w %.old
"myfile.old" 698 lines, 24113 characters
:
```

The use of % as an abbreviation for the current file is extremely useful when you are obeying UNIX system commands from within the editor.

The current file name can be displayed with the **f** (for **f**ile) command:

```
: f
"myfile" [Modified] line 465 of 698 --66%--
:
```

As you can see, **ex** tells you more than the file name. It tells you where you are in the file, and whether the buffer has been modified since the last **w**rite operation.

The **f** command can also be used to change the remembered filename:

```
: f otherfile
"otherfile"[Not Edited][Modified]line 465 of 698 --66%--
:
```

The new state of affairs is displayed automatically. The file is considered to be "not edited" because there is no request to edit the file. This only becomes important when you try to write the file away. If there is no existing file of the remembered name, everything is fine. But if a file of the same name already exists, **ex** warns you about it, and you must use the **w!** command variant to write the file.

Whenever you ask to edit another file, by giving the **e**, **n** or **rew** operations, the new file name becomes the remembered filename. The new file is considered to be "edited" (as is the file you call up on the **ex** command line), and you have no problem writing the file away.

There is another file that **ex** remembers the name of, called the "alternate file". When you change the remembered file name, the previous file becomes the alternate file. The alternate file can be accessed with the shorthand notation **#**. If there are two files you want to edit, you can easily swap from one to another by using the command **e #**. If your request to edit a new file is unsuccessful, because you haven't written out the current file, then the file name you specify on the **e** command becomes the alternate filename. This means that after writing the current file, you don't have to specify the new file name in full, but you can simply say **e #**. When you specify a file name on a **r**ead or **w**rite operation, that file becomes the alternate file too.

8.1.10 Getting Out of the Editor

As with **ed**, the command to exit from **ex** is **q**, for quit. If you try to exit without having written your changes away to a file, **ex** warns you:

```
: q
No write since last change (quit! overrides)
:
```

If you really don't want your changes saved, you can use the command variant **q!** (or you can spell out in full "quit!") to exit.

If you specified several files on the calling **ex** command, and try to quit before you have dealt with them all, you get:

```
: q
2 more files to edit
:
```

Again, the **q!** command variant will get you out.

For convenience, the write and quit operations can be combined:

```
: wq
"myfile" 701 lines, 24289 characters
$
```

8.1.11 Cut and Paste Operations

In the chapter on **ed** we showed how you can move lines around in the buffer, and copy lines in the buffer, with the operations transpose and **m**ove. These operations exist in **ex** too, and there are some additional commands which are useful for cut and paste type of changes.

One of the additional commands is **co** for **co**py. This works identically to the **t** command in **ed**, but "co for copy" is a bit easier to remember than "t for transpose". However, if you are used to using **t**, or are too lazy to type two-letter commands, then **t** is still around and does the same job.

Another command for which you have a choice of two names is the command used to mark lines for later addressing. The **k** command of **ed** still exists in **ex**, but you can also use **ma** (for **ma**rk), which may be easier to remember.

These commands are not really new commands, they are simply aliases for old **ed** commands. But there are some truly new commands, and also some variations of old commands, which make it easier to do cut and paste editing.

8.1.11.1 Joining lines with the 'j' command   The **j** operation takes the addressed lines and joins them together to form one line. If only one line address is given, then that line and the one following it are joined. If no line addresses are given, the current line and the next line are joined.

To show an example of this, let's go back to the memo we were writing,

```
$ ex memo
"memo" [New file]
a
From: Bill Williams

To: Fred Bloggs

Date:
.
: r !date
!
Wed Mar 17 09:33 PST 1982
:-j
Date: Wed Mar 17 09:33 PST 1982
:
```

We added the text "Date:", then used **r** to get the current date as the next line. We then used **j** to get these two things together on the same line.

The join operation automatically provides a reasonable amount of space. Usually this is one space, but if one of the lines joined together ends with a period (or any other end of sentence character), then two spaces are provided. Also, if one of the lines to be joined starts with a closed parenthesis ")", no spaces are left.

There is a variant of this command, **j!**. When you use the variant, no spaces are left between the joined lines.

8.1.11.2 Copying Text with 'yank' and 'put' **ex** has two commands which be used to copy text from one place to another in the edit buffer. They can also be used to copy text from one file to another.

The **ya** (for **ya**nk) command causes the specified lines to be copied into a buffer area. This buffer is separate from the buffer area where the file is being edited. The lines are not deleted from the "main" buffer where the file is being edited.

The **pu** (for **pu**t) command causes the lines in the separate buffer to be put in the file after the specified line.

For instance, if you wanted the last two lines of a file to be a copy of the first two, you would use the commands:

```
: 1,2ya
: $pu
I am the only God of Wine
:
```

The **yank** command can also be given a starting line and a trailing count, so that:

```
: 1ya  2
:
```

is another way to get the first two lines into the buffer.

With the 'autoprint' option set, the last line **put** from the buffer is printed. The lines are not printed when they are yanked into the buffer.

The contents of the buffer are affected by other **ex** commands, so no other changes should be made between the yank and the put. However, there are other buffers which are not affected by **ex** commands unless specifically requested. These are called the "named buffers", and there are 26 of them named 'a' through 'z'. To use one of these buffers, you simply tack the name on the end of the **yank** and **put** commands:

```
: 1,2ya  g
: $pu  g
I am the only God of Wine
:
```

The above example uses the buffer 'g'. If you specify an uppercase letter in a **ya**nk command:

```
: 3ya  G
:
```

the specified lines are appended to anything that might already be in the buffer, in our case buffer 'g'.

When you use the format of **ya**nk which takes a trailing count to put lines in a named buffer, the name of the buffer must precede the count:

```
: 1ya  g  3
:
```

If you put things in the wrong order you get a message:

```
: 1ya  3  g
Extra characters at end of command
:
```

When a named buffer is used, the contents are not affected by other **ex** commands, so you can do other changes between the yank and put. In particular, the contents of named buffers are not affected by **e**dit or **n**ext operations, so you can copy lines from one file to another without writing temporary files.

8.1.11.3 Transposing Lines with 'delete' and 'put' In **ex**, when you delete some lines, they don't disappear completely. They are placed in the same buffer that lines get yanked into, and they can be retrieved with the **pu** operation. Again, there should be no other changes between the **d** and the **pu**, unless you use a named buffer. You can use these operations to move stuff around in a file, or to transfer lines from one file to another.

Reverting to our files containing names and phone numbers, let's suppose we want to transfer Maryann from *'adminpeople'* to *'softpeople',* and put someone else in her place. Here's how we can use **ex** to do it:

```
$ ex adminpeople softpeople
"adminpeople" 2 lines, 40 characters
: /Maryann
Maryann Clark    101
: d m
Bill Williams    100
: a
Ethel Snerge     101
.
: w
"adminpeople" 2 lines, 40 characters
: n
"softpeople" 5 lines, 100 characters
: pu m
Maryann Clark    101
: s/01/15
Maryann Clark    115
: wq
"softpeople" 6 lines, 120 characters
$
```

First we dealt with the *'adminpeople'* file; we deleted the line containing Maryann into the buffer named 'm', then we added a new line for Ethel. After saving the changes, we moved to the *'softpeople'* file; we **put** the line containing Maryann, then changed her phone number.

8.1.12 Running UNIX system Commands
from Inside 'ex'

If you want to use a UNIX system command while you are in the editor, you can use the ! operation, the same as you could in **ed**. This is where the use of % to mean the current file comes in handy. For instance you can compile your C program by:

    : !cc %

or you can format your document for proof reading by:

    : !nroff %

Another useful shorthand notation is the double !!, which means "repeat the last system command". So when you have corrected your compilation errors, you can recompile your program simply by saying !!.

A point to note is that the last command includes the expanded filename. So if you edit *'program1'*, and compile it with !cc %, then switch to editing *'program2'*, the !! still refers to *'program1'*.

When you run a command in this fashion, **ex** warns you if you have changed the buffer since you last wrote it away. In the examples we have been discussing, this is very useful. There is no point in re-formatting your document if the changes you have made haven't got into the file yet. However, this warning is under control of the 'warn' option, so if you don't want it you can turn it off by:

    : set nowarn

The default setting of the option is 'warn'.

Sometimes you may want to run many commands without terminating your edit session. The **sh** command temporarily suspends your edit session and puts you at UNIX system command level. You see the system prompt, and can execute any commands you want, including another **ex** to edit another file. When you have finished you type control-D, just as if you were logging out. You then return to your suspended edit session, where you see the **ex** prompt once more. This is called "forking out of the editor". Some UNIX system installations have the capability to give you a different prompt under these conditions, to remind you that you have a suspended edit session.

We have seen that you can get the result of a command into the edit buffer using a variation of the **r** operation. Also we saw that you can pass lines from the buffer as input to command with a variation of the **w** operation. But the buffer itself is unaffected by the write operation. For instance, suppose we were editing our 'people' file, and we gave the command:

```
: 1,$w !sort
```

The sorted names appear on the terminal screen, but the lines in the buffer are in their original unsorted order.

However, there is a way of telling **ex** to use a UNIX system command to transform the contents of the edit buffer. To illustrate this let's continue our earlier example of the memo:

```
: a

cc:
Sylvia Dawson
Jack Austen
Joe Mugg
Pat Manders
.
: ?Sylvia?,.  !sort +1
!
Joe Mugg
: ?cc?j
cc: Jack Austen
: 1,$p
From: Bill Williams

To: Fred Bloggs

Date: Wed Mar 17 09:33 PST 1982

cc: Jack Austen
Sylvia Dawson
Pat Manders
Joe Mugg
:
```

We wanted the "copies to" list to be in alphabetical order by last name, so we entered them on separate lines from the "cc:" heading. Then we used the **sort** command to get them into alphabetical order, by giving the range of lines and preceding the **sort** command with !. The output of **sort** replaced the original lines in the buffer. Finally we got everything together by using the **j** operation to put the first name on the same line as "cc:"

8.1.13 Open and Visual Modes

All the commands we have talked about so far deal with lines. The only way to affect parts of a line is with the substitute command. This is because **ex**, like **ed**, is basically a line oriented editor. However, **ex** has two commands which provide intraline editing. This means that you can add characters in the middle of a line, or delete characters from a line.

The **vi** editor command switches the editor into **vi**sual mode. While in visual mode, **ex** is identical with the **vi** editor described in the latter part of this chapter. The screen of text displayed usually starts at the line specified, for example **10vi** displays a screen which starts at line 10. However the screen display can also be specified backwards from the specified line or on either side of it. This is achieved by following the **vi** command with a −, or with a period character **.**, similar to the context display command **z**. To exit from visual mode and revert to the line oriented mode, you type **Q** (uppercase Q). *

Open mode gives the same capabilities as visual mode, but only one line is displayed at a time. To enter open mode you use the **o** command. The specified line is displayed, and you can use any command that is available in visual mode. Open mode is useful for "dumb" terminals, or hard copy terminals, such as the TI-700.

8.1.14 Recovery from System Crashes

One of the most annoying things that can happen when you are using an editor, is for the system to crash before you have had a chance to write away your modified (or new) file. Just as bad from the user's point of view, is an accidental disconnection from the system. In either case, there is the possibility of hours of work being wasted because a modified file was not saved.

ex provides a means of recovering from this situation. When your system recovers, and when you get reconnected, you may have mail telling you that files have been saved to help you recover your changes. Even if you don't get mail, it is worth trying the recovery operation.

---

* On some older versions of **ex**, you exit from visual mode, back into line mode, by typing **q** (lowercase q).

Change directory into the same directory you were in when the interruption occurred, and give the command:

```
$ ex  -r  myfile
"myfile" [Dated: Wed Mar 19 09:41:23] 10 lines, 135 characters
:
```

The filename you specify must obviously be the name of the file you were editing when the interruption occurred.

You will not necessarily recover all the changes you had made, but you will get most of them. In particular, if you had yanked or deleted stuff into a buffer (even a named buffer), those buffer contents are lost.

8.1.15 Different Versions of 'ex'

As we said way back at the beginning of this chapter, there are different versions of **ex** around. Some of the older version do not have all the features that we have described, or that are described in the document "Ex Reference Manual". You can use the editor command **ve**:

```
: ve
Version 2.13, 9/5/80
:
```

to check which version of **ex** you are using.

8.2 The Display Editor 'vi'

Closely associated with the **ex** text editor is another editor called **vi**. This is the type of editor sometimes called a "visual" editor (hence the name), or a "screen" editor, or a "display" editor. What happens is that a portion of the file you wish to modify is displayed on your terminal screen. This is often termed a window on the file.* Within that window you can move the cursor around to control where changes are to be made, and then you can make changes by replacing text, adding text or deleting text. The portion of the file displayed in the window can be changed, so you have access to the whole file.

---

* In fact, **vi** uses an edit buffer, so what you see is actually a window on the buffer. But in this chapter we use the more common term "window on the file".

The behavior of the different screen editors varies widely in the way in which they handle text which you just type then and there. Some screen editors (such as the RAND editor) replace what is already on the screen with what you type, and you have to tell them something special when you want to insert new text. Other screen editors (such as EMACS) insert new text by default, and you have to do something different to change or replace text. Unlike these other editors, **vi** has no default mode. Everything you want to change, insert, replace, or delete, you have to tell **vi** explicitly what to do.

From within **vi** you have access to all of the **ex** line-oriented commands, as well as the display editing capabilities. This makes **vi** a very powerful editor indeed.

vi has a wide range of commands for positioning the cursor at the spot you want changed — too many to learn them all easily. In this section, we introduce the most generally useful ones first. You should practice using these until you are thoroughly familiar with them, before advancing to the more specialized ones.

Practice is the key to using a display editor. You must become so familiar with the commands that you don't have to think about them: they just flow out of your fingertips.

It is difficult to learn how to use a display editor by reading a book, you really need to get on a terminal and *use* the editor. It is also difficult to give examples of a screen oriented editor on paper, but we will do so as far as possible.

We don't cover all the features of **vi** in this section. As is our wont, we only show you how to perform the more common useful functions. More details of using **vi** can be found in the paper "An Introduction to Display Editing with Vi" by William Joy. There is also a "Ex/Vi Quick Reference" card, which is useful for the experienced user who needs a memory-jogger.

8.2.1 Calling Up 'vi'

Depending on your UNIX installation, and the Shell you are using, you may have to tell **vi** the type of terminal you are using. This is done with the command **setenv**, or with the **ex** operation **set**. We described how to do this earlier, when we discussed **ex**. If you skipped that bit, you should refer to it now. An important fact is that, although you can use the **set** command from within **vi**, you cannot use it to set your terminal type. So if you do not have your terminal type set up prior to entering the editor, you have to enter **ex**, set your terminal type, then call up visual mode from within **ex**.

The **vi** editor can be called from within the **ex** editor, as we described in the last section. It can also be called up by the **vi** command:

```
$ vi myfile
```

After you have issued this command, your file is read into the edit buffer, the terminal screen is cleared, the window is set at the first lines of the buffer, and the cursor is initially set at the first character of the first line in the window.

As with **ex**, you can specify multiple file names on the command line:

```
$ vi thisfile thatfile theotherfile
```

The first file is read into the edit buffer, and the first lines of it are displayed in the window.

The size of the window is dependent on two things, namely the speed of your terminal, and the setting of the 'window' option. For slow speeds (600 baud or less) the default window is 8 lines; for medium speed (1200 baud) it is 16 lines; for higher speeds the window is the full screen size, less one line (this usually works out to be 23 lines).

The name of the file, and its length in characters and lines, is shown on the last (bottom) line of the screen.

The default window size can be changed by using the **set** command to set the required window size, for example:

```
: set window=12
```

In all the examples we give, we assume a window of 8 lines, although usually you would use the full screenful. Use of an 8-line window is only a device to make our examples fairly short, and in fact we show them as though the screen itself were only 9 lines long — an 8 line window on a standard 24 line screen would not behave exactly like we've shown.

So, if we have an 8-line window and we call up **vi**:

```
$ vi   omarkhayyam
```

what we see is:

```
How long, how long, in infinite Pursuit
    Of This and That endeavour and dispute?
    Better be merry with the fruitful Grape
    Than sadden after none, or bitter, fruit.

You know, my Friends, how long since in my House
    For a new Marriage I did make Carouse:
    Divorced old barren Reason from my Bed,
"omarkhayyam" 19 lines, 715 characters
```

The bottom line of the screen shows statistics about the file we are editing, the first eight lines of the file are shown in the window. The cursor is sitting at the very first character in the file.

The width of the window is always the full width of the screen (80 columns). If you have a file with lines that are longer than 80 characters, they can still be edited. The characters over 80 look as though they were another line, because the display wraps round. This can be a little confusing, but isn't as bad as it sounds. It is relatively easy to tell when you have a wrapped line by the way the cursor moves.

The file statistics that appear at the bottom of the screen disappear when the window on the file is moved. Some **vi** commands also use this space, and the file statistics go away if one of these commands is typed.

Another way of invoking **vi** is with the **+** flag:

    $ vi + omarkhayyam

When you call **vi** this way, the last part of the file is displayed on the screen, and the cursor is positioned at the beginning of the last line. A variation of this is:

    $ vi +10 omarkhayyam

which displays the initial window such that line 10 (or whatever number you specify) is in the middle of the screen, and the cursor is positioned at the beginning of that line.

When you call up **vi** with more than one file name, you first get the "N files to edit" message as in **ex**, then the first of the N files is read into the buffer, with the same effect as if it were the only file.

As in **ex**, there is a **–r** option for recovery from system crashes. If the system goes down, or you get disconnected from it, while you are using **vi** to edit *'myfile'*, you can recover most of your changes by giving the command:

```
$ vi -r myfile
```

when you get back on the system.

8.2.2 Getting Out of 'vi'

As usual, we're putting this information first, because getting out of the editor, especially when you have made many mistakes and want to start over, is very important.

There are many different ways of getting out of **vi**. Which one you use depends, in part, on whether you want to save the changes you have already made.

If you want to save your changes, you can exit the editor by typing any of the following:

        :wq<CR>

or

        :x<CR>

or

        ZZ

The notation <CR> indicates that you have to press the key marked RETURN. You have to do it in the first two cases (the reason for this will become clear in the next paragraph), but not in the third.

If you do not want to save your changes, you exit the editor by typing:

        :q!<CR>

Again, the <CR> indicates that you have to press the key marked RETURN.

If you called up **vi** from within **ex**, and now want to return to **ex**, the command to do this is simply an uppercase **Q**. You can also use this if you entered **vi** in the first place, but would now like to use **ex**.

8.2.3 Command Structure

We said earlier that **vi** has no default mode, you have to give it specific commands. Just about every key on the keyboard is some command to **vi**. So are combinations of the SHIFT key and the other keys, and combinations of the CONTROL key and the other keys. This is particularly important in the case of the SHIFT key. In the following paragraphs, when we talk about the **W** command, we really do mean uppercase "W". Lowercase "w" is another command, and does something different.

For the most part, the commands are mnemonic. There are some exceptions, and in some cases the mnemonic is a little strained.

There are some keys for which there is no function. If you type one of these, **vi** will "beep" at you; that is, it will ring the terminal bell. The "beep" is not restricted to this error, it is **vi**'s general signal that you are doing something wrong, like trying to move the cursor further than it can go.

The general structure of most **vi** commands is:

```
[count]operator[count]object
```

The distinction between operators and objects is sometimes blurred, because an object can also be a command. For example, the command **w** moves the cursor forward one word of text, while the command **dw** deletes the next word of text. The **w** acts as the operator in the first case, and as the object in the second.

The optional count can appear in either place in the command, either before the operator, or after the operator and before the object. For instance, to delete three words we could say either **3dw** or **d3w**.

 You can also place the count in both places, before the operator *and* before the object. If you place the count in both places, the effect is multiplicative. In other words, the command **3d3w** deletes nine words.

With a few exceptions, **vi** commands are not echoed to the screen, but are simply obeyed. You see the result of them by either a movement of the cursor, or a change in the text that appears on the screen.

A very important key is the escape key. On most terminals it is labelled ESC, but on some it is marked ALT. For any commands which require text to be entered, you tell **vi** when you have finished entering text by pressing the ESC (or ALT) key. Also, if you start to type a **vi** command, and then change your mind before you finish, you cancel the partial command by hitting ESC. There is no command associated with the ESC key, so it is the safest key to press. If you are not sure what state you are in, hit ESC until **vi** beeps. You then know that **vi** is listening for your commands. The combination control-[is the equivalent of ESC, and performs the same function. However, it is a lot easier to use the ESC key.

8.2.4 Accessing 'ex' Commands

One command that deserves special attention right now is the colon : character. When you type : the character is echoed at the beginning of the bottom line of the screen. Whatever you now type, up to

RETURN, is interpreted as an **ex** command, and acted upon accordingly. The command you type is echoed on the last line of the screen as you type it. This is how **vi** has access to all of **ex**'s powerful features, like global substitution. It is also the way in which many **vi** features are implemented. For example, to save your file you say:

```
:w<CR>
```

the "w" in this case is the **ex w**rite operation, and has no connection with the **vi w** operator which moves the cursor a word. Similarly, to exit from **vi**, you can say:

```
:q<CR>
```

which is the same as giving the **q**uit command in **ex**.

To set an editor option, you type, for example:

```
:set ai<CR>
```

A fuller description of the **ex** set command is given in the previous section. In this section we merely mention those options which are useful, or only applicable, in **v**isual mode.

8.2.5 Positioning the Cursor within the Window

There are many ways of changing the position of the cursor. It can be moved left and right along the screen a character at a time, a word at a time, or directly to the beginning or end of a line. It can be moved up and down the screen. You can specify a line number to go to, or a string to search for. Sometimes this may change the window on the file.

8.2.5.1 Basic Cursor Movements The simplest way to position the cursor is a character at a time. How you do this depends somewhat on the type of terminal you are using. If you have four keys marked with arrows, they should have the effect:

    ←   move the cursor one character to the left
    ↓   move the cursor down one line
    ↑   move the cursor up one line
    →   move the cursor one character to the right

If you don't have keys with arrows on them, then the four keys h, j, k, l should be capable of being used in their place, that is:

h	(same as ←)	move the cursor one character to the left
j	(same as ↓)	move the cursor down one line
k	(same as ↑)	move the cursor up one line
l	(same as →)	move the cursor one character to the right

We suggest you mark arrows on these keys (they are already so marked on adm3a terminals).

On some older versions of **vi**, these keys don't work on all terminals, so you may have to resort to the following:

control-H	move the cursor one character to the left (backspace)
control-N	move the cursor to the next line
control-P	move the cursor to the previous line
space	move the cursor one character to the right

These characters are not so easy to use — you might want to find yourself another terminal, or another editor. If you have a key marked BACKSPACE (sometimes abbreviated BS), that is the same as control-H, and it can be used to move the cursor to the left. Sometimes, just typing "h" without holding the control key will work too. Control-J can be used in place of control-N to move the cursor down to the next line (but it isn't mnemonic). If you have a key marked LINEFEED, that is the same as control-J, so you can move the cursor down with that key instead.

Investigate your terminal and find out which keys you use to perform these cursor moving functions before you proceed any further. They are the most basic commands in the editor, and you won't become proficient until you are thoroughly familiar with them.

Each time you press one of these four keys, the cursor moves one unit in the required direction. You can move several lines or characters by pressing the key repeatedly. Some terminals have an automatic repeat function, so that if you hold a key down it will repeat until you let go. Other terminals have a key marked REPEAT, if you hold this key down while typing some other character, that character is repeated until you let go. These features can be used when you have long distances to move the cursor, but be careful if you are working at a low baud rate — it's very easy to go too far.

The cursor positioning commands can be given a preceding count, the cursor will move the specified number of characters or lines. For instance, **8→** moves the cursor eight characters to the right; **4↑** moves it up four lines.

When you are moving the cursor in a horizontal direction, it will not go beyond the end of the line when you're moving it to the right, or beyond the beginning of line when you are moving it to the left. This is how you can tell that you have a long line that is wrapped round the display, the cursor keeps moving beyond the apparent end of line.

When you are moving the cursor vertically up or down, the horizontal position of the cursor is unchanged, as far as possible. If the cursor is towards the end of a line, and you move it down to a shorter line, then the cursor is placed at the end of that shorter line. However it will revert to its original horizontal position on any line that is long enough. The following diagram illustrates the position of the cursor on three successive ↓ movements.

```
How long, how long, in infinite Pursuit
    Of This and That endeavour and dispute?
    Better be merry with the fruitful Grape
    Than sadden after none, or bitter, fruit.

You know, my Friends, how long since in my House
    For a new Marriage I did make Carouse:
    Divorced old barren Reason from my Bed,
"omarkhayyam" 19 lines, 715 characters
```

If you are on the last line of the window and you try to move the cursor down, the window will move down the file one line. An alternative way of saying this is that the lines on the screen scrolls up one line. That is, the top line disappears from the display, and the next line in the buffer appears at the bottom of the display. You cannot go past the end of the file, there is no wrap around to the beginning. Similarly, if you are on the top line of the window and you try to move the cursor up, the window will move up the file one line (the lines on the screen scroll down one line). Again, there is no wrap around from beginning to end of file, you cannot move past the first line of the file.

When you do something that causes the window on the file to change, the bottom line of the screen, which initially shows the filename and length, goes blank. Some of the **vi** commands use this space, and we'll describe these in the next few paragraphs.

There are a few other basic cursor positioning keys. For horizontal motions along the lines, two useful functions are:

^	move cursor to beginning of line
$	move cursor to end of line

For those who are used to using regular expressions, these should be easy to remember. When moving the cursor vertically up and down the screen,

RETURN   move to beginning of next line

–   move to beginning of previous line

can be useful. The key combination control-M is the equivalent of RETURN, and has the same effect.

"Beginning of line" is not always the real beginning of line. Leading spaces and tabs are ignored, so the cursor moves to the first non-blank character. Most of the time this is where you really want to be; but if it isn't, you can get to the very first character on the line by using ←. Alternatively, the **0** (that's the figure zero) command puts the cursor on the very first character of the line.

Three more basic cursor movements are:

H   home

M   middle

L   last

The **H** command homes the cursor onto the top line of the screen, **M** moves the cursor to the middle line of the screen, and **L** moves it to the last line of the screen. Note that these commands must be uppercase letters. All three commands position the cursor at the "beginning of line" (that is, at the first non blank character). **H** and **L** take preceding counts — **3H** moves to the 3rd line on the screen, **2L** moves to the second line from the bottom. If you have a key marked HOME on your terminal, this will probably achieve the same as the **H** command.

Once you know these basic cursor positioning commands, you can use **vi** to change existing files. It is probably a good idea at this stage to move on to learning how to do simple text changes, and to use the editor for a while, before progressing to the other types of cursor movements. A good indication that you are ready to learn more about **vi**, is a growing impatience with the slowness of what you already know.

8.2.5.2 Moving over Words and other Text Objects

So far we have seen how to get to the beginning and end of line quickly, but otherwise movements are mostly a character at a time. You can tell **vi** to move over the text a word at a time by using the commands:

w   move forward to beginning of next word

e   move to end of this word

b   move back to beginning of word

If you are already at the beginning of a word when you issue the **b** command, the cursor will go to the beginning of the previous word. If you are at the end of a word when you give a **e** command, the cursor will move to the end of the next word.

The definition of a "word" is:

> Anything consisting of letters, digits and underscores; surrounded by anything which is not a letter, a digit or an underscore.

This definition covers variable identifiers in most programming languages, so the commands are useful for editing both programs and documentation. The following picture shows the position of the cursor on five successive w commands:

```
The source code for the program is in the file
/aa/widget/henry/progs/c/thingummy.c.  documentation
is in directory /aa/widget/henry/docs -  thingspec
is the specification, it needs to be formatted
using -ms; thinguser is the user's guide, it also
requires -ms.
~
~
"thinginfo", 6 lines, 251 characters
```

In the above example the file is shorter than the window. Lines in the window that are in excess are indicated by the tilde character ˜ to avoid confusion with blank lines in the file.

You can also move the cursor forward a word by the command **W**. When you use **W** instead of **w**, a word is any sequence of characters surrounded by spaces. So if we had started with the cursor in the same position as in our previous example, the position of the cursor on the same number of successive **W** commands is:

```
The source code for the program is in the file
/aa/widget/henry/progs/c/thingummy.c.  Documentation
is in directory /aa/widget/henry/docs -  thingspec
is the specification, it needs to be formatted
using -ms; thinguser is the user's guide, it also
requires -ms.
~
~
"thinginfo", 6 lines, 251 characters
```

There are commands **B** and **E** which are similarly related to **b** and **e**.

All the commands **w**, **b**, **e**, **W**, **B** and **E** move past the end of a line, as is demonstrated in the above examples. If you use them to move past the upper or lower limits of the window, the lines scroll up the screen accordingly.*

These commands can take a preceding count, so the command **5w** moves the cursor forward five words, as if you had issued five separate **w** commands. This means you have to count the number of words to move. The easiest way of doing this is to mark each one by placing the cursor over it. The net result is that this is not a particularly useful feature under most circumstances. It is useful if you are working in what is termed "slow open" mode, which is what you get if you call up **vi** on a dumb terminal.

With **vi** you are not restricted to moving forward or backward a word, or groups of words, at a time. You can move forward whole sentences. A sentence is defined as string of words ending with one of the characters ".", "!" or "?" followed by two spaces, or occurring at the end of a line. The commands which move the the cursor over sentences are (and). Typing) moves the cursor to the beginning of the next sentence, and (moves the cursor to the beginning of the previous sentence.** The commands can be given counts, so 2) moves forward 2 sentences; 3(moves back three sentences.

You can also move the cursor whole paragraphs at a time by the commands } (beginning of next paragraph) and { (beginning of previous paragraph). Every time there is a blank line, the next line is considered to be the start of a new paragraph. However, if your file is text to be input to the **nroff** text formatter using the macro packages **−ms** or **−mm**, **vi** recognizes the "start of paragraph" macros available in these packages, and positions the cursor accordingly.

If the file you are editing contains text to be formatted using one of the **nroff** macro packages, you can also tell **vi** to move forward or backward whole sections. The command to move forward a section is]], to move back a section you type [[. **vi** makes you type the double character in each case, because it is not so easy to type two]'s or ['s by accident. In the case of sentences or paragraphs, you will not move very far, so if you move by accident it is not too difficult to get back to where you started. But sections can be huge, and it would be

---

* On some older versions of **vi**, these commands will not move past beginning or end of line.

** If the file you are editing contains a LISP program, you may want to change the meaning of these commands by setting the option **lisp**. When this option is set, (and) move backward and forward over s-expressions. The meaning of { and } is changed too.

easy to get completely lost by mistake, hence the precaution of double characters.

If the text you are editing is source text in the C programming
language, the section positioning commands [[and]] move forward
or backward over whole procedures.

vi recognizes the paragraph and section macros provided by the
–ms and **–mm** macro packages, but if you want to provide your own
definitions, you can do it with the 'para' and 'sect' options.

8.2.5.3 Moving to Specific Characters or Columns   Suppose that you
have the cursor positioned at the beginning of a line, and you want
to position the cursor to the character "n". This can be done by saying "find n" — the **f** command followed by the character you want to
find, in other words **fn**. This command positions the cursor to the
first character "n" following the current cursor position. The following example shows the different cursor positions from initial beginning of line to after the **fn** command:

```
How long, how long, in infinite Pursuit
    Of This and That endeavour and dispute?
    Better be merry with the fruitful Grape
    Than sadden after none, or bitter, fruit.
```

If you then want to find the next "n" character, you can repeat the **fn**
command. However there is a shorthand command **;** which says, in effect,
"search forward for the same character as you looked forward for before".
So, having found the first "n", giving four **;** commands will position the
cursor at the following points in turn:

```
How long, how long, in infinite Pursuit
    Of This and That endeavour and dispute?
    Better be merry with the fruitful Grape
    Than sadden after none, or bitter, fruit.
```

If you go too far, and want to go back one or more "n"s, there is a command
, which says, effectively, "look for the same character as you did last time,
but in the other direction".

The "find" command **f** will not go past the end of line. To find the same
characters on the next line you have to first type the RETURN key to get
you to the next line, then you can issue more **;** commands to find the
character.

The reverse of the **f** command is **F,** which searches the line backwards for the specified character. Again, there is a shorthand form **;** which
continues the search for the same character. So if we started

off with the cursor positioned as at the end of our last example, then gave a **Fo** command followed by three ; commands, the positions taken by the cursor at each step would be:

```
How long, how long, in infinite Pursuit
     Of This and That endeavour and dispute?
     Better be merry with the fruitful Grape
     Than sadden after none, or bitter, fruit.
```

The , command can be used to reverse the direction of the search. As for **f**, the **F** command will not move past the beginning of line.

To summarize these commands:

f*a*	search forward on line for character *a*
F*a*	search backward on line for character *a*
;	search for same character in same direction
,	search for same character in opposite direction

You will notice that, if you start off with an **f** then ; goes forwards whereas , goes backwards. However, if you start off with **F** then , goes forwards and ; goes backwards. Try not to let this confuse you.*

All the commands can be given leading counts. If the cursor is sitting at the beginning of a line, you can find the fourth "c" character by the command **4fc**. If you use a simple **fc** to get to the first, you can get to the third next "c" by the command **3;**. If this takes you two "c"s beyond where you want to be, you can say **2,** to get back to the correct position. Similarly for moving in the other direction with **F**.

Even with the count, the commands will not go beyond the end of line. If you ask to move **4;** and there are only two of them on the line, the cursor will not move and **vi** will beep at you.

These commands are useful for positioning yourself at punctuation marks, or at some unusual characters in the line. The best way to use them when giving letters to look for, is to give the initial letter of the word you want, then use **e** to get to the end of that word, or → to get to somewhere in the middle of it.

There are two other commands that are similar to **f** and **F**, these are **t** and **T**. Lowercase **t** is similar to **f**, but instead of placing the cursor on top of the specified character, the cursor is placed on the character just to the left of the specified character. In a similar way,

---

* Those who have used the screen editor in the UCSD P-system can probably cope with this.

T is like **F**, but puts the cursor over the character immediately to the right of the specified character. The reason for having these two commands, in addition to **f** and **F**, will be made plain when we talk about deleting and changing partial lines.

Yet another way to move the cursor to a point on the line, is to move it to a specified column number. To position the cursor at a particular column in a file, the command to use is **|** . For example, to place the cursor in column 40, you give the command **40|** .

8.2.6 Changing the Window

So far, all the cursor movements we have shown you have been within the current window on the file, or have adjusted it by only one line. There are commands which affect the window without changing the position of the cursor on the line.

The **z** command redraws the screen with the current line positioned at the top, or in the middle, or at the bottom of the screen:

z <CR>   current line is at the top of the screen

z .   current line is in the middle

z -   current line is at the bottom

So, if our screen initially looked like this:

```
How long, how long, in infinite Pursuit
    Of This and That endeavour and dispute?
    Better be merry with the fruitful Grape
    Than sadden after none, or bitter, fruit.

You know, my Friends, how long since in my House
    For a new Marriage I did make Carouse:
    Divorced old barren Reason from my Bed,
"omarkhayyam" 19 lines, 715 characters
```

and we issued the command **z**, the screen would be changed to look like:

```
    Than sadden after none, or bitter, fruit.

You know, my Friends, how long since in my House
    For a new Marriage I did make Carouse:
    Divorced old barren Reason from my Bed,
    And took the Daughter of the Vine to Spouse.

For "Is" and "Is-not" though with Rule and Line,
```

There are other commands which change the window on the file, they also change the cursor position with respect to the line (it stays constant with respect to the window):

control-D   scroll down half window

control-U   scroll up half window

If you type control-D, the top half of the text in your window moves off the screen, the bottom half moves into the top half, and the next lines in the buffer are displayed in the bottom half. The cursor stays in the same position on the screen. So if we issued a control-D command from the position shown in the previous example, the result would be:

```
Divorced old barren Reason from my Bed,
And took the Daughter of the Vine to Spouse.

For "Is" and "Is-not" though with Rule and Line,
    And "Up-and-Down" without, I could define,
    I yet in all I cared to know,
    Was never deep in anything but - Wine.
```

In other words, the window has moved down the file. Control-U has the same effect in the reverse direction, it moves the window up the file.

The window can be also be moved up and down the file with:

control-F   move the window forward through the file

control-B   move the window backward through the file

If you type control-F the whole window moves forward (down) in the file, apart from 2 lines retained for continuity. So the last two lines of the screen become the first two lines. The cursor is placed at the beginning of the first line on the new screen display. Control-B does the same thing in the reverse direction, the two top lines become the bottom lines and the cursor is placed on the bottom line of the screen.

8.2.7 Line Numbers, Search Strings and Marking

If you are aware of the line numbers of the lines in the file you are editing, you may wish to position the cursor at some specific line. The command you use to do this is **G**, the "go to" command. This is uppercase "G", there is no command for lowercase "g". For example, to go to line number 432 you type **432G**. The cursor is moved to the beginning of the requested line. If necessary, the window on the file

is changed, so that the requested line appears in the middle of the screen.

Typing the **G** command with no preceding line number moves the cursor to the last line of the file.

Another way of going to a specific numbered line, is to use : to call up the **ex** command. Typing ":432" followed by the RETURN key also moves the cursor to the beginning of line 432. The legend ":432" appears at the bottom of the screen while you are typing it. To get to the last line by this method, you would use the **ex** notation $ for last line and you would type :$ followed by RETURN.

To find a particular character string anywhere in the file, you use the / command. When you type / it is echoed at the bottom line of the screen. You then type the string you want to search for, either as a fixed character string, or as a regular expression. Regular expression metacharacters are the same as in **ex**, and are subject to the setting of the 'magic' option. To signal the end of the character string, you type either ESC, or RETURN.

vi places the cursor at the start of the next string that matches what you typed, going forward through the file. The following example shows the starting and ending positions of the cursor, for the search indicated at the bottom of the screen:

```
How long, how long, in infinite Pursuit
Of This and That endeavour and dispute?
Better be merry with the fruitful Grape
Than sadden after none, or bitter, fruit.

You know, my Friends, how long since in my House
For a new Marriage I did make Carouse:
Divorced old barren Reason from my Bed,
/fruit
```

If the string is not in the current window, the window is changed to display that part of the file which contains the string. If we entered the search command **/though** from the position shown in the previous example, the window when the search was completed would look like:

```
For a new Marriage I did make Carouse:
Divorced old barren Reason from my Bed,
And took the Daughter of the Vine to Spouse.

For "Is" and "Is-not" though with Rule and Line,
And "Up-and-Down" without, I could define,
I yet in all I cared to know,
Was never deep in anything but - Wine.
```

The search wraps around the file. That is, if the string isn't found between the current position and the end of the file, the file is searched from the beginning up to the current position. This feature is under control of the 'wrapscan' option, as we described in **ex**. If the string doesn't exist in the file at all, the message

```
Pattern not Found
```

is displayed on the bottom line of the screen.

A search forward through the file can also be accomplished by giving the : command, and then using **ex**'s search commands. These also start with the / character, so you type :/, followed by the string or pattern you want to search for, followed by RETURN. The difference between this and using / on its own is illustrated by the following example, which repeats one of the previous searches, but using :/ instead of / on its own:

```
How long, how long, in infinite Pursuit
    Of This and That endeavour and dispute?
Better be merry with the fruitful Grape
    Than sadden after none, or bitter, fruit.

You know, my Friends, how long since in my House
    For a new Marriage I did make Carouse:
    Divorced old barren Reason from my Bed,
:/fruit
```

You can see that whereas :/ places the cursor at the beginning of the line containing the string, / on its own places the cursor at the start of the string itself. Both functions are useful under different circumstances.

If you want to search backward through the file instead of forward, you can do this by typing the ? command, followed by the string (or pattern) you want, terminated by either ESC or RETURN. Again, what you type is echoed on the bottom line of the screen. Alternatively, you can use :? to find the beginning of the line containing the string. Both ? and :? act in a similar manner to / and :/, the only thing different is the direction of the search.

If you want to search forward again for the same string, you can do it by typing // (or ://). Similarly, if you want to search backward for the same string, you use ?? or :?? However there are two other commands you can use:

n	find next occurrence of same string in same direction
N	find next occurrence of same string in reverse direction

If you did your initial search with /, the **n** command will do the next search forward, and **N** will search backward. On the other hand, if you did your initial search with **?**, **N** will go forward and **n** will search backward. You might find it less confusing to use **//**, which always goes forward, and **??** which always goes backward.

You can mark a place in the file using the **m** (**m**ark) command. The command is followed by a single letter, which is the mark or label. For example **mz** marks the character under the current cursor position with the label "z". If you move away from that position, you can return to it with the command `z. The ` character is a grave accent, on most terminals it is SHIFT-@.

A special case of the ` command is ` `. This returns you to the place you were at before the last search or "goto" command.

Another way of returning to the marked place is by using the ' command, that is the apostrophe character. The difference between ' and ` is that ` places the cursor exactly over the marked position, while ' puts the cursor at the beginning of the line containing the marked position.

8.2.8 The 'Undo' and 'Repeat' Commands

We have now shown you many ways to get the cursor to the position in the file where you want to make changes. But we haven't yet shown you how to make any changes. Before we do that, we're going to tell you about the "undo" commands, so that if you make any mistakes while doing the changes, you can take corrective action.

There are two "undo" commands, namely **u** and **U**. The lowercase **u** simply undoes the last change you made. If you have moved the cursor away from the position at which you did the change, the cursor is repositioned to its original place after the change has been undone. Similarly, if the window has been moved since you did the change, it is moved back to its original display. The **u** command undoes any change to the edit buffer, even if that change affected many lines.

If you give another **u** command, it DOES NOT undo the change before the last one: it undoes the original "undo" command, thus applying the change all over again.

The uppercase **U** command is different: it can undo several changes, but only those made on the same line. **U** undoes all the changes you have made to the current line, that is, the line the cursor is currently sitting on. If you move the cursor away from that line, **U** doesn't do anything. **U** will not undo itself, so typing a second **U** has no effect.

In general, **u** is more useful than **U**. However, there are cases where you need **U**, and we show an example of the different actions of the two in the next paragraph. Beware of using **u** and **U** in succession, the one will not undo the effects of the other.

Another special command is **.** the period character, called "dot". While **u** says "undo that which I just did" **.** says "do it again". Regardless of the change you made, whether it changed a word, added a new sentence, or deleted two lines, if you change the position of the cursor and say **.** the same change will be done at the new position. Again, we show some examples in the next paragraph.

8.2.9 Simple Text Additions, Changes, and Deletions

In this paragraph, we talk about making changes at a character level. We introduce commands for deleting characters, changing characters, and adding new text. Since these commands are often used to alter only a single line, most of the examples given only show one line of text. Your imagination will have to supply the rest of the window.

8.2.9.1 Deleting Text with 'x' and 'X' The simplest command to use is the "delete character" command **x**. This command is sometimes called "x-out" or "gobble". If you have a line, with the cursor positioned like this:

```
Use not vain repetition, as the heathen do.
```

and you "gobble" a character, the result is:

```
Use not ain repetition, as the heathen do.
```

If you want to gobble five characters, you can do it in two different ways. You can either repeat the **x** five times (so you say **xxxxx**), or you give the command a leading count and say **5x**. In either case, the result is the same (assuming you started with the cursor placed on the "v" of "vain" as in the last example):

```
Use not repetition, as the heathen do.
```

However, if you change your mind, and want the characters replaced, the command you gave in the first place matters a lot. If you gave the **5x** command, you can get them all back with an undo command of **u**. However, if you said **xxxxx**, the **u** command will undo only the last **x** command:

```
Use not  repetition, as the heathen do.
```

In order to restore the line to its original state, you have to use **U**.

The difference between **xxxxx** and **5x** is also important if you are going to use **.** to repeat changes. If you said **xxxxx** to start with, typing **.** gives you:

```
Use not epetition, as the heathen do.
```

that is, one more character has been deleted. But, if you initially said **5x** and now say **.** the result is:

```
Use not ition, as the heathen do.
```

another 5 characters have been deleted.

The **x** command will not gobble characters beyond the end of a line. Normally, after a character has been deleted, the cursor is left sitting on top of the character after (that is, to the right of) the deleted character, this is illustrated by the examples above. However if you use **x** to gobble the last character on a line:

```
Use not vain repetition, as the heathen do.
```

the cursor is left sitting on the new last character on the line:

```
Use not vain repetition, as the heathen do
```

So another **x** command would gobble that one:

```
Use not vain repetition, as the heathen d
```

This has the effect of making **x** gobble characters backward along the line, rather than forward in its usual fashion. If you use repeated **x**'s (either with the REPEAT key, or with the automatic repeat feature of your terminal), be careful, because it's very easy to gobble up an entire line without meaning to. However, things are not too bad, **x** will not go past the beginning of the line, and the entire line can be restored using **U**.

Another command which deletes characters is **X** (uppercase "X"). This is similar to the lowercase **x** command that we have been discussing. Instead of deleting the character under the cursor (and moving the cursor to the right), it deletes the character to the left of the cursor. The cursor is left sitting over the same character. It can therefore be considered the reverse of **x**, deleting characters backward along the line instead of forward. **X** can also be given a preceding count, for example **3X** deletes three characters to the left of the cursor. The "reverse gobble" command **X** will not go further back than the beginning of the line, neither will it reverse direction like **x** does.

8.2.9.2 Replacing Characters with 'r' and 'R' The command to replace (change) a single character is **r**. You first position the cursor on top of the character you want to replace, then you type **r** followed by the character you want at that position. So if you started out with the cursor positioned:

```
Use not vain repetition, as the heathen do.
```

and issued the command **rV**, the result would be:

```
Use not Vain repetition, as the heathen do.
```

The cursor remains over the same character, so if you want to replace it by something else again, all you have to do is type another **r** command. The character you put in place of the one under the cursor can be a newline character. So if you want to split a line, you can first position the cursor:

```
Use not vain repetition, as the heathen do.
```

then type **r** followed by the RETURN key. The result is:

```
Use not vain repetition,
as the heathen do.
```

The **r** command can be given a preceding count. For example, if we started with our cursor on the "v" of "vain", and typed **4rV**, the result would be:

```
Use not VVVV repetition, as the heathen do.
```

This is not a very useful feature, except under some specialized circumstances.

More useful is a variation of the **r** command: the uppercase **R** replaces characters until you tell it to stop. You tell it to stop by hitting the ESC (escape, on some terminals labelled ALT) key. So if you started with the cursor:

```
Use not vain repetition, as the heathen do.
```

and typed "**R**You use <ESC>", the result would be:

    You use vain repetition, as the heathen do.

The cursor is left sitting on top of the last character which was replaced. We have just used **R** to change two words. We were lucky, in that the total length of the new words we wanted was the same as the total length of the words we were replacing. A better way of changing words is described in the next paragraph.

The **R** command is useful when you have a fixed format, where you want to preserve column alignment for example.

Another useful command is ~, the tilde character.* This command has the effect of changing the case of the letter under the cursor. For example, if the character under the cursor is "V", the ~ command will change it to "v", and will move the cursor to the right one position. If the character under the cursor is "a", then ~ changes it to "A", and moves the cursor one character to the right. The command does not take a preceding count, but because the cursor is moved one place to the right after the command is executed, it is easy to change a whole word to upper or lower case by giving repeated ~'s.

8.2.9.3 Entering New Text with 'a', 'i', and 's' There are two basic commands that can be used to enter new text into a file, They are **a**, which appends text after the current cursor position, and **i** which inserts text before the current cursor position. The **a** command is the equivalent of →**i** ; when you give the command, the first thing that happens is that the cursor moves one place to the right, then text gets inserted before it.

When you give either of these commands, any following text you type gets put in the file. To stop text entry you hit the ESC key. So, for example, if you had a line:

    The good, and the ugly

with the cursor positioned on the "," as shown, if you type "**a** and the bad<ESC>", the result is:

    The good, and the bad and the ugly

Whereas, if you start from the same position and type

---

* Older versions of **vi** do not support this command.

"i and the bad<ESC>", what you get is:

```
The good and the bad, and the ugly
```

If you are using what is called a dumb terminal, when you type in the additional text, it might look as if you are over-typing the existing text. However, as soon as you hit ESC, it all gets straightened out. What you see when you are inserting new text on a dumb terminal depends on an option called 'redraw'. If this option is set, then as you type in new text, the rest of the line gets shuffled along to the right, and you can see exactly where you are. If the redraw option is not set, the text you insert gets displayed on top of the original display, and it looks like you are overwriting it. So when we did the insert in the previous example, just before we hit ESC, the text would look like this:

```
The good and the badly
```

but as soon as we typed ESC, the line would show in its final form. The redraw option makes **vi** do a lot of work, and slows down the editor quite a bit. For this reason, the default value of the option is **noredraw**.

If you make a mistake while entering new text, you can backspace to correct it in the usual way, by typing control-H (assuming that you have made this your erase character). Another correction feature, only usable in the editor, is control-W. This backspaces over and erases a whole word, so you can correct it. The erased characters don't disappear from the screen at the time you backspace, but your corrections over-type them. This feature is independent of the "redraw" option.

Both the **a** and **i** commands can take a preceding count. In this case, whatever gets typed between the command and ESC is entered into the text the specified number of times. So if we take the result of the last example, and place the cursor at the beginning of "bad":

```
The good and the bad, and the ugly
```

If we then type the command "**2i**very <ESC>", the result is:

```
The good and the very very bad, and the ugly
```

This does not appear to be a very useful feature, but it makes for a certain amount of consistency in the editor commands.

Another command which can be used to enter new text is **s**. There are two ways of looking at this command. In the **vi** documents the command is described with the **r** and **R** commands. The "s" stands for substitute, and it replaces a single character with lots of characters, until you type ESC. Another, but less mnemonic, way of describing it, is as a "gobble" followed by an insert. Typing "**s**text" has the same effect as typing "**x**itext". So if we start with our original line:

```
The good, and the ugly
```

with the cursor over the "," as usual, and type "**s** and the bad<ESC>", the result is:

```
The good and the bad and the ugly
```

The comma has been deleted and the new text inserted in its place. Or, if you prefer, the text "and the bad" has been substituted for the comma.

All the commands used for text entry consider the newline character as part of the text being entered. So you can split a line simply by typing RETURN at the appropriate point. If we start, as usual with:

```
The good, and the ugly
```

and type "**a**<CR>and the bad,<CR> <ESC>" we end up with three lines:

```
The good,
and the bad,
and the ugly
```

If you want to insert completely new lines of text, all you have to do is position the cursor to the end of the line they have to go after, give the **a** command, then type RETURN as the first character of the new text you want to put in.

There are two other simple commands for entering additional text:

    I   insert text at the beginning of the line
    A   append text at the end of the line

Regardless of where the cursor is positioned on a line, the **I** command will insert text at the beginning of that line. It is as if you had typed ^i (we don't mean control-I, we mean the two characters "^" and "i"). Similarly, **A** has the same effect as typing $a — text is added at the end of the line, regardless of the cursor position.

New lines of text can be inserted by using the **A** command and making the first character you enter a RETURN. There are also two other commands that can be used to add new lines of text, these are the "open lines" commands, **o** and **O**. When you give the **o** command, regardless of the position of the cursor on the line, a blank line is opened up following the current line, and the cursor is placed at the beginning of the new line. Anything you type from now on, until you type ESC, becomes the new line or lines. You don't have to enter any text; if all you want is a blank line, you can type ESC immediately following the **o**.

It is a fairly simple process to make a file double spaced. Simply place the cursor at the beginning of the file and type **o<ESC>**, then type a sequence of repeated "**<CR> .**" to apply the same change to the rest of the file. If the file is a long one, this method is not recommended. It is better to use : to access **ex**'s global command to add the blank lines, as we described in the previous section.

The **O** command is similar to the **o** command, except that it opens a line above the current one, instead of below.

8.2.9.4 Creating a New File   You can now see that it is quite a simple matter to create a new file. You simply call up **vi** with the name of the file you want to create:

    $ vi somejunk

The screen goes almost completely blank:

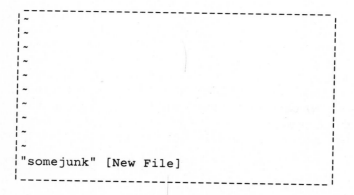

```
| ~
| ~
| ~
| ~
| ~
| ~
| ~
| ~
| ~
| ~
|"somejunk" [New File]
```

The cursor is positioned in the top left hand corner; there are a row of ~ characters down the left hand edge of the screen. These indicate that there are no lines in the file corresponding to these lines on the display. At the bottom of the screen there is displayed the name of the file you are creating, and an indication that it is a new file.*

You give the **a** command (or it could be the **i** command, it doesn't really matter), then type in all the text you want. When you have finished, you type ESC.

In the unlikely event that you don't make any mistakes, all you then have to do is write the file away and quit the editor by typing **:wq**. When you write the file away, a message looking something like:

```
"somejunk" 50 lines, 3172 characters
```

appears at the bottom of the screen. After you have quit the editor, you see the UNIX system prompt again.

If you make mistakes while entering text, you can correct them at any time. Remember to type ESC to stop the current text addition, before moving the cursor to the place where the correction is needed. When you have made the corrections, to continue adding more text you simply put the cursor at the end of your previous text, type another **a** command, and repeat the whole process. When all is to your satisfaction, write the file away and quit the editor, as we described above. It is a good idea to save the file periodically with the **:w** command — you have less to recover if the system crashes when you are creating a new file, or even editing an old one.

If you want to enter a control character in the file (for example, you might want to put control-L, which is the form feed character, at strategic places) you have to escape it by preceding it by the **vi** escape character control-V. In other words, to get control-L into the file you have to type control-V first, then immediately follow it by control-L. Control characters in the file are displayed by the notation ^L, for example. They look like two characters, but you can tell that they are only one because the cursor moves over them as one unit, never coming to rest on the ^.

When you are entering a great deal of text, you can get **vi** to insert newline (RETURN) characters automatically. This provides for fast text entry, since you don't have to watch the screen and type RETURN at the appropriate places. This feature is controlled by an option called 'wrapmargin', which has a value associated with it. If the value is zero, the feature is turned off (this is the default case). If the value is set to some value other than zero, for example:

---

* On older versions of **vi**, it says
  "somejunk" No such file or directory
  Don't let this worry you, it means the same thing as "New file".

```
:set wrapmargin=8
```

then every time a space is typed at a position less than 8 places from the right hand edge of the screen, the previous space is converted into a newline character. The result is that you can just keep typing, and your file will be such that none of the lines exceed 72 characters. So you only need to type RETURN when you deliberately want to start a new line.*

This feature is useful when typing text for document preparation, it is not so useful when typing computer programs.

An option which is useful if you are entering program source code is 'autoindent', and the associated option 'shiftwidth'. These options are also effective in **ex**, and they are described in some detail in the previous section. The default setting for the option is no auto-indentation.

Another option which can be useful when entering program source code is 'showmatch'. When this option is set, each time a closing parenthesis), closing bracket], or closing brace } is typed, the cursor moves to the matching (, [, or { for one second, if the matching character is on the screen. The abbreviation for the 'showmatch' option is **sm**, and it can be set by typing:

```
:set sm
```

The default is to not show matches (**nosm**).

Even if you don't have the 'showmatch' option set, you can show matching pairs of parentheses, brackets, or braces with the % command. If you place the cursor over any of (, [, or {, and then type %, the cursor will move to the matching),], or }. Similarly if the cursor is placed on the closing character of such a pair, the % command moves the cursor to the corresponding opening character. Remember to type ESC to stop text entry before using this command.

8.2.10 Operating on Words and Other Text Objects

In a previous paragraph we showed you how you could move the cursor whole words by typing the commands **w** or **W** to go forward, or the commands **b** or **B** to go backward. These "commands" are actually descriptions of text objects, and they can be affected by various **vi** operators, which can in themselves be considered "commands".

---

* Beware — on some older versions of **vi** this option does not work fully, it is safest not to use it.

The operators are

    d   delete

    c   change

    y   yank

The **y** operator is covered in a later paragraph, we deal with **d** and **c** here.

8.2.10.1 Deleting Words, Sentences and Paragraphs This is quite simple. To delete a word, you just place the cursor at the beginning of it and type the **dw** command (delete word). **vi** takes care of spacing, so you don't get left with a double space where you only want one. For example:

```
Use not vain repetition, as the heathen do
```

after a **dw** command, looks like:

```
Use not repetition, as the heathen do
```

To delete a number of words, we give a count. The count can precede either the **d** operation, or the **w** object, so **2dw** or **d2w** both have the same effect, namely, delete two words:

```
It was a dark and stormy night
```

becomes:

```
It was a stormy night
```

If the words you want to delete are not all on the same line, **vi** joins the lines together. For example, suppose you want to delete three words starting from:

```
It was a dark and stormy night;
the young boy said to his
uncle "Tell me a story, Uncle"
```

the result would be:

```
It was a dark and stormy night;
the young boy said "Tell me a story, Uncle"
```

This might result in a very long line. To split it you would have to move the cursor to some suitable place and insert a RETURN character.

If the cursor is not at the beginning of a word when you type the **dw** command, the partial word from the cursor position to the end of the word is deleted. For example:

```
With all due pomposity and circumstance
```

after a **dw** command, becomes:

```
With all due pompand circumstance
```

This unfortunately deletes the space between words as well, however the cursor is left in just right position for inserting a space by typing "i <ESC>".

In the same way you can delete "Words" — objects found by the **W** command rather than the **w** command. You can also delete words to the left of the cursor, by saying **db** or **dB**.

Using **vi**, you can easily delete whole sentences, or parts of sentences. This works in much the same way as it does for words. To delete a whole sentence, first move your cursor to the beginning of the first word of the sentence, then type the **d)** command. **vi** joins the sentences on either side of the deleted sentence. To delete several consecutive sentences you give a count, in the same way as you do for words: **2d)** or **d2)** for instance.

Exactly what you see displayed when you delete large amounts of text depends on the type of terminal you are using. On an an intelligent terminal, the undeleted text is rearranged. However, if you are using a dumb terminal, this does not happen unless you have the "redraw" option set. Instead, whole lines that get deleted are indicated by a @ in the first column, the remainder of the line is blank. These lines are blank line on the screen, but there is no corresponding blank line in the edit buffer. If you get too many of these lines, it is hard to see what you are doing. At this point, you can ask **vi** to redraw the screen by typing **^R** (control-R).

You can delete parts of sentences by placing the cursor part way through the sentence before giving the command, but you will probably have to do other small cosmetic changes too.

The command **d(** deletes the sentence before the cursor, or several sentences if a count is given. It can also be used to delete part of a sentence, but again you will probably have to make some cosmetic changes to repair punctuation and initial capital letters on sentences.

After deleting large portions of text you might wish to make further changes to adjust the length of the lines so that they are all more or less the same. However, if the text you are entering is to be passed through the **nroff** text formatter it is a waste of time and effort to do this. Adjusting the line lengths so that they are all much the same is one of the formatter's most basic functions.

Paragraphs and larger text objects can also be deleted. The **d}** command deletes the following paragraph, **d{** deletes the preceding one. Similarly, sections can be deleted by **d]]** and **d[[**. Definitions of paragraphs and sections were given earlier when we described cursor movements.

8.2.10.2 Changing Words and Sentences If you want to replace one word by a different word, or by several words, you move the cursor to the start of the word, then give the **cw** command. At this point, the symbol $ appears to mark the extent of the change. In the case of **cw**, it appears over the last character of the word. You then type in the new word or words that you want, then press the escape key (ESC) to finish text entry. Suppose we wanted to change:

```
It was a dark and stormy night
```

to:

```
It was a dark and turbulent night
```

we would have to type "**cw**turbulent<ESC>".

If you want to replace more than one word, you give a count: **3cw** or **c3w** for example. The $ sign appears to mark the end of the text you are going to replace by the text you enter. If we have this:

```
It was a dark and stormy night
```

to get this:

```
It was an inky and stormy night
```

type "**c2w**an inky<ESC>".

So far we have replaced words with the same number of words, but it doesn't have to be that way. You can replace one word with many or many words with one. You can get:

```
It was an incredibly inky, black, rain-filled,
wind-blown, and stormy night
```

from:

    It was a dark and stormy night

simply by typing the **c2w** command then typing the text

    an incredibly inky, black, rain-filled,
    wind-blown,

followed by ESC. Or you can change

    It was a dark and stormy night

to

    It was raining

by typing "**c5w**raining <ESC>".

As is the case when deleting words, the words we want to change don't have to be all on the same line.* So to change:

    It was an incredibly inky, black, rain-filled,
    wind-blown, and stormy night

to something simpler, we can type "**c2W**rainy", to get

    It was an incredibly inky, black, rainy and stormy night

The action taken by **vi** is a little different in this case. Before you start entering the replacement text, the words that will be replaced disappear from the display, and the remaining parts of the two lines are joined together on the display. There is no $ sign to indicate the end of the replacement. This is exactly as if you had typed the commands **d2wi**.

Notice that in the last example we used "Words" rather than words. If we had used **w** instead of **W**, the result would have been:

    It was an incredibly inky, black, rainyfilled,
    wind-blown, and stormy night

---

* On some older versions of **vi** you cannot change words over a line boundary — all the words do have to be on the same line. If you give a count that will take you beyond the end of the line, the rest of the line is changed, but nothing is changed on the following line.

because according to the definition of **w** words "rain" is a word, so is "-", so is "filled", so is ",", and so on. To use **w**, we would have had to give a count of 8.

This is the sort of situation where that $-sign comes in handy. As soon as you have typed the command, before you enter text, look for that $ sign. If it isn't sitting on top of the last character you want to replace, you need to take some sort of corrective action. In our example, after typing **c2w** we would see the $ sign sitting on the "-" of "rain-filled". If we now type ESC, we effectively delete those two words (replace them with nothing). Since a **word** is a subset of a **Word**, we can still use the same count and say **c2W**, which is the correct command.

The command **cw** doesn't have to be used to change whole words, it can change partial words. Given the phrase:

```
with all due pomposity and circumstance
```

by typing "**cw**locution<ESC>", we get a different phrase:

```
with all due pomposity and circumlocution
```

In a similar way the change operator can be applied to the objects **b** and **B**, although these are not so commonly useful, since it's not so easy to envision changes backward along a line. The command **cb** changes the word before the cursor, **cB** changes the Word before the cursor. Both can be given counts. The extent of the text that will be replaced is indicated by the cursor moving to the leftmost character that will be replaced, and the $ sign sitting over the rightmost character (actually the one just to the left of where the cursor was when you gave the command). When changing words in this way, if you start with the cursor at the beginning of a word, you will have to supply the space between that word and the one before it as part of the text you enter.

Just as the change operator can be applied to words in either direction from the cursor, it can be applied to sentences. The **c)** command, followed by some text and the ESC character, changes the next sentence, or the last part of the current sentence. **2c)** or **c2)** changes the next two sentences. When changing sentences, the old sentences are deleted from the display, a blank line is opened up, and you start typing the new sentences in that line. In a like manner, **c(** will change the previous sentence, or the first part of the current sentence.

For those users brave enough to try it, the **c** operator can also be applied to paragraphs and sections.

8.2.11 Changing Lines of Text

So far we have been dealing with language constructs, such as words and sentences. Sometimes it is inconvenient to consider things in this way, it is easier to work simply with lines of text. This is especially true when the text you are editing is not documentation, but program source code. However, even during document preparation, it is often convenient to be able to say "delete the rest of this line", rather than "delete the next 4 words", or "delete the rest of the sentence". **vi** has commands for dealing with partial lines, and also for dealing with whole lines, in blocks if necessary.

8.2.11.1 Changing and Deleting Parts of Lines   In the previous paragraph we saw that to delete a word, we simply applied the **delete** operator to the cursor positioning command **w**. The same principle applies to the commands used to delete parts of lines. For example, **d$** deletes all characters from the current cursor position to the end of line,

```
#define LINES 66   /* number of lines on each page */
```

becomes

```
#define LINES 66
```

There is also a **D** command which does the same thing, that is, deletes to end of line. The character that is under the cursor is included in the definition of "here to end of line".

In the same way, the **d^** command means "delete from beginning of line to here". For example:

```
#define LINES 66   /* number of lines on each page */
```

ends up as:

```
/* number of lines on each page */
```

In this case the character under the cursor does NOT get deleted, but becomes the first character of the new line.

Changing parts of lines is similar, the **c** operator is applied to $ and ˆ. The **C** command is identical to **c$**. After the command is given, the last character that will be replaced is indicated by a $ sign (in the case of **cˆ**, the cursor position is adjusted too). The new text you type in can be shorter than, or longer than the text you are replacing. It can contain RETURN characters, in which case you create new lines of text. You signal the end of text entry by typing ESC, as usual.

Another cursor positioning command that the **d** and **c** operators can be applied to is the "find character" command. There are actually four of these, as we discussed earlier. **f** and **t** find characters forward, **F** and **T** find characters backward on the line. Let's take an example from way back:

```
The source code for the program is in the file
/aa/widget/henry/progs/c/thingummy.c.  Documentation
is in directory /aa/widget/henry/docs - thingspec
is the specification, it needs to be formatted
using -ms; thinguser is the user's guide, it also
requires -ms.
```

If we want to change the full pathname of the program into a simple filename, we can do this with a **d5f/** command; this deletes everything from the current cursor position, up to and including the fifth / character. So the second line looks like this:

```
thingummy.c.  Documentation
```

We could also have put the count in front of the **d** operator: **5df/** does the same thing. **df5/** will not work, however, because that is telling **vi** to delete characters up to "5". There is no character "5" on that line, so **vi** beeps at you before you get a chance to type the "/".

The difference between **f** and **t** becomes important when applying the **d** and **c** operators. Suppose that we decided to use this method of deleting the remainder of the sentence containing the full pathname. If we say **dfD** what we end up with is:

```
ocumentation.
```

We should in fact have used a **dtD** command. The **f** and **F** commands include the character they find. The **t** and **T** commands are exclusive (in either direction) of the character specified.

Changing things is similar. For example, to change the full path-name of the program, we would say something like "**c5t/** /ab/blivet/ joe/c-progs<ESC>". We used **t** rather than **f** for the change, it saves us one keystroke (big deal) because we don't have to enter the final "/". As usual, the last character that will be replaced is marked with a $ sign, and in the case of **F** and **T** the position of the cursor is adjusted.

8.2.11.2 Operating on Whole Lines   Whole lines can be deleted or changed, by the simple expedient of typing the **d** or **c** operator twice. Thus the command **dd** deletes one line, the line that the cursor is positioned on. The cursor is left sitting at the beginning of the line after the deleted line. Several lines can be deleted by giving a count, for example **10dd** deletes the current line and the following nine lines.

If you are working on an intelligent terminal, or if you have the "redraw" option set, the lines following the deleted lines will shuffle up the screen to take the place of the deleted ones. However, if you are using a dumb terminal without the "redraw" option set, this does not happen. Instead, the deleted lines are displayed as lines consisting only of the @ character in the first column. So that if you have:

```
He served out some grog with a liberal hand,
 And bade them sit down on the beach:
And they could not but own that their Captain looked grand,
 As he stood and delivered his speech.
```

then after typing a command of **2dd**, the screen will look like this:

```
He served out some grog with a liberal hand,
@
@
As he stood and delivered his speech.
```

Mostly this is no inconvenience, but if you have done many deletions in the same window of text, the remaining text may become rather sparse on the screen. At this point you may wish to redraw the screen, this can be done by typing control-R.

Changing lines is similar, **cc** changes one line, while **5cc** changes five lines. The effect of a **5cc** command is the same as that of the commands **5ddO**, that is, 5 lines are deleted, then a line is opened up with the cursor at the beginning of it. At this point, you type the text for the new line or lines, text entry is stopped in the usual fashion by typing ESC. As with delete, exactly what you see on the display depends on your terminal type and the setting of the "redraw" option.

8.2.11.3 Search Strings The **df** command deleted parts of lines between the cursor and a specified character. An extension of that is the ability to delete lines up to a specified character string (which may be expressed as a pattern, our old friend regular expressions). If we have the text:

```
He served out some grog with a liberal hand,
  And bade them sit down on the beach:
And they could not but own that their Captain looked grand,
  As he stood and delivered his speech.

`Friends, Romans, and countrymen, lend me your ears!´
  (They were all of them fond of quotations:
So they drank to his health, and they gave him three cheers,
  While he served out additional rations.)
```

and we type the command "**d/** he <ESC>", the text between the current cursor position and the next word "he" is deleted to give:

```
He served out some grog with a liberal hand,
  And bade them sit down on the beach:
And they could not but own that their Captain looked grand,
  As he served out additional rations.)
```

After you have typed the **d/**, the "/" character appears on the last line of the screen. The search string is echoed as you type it, so you can check it and correct it if necessary.

You can do the same thing with a backward search:

```
He served out some grog with a liberal hand,
  And bade them sit down on the beach:
And they could not but own that their Captain looked grand,
  As he stood and delivered his speech.

`Friends, Romans, and countrymen, lend me your ears!´
  (They were all of them fond of quotations:
So they drank to his health, and they gave him three cheers,
  While he served out additional rations.)
```

After typing the command "**d?**they <ESC>" the result is:

```
He served out some grog with a liberal hand,
  And bade them sit down on the beach:
And they drank to his health, and they gave him three cheers,
  While he served out additional rations.)
```

Notice that the deletion is always to the start of the string that is found. So the specified string is not included in the deleted material for forward searches, but is deleted on backward searches.

Changes can also be made with a **c/** (or **c?**) command, followed by a search string. When you do this, you have to type ESC twice, once to terminate the search string, and again to finish text input.

8.2.11.4 Position Markers
Another way of specifying changes or deletions that can cover many lines, is to make use of character positions previously marked with the **m** command. As we have seen, there are two ways of getting at these positions: with ` (the grave accent) and with ' (apostrophe). The difference is shown in the following examples. Suppose we have the text:

```
They sought it with thimbles, they sought it with care;
   They pursued it with forks and hope;
They threatened its life with a railway share;
   They charmed it with smiles and soap.
```

and that we mark the "w" of "with" on the third line with the letter "z". We do this by placing the cursor over that letter and typing **mz**. If we move the cursor over the "w" of "with" on the second line, and give the command **d`z** (using the grave accent) the result is:

```
They sought it with thimbles, they sought it with care;
   They pursued it with a railway share;
   They charmed it with smiles and soap.
```

whereas if we used the command **d'z** (using the apostrophe) from the same position, we would get:

```
They sought it with thimbles, they sought it with care;
   They charmed it with smiles and soap.
```

The ` deletes from the current cursor position up to, but not including, the marked position. The partial lines left by this are joined together. The ' command deletes whole lines from the current line up to and including the line containing the marked position.

In these examples we have deleted text when the cursor has been before the marked position. Deletions can also be done when the cursor is after the marked position. If we marked the "s" of the *first* "sought" on line 1 with the letter "x", then moved the cursor on to the beginning of "charmed" in the last line, the command **d`x** would produce:

```
They charmed it with smiles and soap.
```

The **change** operator can also be applied to the ` and ' commands. **c`x** means "change all text between here and the place marked 'x'", if the cursor is before the marked place. If the marked place is before the cursor position, the meaning becomes "change all text between the place marked 'x' and here". In either event, the new text to replace the old text is then typed, terminated by ESC as usual.

The use of marks is very useful when you have large amounts of text to delete or change. It is relatively simple to find the beginning of the text you want deleted, mark it, find the end of the text, then issue the delete command. This is especially so when the text to be deleted or changed covers many windows on the file. It is less prone to error than using search strings, since you can pin-point exactly where you want the limits of the action, and don't have to rely on correctly specifying a character string or regular expression.

8.2.11.5 Joining Lines Together   In an earlier paragraph we told you that the "gobble" command **x** would not gobble characters beyond the end of line. Although you can split one line into two by finding a suitable space character and replacing it with a carriage-return, you can't reverse the process and join two lines together by **x**-ing out the carriage-return.

There is a special command for joining lines together. It is the **J** (for **Join**) command. This is an uppercase "J"; lowercase "j" moves the cursor down one line, on most terminals. When you issue the **J** command, the cursor can be anywhere on the line. The effect of the command is that two lines, the one the cursor is sitting on and the one following it, are joined together to form one line. So if you have:

```
The good,
and the bad,
and the ugly
```

the result of the command will be:

```
The good, and the bad,
and the ugly
```

Notice that **vi** automatically provides the necessary space between the last word on the first line and the first word on the second line. If the end of the first line is an end of sentence indicator, such as **.** or **!** or **?**, then **vi** will provide two spaces. In some contexts, the spaces provided by **vi** are inappropriate. In this case you have to get rid of them by using the **x** command; the cursor is left in just the correct place for issuing this command.

The **J** command can be given a preceding count, in this case the specified number of lines is joined together, instead of just two. So if our command had been **3J** rather than simply **J**, we would have got:

```
The good, and the bad, and the ugly
```

All three lines are joined together to make one line.

8.2.12 Cut and Paste and Copy Operations

Very often updating text, whether it be documentation or program, involves more than simple changes, additions, and deletions. Text needs to be rearranged, chunks of it need to be moved from one place to another.

When you have lots of text which is very much repetitive, with only minor changes in each repetition, it is nice to be able to just copy the first one, then make those minor changes.

Both of these things can be achieved in **vi** by using the **delete** operator, which we have already described, and two new commands "yank" and "put". Another feature of **vi** that aids cut and paste operations, is the presence of named buffers.

8.2.12.1 Moving Text with 'delete' and 'put'   Let's start off with an example. Suppose we take the first two verses of Robert Herrick's poem:*

```
The glorious lamp of heaven, the sun,
   The higher he's a-getting,
The sooner will his race be run,
   And nearer he's to setting.

Gather ye rosebuds wihle ye may,
   Old Time still is a-flying:
And this same flower that smiles to-day
   To-morrow will be dying.
```

If you check with your poetry book, you will see that we have put these verses in the wrong order. The problem is to correct this situation. Obviously we can remove the "first" verse and the following

---

* For the unliterary, the title of this poem is "To the Virgins, to make much of Time"

blank line by the command **5dd**, but do we have to retype them after the last blank line? The answer is no. When you delete something in **vi** it doesn't go away completely, at least not immediately. It goes into a buffer, from which it can be retrieved by a "put" command. This buffer is called the "un-named" buffer in order to distinguish it from the "named" buffers which we discuss below. It behaves in a different manner from the named buffers, as we shall show.

What the "put" commands do depends on the way the text was placed into the un-named buffer. If the text was deleted as whole lines, it is put back as whole lines. The lowercase **p** command puts the lines back after the current line. Uppercase **P** puts the lines before the current line.

In our example, we deleted five whole lines. To get them to the place we want them, we must move the cursor down to the last line (which is a blank line), then give the command **p**:

```
Gather ye rosebuds wihle ye may,
   Old Time still is a-flying:
And this same flower that smiles to-day
   To-morrow will be dying.

The glorious lamp of heaven, the sun,
   The higher he's a-getting,
The sooner will his race be run,
   And nearer he's to setting.
```

After we deleted the first five lines, the cursor was placed on the line starting "Gather". There is a spelling mistake in that line. Suppose that we had at that point corrected the mistake, by moving the cursor forward three words and then retyping the word correctly with the command "**cw**while<ESC>". Then, when we moved the cursor to the last line and gave the **p** command, what we would have gotten is:

```
The glorious lamp of heaven, the sun,
   The higher he's a-getting,
The sooner will his race be run,
   And nearer he's to setting.
wihle
```

which is not what we wanted. The cause of the trouble is that the **cw** command that we did, is the equivalent of a **dw** command followed by some text entry. The named buffer always contains the last thing that was deleted. So the "put" commands always put the last thing that was deleted, in this case the incorrectly spelled word "wihle".

The moral is: once you have deleted something, always put it in its new place immediately, ignoring all distractions. This is not easy to achieve when the new place is not in the window. As you are scrolling through the file, you are very likely to notice typos and we all know that it's best to correct a typo as soon as you see it (you might not notice it a second time). If you are moving text a long way from its original place, it is best to use the named buffers, which we describe below.

The word we put appeared, not on the line following the last blank line, but on the blank line itself. This is because it was a word deletion. When dealing with text objects, rather than whole lines, the actions of the put commands are different. In this case, **p** puts the objects back after the cursor, **P** puts them back before the cursor.

Let's illustrate this by correcting yet another error in the poem as we have typed it. We have the line:

```
Old Time still is a-flying:
```

The words "still" and "is" are in the wrong order. We can correct this by placing the cursor at the beginning of the first misordered word, as shown, and typing the sequence of commands **dwwP**, to give the result:

```
Old Time is still a-flying:
```

The **dw** deletes "still" and the space following it, the cursor is left at the beginning of the second word, **w** moves to the next word, and **P** puts the deleted text before the cursor. We use **P** rather than **p** because **p** wouldn't give the right spacing.

8.2.12.2 Character Transposition This is really just a special case of delete and put, we are putting it in a separate paragraph for emphasis.

In the example in the last paragraph, we had misspelled "while" as "wihle". Character transposition is a very common form of typing error, and the simplest way of correcting it is not obvious. The obvious way is to replace (or **R**eplace) the two characters in the right order. However, unless you have a long word, it's almost as easy to retype the whole thing, as we did in the example.

The easy way to make the correction, is to place the cursor over the first of the two transposed characters, then give the command **xp**. The **x** deletes the first character, and leaves cursor sitting on the second character. The deleted character has gone into the un-named buffer, the **p** puts it back in the word after the second character, so reversing the order of the two characters.

Simple, once you know how.

8.2.12.3 Copying Text with 'yank' and 'put' Some documents have
the same text appearing in many places. For instance, if you are
writing a user guide to a text editor, you might use the same text in
all, or most, of your examples. Suppose you were given the task of
entering the following verses:

```
Old McDonald had a farm,
and on that farm he had some cows.
With a moo-moo here and a moo-moo there,
here a moo, there a moo, everywhere a moo-moo....

Old McDonald had a farm,
and on that farm he had some ducks.
With a quack-quack here and a quack-quack there,
here a quack, there a quack, everywhere a quack-quack,
here a moo, there a moo, everywhere a moo-moo....
```

and so on for all umpty-ump verses.

Obviously, you wouldn't want to type every character, because the
stuff is repetitive with only minor changes. So you start off by typing just the first verse. Now you want to copy it. We know that if
you move the cursor to the end and "put", you will get the contents
of the buffer appended to the file. But how do you get things into
the buffer without deleting them? The answer lies in the "yank"
command.

"Yank" is actually an operator. Like **d** and **c** it can be applied to
text objects and other things. So for example, **yw** yanks the following word into the unnamed buffer. We can make use of that when
were constructing the first verse. If we enter the first three lines
and just a part of the last:

```
Old McDonald had a farm,
and on that farm he had some cows.
With a moo-moo here and a moo-moo there,
here a moo
```

we can now move to the beginning of that last line and yank three
words with **y3W** (or **3yW**), then move to the end of the line and
repeat those three words twice with **pp**. The last line now looks like:

```
here a moo,here a moo,here a moo
```

The first "put" command didn't destroy the contents of the buffer, so that we can put them again with another **p** command. In fact we can repeat them as many times as we like by issuing the appropriate number of **p**'s (or **P**'s). After the initial put command, we can't repeat it with the **.** command. When used after **p** or **P**, the "repeat last change" command works differently from usual, and doesn't simply put the same thing again.

It is an easy matter to use **i** to insert " everyw" before the last "here", and " t" before the middle "here", and **s** to add the other bits at the end of the line, to give the final line of the verse:

```
Old McDonald had a farm,
and on that farm he had some cows.
With a moo-moo here and a moo-moo there,
here a moo, there a moo, everywhere a moo-moo...▓
```

Now that we have the first verse, we can get the second verse by making a copy of it and making some minor modifications to the copy.

As with the other operators, doubling **y** makes it affect lines, so **yy** yanks the whole of the current line. In addition, there is a command **Y** which is the equivalent of **yy**. So, after we position the cursor to the start of the first line, we can yank the first verse, plus the following blank line, into the buffer with the command **5yy** or with **5Y**. Then we can move to the last line and make a copy of the verse, to give:

```
Old McDonald had a farm,
and on that farm he had some cows.
With a moo-moo here and a moo-moo there,
here a moo, there a moo, everywhere a moo-moo....

Old McDonald had a farm,
and on that farm he had some cows.
With a moo-moo here and a moo-moo there,
here a moo, there a moo, everywhere a moo-moo....
```

It is a relatively simple matter to do the changes necessary to turn "cows" into "ducks" and "moo" into "quack". The second verse also repeats a line of the first verse, so we go back and yank it, then put it in the appropriate place in the second verse.

To get the third verse, we yank the first one again, put it at the end of the file, make the necessary changes, and so on ad nauseam. We have to go back and yank the first verse again, because the changes we did in the meantime have destroyed the buffer that it was yanked into.

An alternative approach would have been to make as many copies of the first verse as were required in total in the first place, then go back and alter them, instead of altering them on the fly as we did.

Of course, if you used a named buffer for the initial yank, you could put it again at any time, regardless of any changes you had done in the meantime. In our particular example, to get the third verse, it probably makes more sense to take a copy of the second verse, and alter that to form the third.

Although we have only shown examples of the yank operator used for words and whole lines, it works on other things too, just like the the delete and change operators. For example, **y**) yanks all text to the end of sentence; **y^** yanks everything from the beginning of line to the current cursor position; **y2f;** yanks everything from the cursor position to the second following semicolon.

8.2.12.4 Named Buffers We have seen that the un-named buffer always contains the last text that was deleted, or changed, or yanked. In order to copy text once it has been placed in the buffer, it must be put immediately, there must be no other changes in between. Also, you cannot transfer text from one file to another in this way, because each time you call up a new file into the edit buffer, the un-named buffer gets cleared. Both these shortcomings can be circumvented by using named buffers.

There are 26 named buffers, with allocated single-character names 'a' through 'z'. The buffers are accessed by the notation **"**x, where x is the name of the buffer to be addressed.

For example, to yank 3 lines into the buffer named 'a', we issue the command **"a3yy**. We can them make a copy of those lines by moving the cursor to the appropriate position and typing **"ap**. Any number of other changes can intervene, so long as they don't affect the buffer named 'a'.

The notation **"**X), where X is an uppercase letter, has the effect of appending deleted or yanked text to one of the named buffers. For example **"Add** deletes a line of text from the file being edited, and appends it to the text already in the buffer named 'a'. Using upper-case letters only has meaning when getting text into the named buffers, when putting the text, 'A' is the same as 'a'.

The contents of the named buffers are preserved when you change the file you are editing. So you can copy lines from one file to another by yanking them into one of the named buffers, then changing the file by ":e otherfile", then putting the lines from the named buffer in the appropriate place.

8.3 Summary

If you have made it through this chapter and are still with us, congratulations! The **ex** and **vi** editors provide one of the more complex text editors in the world of UNIX systems. They are not easy to learn, but once learned, they are a powerful tool.

By now, you have at your disposal most of the power of the UNIX system for creating, rearranging, and generally hacking about with text files. If you have recently arrived on small systems from the mainframe world, be aware that a good screen editor, on a responsive system, can enormously improve your productivity.

Of course we did not cover all that **ex** and **vi** can do. We simplified a lot, so it is up to you to explore further. Read the various papers on the **ex** and **vi** text editors. Create some files and experiment with changing them. When you get to the point where your fingers are doing the thinking, you will be using **vi** effectively.

In the next two chapters, we describe the facilities that the UNIX system provides for computer-aided documentation.

9 Formatting Documents

In this chapter and in chapter 10 we talk about utilities for formatting documents. Most of the UNIX system's word processing capabilities revolve around "text formatters", the widely known ones being the **nroff** and **troff** processors. There are a number of supporting facilities in addition to these two.

Before we start in to text formatting, we would like to point out the differences between text formatters and word processors, and their relative strengths and weaknesses. In a word processor, text is entered and formatted by the same program. Text entry commands and text formatting commands are typed on the terminal keyboard. The formatted document is displayed on the terminal screen. The effects of this are often termed "what you see is what you get". A word processor to some extent simulates a typewriter.

With a text formatter, text entry and text formatting are two separate and independent operations. A text file is first prepared, usually using a text editor such as **ed** (or **ex**, or **vi**, or any other editor). The file consists of text to be formatted, interspersed with formatting instructions which control the layout of the final text. This file is then passed to the text formatter, which obeys the formatting instructions contained in the file. The result of the formatting process is a finished document.

The major advantage of word processors is that what you see on the screen is an exact representation of the finished document; the dividing line between entering the text and formatting the text is not apparent. However, there are disadvantages to word processors. In general, a word processor cannot handle large documents of more than a few tens of pages. We know that some people write large manuals and even whole books with word processors, but the process gets painful for large manuscripts. Sometimes a change, such as deleting a sentence or inserting a new one, in the early part of a document can require that the whole document has to be reformatted. A change in the overall structure of the formatting requirements (for example, a changed indentation depth) will also mean that the whole document has to be reformatted. Word processors, in general, cannot cope with automatic chapter and section numbering (of the kind you see in this book), neither can they generate the table of contents automatically. These tasks have to be done manually, and are a potential source of error.

Word processors are eminently suitable for memos and letters, and can handle short documents of, say, up to ten pages. But a larger document requires use of a text formatter.

The disadvantages of text formatters are that you have to run them to find out what the final result will look like. Many people find the idea of embedded "formatting commands" foreign, as they do the idea of two separate processes (an edit followed by a run of the formatter) to get the final document.

The text processing facilities of the UNIX system evolved at a time when there were no such things as word processors, but only hard copy devices. The design of the formatters is to a large extent based upon this historical legacy.

There are several formatters available on the UNIX system. There is a primitive formatter called **roff**, a more advanced formatter called **nroff**, and an advanced program called **troff**, which produces output for a photo-typesetter. **nroff** and **troff** are the "standard" formatters supplied with the UNIX system. Some installations support other, more powerful, formatters such as Scribe (from UNILOGIC) and TEX (from Stanford University).

The most commonly used formatter on the UNIX system is **nroff**, which is what we describe in this chapter. In chapter 10 we describe some of the other facilities that are available for use in conjunction with **nroff**.

The derivation of the name **nroff** goes something like this:

Once upon a time there was a formatter called "runoff", so called because people would say "I will run off a copy" when they intended to format and print a document. On the UNIX system this was abbreviated to **roff**, and a formatter of this name still exists. Then a new improved version was made, called "newroff". This was followed by yet a newer version, but "newerroff" is a very cumbersome name, so it was abbreviated to **nroff**.

We don't guarantee the authenticity of this history, but it's close, and it's as good an explanation of the name as any.

9.1 Basic Ideas of 'nroff'

The **nroff** text formatter reads an input file containing unformatted text which is to be formatted so as to produce a neatly laid out document. First you prepare the input file, using the editor of your choice, then you format that text with an **nroff** command line that looks like this:

```
$ nroff manuscript | lpr
$
```

The **nroff** command formats the document called *'manuscript'*, ready for printing on a line printer. Since **nroff** normally generates its results to the Standard Output, you must either pipe the result to **lpr**, as we show here, or redirect the results to a file for printing later.

The input file might, or might not, contain **nroff** "requests" interspersed with the text to be formatted. In the absence of any formatting requests, **nroff**'s basic action is to tidy up the input to produce neatly formatted output. It makes all output lines the same length, as far as possible, and adjusts the spacing so as to make both the left and right margins regular. However, if you leave blank lines in the input they are transferred to the output. If you put leading spaces on a line, they are also transferred to the output. So if you type paragraphs separated by blank lines, with the first line indented five spaces, the output from **nroff** is also paragraphs separated by blank lines, with the first line of each paragraph indented five spaces. But the paragraphs produced by **nroff** look much neater than those you typed. Later in this chapter we show an example of input to **nroff** without any formatting requests, and the formatted version. This example shows how **nroff** tidies up your typing.

There is more to formatting a manuscript than this, however, and **nroff** provides very tight control over the final appearance of a document. **nroff** lets you select your page size: number of lines on the page, length of the lines, size of margins. You can select your text to be both left and right justified, or some other layout, or you can tell **nroff** to leave it exactly as you typed it. You have complete control over indentation, so you can have any style of paragraphing that you require. **nroff** can center headings, and underline things. With the help of "macros" you can get footnotes, automatic page numbering and titles, automatic paragraph numbering, and automatic generation of table of contents.

nroff accepts very low level formatting requests. For example, when you begin a new paragraph you might want to take the following steps:

1. leave one or more blank lines

2. make sure that you don't get an "orphan" (that is, the first line of the paragraph at the bottom of a page and the rest of it on the next page).

3. indent the first line of the paragraph by 5 spaces

You have to specify each of these steps separately to **nroff**, you can't simply say "start a new paragraph". However, **nroff** does give you the capability to design your own high-level formatting instructions. So you could create for yourself a "start new paragraph" request, which could be made up of some, or all, of the steps outlined above, plus anything else you wanted to do at each new paragraph. Such a self-made request is called a "macro".

Macro definitions can be quite complex. There are available several sets of macros that have already been defined. These are called "macro packages", and we describe some of them in chapter 10. Because fairly important things like page numbering are not automatically done by **nroff**, it is usual to use such a macro package which will provide the basics. However, it is still important to know the low-level **nroff** requests because you will need to use these in conjunction with the macros.

In this chapter we will show you how to use **nroff** to do fairly simple things. We do not go into details of how to design macros for paragraph numbering, footnotes and such, but we show you a fairly simple macro for page numbers. For more details of the formatter, refer to "**nroff/troff** User's Manual" by Joseph F. Ossanna.

9.2 Format of nroff Requests

An **nroff** "request" is embedded in the text of the document to be formatted. Requests control the overall layout of the formatted document, or establish conditions for the formatter itself. Each request to **nroff** must appear by itself at the beginning of a line. A request cannot appear on the same line as the text to be formatted (although sometimes part of the text to be formatted can be given as an argument to a request).

A formatting request consists of a basic **nroff** instruction, or a call to an **nroff** macro, optionally followed by one or more arguments separated by spaces.

An **nroff** instruction consists of a period or "dot" (.), followed by one or two characters. There is an alternative form of **nroff** instruction that starts with a single quote (') rather than the dot. We explain what this means when we talk about text filling.

Here are some examples showing what **nroff** requests look like:

```
.pl 72
.po 8
.bp
.in 5
.ti -3
.in +5
.ce 4
'ul
.AU
.IP "first stanza:" 14
```

The last two examples are macro references. The remainder are basic **nroff** instructions.

A reference to an **nroff** macro looks exactly the same as a regular **nroff** instruction. All **nroff** instructions consist of lower case letters. Conventionally, macro packages (such as the **ms** macro package) use uppercase letters to distinguish them from the basic **nroff** instructions. Note that this is only a convention; some macro packages might ignore it and use lowercase letters for the macros.

In all our examples we show a space between the instruction and any numerical value that an argument may take. In practice, it is not necessary to have the space between the request and the first argument. Some of the above examples could have been written:

```
.pl72
.po8
.ce4
```

These work just as well, but are not so easy to read. We use spaces in our examples for enhanced readability.

The form that the arguments can take depend on the instruction or macro, but in many cases the arguments are numeric. There are three different possible forms of numeric arguments. A number may be given as an unsigned number, this means that it is to be taken as an absolute value. For instance,

```
.in 4
```

means indent the margin 4 spaces.

An argument may also be a number preceded by a plus sign or a minus sign. This means a change relative to the existing value of whatever it is you're altering. For example

```
.in +4
```

means indent the margin 4 spaces more than what it is now, and similarly

```
.in -5
```

means back off that indent by 5 spaces.

9.3 Specifying Page Layout

The page size that **nroff** provides is intended to fit U.S. letter size paper. There are 66 lines on each page, each line being 65 characters long. The line length is such that there is room for a margin on both sides of the paper, but **nroff** doesn't provide a left margin.

9.3.1 Setting the Page Offset

nroff starts off with the left-hand edge of the printing right up against the left-hand edge of the paper. This is not normally a desirable situation, since you usually want some margin on the left side of the paper. The **.po** request changes the **p**age **o**ffset, which is the distance between the left-hand edge of the paper and the left-hand edge of the printing. For instance,

```
.po 8
```

sets the page offset to 8 characters. This is a reasonable value for the page offset, it gives more or less equal left and right margins with the default line length.

The current page offset can be changed by giving a number preceded by a plus sign or a minus sign. For example **.po +2** increases the left margin by 2 spaces, and **.po −5** reduces the left margin by 5 spaces. If you do not supply any argument to the **.po** request the page offset is reset to what it was before you last changed it.

You will almost certainly want to change the default value of 0, unless you are using a macro package which includes a reasonable page offset. Some macro packages adjust the margins to be different on even and odd pages, so that the resulting document is suitable for double-sided copying.

Once you have set the page offset for a document, you should not change it except under very unusual circumstances. One situation where you might need to adjust the page offset temporarily is if you have a table or diagram which is wider than the normal line length, in that case you may need to ease the left margin a little more leftwards.

9.3.2 Setting the Line Length

The **.ll** request alters the line length. The line length and the page offset together determine the width of the right margin. The length of the lines of text produced by **nroff** can be set to a given value:

```
.ll 60
```

sets the length of each line to 60 characters. Alternatively, the line length can be increased or decreased: **.ll +5** increases the length of each line by 5 characters, and **.ll −20** reduces the line length by 20 characters.

Omitting the argument to the **.ll** request sets the line length to what it was before you last changed it.

You may wish to change the line length, depending on the layout of the text you are formatting. For example, if you want to shrink both margins, you would use **.ll** and also adjust either the page offset or the indentation depth.

9.3.3 Setting the Page Length

The **.pl** request adjusts the **page length** of the printed page. You can set the page length to 72 lines, which fits European A4 size paper, by this request:

```
.pl 72
```

The current page length can be changed: **.pl −6** reduces the number of lines on a page by 6, and **.pl +10** increases the number of lines on a page by 10.

Omitting the argument to the **.pl** request resets the page length to its standard value of 66 lines per page.

You will probably never want to change the page length unless you have to use a different size of paper.

☛ If the number of lines on a page do not match the physical size of the paper you are using, your output will probably be a mess.

9.3.4 Changing the Page Number

nroff does not automatically provide page breaks and page numbering. This must be done under control of a macro, either one you have defined yourself (we show you how later), or by using a macro package. However, the current page number is kept in a "page number register", which is incremented each time a pageful of formatted text has been created.

The **.pn** request alters the value of the **page number** held in the page number register:

```
.pn 23
```

sets the value in the register to 23; **.pn +1** adds one to the page number in the register, and **.pn −2** subtracts 2 from the page number register.

If you enter a **.pn** request with no argument **nroff** just ignores the request completely, with no effect on the page number register.

When **nroff** starts work on a document, the initial value of the page number register is set to 1.

9.3.5 Producing Page Breaks

You can do your own page breaks by inserting the **.bp** request to begin a new page at strategic points in your document:

```
.bp
```

simply starts a new page. **nroff** produces enough blank lines to fill the current page, and continues the formatted text output on a new page. The page number register is incremented. You will probably want to follow this with some blank lines to form a top margin, unless you have a macro to provide automatic page control. Even when you are using macros to give automatic page breaks, **.bp** can be used to force the start of a new page.

You can specify the page number at which the new page is to start, by giving an argument to the request: **.bp 10** starts a new page and sets the page number register to 10. If the number given to **.bp** is preceded by a plus sign or minus sign, the page number register is incremented or decremented by that amount when the new page is started.

9.3.6 Keeping Blocks of Text Together

Sometimes you have the situation where you want to make sure that some lines will all appear on the same page. A table of figures, for instance, should not start at the bottom of one page and be continued on the next.

The **.ne** request tells **nroff** that you **ne**ed the next **N** lines all to appear on the same page. So a request like this:

```
.ne 5
```

starts a new page if there are less than 5 lines left on the current page.

A **.ne** request with no argument is taken to be **.ne 1**, which has the same action as if the **.ne** request wasn't there.

Most macro packages provide a "new paragraph" macro which uses the **.ne** request to avoid orphans.

9.4 Filling and Adjusting Text Lines

Perhaps the most important reason for using **nroff** is to use its filling and adjusting capabilities. Filling means that **nroff** produces output lines that are all as long as they can be without overflowing the line length. Filling continues until something happens to break the filling process, such as a blank line in the text.

Adjusting means that filled lines are then padded with spaces between words so that both the left and the right margins come out straight.

Suppose your input looks like this:

```
On the edge of a great forest lived
a poor woodcutter with his wife and two children.
The boy's name was Hansel and the girl's name was Gretel.
They had little enough of crust or crumb,
and once, when there was great famine in the land,
they could not even find their daily bread.
```

In all the examples we show in this chapter, we have set the line-length to 55 characters (so as to set the examples off from the body of this chapter). Given the above input text and a 55 character line-length, **nroff** will fill these lines to look like this:

```
On the edge of a great forest lived a poor woodcutter
with his wife and two children.  The boy's name was
Hansel and the girl's name was Gretel.  They had little
enough of crust or crumb, and once, when there was
great famine in the land, they could not even find
their daily bread.
```

Notice that **nroff** is clever enough to put two spaces after a period at the end of a sentence. It will do the same after the other sentence terminators like "?" and "!". The output produced by filling is some-times called "flush left, ragged right", or simply "ragged right".

Adjusting, in **nroff**, usually means justification. The spacing be-tween words in the filled output lines, is adjusted to completely fill the line length. This produces straight (flush) margins on both the right and left edges of the printing. If we asked **nroff** to justify our document, the results, (for 55 character line length) would look like this:

```
On the edge of a great forest lived a  poor  woodcutter
with  his  wife  and  two children.  The boy's name was
Hansel and the girl's name was Gretel.  They had little
enough  of  crust  or  crumb,  and once, when there was
great famine in the land,  they  could  not  even  find
their daily bread.
```

Justification implies filling — it makes no sense to adjust lines with-out also filling them. Notice that the last line is not justified. Justi-fication stops when a break occurs in the filling process.

In the absence of any other information, **nroff**'s standard behavior is to fill lines and adjust for straight left and right margins, so it is quite possible to create a neatly formatted document which only con-tains lines of text, and no formatting requests.

You can ask **nroff** to adjust the position of your lines in four differ-ent ways. One way is both margins straight, which we have just described. Another way is the "flush left, ragged right", which is what you get when you have filling without adjusting. A third way is the reverse of that, "flush right, ragged left", so your output would look like this:

```
    On the edge of a great forest lived a poor woodcutter
      with his wife and two children.  The boy's name was
Hansel and the girl's name was Gretel.  They had little
      enough of crust or crumb, and once, when there was
      great famine in the land, they could not even find
                                      their daily bread.
```

The fourth way is to have each line centered, this gives both left and right ragged margins:

```
 On the edge of a great forest lived a poor woodcutter
   with his wife and two children.  The boy's name was
Hansel and the girl's name was Gretel.  They had little
   enough of crust or crumb, and once, when there was
   great famine in the land, they could not even find
                       their daily bread.
```

This last method is an unusual way of formatting text, and you probably won't use it very often. Mostly you use centering only for headings. There is a separate **nroff** request for centering, described under "Centering and Underlining".

9.4.1 No Adjusting

If you don't specify otherwise, **nroff** justifies your text so that both left and right margins are straight. This can be changed if necessary, and one way is to request no adjusting at all, with the **.na** request:

```
.na
```

requests **n**o **a**djust. Adjusting of output lines is turned off.

Output lines will still be filled, providing that filling hasn't also been turned off (see **.nf** below). If filling is still on, **nroff** produces flush left, ragged right output.

9.4.2 Specifying Adjusting Styles

The **.ad** (**ad**just) request specifies one of the four different methods, described above, for adjusting text:

```
.ad l
```

produces flush left, ragged right output, which is the same as filling with no adjustment. The

```
.ad  r
```

request produces flush right, ragged left output, and the

```
.ad  c
```

request centers each output line, giving both left and right ragged margins. Finally either of the requests:

```
.ad  b
.ad  n
```

(**b** for **b**oth, or **n** for **n**ormal) gives complete justification of both left and right margins.

```
.ad
```

on its own simply turns on adjusting of lines in the last mode requested.

It makes no sense to try to adjust lines when they are not being filled, so if filling is off when a **.ad** request is seen, the adjusting is deferred until filling is turned on again.

9.4.3 Turning Filling On and Off

The **.nf** (**n**o **f**ill) request turns off filling. Lines in the result are neither filled nor adjusted. The output text appears exactly as it was typed in, this is often called "as-is text", or "verbatim".

The **.fi** request turns on filling. If adjusting has not been turned off by a **.na** request, output lines are also adjusted in the prevailing mode set by any previous **.ad** request.

9.5 Hyphenation

When **nroff** fills lines, it takes each word in turn from the input text line, and puts it on the output text line, until it finds a word which will not fit on the output line. At this point **nroff** tries to hyphenate the word. If it can, the first part of the hyphenated word is put on the output line followed by a "-", and the remainder of the word is put on the next line.

There were no hyphenated words in our example, but had we specified a line length of 50 rather than 55, we would get:

```
On the edge of a great forest lived a  poor   wood-
cutter  with his wife and two children.  The boy's
name was Hansel and the girl's  name  was  Gretel.
They  had  little  enough  of  crust or crumb, and
once, when there was great  famine  in  the  land,
they could not even find their daily bread.
```

Now we see that the word "woodcutter" has been hyphenated. It is the only word in the short passage that does get hyphenated, but there aren't many long words in the passage. Automatic hyphenation can be turned off, in which case our example would look like:

```
On the  edge  of  a  great  forest  lived  a  poor
woodcutter  with  his  wife and two children.  The
boy's name was Hansel  and  the  girl's  name  was
Gretel.  They had little  enough of crust or crumb,
and once, when there was great famine in the land,
they could not even find their daily bread.
```

You can see that the first line has been spread out to fill the entire 50 characters, and "woodcutter" is left intact on the second line.

At this point we should emphasize that, although we have been showing the examples both filled and justified, it is the filling process that causes **nroff** to hyphenate words, not the process of adjusting.

If you have in your input text words containing a hyphen (such as jack-in-the-box, or co-worker), **nroff** will if necessary split these words over two lines, regardless of whether hyphenation is turned off.

9.5.1 Controlling Hyphenation

Normally, when you invoke **nroff**, hyphenation is turned on, but you can change this. The

```
.nh
```

request (**no hyphenation**) turns off the automatic hyphenation process. The only words that are split over more than one line are those which already contain "-". Hyphenation can be turned on again with the **.hy** request.

.hy can be given an argument to restrict the amount of hyphenation that **nroff** does. The argument is numeric. The request **.hy 2** stops **nroff** from hyphenating the last word on a page. **.hy 4** instructs **nroff** not to split the last two characters from a word; so, for example, "repeated" will never be hyphenated "repeat-ed". **.hy 8** requests the same thing for the first two characters of a word; so, for example, "repeated" will not be hyphenated "re-peated".

The values of the arguments are additive: **.hy 12** makes sure that words like "repeated" will never be hyphenated either as "repeat-ed" or as "re-peated". **.hy 14** calls up all three restrictions on hyphenation.

A **.hy 1** request is the same as the simple **.hy**, it turns on hyphenation everywhere. Finally, a **.hy 0** request is the same as the **.nh** request, it turns off automatic hyphenation altogether.

If there are words that you want **nroff** to hyphenate in some special way, you can specify them with the **.hw** request (hyphenate words). This request tells **nroff** that you have special cases it should know about, for example:

```
.hw pre-empt ant-eater
```

Now, if either of the words "preempt" or "anteater" needs to be hyphenated, they will appear as specified on the **.hw** request, regardless of what **nroff**'s usual hyphenation rules would do. If you use the **.hw** request, be aware that there is a limit of about 128 characters in total, for the list of special words.

9.5.2 Controlling Line Breaks

Earlier we said that when filling is turned on, words of text are taken from input lines and placed on output lines to make them as long as they can be without overflowing the line length, until something happens to break the filling process. When a break occurs, the current output line is printed just as it is, and a new output line is started for the following input text. There are various things that cause a break to occur:

A **.br** request   A **br**eak request can be used to make sure that the following text is started on a new line.

nroff requests   Many **nroff** requests cause a break in the filling process. However, there is an alternate format of these requests which does not cause a break. That is the format where the initial period character (**.**) in the request is replaced by the apostrophe or single quote character (**'**).

end of file   The filling process stops when the end of the input file is reached.

spaces   at the beginning of a line are significant. If there are spaces at the start of a line, **nroff** assumes you know what you are doing and that you really want spaces there. Obviously, to achieve this, the current output line must be printed and a new line begun. Avoid using tabs for this purpose, since they do not cause a break.

blank line(s)   If your input text contains any completely blank lines, **nroff** assumes you mean them. So it prints the current output line, then your blank lines, then starts the following text on a new line.

It is these last two things that enable you to take advantage of the filling and justification features provided by **nroff** without having to use any **nroff** requests in your text. Figures 9.1 and 9.2 show an example of this.

Figure 9.1 shows a memo as it was input to **nroff**. Notice that there are no formatting requests in the document at all. Figure 9.2 shows the output that **nroff** generated. You can see how the appearance has improved, merely because the lines are filled and adjusted.

9.6 Line Spacing

nroff normally produces its output single spaced, but this can be changed, either by explicit line spacing requests, or by embedded blank lines in the text.

9.6.1 Setting Line Spacing

The **.ls** request adjusts line spacing. If there is an argument of N on the request, $N-1$ blank lines appear after each line of text is produced. For example, the request:

```
.ls 2
```

sets double line spacing. There is one blank line following each line of text in the output. Similarly, **.ls 3** sets triple spacing.

A **.ls** request without any argument returns the line spacing to what it was before you last changed it.

The default value when **nroff** is invoked is equivalent to **.ls 1**, or single spacing.

```
From: Bill Williams

To: Fred Bloggs

Date: Wed Mar 17

cc: Jack Austen
    Sylvia Dawson
    Pat Manders
    Joe Mugg

Subject: Personnel Changes

    I am pleased to announce that Maryann Clark is being
transferred to our software development team,
where she will take up duties as a programming assistant,
effective next Monday, March 22nd.

    Maryann has been our department secretary for two
years, and we have all admired her cheerful efficiency.
I feel sure she will carry these qualities to her new
position.
Maryann will be attending outside classes in programming
concurrent with taking up her new tasks,
please give her all the assistance you can.
    Maryann's secretarial duties will be taken over by
Ethel Snerge.
Ethel brings considerable experience to the job,
please join me in welcoming her to our department.




                              Bill Williams
```

Figure 9.1   A Memo as Input to nroff

From: Bill Williams

To: Fred Bloggs

Date: Wed Mar 17

cc: Jack Austen
    Sylvia Dawson
    Pat Manders
    Joe Mugg

Subject: Personnel Changes

   I am pleased to announce that Maryann Clark is
being transferred to our software development team,
where she will take up duties as a programming assistant,
effective next Monday, March 22nd.

   Maryann has been our department secretary for two
years, and we have all admired her cheerful efficiency.
I feel sure she will carry these qualities to her new
position. Maryann will be attending outside classes in
programming concurrent with taking up her new tasks,
please give her all the assistance you can.

   Maryann's secretarial duties will be taken over by
Ethel Snerge. Ethel brings considerable experience to the
job, please join me in welcoming her to our department.

                    Bill Williams

Figure 9.2   The Memo After Processing by nroff

9.6.2 Generating Blank Lines

Blank lines can be produced in the output by using the **.sp** request. The appropriate number of blank lines are left in the output text. For example, a **.sp** request like this:

```
.sp 5
```

leaves five blank lines. A **.sp** request with no argument is the same as **.sp 1**, one blank line is left in the output.

Blank lines can also be produced by just leaving blank lines in the input text. The advantage to using the **.sp** request, instead of leaving blank lines in the input, is that it is easier to change. For instance, suppose you had left two blank lines before each paragraph, then decided your document would look better with three blank lines. With a text editor it is much easier to change all occurrences of ".sp 2" to ".sp 3", than it is to find all sequences of two blank lines and add another one.

To illustrate these requests, consider the following text input to **nroff**:

```
.nf
.ls 2
O what can ail thee, knight-at-arms,
Alone and palely loitering?
The sedge is wither'd from the Lake,
And no birds sing.
.ls 1
O what can ail thee knight-at-arms,
So haggard and so woe-begone?
The squirrel's granary is full,
And the harvest's done.
.sp 1
.ls
I see a lily on thy brow
With anguish moist and fever dew,
And on thy cheeks a fading rose
Fast withereth too.
```

When the above text is formatted, it produces the following output:

```
O what can ail thee, knight-at-arms,

Alone and palely loitering?

The sedge is wither'd from the Lake,

And no birds sing.


O what can ail thee knight-at-arms,
So haggard and so woe-begone?
The squirrel's granary is full,
And the harvest's done.

I see a lily on thy brow

With anguish moist and fever dew,

And on thy cheeks a fading rose

Fast withereth too.
```

In double-spacing mode (.ls 2) there is one blank line following each line of text. In single spacing, there are no blank lines. To leave a blank line between the second and third stanzas we have to deliberately say **.sp 1**. The second **.ls** request returns the line spacing to its previous value of **.ls 2**.

The **.ls** request does not cause a break in the filling process. The previous example doesn't show this, since we requested no filling. You usually only change line spacing for whole paragraphs, so there is no problem for the most part.

9.7 Centering and Underlining

The subjects of centering lines of text and underlining text are grouped together, because these two ways of dealing with text are frequently used to produce different styles of headings. Apart from that, there is no logical connection between them. In the "Nroff User's Manual" centering and underlining are described in different sections.

9.7.1 Centering Lines of Text

When we described "Filling and Adjusting", we showed how the text produced by **nroff** could be centered by using the **.ad c** request. Setting text adjustment for centering is a fairly unusual way of getting centered text. When you only want a few lines centered, it is not necessary to change your usual adjusting mode. Instead, you can use the .ce request, which centers lines of text.

If you just use a .ce request without an argument, one line is centered:

```
.ce
```

centers the following line of text, whereas:

```
.ce 5
```

centers the following five lines of text. Filling is temporarily turned off when lines are centered, so each line in the input appears as a line in the output, centered between the left and right margins. For centering purposes, the left margin includes both the page offset and any indentation that may be in effect.

An argument of zero to the .ce request simply stops the process of centering. So, if you don't want to count how many lines you want centered, you can say **.ce 100** (or some large number) before the first, then stop centering by putting **.ce 0** request after the last line you want centered.

Note that the argument to the .ce request only applies to following text lines in the input. Lines containing **nroff** requests are not counted.

The input:

```
.ll 50
.ce 3
Courtship Rituals of Old Moldavia
A Treatise
by Horace Postlethwaite
```

produces the output:

```
        Courtship Rituals of Old Moldavia
                   A Treatise
            by Horace Postlethwaite
```

If you want to space this out a bit, you could change the input text to look like this:

```
.ll 50
.ce 3
Courtship Rituals of Old Moldavia
.sp
A Treatise
by Horace Postlethwaite
```

and when that text is formatted, it generates:

```
        Courtship Rituals of Old Moldavia

                  A Treatise
            by Horace Postlethwaite
```

The **.sp** does not affect the number you give to the **.ce**; only text lines to be centered are counted.

You can stop the centering process by putting a **.ce 0** request after the **.sp** request, in which case the results look like:

```
        Courtship Rituals of Old Moldavia

    A Treatise by Horace Postlethwaite
```

Now, only the first line is centered, and the next two input lines appear on the same output line, because filling is resumed after centering stops.

9.7.2 Underlining Text

Sometimes headings are underlined, rather than centered. There are two types of underlining that **nroff** can do. The **.ul** request only underlines alphanumeric characters. As with the **.ce** request, **.ul** with no argument underlines a single line of text, so:

```
.ul
```

simply underlines the following line of text. A numeric argument to the **.ul** request specifies the number of text lines you want underlined, so:

```
.ul 3
```

underlines the next 3 lines of text. As with centering, an argument of zero (**.ul 0**) cancels the underlining process.

The other form of underlining is called up with the **.cu** request, and asks for continuous underlining. This is the same as the **.ul** request, except that *all* characters are underlined.

As with **.ce**, only lines of text to be underlined are counted in the number given to the underline request. **nroff** requests interspersed with the text lines are not counted.

The difference between the two types of underlining is shown by the following input:

```
.cu
1.0 General Introduction
.sp
.ul
1.1 Historical Background
```

which produces the output:

1.0 General Introduction

1.1 Historical Background

In the first call for underlining (the .cu request), all characters including spaces are underlined. In the second (the .ul request), only letters and numbers are underlined.

Centering and underlining can be combined, and the combination is frequently used to produce headings:

```
.ll 50
.ce 4
.cu 2
Courtship Rituals of Old Moldavia
.sp
A Treatise
by
.ul
Horace Postlethwaite
```

The above example produces this result after formatting:

Courtship Rituals of Old Moldavia
A Treatise
by
Horace Postlethwaite

Underlining is not used just for headings, but is often used in paragraphs of text to add emphasis to individual words. The input:

```
.ll 55
One thing was certain, that the
.ul
white
kitten had had nothing to do with it: it was the
.ul
black
kitten's fault entirely.
```

gives this output:

```
One thing was certain, that the white  kitten  had  had
nothing  to do with it: it was the black kitten's fault
entirely.
```

Notice that we had to arrange our input so that each of the two words we want underlined appears on a line of its own. This is because the **.ul** request underlines all of the following input line.

In some older versions of **nroff**, the underline requests cause a break in the filling process. This is one case where you would have to use the alternative form of the request, **'ul**, to indicate that filling is to continue.

Sometimes you may want to underline a whole block of text. Here is a formatted fragment of a document:

```
Since they only work a  six-hour  day,  you   may   think
there must be a shortage of essential goods.
On the contrary, those six hours are enough,  and   more
than   enough,  to  produce  plenty of everything that's
needed for a comfortable life.
```

The above formatted output was produced from the input text below:

```
.ll 55
Since they only work a six-hour day,
you may think there must be a shortage of
essential goods.
.br
.cu 4
On the contrary, those six hours are enough,
and more than enough,
to produce plenty of everything
that's needed for a comfortable life.
```

Notice that although the block of text that is underlined occupies three lines in the output, it occupies four lines in the input. It is the number of input lines which is the figure given to the underline request. When you think about it, this is a fairly obvious way to do things. Until the text has been formatted, you don't know (and usually don't care) how many lines it will occupy in the output, but you do know how many input lines it occupies.

If you don't want to count the number of input lines in the passage to be underlined, you can specify some number on the **.cu** request which you know is larger than the number of input lines, then stop the underlining process with a **.cu 0** request. If we format the following block of text:

```
.ll 55
Since they only work a six-hour day,
you may think there must be a shortage of
essential goods.
.br
.cu 10
On the contrary, those six hours are enough,
and more than enough,
to produce plenty of everything
that's needed for a comfortable life.
.cu 0
```

the result is exactly the same as in the example that went before.

9.8 Paragraphs and Indenting

Paragraphs are the basic elements of manuscripts. Most documents (other than poetry maybe) are built around paragraphs. There are various styles of paragraphing. Some of the styles are illustrated in figure 9.3.

First we show simple blocked paragraphs; then we show indented paragraphs, where the first line of each paragraph is indented by some amount. Then there is the layout where a whole paragraph is indented from the surrounding paragraphs; this is called a "display". We have shown both the display and the surrounding paragraphs as blocked, but they could also be indented paragraphs. Frequently the display paragraph is non-filled, as are the examples we use throughout this book, for instance. A variation of a display is a "quotation", where the paragraph is indented from the surrounding paragraphs on both left and right margins. Finally we show the "hanging indent" style of layout, where the whole paragraphs are indented, but

the first line of each extends to the left a little. This layout is used
for producing lists of items.

Blocked paragraphs are easy to achieve using **nroff**; you simply
insert blank lines where you want to start a new paragraph:

```
.ll 50
These people are most excellent mathematicians,
and arrived to great perfection in mechanicks,
by the countenance and encouragement of the emperor,
who is a renowned patron of learning.
.sp 1
This prince hath several machines fixed on wheels,
for the carriage of trees and other great weights.
He often buildeth his largest men of war,
whereof some are nine foot long,
in the woods where the timber grows, and has them
carried on these engines three or four hundred yards
to the sea.
.sp 1
Five hundred carpenters and engineers were immediately
set to work to prepare the greatest engine they had.
```

When the above text is formatted, it results in block paragraphs, like
this:

```
These people are  most  excellent  mathematicians,
and  arrived to great perfection in mechanicks, by
the countenance and encouragement of the  emperor,
who is a renowned patron of learning.

This prince hath several machines fixed on wheels,
for the carriage of trees and other great weights.
He often buildeth his largest men of war,  whereof
some  are  nine foot long, in the woods where  the
timber grows, and has them carried  on  these  en-
gines three or four hundred yards to the sea.

Five hundred carpenters and engineers were immedi-
ately  set  to work to prepare the greatest engine
they had.
```

To achieve the other paragraph styles, we have to use the **nroff**
indentation requests.

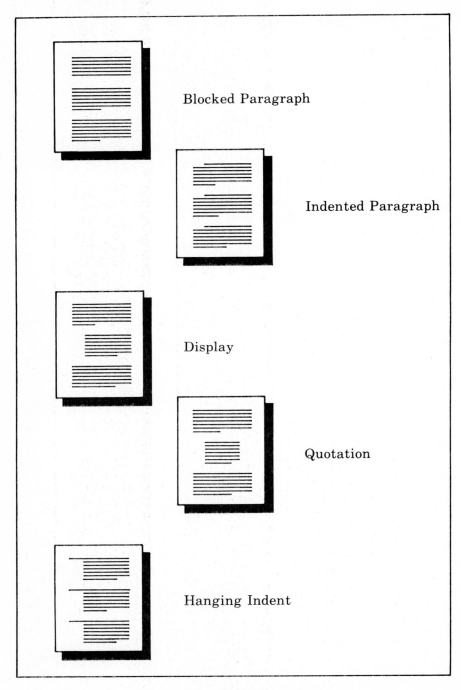

Figure 9.3   Paragraph Styles

9.8.1 Indenting Lines of Text

There are two ways to indent text. The **.in** (indent) request indents all following lines of text by a specified amount, until another indent request changes it. The **.ti** (temporary indent) request indents only the single line following the request. Both forms indent the text lines relative to the page offset.

The plain **.in** request indents the following lines in the output text by the specified number of spaces:

```
.in 5
```

indents all lines by 5 spaces from the left hand edge of the printing on the page. The argument given to the **.in** request can be relative to the previous indent. For instance **.in +5** indents all lines by 5 spaces to the right of the current indentation depth, and similarly **.in −5** indents all lines by 5 spaces to the left of the current indentation depth.

In common with many similar requests, a **.in** request with no argument makes the indentation depth revert to what it was before it was last changed.

If you type an argument of zero to the **.in** request, **.in 0**, it means that there is no indentation, and so the output text appears on the page at the position of the page offset (specified by a previous **.po** request).

When **nroff** is first invoked, the indentation depth is zero, so all lines are aligned at the page offset. The page offset is also zero at the start of a document.

The difference between page offset and indentation is illustrated in figure 9.4.

The length of the printed line includes indentation depth, but does not include page offset.

9.8.2 Temporary Indent of One Line

The **.ti** request differs from the **.in** request in that it requests a temporary indent. Only the first line of output text following the **.ti** request is indented. The remainder of the output text remains at the indentation depth set by the previous **.in** request. The interpretation of arguments to **.ti** is as described for **.in**.

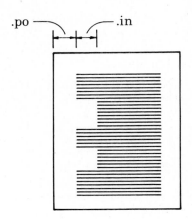

Figure 9.4   Relationships Between Page Offset and Indentation

9.8.3 Paragraph Styles

The various styles of paragraphing illustrated can be achieved by using combinations of the indent (**.in**) and temporary indent (**.ti**) requests described above.

For instance, indented paragraphs can be produced using temporary indentation. If we give **nroff** this input text:

```
.ll 50
.ti 5
These people are most excellent mathematicians,
and arrived to great perfection in mechanicks,
by the countenance and encouragement of the emperor,
who is a renowned patron of learning.
.sp 1
.ti 5
This prince hath several machines fixed on wheels,
for the carriage of trees and other great weights.
He often buildeth his largest men of war,
whereof some are nine foot long,
in the woods where the timber grows, and has them
carried on these engines three or four hundred yards
to the sea.
```

```
.sp 1
.ti 5
```
Five hundred carpenters and engineers were immediately
set to work to prepare the greatest engine they had.

This produces the formatted output:

      These people are   most   excellent   mathemati-
cians,   and arrived to great perfection in mechan-
icks, by the countenance and encouragement of   the
emperor, who is a renowned patron of learning.

      This prince hath several   machines   fixed   on
wheels,   for the carriage of trees and other great
weights. He often buildeth his   largest   men   of
war, whereof some are nine foot long, in the woods
where the timber grows, and has   them   carried   on
these   engines   three or four hundred yards to the
sea.

      Five hundred carpenters   and   engineers   were
immediately   set   to   work to prepare the greatest
engine they had.

A display, where an entire paragraph is indented from the surrounding paragraph, is achieved using the **.in** request. Consider the
following piece of formatted text:

In the opening sentence of "The   Vicar   of   Wakefield",
the leading character opines:

    "I was ever of the opinion, that   the   honest   man
who   married   and   brought   up a large family, did
more service than he who continued single and only
talked of population."

It is not known if Goldsmith was expressing the popular
feeling of his time, but if so - how things are changed
in the 200 or so years since those words were written.

This was produced from the **nroff** input:

```
.ll 55
In the opening sentence of "The Vicar of Wakefield",
the leading character opines:
.sp
.in +5
"I was ever of the opinion, that the honest man who
married and brought up a large family, did more
service than he who continued single and only talked
of population."
.in -5
.sp
It is not known if Goldsmith was expressing the
popular feeling of his time, but if so - how
things are changed in the 200 or so years since
those words were written.
```

To indent the middle paragraph we used a **.in +5** request. This takes it five spaces to the right from the current indentation depth. The current indentation depth was zero, so in this case **.in 5** would have exactly the same effect. However, using the relative form of the request is more flexible. We might decide later that all of the above text should be an insert in an outer surrounding paragraph, to get the effect shown in figure 9.5.

Figure 9.5   Nested Indented Paragraphs

Had we used the absolute form of the request in our original text, we would now have to change it to **.in 10**, whereas our relative form of the request requires no change. The same reasoning lies behind the use of **.in −5** to move the left margin back. We could also have used a plain **.in** to make the margin revert to what it was previously.

The display in our previous example is a quotation from a book. Let's reformat the text to produce a "quotation" style of paragraph, where the text is indented from both left and right margins. We achieve this by a combination of indenting and changing line length. By simply adding two **.ll** requests:

```
.11 55
```
In the opening sentence of "The Vicar of Wakefield",
the leading character opines:
```
.sp
.11 -5
.in +5
.ti -1
```
"I was ever of the opinion, that the honest man who
married and brought up a large family, did more
service than he who continued single and only talked
of population."
```
.in -5
.11
.sp
```
It is not known if Goldsmith was expressing the
popular feeling of his time, but if so - how
things are changed in the 200 or so years since
those words were written.

and the resultant output now looks like this:

In the opening sentence of "The   Vicar   of   Wakefield",
the leading character opines:

>   "I was ever of the opinion,   that   the   honest
>   man   who married and brought   up a large fami-
>   ly, did more service than   he   who   continued
>   single and only talked of population."

It is not known if Goldsmith was expressing the popular
feeling of his time, but if so - how things are changed
in the 200 or so years since those words were written.

One other small change we made was to insert a

```
.ti -1
```

to make the initial quote mark of the insert lie outside the indentation depth. This is common practice in manuscripts forms, and looks
better.

9.8.4 Lists and Descriptions

The hanging indent paragraph style is not often used exactly as
shown, except possibly when quoting poetry:

```
O what can ail thee, knight-at-arms,
    Alone and palely loitering?
    The sedge is wither'd from the Lake,
    And no birds sing.

O what can ail thee knight-at-arms,
    So haggard and so woe-begone?
    The squirrel's granary is full,
    And the harvest's done.
```

This form of document is produced by using both **.in** and **.ti** requests:

```
.nf
.in 4
.ti -4
O what can ail thee, knight-at-arms,
Alone and palely loitering?
The sedge is wither'd from the Lake,
And no birds sing.
.sp
.ti -4
O what can ail thee knight-at-arms,
So haggard and so woe-begone?
The squirrel's granary is full,
And the harvest's done.
```

However, the general layout has other possibilities. For instance, it can be used to produce an indented list of items, each item being marked with a "bullet". Consider this fragment of a formatted document:

```
In all our examples of the text formatter, we have used
a line length which is 10 or 15 spaces shorter than the
normal (default) line length.  There are   various   rea-
sons for doing this:

    - When giving formatted examples,   it   is   desirable
      that the text be of a reasonable size.  Paragraphs
      should be more than two lines, and 4 or 5 lines if
      possible.  On the other hand, we want to avoid ex-
      amples that   are   too   lengthy.   A   shorter   line
      length  helps to achieve a reasonable body of for-
      matted text with a smaller amount of input text.
```

- Examples should stand out clearly - ideally they should be "indented" from both left and right margins of the explanatory text. Using a line length which is shorter than usual achieves this without distorting the action taken by the formatter.

- By adjusting the line length, it is possible to highlight some actions taken by the formatter (for example, hyphenation) which would not occur if a "standard" line length were used.

Here we have used the hyphen character "-" as our "bullet". This formatted output is produced from the input text:

```
In all our examples of the text formatter,
we have used a line length which is 10 or 15 spaces
shorter than the normal (default) line length.
There are various reasons for doing this:
.sp
.in 5
.ti -2
- when giving formatter examples, it is desirable that
the text be of a reasonable size.
Paragraphs should be more than two lines, and 4 or 5
lines if possible.
On the other hand, we want to avoid examples that are
too lengthy.
A shorter line length helps to achieve a reasonable body
of formatted text with a smaller amount of input text.
.sp
.ti -2
- Examples should stand out clearly - ideally they
should be "indented" from both left and right margins of
the explanatory text.
Using a line length which is shorter than usual achieves
this without distorting the action taken by the
formatter.
.sp
.ti -2
- By adjusting the line length, it is possible
to highlight some actions taken by the formatter
(for example, hyphenation) which would not occur if a
"standard" line length were used.
.in -5
```

A variation of this paragraph style is the so-called "description list", usually used when describing (say) a list of commands:

Summarizing the UNIX system commands that are used for directory manipulation:

pwd   prints the pathname to the current working directory.

cd   changes the working directory to that speci-fied.

ls   lists the contents of the specified directory. If none is specified, the contents of the current directory are listed.

mkdir   creates a new directory of the specified name or pathname.

rmdir   removes the specified directory, which must be empty.

Such a list is produced by formatting input text which looks like this:

```
.ll 55
Summarizing the UNIX system commands
that are used for directory manipulation:
.in +8
.sp
.ti -8
pwd     prints the pathname to the current working
directory.
.sp
.ti -8
cd      changes the working directory to that specified.
.sp
.ti -8
ls      lists the contents of the specified directory.
If none is specified, the contents of the current
directory are listed.
.sp
.ti -8
mkdir   creates a new directory of the specified name
or pathname.
.sp
.ti -8
rmdir   removes the specified directory, which must
be empty.
.in -8
```

You should be aware that some older versions of **nroff** do not pre-serve the spaces which we typed between the described items and the describing paragraph in the example input above. If you have such a version of **nroff**, you either must use the special character sequence for an unpaddable space, or use the \c continuation indicator, both of which we describe later in this chapter.

9.9 Simple Macros and Traps

We have said several times that it is possible to define your own **nroff** formatting requests. These special user-defined requests are called macros.

A macro is a shorthand form, wherein one request is a synonym for a number of other requests. You use macros in situations where the same detailed sequence of requests keeps appearing. At the begin-ning of the chapter we gave an example of the actions you need to take each time you start a new paragraph: leave a blank line, make sure you won't get an orphan, indent the first line. If you define a "new paragraph" macro, it will save you the tedium of doing these things for each new paragraph. It will also ensure that all your paragraphs look the same: that there is the same vertical space between them, and they are all indented the same amount.

Of course, before you start defining your own macros, you might want to look at some of the macro packages already in existence, since it is highly likely that the macros you want are already defined somewhere. In the next chapter we describe one of the more readily available macro packages, the **ms** macro package.

In this section we show you some very easy macros, just to give you some idea of what they can do for you. We show you how to pro-vide simple page numbering, so that you will be able to get that fea-ture without having to use a macro package.

9.9.1 Defining a Macro

The **.de** request defines (introduces) a new macro. To define a new macro named 'XY', you use the request like this:

```
.de XY
```

The end of a macro definition is signalled by two periods at the start of a line, on their own

```
..
```

All input lines, between the **.de** request and the **. .** constitute the definition of the macro.

To use the 'XY' macro in **nroff** input text, simply type it like any basic **nroff** request:

```
.XY
```

The body of the macro is substituted in place of the macro call.

Macro names are usually two characters long. By convention people use uppercase letters to distinguish macros from basic **nroff** formatting requests.

A macro must be defined before it can be used. If **nroff** sees a line beginning with a dot " **.** ", but can't identify the following two characters as either a basic request, or as a defined macro, it simply ignores the line.

This example below illustrates a simple **nroff** macro to start a new paragraph. We call the new macro 'NP' for **New Paragraph**:

```
.de NP
.sp 2
.ne 3
.ti +5
. .
```

Now, every time you want to start a new paragraph, you just place the **.NP** macro reference before the paragraph, and **nroff** will automatically perform the defined actions.

But just what are these actions? It's not always easy to remember what all the detailed requests mean, so let's re-write the 'NP' macro, putting in some comments:

```
.de NP     \"New Paragraph macro
.sp 2      \" leave 2 blank lines
.ne 3      \" make sure 3 lines will fit on page
.ti +5     \" indent first line 5 spaces
. .        \"End of New Paragraph macro
```

There are many special character sequences, each one starting with the reverse slash \, which have a special meaning to **nroff**. We describe some of the more useful ones later in this chapter.

The special character sequence \" means that the rest of the line is ignored, and does not appear in the **nroff** output. The \" sequence can therefore be used to put comments in **nroff** input text. Comments are not generally useful in ordinary **nroff** requests. Macro definitions, on the other hand, usually contain many ordinary

nroff requests, and often call other macros. It is therefore a good idea to put comments in macro definitions, so that they can be read and understood more easily.

Now let's see an example of using these macros. If we run **nroff** on this input file, with **.NP** macros instead of regular requests:

```
.de NP     \"New Paragraph macro
.sp 2      \" leave 2 blank lines
.ne 3      \" make sure 3 lines will fit on page
.ti +5     \" indent first line 5 spaces
..         \"End of New Paragraph macro
.ll 50
.NP
These people are most excellent mathematicians,
and arrived to great perfection in mechanicks,
by the countenance and encouragement of the emperor,
who is a renowned patron of learning.
.NP
This prince hath several machines fixed on wheels,
for the carriage of trees and other great weights.
He often buildeth his largest men of war,
whereof some are nine foot long,
in the woods where the timber grows, and has them
carried on these engines three or four hundred yards
to the sea.
.NP
Five hundred carpenters and engineers were immediately
set to work to prepare the greatest engine they had.
```

the result produced is this formatted output:

```
        These people are  most  excellent  mathemati-
cians,  and arrived to great perfection in mechan-
icks, by the countenance and encouragement of  the
emperor, who is a renowned patron of learning.

        This prince hath several  machines  fixed   on
wheels,  for the carriage of trees and other great
weights.  He often buildeth  his  largest  men   of
war, whereof some are nine foot long, in the woods
where the timber grows, and has  them   carried   on
these  engines  three or four hundred yards to the
sea.

        Five hundred carpenters  and  engineers   were
immediately  set   to   work to prepare the greatest
engine they had.
```

Much more complex macros are possible. For example, you might find that you are generating lots of numbered lists. In such a case, you might define a "start numbered list" macro, a "finish numbered list" macro, and a "next item" macro. Then, each time you use the macros, you would be assured that the same sequence of **nroff** requests would get generated. Most of the available macro packages contain such macros.

9.9.2 Setting a Trap

We also said at the beginning of this chapter that **nroff** does not automatically handle page control and page numbering. These can only be achieved by using macros and traps.

A trap defines a place on the page at which a macro is to be called up. A trap can be set to invoke a predefined macro at any position on the page. A trap is set by using a **.wh** (for **wh**en) request, whose general form is:

```
.wh N xx
```

where N is the line number at which the trap is to take place, and xx is the name of the macro to be called at that point.

If the line number N is a positive number, it means that number of lines down from the top of the page. If the line number N is negative, it means that number of lines up from the bottom of the page. A line number N of zero means top of page.

If you set a trap in the form **.wh N**, without a macro name specified, any trap previously set at line number N is removed.

Let's look at an example of some traps:

```
.wh 0   HD      \"invoke macro HD at top of page
.wh -5  FT      \"invoke macro FT at foot of page
```

We have called two macros **.HD** and **.FT** at the head and foot of each page. Notice that while **.HD** is called exactly at the top of each page, **.FT** is called a little before the bottom of the page, so that there will be some blank space at the bottom of each page.

The definitions of the macros HD and FT can be as simple as:

```
.de HD          \"Head of page macro
.sp 5           \"    leave some blank space at top of page
..
.de FT          \"Foot of page macro
.bp             \"    start a new page
..
```

Note that these macro definitions must be defined before the trap **.wh** is activated. In practice it is usual to define the macros before setting the trap with the **.wh** request.

When a point 5 lines from the bottom of a page is reached, the macro **.FT** is called. This immediately starts a new page, so there are 5 blank lines at the bottom of the page. But as soon as the new page is started, the macro **.HD** is called, which spaces down 5 lines. So now you have a top and bottom margin of 5 lines each on every page of your document.

More complex macros can be defined to put running titles and folios on a page, and to do automatic numbering of pages.

9.10 Titles and Page Numbers

A nice feature of **nroff** is the provision for three part titles. A title line can consist of three fields: left, right and center. Any one of the fields may be left blank. The length of title lines can be set independently of the usual line length, so you can have titles that are longer or shorter than the body of the text.

9.10.1 Setting the Text and Length of a Title

The **.tl** (for title line) request defines a title string. The **.tl** request is in the form of:

```
.tl  'left part'center part'right part'
```

The title consists of the three parts separated by single quotes. The *left part* is left justified on the line, the *right part* is right justified on the line, and the *center part* is centered in the gap between the left and the right parts. Any of the strings may be blank.

The length of subsequent title lines can be defined with the **.lt** (for length of title line) request. The form of the request is:

```
.lt   N
```

where *N* is the length required. As with the **.ll** request, preceding the *N* with a plus or minus sign increments or decrements by *N*.

The title length is initially set to be the same as the text line length, 65 characters.

Let's take a look at some examples of titles:

```
.lt 55
.tl 'The Vicar of Wakefield'A Novel'Oliver Goldsmith'
.tl 'The Vicar of Wakefield''Oliver Goldsmith'
.tl ''The Vicar of Wakefield'Oliver Goldsmith'
```

These three **.tl** requests show variations on the same title. In the first one we have used all three fields; in the second variation we have left out the center field; in the last we have moved the left field into the center field. When this input is **nroff**-ed, the result is:

```
The Vicar of Wakefield  A Novel         Oliver Goldsmith
The Vicar of Wakefield                  Oliver Goldsmith
            The Vicar of Wakefield Oliver Goldsmith
```

The next three **.tl** requests define a 3-line title. The first line contains only the left field; the second line only the center field; and the last line only contains the right field:

```
.lt 55
.tl 'Courtship Rituals of Old Moldavia'''
.tl ''A Treatise''
.tl '''by Horace Postlethwaite'
```

When **nroff** has formatted these three title definitions, the results are like this:

```
Courtship Rituals of Old Moldavia
                    A Treatise
                            by Horace Postlethwaite
```

Notice that two of the fields touch in this title, and the left field actually overlaps the other two. **nroff** makes no check for overlapping fields, it just goes ahead and prints one on top of the other. Had we tried to put our title and author on one line, like this:

```
.lt 55
.tl 'Courtship Rituals of Old Moldavia'by Horace Postlethwaite'
```

the output on the terminal screen would look like this:

```
Courtship Ritualby Horace Postlethwaite
```

and a hard copy would show overprinting where the three parts of the title overlap. You must design your title so that the fields don't overlap within the length of the title line.

9.10.2 Getting Page Numbers in Titles

Within a title defined with **.tl**, the percent sign character % means something special. Everywhere % appears inside a **.tl** request, it is replaced by the current value of the page number register. To show an example in this book without taking up a lot of space, we have to pretend we have a very short page (only 2 lines, in fact):

```
.pl 2
.lt 55
.bp 1
.tl 'Courtship Rituals of Old Moldavia''Page %'
.bp
.tl 'Courtship Rituals of Old Moldavia''Page %'
```

when **nroff** has processed the above file, it produces this result:

```
Courtship Rituals of Old Moldavia                Page 1
Courtship Rituals of Old Moldavia                Page 2
```

This is how you can get automatic page numbering. Now we can expand the header and footer macros that we defined above:

```
.de HD          \"Head of page macro
.sp 3           \"    leave some blank space at top of page
.tl 'Courtship Rituals of Old Moldavia'''
.sp 2           \"    space between title and text
..
.de FT          \"Foot of page macro
.sp 2           \"    put some blank lines
.tl ''%''       \"    then the page number
.bp             \"    start a new page
..
```

Our document will now have a title at the top of each page and the page number centered at the bottom of each page.

Much more complex macros than this are possible. For instance, it is possible to have page numbers on the right-hand side of the page on odd numbered pages, and on the left for even pages; this makes the document suitable for double-sided copies. However, a detailed description of how to write **nroff** macros is beyond the scope of this book.

For the most part, you probably won't want to write your own macros, but will more likely use one of the available macro packages.

9.11 Special Character Sequences

When we introduced macros, we also introduced the special character sequence \\", which enabled us to put comments within the macro definition. There are many of these special character sequences, which are also known as "escape sequences". We describe some of the more useful ones in the following paragraphs.

9.11.1 Unpaddable Space '\\'

It sometimes happens that you have a sequence of words that you would like to appear all on one line, but which occur in the text in such a way that **nroff** splits them over 2 lines. For instance, consider the appearance of this block of formatted text:

```
Tucked away behind the busy  thoroughfare  of  St.
Helens  Avenue,  we  find the bijou restaurant "Le
Coq d'Or".  The ambience  is  very  intimate,  the
menu  is  tres  French,  the  food  is  absolutely
divine!!
```

This schmaltzy restaurant review would look better if the street name, "St. Helens Avenue", and the name of the restaurant, "Le Coq d'Or", were not split across lines. We can tell **nroff** to keep these words together by using the special character sequence known as the "unpaddable space". This sequence is simply the reverse slash \\ followed by a space.

If we use this sequence in place of ordinary spaces, **nroff** makes sure that the words on either side of the unpaddable spaces are not split over more than one line. **nroff** also ensures that each unpaddable space in the input text is replaced by one space in the formatted output, so if you have some special spacing requirements, "\\ " can be used for this too.

If our example uses "St.\\ Helens\\ Avenue", and "Le\\ Coq\\ d'Or" everywhere in place of the straightforward "St. Helens Avenue", and "Le Coq d'Or", our formatted output looks like this:

```
Tucked   away   behind   the   busy  thoroughfare  of
St. Helens Avenue,  we  find  the bijou restaurant
"Le Coq d'Or".  The ambience is very intimate, the
menu  is  tres  French,  the  food  is  absolutely
divine!!
```

Now at least the appearance of the review is better.

9.11.2 The Zero Width Character '\&'

In the section on "Paragraphs and Indenting" we gave an example of a description list which itemized directory manipulation commands. Suppose we want to show a similar list which itemizes **nroff** requests. One item in the list might be:

```
.fi   filling is turned  on,  output  lines   are
filled.  If  adjusting has not been turned
off by ".na", the output lines are adjust-
ed in the prevailing mode.
```

We cannot achieve this by the straightforward input text shown here:

```
.ll 50
.in +8
.ti -5
.fi  filling is turned on, output lines
are filled. If adjusting has not been
turned off by ".na", the output lines are
adjusted in the prevailing mode.
```

Because the **.fi** on the fourth input line is seen as a formatting request, the rest of the line is ignored, and the output text looks like this:

```
are filled. If adjusting has  not  been  turned
     off by ".na", the output lines are adjust-
     ed in the prevailing mode.
```

To stop **nroff** interpreting the .fi as a request, we use the special character sequence \&. This is a non-printing zero-width character; nothing appears in its place in the formatted output. The text:

```
.ll 50
.in +8
.ti -5
\&.fi   filling is turned on, output lines
are filled. If adjusting has not been
turned off by ".na", the output lines are
adjusted in the prevailing mode.
```

produces the results we want. The line containing .fi is now seen as a plain text line, since it doesn't start with a dot.

Another example we showed was an itemized list with each item introduced by a "bullet". We used the character "-" as a bullet in that example. If we want to use "." as the bullet we have to use the \& character sequence before each bullet in the input text.

9.11.3 Preventing Extraneous Line Breaks

In the section on "Centering and underlining" we showed how you could underline individual words in a sentence using .ul or .cu requests. What if you wish to underline only part of a word, for instance:

```
The nroff request ".ce" produces centered
output lines from the input text.
```

If you try to underline a part of a word with this simple input:

```
.ll 45
The nroff request ".ce" produces
.ul
ce
ntered output lines from the input text.
```

what you actually get is this:

```
The nroff request ".ce" produces ce ntered
output lines from the input text.
```

because **nroff** assumes there are full words on the input text lines, and it puts spaces between them in the output text. Worse still, **nroff** might even split the word across two lines, so that the resultant output looks like this:

```
The nroff request ".ce" produces ce
ntered output lines from the input text.
```

You can stop this behavior by using the special character sequence \c, which tells **nroff** that the following input line is a continuation of the current input line. The input:

```
.ll 45
The nroff request ".ce" produces
.ul
ce\c
ntered output lines from the input text.
```

gives us the result we want.

9.11.4 Half Line Motions with '\u' and '\d'

Two special character sequences worth mentioning are **\d** (for **down**), and **\u** (for **up**). These cause the output to go half a line-space down, and half a line-space up. They give you the capability of doing subscripts and superscripts. Supposing you want an equation formatted like this:

$$y = c_1x^2 + c_2x + c_3$$

You can get that result from this **nroff** input:

```
y = c\d1\ux\u2\d + c\d2\ux + c\d3\u
```

It should be emphasized that these character sequences can only be used if you have a printer which is capable of vertical motions of less than one line. If your input text contains **\u** or **\d**, you should use the **–T** option (described later) when invoking **nroff**.

9.11.5 Multi-Line Nroff Requests

One last special character sequence to be aware of is **** followed by a newline. This escape sequence is for continuing an **nroff** request onto another line, in much the same way as you can type a UNIX system command on more than one line. Since most **nroff** requests are short, you don't need to use it very often.

9.12 Running the Formatter

So far, we have shown you the kinds of things you can do with the various **nroff** requests, macros, and traps. Now we get to the business of actually using the **nroff** utility to format the text, and some of the options which can appear on the command line.

When you have created your file containing text to be formatted interspersed with formatting requests, you produce the formatted output by typing the the **nroff** command line:

```
$ nroff file
```

The formatted document is produced on the Standard Output (the terminal screen), so you can proof-read it. When you are satisfied that it is correct, you can print it by piping the output to the printer:

```
$ nroff file ¦ lpr
$
```

The process of formatting text can take some time, so you might want to run **nroff** in the background:

```
$ nroff file ¦ lpr &
2042
$
```

as we described in chapter 4, "Commands and Standard Files".

In practice, the **nroff** command line might not be quite that simple. The general format of the **nroff** command is:

```
nroff   [options]   file   ....
```

There are some options you can use if you want, and you can format more than one file at a time.

If you give more than one file to **nroff**, all the files are concatenated and the resulting text formatted. This means that it is not a good idea to try to format separate documents with a single **nroff** command.

Suppose you have three separate memos called 'memo1', 'memo2', and 'memo3'. You should not format these with a single **nroff** command:

```
$ nroff   memo[123] ¦ lpr
$
```

because this could cause problems.

For instance, **nroff** automatically starts at the top of the first page, so you do not normally put a **.bp** at the front of each memo. So if you format all three memos in a single **nroff** run, 'memo2' will follow immediately after 'memo1' without starting a new page, and the same for 'memo3'. A **.bp** at the front of each memo will avoid this problem, but will produce an extra blank sheet at the start of each memo when it is formatted separately.

Other possible sources of trouble are page offsets and indentations. Suppose you have a **.po +6** request at the start of each memo. Now 'memo1' will be printed 6 spaces in from the left hand edge of the paper, 'memo2' will be 12 spaces in, and 'memo3' will be 18 spaces in. This can be avoided by using **.po 6** rather than **.po +6**.

You may have used **.in 40** to put the author's name over on the right hand side, just below a space for signature. Since it is at the end of the memo, it is quite common to leave that indentation rather than cancelling it with **.in 0**. Imagine the result of trying to format two such memos together!

All these problems can be avoided with due care and attention, but the general rule is:

☞ if files represent separate documents, they should be formatted separately.

In our example, we should use the three separate commands:

```
$ nroff   memo1 ┊ lpr
$ nroff   memo2 ┊ lpr
$ nroff   memo3 ┊ lpr
$
```

Sometimes it is desirable to hold a large document in more than one file. It may be just because it's easier to organize things that way; or it might be that if the document was all in one file, that file would be too big for the editor to cope with. For instance, you might have a document consisting of six sections called *'section1'* through *'section6'*, and three appendices called *'appendixA'* through *'appendixC'*. To format and print the entire document, you type this **nroff** command:

```
$ nroff section[1-6] appendix[A-C] ┊ lpr
$
```

Another reason for using more than one file might be that you have defined your own macros, and you use them in many of your documents. Rather than repeating the macro definitions in each file, you can keep them in a separate file, then use them by:

```
$ nroff macros memo1 ┊ lpr
$
```

The document in the file *'memo1'* is formatted using the macro definitions held in file *'macros'*.

If the "–" character appears in the list of files to be formatted, **nroff** reads the Standard Input at that point:

```
$ nroff letterhead - letter ┊ lpr
$
```

This **nroff** command takes the contents of the file *'letterhead'*, followed by the Standard Input, followed by the contents of the file *'letter'*, and formats the resulting text. Here, the Standard Input is taken from the terminal keyboard, so **nroff** formats whatever you type, until you type a control-D to end input from the keyboard.

This could be used to create a "personalized" form letter, by repeating the command for each person to receive it, and entering the name at the appropriate point. However, this sort of thing is much better done with the **nroff** **.rd** (for **read**) request, described under "Switching Input to **nroff**".

Using "−" to get the Standard Input is more commonly used in conjunction with piping. For instance, suppose you have a list of people that you want printed in alphabetical order, double spaced, and with a nice header on each page. You can keep a file of people in any order, then produce the list you want with the command:

```
$ sort + 1 lotsofpeople ¦ nroff peoplehead - ¦ lpr
$
```

The file *'peoplehead'* should contain macros for pagination and titles, and the line spacing requests.

9.13 Options to the 'nroff' Command

There are quite a few options that can be specified on the **nroff** command line. Some of these are connected with some of the advanced features of **nroff** which we haven't described, so we don't describe those options either. If you are interested in the advanced features of **nroff** (and possibly **troff**), refer to the various papers quoted in the bibliography. Here we discuss some of the more useful **nroff** options.

9.13.1 Printing Specific Pages Only

Suppose that you have just printed out a 100-page document, and then you notice a spelling mistake on page 10. The correction of the mistake won't affect any of the other pages, so you really don't want to print the whole thing out again. You can print only the page you want by using the −o (for output) option:

```
$ nroff -o10 document ¦ lpr
$
```

There must not be any spaces before the −o and the number of the page you want. If there several pages that need reprinting, you can specify them all in the same −o option, with the page numbers separated by commas:

```
$ nroff -o10,19,47,95 document ¦ lpr
$
```

If there are some consecutive pages to be printed, you can specify them as a range by separating the first and last page numbers by a "–" character:

```
$ nroff -o3-6 document | lpr
$
```

which is the same as saying:

```
$ nroff -o3,4,5,6 document | lpr
$
```

The two different methods of specifying page numbers (lists and ranges) can be combined:

```
$ nroff -o3-6,10,47-50,95 document | lpr
$
```

This prints pages 3 through 6, page 10, pages 47 through 50, and page 95 of the document. If the first page of a range of pages is the very first page of the document, it can be omitted:

```
$ nroff -o-9 document | lpr
$
```

prints the document from the beginning (page 1) up to and including page 9. In a similar way:

```
$ nroff -o95- document | lpr
$
```

prints from page 95 through to the last page of the document. In all cases, the entire document is formatted, but only the specified pages are sent to the output. No formatting time is saved, only printing time, and paper.

9.13.2 Specifying the Starting Page Number

By using the **–n** (for **n**umber) option, you can specify what number you want the first page to be. So if you have a large document held in several files, you can format the files separately and still have continuous page numbering throughout the document.

Suppose the first section of your document takes 15 pages. To preserve the page numbering you can format the second section by:

```
$ nroff -n16 section2 ¦ lpr
$
```

If you are using the automatic table of contents feature provided by some macro packages, it is not a good idea to format the sections of a document separately in this way, because the table of contents gets clobbered.

9.13.3 Pause between Pages

If you are using separate sheets of paper in your printer, instead of the more usual fan-fold paper, you will want **nroff** to pause when you want to change sheets. To achieve this you use the –s (for stop) option:

```
$ nroff -s document
$
```

so that **nroff** waits between pages. When you have inserted the next sheet of paper, you type RETURN to tell **nroff** to continue.

You don't have to stop every page, you stop every "n" pages by giving a number on the –s option:

```
$ nroff -s5 document
$
```

which stops after every 5 pages have been processed.

9.13.4 Specifying Type of Printer

nroff can handle a variety of printing devices. If your document uses features which rely on special printer capabilities (for example \u and \d for superscripts and subscripts), you must tell **nroff** the type of printer on which the document is to be printed.

More to the point, if the device which is to print your document cannot handle things such as half-line motions, you must also indicate this to **nroff**.

You use the –T (for Terminal, or maybe Typewriter) to indicate the type of printer the document is to be printed on. For example, if your document contains half-line motions as specified by \u and \d character sequences, you might want to print the result on a Diablo printer of some sort:

```
$ nroff -T450 document ¦ lpr
$
```

specifies that your printer (the one that **lpr** sends printouts to) is a DASI-450 (or Diablo Hyterm). Note that the −T option must be uppercase **T**; lowercase **t** is not an **nroff** option.

In practice, the type of terminal or printer that you specify with the −T option depends on your installation. It is advisable to consult with your system administrator, or some other local expert, before you use this option.

One device which is nearly always available is some kind of "Line Printer". You frequently use the line printer as a proofing device, that is, a quick and dirty way to look at a document to see if the overall layout is good, before formatting the document to a higher quality printer. The line printer device is called "lp", so you would use the −**Tlp** option to indicate to **nroff** that that is the device you want:

```
$ nroff -Tlp document | lpr
$
```

Normally **nroff** justifies words in a line by adding spaces between words as required to fill out the line to its full length. If you have a printer that is capable of horizontal movements of less than a space width, **nroff** can use this feature to adjust the spacing more evenly, which results in a better appearance of the output text. To take advantage of this you use the −**e** (for **e**ven) option. In general, the −**e** option requires special printers, so you should also use the −**T** option to specify the printer type.

Although this is not an exhaustive list of all the printer types supported, here is a list of some printers which **nroff** knows about, as specified on the −T option:

37	Teletype Corporation Model 37
tn300	GE TermiNet 300
300S	DASI 300S
300	DASI 300
450	DASI 450
5512	NEC 5512 Spinwriter
lp	Plain line printer

9.13.5 Using Macro Packages

The −**m** option to **nroff** is used to call up standard packages of predefined macros. The command:

```
$ nroff -ms document | lpr
$
```

has the same result as if you had said:

```
$ nroff /usr/lib/tmac/tmac.s document ¦ lpr
$
```

It is the **−m** option which gives the names by which the macro packages are known (**ms**, **mm**, **me**, and so on).

   If you have your own set of macros which you would like to call up
in this way, you must put them (or persuade your system administrator to put them) in the system directory */usr/lib/tmac* with a filename
which begins with *'tmac.'*. For example, if the macros were in a file
'tmac.blurb' in the */usr/lib/tmac* directory, you could call them up by:

```
$ nroff  -mblurb  document ¦ lpr
$
```

9.14 Switching Input to nroff

We now describe two **nroff** requests that we omitted earlier, because
their usefulness is more apparent when you understand the **nroff**
command line. Normally **nroff** takes its input from the files given
when it is called up. However there are ways in which the formatter
can be made to take part of its input from elsewhere, using **nroff**
requests embedded in the document text.

   One of these is the **.so** request, which tells **nroff** to switch over and
take its source from the named file. For example, suppose you have
a set of macros that you have defined, and you have them in a file
called *'macros'*. We can call them up from the **nroff** command line:

```
$ nroff macros document
$
```

as we showed earlier, but it's a bit of a nuisance having to do this all
the time. Also, if only some of our documents use the macros, and
others don't, it can be difficult to remember which is which. An
alternative is to make the first line of the *'document'* file look like
this:

```
.so macros
```

Now we can format the document by:

```
$ nroff document
$
```

The first thing **nroff** sees in the file *'document'* is the request

.so macros which tells it to read input from the file called *'macros'*. When it finishes taking input from *'macros',* **nroff** continues to read the original file *'document'*.

Another way of using the **.so** request lets you format a complete document, held in several files, by only giving one filename to the **nroff** command. Let us create a file called *'document'* containing:

```
.so macros
.so section1
.so section2
.so section3
    <etc>
.so appendixC
```

We can now format it with the **nroff** command line:

```
$ nroff document | lpr
$
```

This is a lot easier than typing all the filenames each time you format the document, and a lot less prone to error.

This technique is especially useful if your filenames reflect the contents of the various sections, rather than the order in which they appear. For instance, look at this file which describes a whole book (something like the one you are reading):

```
$ cat book
.so bookmacros
.so preface
.so intro
.so login      \"Getting Started on the UNIX System
.so directs    \"Directories and the File System
.so stdio      \"Commands, Processes, and Standard Files
         <etc...>
.so biblio     \"Bibliography
$
```

It is obviously much easier to format the whole thing with an **nroff** command line like this:

```
$ nroff book | lpr
$
```

than it would be if you had to supply all the filenames in the right order. Notice that we used the comment feature of **nroff** to tie chapter titles to filenames.

Another **nroff** request that switches input from the file you specify is **.rd** (for **read**). The **.rd** request reads an insertion from the standard input. When **nroff** encounters the **.rd** request, it prompts for input by sounding the terminal bell. A visible prompt can be given by adding an argument to **.rd**, as we show in the example below.

Everything typed up to a blank line (two newline characters in a row) is inserted into the text being formatted at that point. This can be used to "personalize" form letters. If you have an input file with this text:

```
.po 10
.nf
.in 20
14th February
.in 0
Dear
.rd who
        Will you be my Valentine?
        If you will, give me a sign
        (I like roses, I like wine).
```

then when you format it, you will be prompted for input:

```
$ nroff valentine | lpr
who:Peter

$
```

After typing the name Peter you have to hit the RETURN key twice, since **nroff** needs a blank line to end input. The result of formatting that file is:

```
                    14th February
        Dear Peter
            Will you be my Valentine?
            If you will, give me a sign
            (I like roses, I like wine.)
```

To get another copy of this for Bill, you just run the **nroff** command again:

```
$ nroff valentine | lpr
who:Bill

$
```

and again for Joe, and for Manuel, and Louis, and Alphonse, and ....

Since **nroff** takes input from the terminal up to a blank line, you are not limited to a single word, or even a single line of input. You can use this method to insert addresses or anything else into form letters.

9.15 Dimensioned Arguments in nroff Requests

In all the examples we showed using requests such as

```
.ll 55
.po 8
.in +5
.sp 3
```

we have assumed that the numbers refer to spaces (or columns) for horizontal movements, and lines for vertical movements.

In practice, you are not restricted to columns and lines. You can request movements in terms of inches or centimeters:

```
.po 1i      \" page offset 1 inch from left hand edge
.ll -0.5i   \" reduce line length by 0.5 inches
.in +1.5c   \" increase indentation by 1.5 centimeters
.sp 3.5c    \" leave 3.5 centimeters vertical space
```

Because we have specified units on these requests, they are said to be "dimensioned". The dimensions (units) that **nroff** understands are:

i	inch
c	centimeter
m	m-space
n	n-space
v	vertical line space (v-space)

If you don't put any dimension on your request, the formatter assumes a default dimension of 'm' on horizontal, and 'v' on vertical requests.

The actual distances taken by m-spaces, n-spaces and v-spaces depend on the device that your document will be finally produced on. The distances produced by **troff** are different from those produced by **nroff**. In particular, in **nroff** an m-space is the same as an n-space, while in **troff** an m-space is twice as wide as an n-space.

If there is any possibility that your document may be formatted by **troff** at any time, it will pay you to specify your spacing in centimeters or inches. These quantities are the same regardless of the type of output device.

You often need to be aware of dimensions when you use a macro package. Most of the macro packages are primarily designed for use with **troff**. If you are using them with **nroff**, and you change the overall document layout, you must give nroff-type dimensions to the macros. When you read about the **ms** macro package in the next chapter, you will see some examples of this.

9.16 Summary

In this chapter we have shown you the basic facilities of the **nroff** text formatter, and the ideas of page layout, paragraphing styles, page headers and footers, titles, and page numbers. Read the documentation on **nroff** and **troff**. You should try typing some documents, and formatting them using **nroff**'s facilities. Experiment with different paragraph styles, try defining some simple macros.

But before you get to deep into macro definitions, scan the next chapter. In chapter 10, we describe the **ms** macro package, one of the more widely available macro packages.

The adventurous may want to get deeper into macro definitions. Investigate some of the more advanced features such as tab-leaders, number registers, strings, diversions. These facilities mean you can define macros for automatically numbering headings or list items, for producing footnotes, and for generating tables of contents automatically.

10 More Formatting Tools

In the previous chapter we described the **nroff** text formatter in some detail. **nroff** can and does make a reasonable job of a document without any formatting requests at all. But, if you want any kind of text structures other than straight paragraphs, **nroff** can be quite cumbersome to use, since you have to give it detailed instructions as to exactly how you want your document laid out. To assist the user with the fine details of **nroff** and **troff**, a number of extra facilities have evolved over the years.

Firstly there are a number of "macro packages" available on the UNIX system. These macro packages supply a relatively high level interface to **nroff** and **troff**, so that you give requests which more closely reflect the layout of the document you are working on. These macro packages contain specific commands for things such as "indented paragraph", "block paragraph", "itemized paragraph", and so on.

Then there is a table layout utility called **tbl** that assists you in laying out tabular material. Using **tbl**, you can get material arranged in columns, with numeric items correctly aligned, and have the entire table enclosed in boxes.

In this chapter, we describe some of these documentation utilities. We cannot hope to do more than scratch the surface, since a complete explanation of the system's documentation aids would end up as a book in its own right. We do try, however, to give you enough of the flavor of what is available so that you can continue to experiment on your own.

10.1 The 'ms' Document Macro Package

Of the many macro packages available for assisting the documentation process, the **ms** macro package is the most widely available, and it is probably the simplest to use. It lacks many of the features available in other macro packages. For instance, although automatic numbering of section and paragraph headings at several levels is provided, there is no capability for automatically generating tables of contents. Also, there is no capability for making automatically numbered lists of items. These capabilities are present in other macro packages, for instance the **mm** macro package.

The name of the macro package, **ms**, derives from the way in which you call **nroff** in order to use the macros, as we showed in the previous chapter:

```
$ nroff -ms document | lpr
$
```

The **−m** option to **nroff** indicates that you want to use a macro package. The letter following the **−m** tells which of the macro packages you want to use. In this section we refer to **ms** as though it were a command in its own right; you must remember that what we really mean is the **nroff** command called up with the **−ms** option.

We describe some of the capabilities that the **ms** macro package provides. The macros are intended for use with both **troff** and **nroff**. However, there are some macros which really only make sense if used with **troff**. Since we are not covering **troff** in this book, we omit those macros.

Calls on **ms** macros look very similar to **nroff** formatting requests. Each consists of a "dot" followed by two characters, optionally followed by arguments to the macro. Some examples of calls on **ms** macros are:

```
.2C
.NH 2
.IP "first stanza" 14
```

All letters are upper case. Each macro call must be on a line of its own.

ms provides page headers and footers, and page numbering. But before we describe the overall page layout, and how you can influence it, we will show how **ms** deals with different paragraph styles, and paragraph and section headers.

10.1.1 Paragraphs and Indentation

In the previous chapter we discussed various formats of paragraphs. You can achieve all these with the **ms** macro package. Many of the formats can be obtained by simple macro calls. Others require that you set values into number registers to get the effect you want.

10.1.1.1 Paragraph Types **ms** provides two basic forms of paragraph, an indented paragraph (that is, the first line is indented), and a block paragraph. To repeat the example of blocked paragraphs that we used in the last chapter:

```
These people are  most  excellent  mathematicians,
and  arrived to great perfection in mechanicks, by
the countenance and encouragement of the  emperor,
who is a renowned patron of learning.
```

```
This prince hath several machines fixed on wheels,
for  the  carriage  of large trees and other great
weights.  He often buildeth  his  largest  men  of
war, whereof some are nine foot long, in the woods
where the timber grows, and has  them  carried  on
these engines  three or four hundred yards  to the
sea.
```

```
Five hundred carpenters and engineers were immedi-
ately  set  to work to prepare the greatest engine
they had.
```

This formatted text was produced from the **ms** input:

```
.LP
These people are most excellent mathematicians,
and arrived to great perfection in mechanicks,
by the countenance and encouragement of the emperor,
who is a renowned patron of learning.
.LP
This prince hath several machines fixed on wheels,
for the carriage of trees and other great weights.
```

```
He often buildeth his largest men of war,
whereof some are nine foot long,
in the woods where the timber grows, and has them
carried on these engines three or four hundred yards
to the sea.
.LP
Five hundred carpenters and engineers were immediately
set to work to prepare the greatest engine they had.
```

The .**LP** macro produces a **L**eft-aligned **P**aragraph, or what we have hitherto called a blocked paragraph. If you actually try this example, what you see will not look exactly like what we've shown. That is because we have used a line length that is shorter than usual, as is our wont. Don't let that worry you, the important thing at this point is that .**LP** gives you a blocked paragraph.

If we did a global substitution on our input file, replacing .**LP** with .**PP**, the output from the formatter would look like this:

```
     These people are   most   excellent  mathemati-
ians,   and arrived to great perfection in mechan-
icks, by the countenance and encouragement of  the
emperor, who is a renowned patron of learning.

     This prince hath several  machines  fixed   on
wheels,  for the carriage of large trees and other
great weights.  He often buildeth his largest  men
of  war,  whereof  some are nine foot long, in the
woods where the timber grows, and has them carried
on  these  engines  three or four hundred yards to
the sea.

     Five hundred carpenters  and  engineers  were
immediately  set  to  work to prepare the greatest
engine they had.
```

This style of paragraph, with the first line indented 5 spaces, is considered the "normal" paragraph type, and is given the name .**PP**.

As you can see, **ms** leaves one line between paragraphs, and for "normal" paragraphs, the first line is indented five spaces. In fact, **ms** talks in **troff** terms, so the indentation is really five n-spaces and the paragraph depth is 1 vertical space (if you are using **troff**, the paragraph depth is 0.3 vertical space). These measurements are controlled by two number registers:

PI - paragraph indent, default value 5n
PD - paragraph depth, default 1v for **nroff**
0.3v for **troff**

If you don't like the paragraph layout that **ms** provides, you can change it by altering the values of these number registers. For instance, if we put the two lines:

```
.nr PI 10n
.nr PD 2v
```

at the beginning of our unformatted file, the output produced by **ms** would look like this:

```
        These people are most excellent mathema-
icians,   and   arrived   to   great   perfection   in
mechanicks, by the countenance  and   encouragement
of the emperor, who is a renowned patron of learn-
ing.
```

```
        This prince hath several machines   fixed
on  wheels,   for   the   carriage of large trees and
other great weights.  He often buildeth his   larg-
```
```
                      .
           <and so on>
                      .
                      .
```

Now we have two blank lines between paragraphs, and the first line of each paragraph is indented 10 spaces.

When you are changing the basic layout provided by **ms**, you must supply dimensions for the new parameters. Saying **.nr PI 10** doesn't give you what you want, you must say **.nr PI 10n**. You could also give a dimension in inches, for example **.nr PI 2i** will cause the first line of each paragraph to be indented 2 inches. To get paragraphs separated by 1 inch, say **.nr PD 1i**

10.1.1.2 Indented Paragraphs The **.IP** macro stands for Indented **Paragraph**. It produces a paragraph which is completely indented from the surrounding text:

```
In the opening sentence of "The  Vicar  of  Wakefield",
the leading character opines:
```

```
    "I was ever of the opinion, that  the  honest  man
    who  married  and  brought  up a large family, did
    more service than he who continued single and only
    talked of population."
```

```
It is not known if Goldsmith was expressing the popular
feeling of his time, but if so - how things are changed
in the 200 or so years since those words were written.
```

The above formatted text was produced from the input:

```
.LP
In the opening sentence of "The Vicar of Wakefield",
the leading character opines:
.IP
"I was ever of the opinion, that the honest man who
married and brought up a large family, did more
service than he who continued single and only talked
of population."
.LP
It is not known if Goldsmith was expressing the
popular feeling of his time, but if so - how
things are changed in the 200 or so years since
those words were written.
```

By default, the paragraph introduced by the **.IP** macro is indented five spaces from the surrounding text. If you want more, or less, you can change the value of the 'PI' number register as we showed in the previous paragraph.

If you want the paragraph indented from the surrounding text at both left and right edges, you use the **Q**uotation **P**aragraph macro **.QP** in place of **.IP** to give you:

```
In the opening sentence of "The  Vicar  of  Wakefield",
the leading character opines:
```

```
    "I was ever of the opinion, that  the  honest
    man  who  married and brought up a large fam-
    ily, did more service than he  who  continued
    single and only talked of population."
```

```
It is not known if Goldsmith was expressing the popular
feeling of his time, but if so - how things are changed
in the 200 or so years since those words were written.
```

The **.QP** macro always indents five n-spaces in from both margins; it is independent of the value in the 'PI' number register.

Another way of achieving this type of paragraph is by changing the line length; how to do this is explained later in the chapter.

10.1.1.3 Lists and Descriptions   The **.IP** macro can be used to create the so-called "hanging indent" type of paragraph. This type of layout is most commonly used for lists of things, where each item in the list is either numbered, or marked by a "bullet". In the previous chapter we gave an example of a bulleted list:

```
In all our examples of the text formatter, we have used
a line length which is 10 or 15 spaces shorter than the
normal (default) line length.  There are  various  rea-
sons for doing this:
```

```
-      When giving formatted examples,  it  is   desirable
       that the text be of a reasonable size.  Paragraphs
       should be more than two lines, and 4 or 5 lines if
       possible.  On the other hand, we want to avoid ex-
       amples that  are  too  lengthy.   A  shorter  line
       length  helps to achieve a reasonable body of for-
       matted text with a smaller amount of input text.

-      Examples should stand out clearly - ideally  they
       should be "indented" from both left and right mar-
       gins of the explanatory text.  Using a line length
       which  is shorter than usual achieves this without
       distorting the action taken by the formatter.

-      By adjusting the line length, it  is  possible  to
       highlight some actions taken by the formatter (for
       example, hyphenation) which would not occur  if  a
       "standard" line length were used.
```

We create a list such as this by giving the character we want to use as the bullet as an argument to each call on the **.IP** macro. The above output was produced from the text:

```
.LP
In all our examples of the text formatter,
we have used a line length which is 10 or 15 spaces
shorter than the normal (default) line length.
There are various reasons for doing this:
.IP -
when giving formatter examples, it is desirable that
the text be of a reasonable size.
               <and so on>
```

```
.IP -
Examples should stand out clearly - ideally they should
be "indented" from both left and right margins of the
                <and so on>
.IP -
By adjusting the line length, it is possible to
highlight some actions taken by the formatter
(for example, hyphenation) which would not occur
if a "standard" line length were used.
```

The character given as an argument to the **.IP** macro appears to the left of the indented paragraph in the output text, thus producing the "hanging indent" effect.

If you compare the formatted output above with the same example in the previous chapter, you will notice that they are not identical. The positioning of the bullets is slightly different: in the previous chapter we have:

```
- When giving formatted examples,  it  is  desirable
```

in the above example we have:

```
   -      When giving formatted examples,  it  is  desirable
```

In order to retain the initial spaces on the line before the bullet, we have to give them as part of the argument to **.IP**. If an argument contains spaces, it must be surrounded by quotes. To exactly repeat the example of the previous chapter, we would have to make all our calls on the **.IP** macro look like:

```
.IP "    -"
```

Because you have to repeat the bullet character for each call on the macro, there is no reason why it has to be the same for each item in the list. In fact, it doesn't have to be a single character. You can make a numbered list:

```
In all our examples of the text formatter, we have used
a line length which is 10 or 15 spaces shorter than the
normal (default) line length. There are  various  rea-
sons for doing this:

(1)  When giving formatted examples,  it  is  desirable
     that the text be of a reasonable size.  Paragraphs
                <and so on>
     matted text with a smaller amount of input text.
```

(2) Examples should stand out clearly - ideally they should be "indented" from both left and right mar-
<and so on>
distorting the action taken by the formatter.

(3) By adjusting the line length, it is possible to highlight some actions taken by the formatter (for example, hyphenation) which would not occur if a "standard" line length were used.

simply by giving the appropriate number on each successive call on the macro:

```
.LP
In all our examples of the text formatter,
we have used a line length which is 10 or 15 spaces
shorter than the normal (default) line length.
There are various reasons for doing this:
.Ip (1)
When giving formatted examples, it is desirable that
the text be of a reasonable size.
                    <and so on>
.IP (2)
Examples should stand out clearly - ideally they should
                    <and so on>
.IP (3)
   By adjusting the line length, it is possible to
highlight some actions taken by the formatter
(for example, hyphenation) which would not occur
if a "standard" line length were used.
```

Unfortunately, with **ms** you have to count the numbers yourself, there is no provision for automatically numbering items in the list.

A variation on this theme is a description list, where you see the name of something on the left of the page, and a paragraph describing it on the right. Again, we gave an example in the previous chapter:

```
Summarizing the UNIX system commands that are used  for
directory manipulation:

pwd       prints the  pathname  to  the  current  working
          directory.

cd        changes the working directory  to  that  speci-
          fied.
```

ls   lists the contents of the specified directory.
          If none is specified, the contents of the
          current directory are listed.

mkdir   creates a new directory of the specified name
          or pathname.

rmdir   removes the specified directory, which must be
          empty.

This output was obtained by formatting the text:

```
.LP
Summarizing the UNIX system commands
that are used for directory manipulation:
.IP pwd 8
prints the pathname to the current working directory.
.IP cd 8
changes the working directory to that specified.
.IP ls 8
lists the contents of the specified directory.
If none is specified, the contents of the current
directory are listed.
.IP mkdir 8
creates a new directory of the specified name
or pathname.
.IP rmdir 8
removes the specified directory, which must be empty.
```

This time we gave two arguments to the calls on .**IP**. The first argument is the name that is to appear on the left, the second argument is the number of n-spaces it is to occupy. If we didn't specify this second argument, then the names would occupy the default amount of five spaces, and our last two items in the list would get all squished together:

mkdircreates a new directory of the specified name or
          pathname.

rmdirremoves the specified directory, which must be
          empty.

Because we want all our descriptions to line up nicely, we expanded the name field to 8 spaces on all items. This is the same as changing the paragraph indent, and we could have achieved it by altering the value in the 'PI' number register, as we described above (and restoring it when we had finished the list). By putting the second argument on **.IP** calls, you can make each item in the list different, so that the name only takes up as much as it needs to.

10.1.1.4 Nested Lists Sometimes you want one item in a list to itself be a list. Suppose we re-phrase the first item in the numbered list we showed in the last paragraph:

```
In all our examples of the text formatter, we have used
a line length which is 10 or 15 spaces shorter than the
normal (default) line length.  There are  various  rea-
sons for doing this:

(1)   When giving formatted examples,  it  is  desirable
      that the text be of reasonable size.  Two criteria
      apply:

      a.   Paragraphs should be more than two lines, and
           4 or 5 lines if possible.

      b.   On the other hand, we want to avoid  examples
           that are too lengthy.  For instance, examples
           longer than a page are awkward to deal with.

      A shorter line length helps to achieve  a  reason-
      able  body of formatted text with a smaller amount
      of input text.

(2)   Examples should stand out clearly - ideally  they
      should be "indented" from both left and right mar-
      gins of the explanatory text.  Using a line length
      which  is shorter than usual achieves this without
      distorting the action taken by the formatter.
```

Here we have two lists, one inside the other. The outer list is numbered (1), (2) and so on; the inner list, which forms part of the first item in the outer list, is "numbered" a., b. We achieve these nested lists by using the **.IP** macro in conjunction with two other macros **.RS** and **.RE**:

```
.LP
In all our examples of the text formatter,
we have used a line length which is 10 or 15 spaces
            <and so on>
```

```
.IP (1)
when giving formatter examples, it is desirable that
the text be of a reasonable size.
Two criteria apply:
.RS
.IP a.
Paragraphs should be more than two lines, and 4 or 5
lines if possible.
.IP b.
On the other hand, we want to avoid examples that are
too lengthy.
For instance, examples longer than a page are awkward
to deal with.
.LP
A shorter line length helps to achieve a reasonable body
of formatted text with a smaller amount of input text.
.RE
.IP (2)
Examples should stand out clearly - ideally they should
be "indented" from both left and right margins of the
                         <and so on>
```

The **.RS** macro can be considered as a **R**ight **S**hift request. All paragraphs following it appear to the right of where they normally would. The amount of the right shift is governed by the paragraph indent number register 'PI'.

The **.RE** macro cancels the effect of the **.RS** macro, it can be thought of as **R**ight-shift **E**nd.

You can have lists, within lists, within lists ... by repeating the **.RS** macro. However, for every **.RS** call there must be a corresponding **.RE**.

When using **.RS** with an indentation depth other than the default, it is best to set the 'PI' register to the value you want, rather than using the second argument on **.IP** calls. If you try to use the second argument on **.IP** to govern the indentation of the outer list, you will probably find that the **.RE** call does not correctly cancel the effect of the **.RS** macro.

10.1.2 Section and Paragraph Headings

The **ms** macro package provides for numbered and un-numbered headings. If you use numbered headings, the numbering scheme allows for five levels of numbering. All headings are underlined by default (headings are made **boldface** if you are using **troff**), and may occupy several lines if required.

10.1.2.1 Un-Numbered Headings
An un-numbered heading is introduced by the macro **SH**, which simply stands for Section Heading. The macro appears on one line of the input text, the actual heading appears on the following line or lines. The first paragraph following the heading must begin with a **.LP** or **.PP** macro, since that signals the end of the heading. For instance, the output:

```
burble burble bumf blurb at end of paragraph.
```

Courtship Rituals in Old Moldavia

```
        A new paragraph  of  burble burble  bumph  blurb,
blurble burp bumf.
```

Was produced from the input:

```
burble burble bumf blurb at end of paragraph.
.SH
Courtship Rituals in Old Moldavia
.PP
A new paragraph of burble burble bumph blurb, blurble
burp bumf.
```

If you omit to put a paragraph macro call after the heading, then the entire paragraph will be taken as the heading. Without the **.PP** call, the above input text will produce:

```
burble burble bumf blurb at end of paragraph.
```

Courtship Rituals in Old Moldavia A new paragraph of
burble burble bumph blurb, blurble burp bumf.

There is one vertical space between the end of a paragraph and a heading. This is independent of the setting of the paragraph depth number register, 'PD'. If you add

```
.nr PD 2v
```

at the beginning of the input text, your output will look like this:

```
burble burble bumf blurb at end of paragraph.
```

Courtship Rituals in Old Moldavia

```
        A new paragraph  of  burble burble  bumph  blurb,
blurble burp bumf.
```

This is not a very satisfactory layout because the vertical distance between paragraphs is greater than the distance between sections.

If you want to make the vertical space between the end of a paragraph and a heading greater than that between paragraphs, you should put one or more **.LP** or **.PP** macros before the **.SH** macro call. For example, the input:

```
burble burble bumf blurb at end of paragraph.
.LP
.LP
.SH
Courtship Rituals in Old Moldavia
.PP
A new paragraph of burble burble bumph blurb, blurble
burp bumf.
```

produces a much better layout:

```
burble burble bumf blurb at end of paragraph.
```

Courtship Rituals in Old Moldavia

```
        A new paragraph  of  burble burble  bumph  blurb,
blurble burp bumf.
```

10.1.2.2 Numbered Headings   Although **ms** doesn't have the capability to count and number items in a list, it does provide automatic numbering of sections and paragraphs. The number is attached to a heading.

The macro used to introduce a **Numbered Heading** is **.NH**. Five levels of numbering are provided. A simple call on **.NH** implies a level 1 heading, the other levels are invoked by giving the level number as an argument to **.NH**. To give an example, let's look at the headings we have used so far in this chapter; they are shown in figure 10.1.

Since we have typed the headings as though it were the whole document, numbering starts at 1.

Each heading is introduced by a **.NH** macro call. The input required to produce the output shown in figure 10.1 appears in figure 10.2.

1. More text Formatting Tools

In this chapter, we burble burble bumf blurb, blurble
burp bumfle blurp

1.1. The 'ms' Document Macro Package

Of the many macro packages blurble burp bumfle blurp,
burble burble bumf blurb

1.1.1 Paragraphs and Indentation

In the previous chapter we burble bumf blurb, blurble
burble burp bumfle

1.1.1.1. Basic Paragraph Types

ms provides two basic bloop burble bumf, blurble blurb
burp bumfle blurp

1.1.1.2. Indented Paragraphs

The macro .IP burble bumf blurb, burble blurble bumfle
blurp

1.1.1.3 Lists and Descriptions

The .IP macro can be used to burble blurble bumfle
blurp bumph

1.1.1.4 Nested Lists

Sometimes you want one item in a list to bloop burble
bumf, blurble blurb

1.1.2 Section and Paragraph Headings

The ms macro package provides burble burble bumf blurb,
blurble burp bumfle blurp

1.1.2.1 Un-numbered Headings

An un-numbered heading is introduced by bumf blurb burble, blurble burp blurp

1.1.2.2. Numbered Headings

Although ms doesn't have the capability to blurble burp
bumfle

Figure 10.1 Examples of Numbered Headings

```
.NH
More text Formatting Tools
.LP
In this chapter, we burble burble bumf blurb, blurble
burp bumfle blurp
.NH 2
The 'ms' Document Macro Package
.LP
Of the many macro packages blurble burp bumfle blurp,
burble burble bumf blurb
.NH 3
Paragraphs and Indentation
.LP
In the previous chapter we burble bumf blurb, blurble
burble burp bumfle
.NH 4
Basic Paragraph Types
.LP
ms provides two basic bloop burble bumf, blurble blurb
burp bumfle blurp
.NH 4
Indented Paragraphs
.LP
The macro .IP burble bumf blurb, burble blurble bumfle blurp
.NH 4
Lists and Descriptions
.LP
The .IP macro can be used to burble blurble bumfle blurp
.NH 4
Nested Lists
.LP
Sometimes you want one item in a list to bloop burble bumf,
blurble blurb
.NH 3
Section and Paragraph Headings
.LP
The ms macro package provides burble burble bumf blurb,
blurble burp bumfle blurp
.NH 4
Un-numbered Headings
.LP
An un-numbered heading is introduced by bumf blurb burble,
blurble burp blurp
.NH 4
Numbered Headings
.LP
Although ms doesn't have the capability to blurble burp
```

Figure 10.2   Input Required to Produce Numbered Headings

The example shows four levels of heading, from 1. through to 1.1.1.1. There is in fact another level, which would give paragraphs numbered 1.1.1.1.1. **ms** keeps track of the numbers at each level, and allocates the next number at the appropriate level for each call on **.NH**. To reset the numbering scheme to 1, you must call the macro with an argument of "0", thus:

```
.NH  0
```

Although **ms** numbers paragraphs for you, it doesn't remember them, so there is no provision for automatically generating a table of contents.

10.1.3 Overall Page Layout

By default, **ms** provides pages which are numbered at the top of each page except the first, page numbering is of the form "-2-" centered at the top of the page. The current date appears at the bottom of each page. The top and bottom margins are set to 1 inch; the line length is set to 6 inches, there is no page offset. Many of these default parameters can be changed.

10.1.3.1 Setting Left and Right Margins The left margin is determined by the page offset, which is initially zero. The right margin is determined by the page offset and the line length. Both the page offset and the line length can be changed to provide the left and right margins you require.

To change the line length, you must adjust the contents of the 'LL' number register. The initial contents of this register is set to give a line length of 6 inches. In all our examples so far, we have used a line length of 55 columns, or n-spaces. In order to achieve this, we set the 'LL' register:

```
.nr  LL  55n
```

The reason for doing it this way, rather than directly using the **nroff** request .**ll 55**, is that **ms** checks the contents of the 'LL' register at the start of each paragraph, and adjusts the line length accordingly. So if we used the .**ll** request, the change of line length would only be effective until the next .**PP**, .**LP**, or .**IP** macro call.

For the same reason, if you want a paragraph to have a shorter line length, you must adjust the 'LL' register *before* giving the paragraph macro.

The page offset can be modified in a similar manner, by setting a value into the number register 'PO'. For instance, the requests:

```
.nr PO 1.5i
.nr LL 5.5i
```

will set up **ms** to give a 1.5 inch left margin and a 5.5 inch line length, which gives a 1.5 inch right margin if your paper is 8.5 inches wide. The page offset can also be given in n-spaces:

```
.nr PO 8n
```

gives a left margin which is 8 spaces wide.

When you change page offset by setting the 'PO' number register, the change is not effective until the next page is started, so you may need to give the basic **nroff** request .**po** as well.

10.1.3.2 Changing Top and Bottom Margins There are two number registers that control the top and bottom margins. The 'HM' register controls the top, or header, margin; the bottom, or footer, margin is controlled by the number register 'FM'.

Initially both are set to give 1 inch margins. These margins can be changed by altering the values in the registers. For example:

```
.nr HM 1.25i
.nr FM 0.75i
```

gives a deeper top margin, and a smaller bottom margin than the default.

```
.nr HM 8v
.nr FM 4v
```

sets the top margin to 8 vertical spaces (approximately 1.25 inches), and the bottom margin to 4 vertical spaces (about 0.75 inches).

Beware of making the header and footer margins too small. If the top margin is not deep enough, the page number gets squished down towards the text, and the result looks horrible. If the bottom margin is too small, you won't get the date printed as is usual.

10.1.3.3 Changing or Suppressing the Date **ms** usually puts the current date at the bottom of every page of your document. This is not always convenient. If you print the document on two successive Mondays, say, you will have two copies of the document with a different date, but the content of the document may not have changed. In practice, it is often better to have a fixed date in the document. That way the printout shows when the text was changed, not when the printout was obtained.

The date that is shown on the bottom of every page can be changed by using the **.DA** macro:

```
.DA 8 June 1982
```

This should go at the beginning of your input text. Another advantage of using the **.DA** macro to set the date is that you can specify the exact format of date that you want, for example:

```
.DA 1982-6-8
```

The format of date usually produced by **ms** is "8 June 1982".

If you don't want the date to appear at all, you should put the macro call **.ND** at the beginning of your input text.

10.1.3.4 Double Column Format   You can ask **ms** to produce its output in two columns, instead of each line going right across the page. This layout is like a magazine:

```
        These people are most
excellent   mathematicians,
and arrived to great   per-
fection   in mechanicks, by
the      countenance     and
encouragement    of     the
emperor, who is a renowned
patron of learning.

        This    prince   hath
several   machines fixed on
wheels, for    the   carriage
of   large   trees and other
great weights.    He   often
buildeth  his   largest men
of war, whereof   some  are
```

```
nine   foot   long,   in   the
woods   where   the   timber
grows,   and   has them car-
ried   on    these    engines
three   or    four   hundred
yards to the sea.

        Five    hundred   car-
penters and engineers were
immediately set to work to
prepare     the     greatest
engine they had.
```

The above output was obtained by inserting the macro call **.2C** at the beginning of the input text we used to illustrate basic paragraph types. We also shortened the page length to give a compact example; if you do the example on a normal page length, the result will be different.

Single column and double column output can be mixed in the same document, the macro call **.1C** reverts to the normal single column format.

When you request double column format in a document, you must filter the output of **nroff** through the **col** utility program, as we describe below. Also, it is a good idea to tell **nroff** the type of output device you are printing the document on, using the **–T** option.

10.1.4 Footnotes and Displays

ms has provision for putting footnotes at the bottom of each page, but the footnotes are not automatically numbered. The macro package also provides ways of keeping text together, either in-line on the same page as the reference to it, or floated to the following page.

10.1.4.1 Footnotes There are two macros that control footnotes: **.FS** marks the start of a footnote, and **.FE** marks the end of it. Any text placed between these two macro calls forms the footnote.

Footnotes are placed at the bottom of the page, and are separated from the body text by a ruled line. Footnote lines are by default slightly shorter than the lines in the body text and, if you are using **troff**, footnotes are printed using a smaller point size.

There is no automatic numbering, or even marking, of footnotes. In order to get a footnote marked with an asterisk, for example, you must say:

```
.nr LL 55n
.PP
We were again fortunate enough to find a very agreeable
family to board with; and soon after breakfast left our
comfortless hotel near the water, for very pleasant
apartments near F. street.*
.FS
* The streets that intersect the great avenues in
Washington are distinguished by the letters of the
alphabet.
.FE
.PP
I was delighted with the whole aspect of Washington;
light, cheerful, and airy, it reminded me of our
fashionable watering places.
```

This produces a page that looks like this (again we have used a short page length to make a compact example):

```
        We were again fortunate   enough   to   find   a   very
agreeable   family   to board with; and soon after break-
fast left our comfortless hotel   near   the   water,   for
very pleasant apartments near F. street.*
```

```
        I was delighted with the whole aspect of  Washing-
ton;   light,   cheerful, and airy, it reminded me of our
fashionable watering places.
```

```
--------------------------
* The streets that intersect the great avenues in Wash-
ington   are   distinguished by the letters of the alpha-
bet.
```

In this example, because we chose a short line length for the body text, the difference between the line length of the footnotes and the length of the lines in the body text is not apparent.

If you wish, you can call other **ms** macros inside the **.FS** — **.FE** pair of macro calls. For instance, if we make the input text for the above footnote look like this:

```
.FS
.IP *
The streets that intersect the great avenues in
Washington are distinguished by the letters of the
alphabet.
.FE
```

then the footnote that is generated will look like:

```
--------------------------
*       The streets that intersect the   great   avenues   in
        Washington are distinguished by the letters of the
        alphabet.
```

If you wanted numbered footnotes, you have to keep track of the numbering yourself. When putting the marks in the text to tie up the footnote, you may find it useful to use the half-line spacing capability of your printer, for instance:

```
apartments near F. street.\u[12]\d
.FS
[12] The streets that intersect the great avenues in
Washington are distinguished by the letters of the
alphabet.
.FE
```

10.1.4.2 Keeping Text Together

Sometimes you want to keep lines of text together on one page. Take the example of a few paragraphs ago, where we had a quotation from Oliver Goldsmith's "Vicar of Wakefield". If that quotation were split over two pages, so that the beginning of it appeared at the bottom of one page, and the rest at the top of the next, it would detract from the appearance of the document.

ms provides two macros for keeping text together: **.KS** marks the start of the text to be kept together (**K**eep **S**tart), and **.KE** (**K**eep **E**nd) marks the end of the text to be kept together. If there is not sufficient room on the current page for the formatted version of the text between these two macro calls, **ms** starts a new page, leaving the remainder of the current page blank. So to make sure that all our quotation got on the same page, we should input the text:

```
.nr LL 55n
.LP
In the opening sentence of "The Vicar of Wakefield",
the leading character opines:
.KS
.IP
"I was ever of the opinion, that the honest man who
married and brought up a large family, did more
service than he who continued single and only talked
of population."
.KE
.LP
It is not known if Goldsmith was expressing the
popular feeling of his time, but if so - how
things are changed in the 200 or so years since
those words were written.
```

It sometimes happens that, although text has to be kept together on one page, it doesn't necessarily have to appear in the output at exactly the same place as it appeared in the input text. Consider a sentence containing the phrase

"...as shown in the following table:"

The table being referred to must follow those words immediately, and must be kept together. However, suppose we rephrase the sentence to say

"... as shown in Table 1a"

Now the table being referred to, although it must be kept together, need not follow immediately; it can appear on the next page. This is called a floating keep, because the text can float from its position in the input text.

ms has a **.KF** (Keep Floating) that copes with this. Material between **.KF** and **.KE** macro calls is kept together on the same page. If there is room on the current page, it appears in the same place as in the input text. If there is not enough room on the current page, the "kept" text appears on the next page. But the remainder of the current page is not left blank; the text that follows the **.KE** call is continued on the current page.

10.1.4.3 Displays In **ms** terms, a "display" is some text that you want to appear as you typed it without any filling of lines, is indented from the surrounding text, and must be kept together on the same page. There are two macros **.DS** (Display start) and **.DE** (Display End); the text that appears between these forms the display.

Consider the following formatted text, which has two displays:

```
He is sometimes unexpectedly mean.  When he describes
the  Supreme  Being as moved by prayer to stop the Fire
of London, what is his expression?

            A hollow crystal pyramid he takes,
            In firmamental waters dipp'd above,
            Of this a broad extinguisher he makes,
            And hoods the flames that to their quarry strove.

When he describes the Last Day, and the decisive tribu-
nal, he intermingles this image:

            When rattling bones together fly,
            From the four quarters of the sky.

It is indeed never in his power to resist  the  tempta-
tion of a jest.
```

This was produced by formatting the input text:

```
.nr LL 55n
.nr PI 2n
.PP
He is sometimes unexpectedly mean.
When he describes the Supreme Being as moved by prayer
to stop the Fire of London, what is his expression?
.DS
A hollow crystal pyramid he takes,
In firmamental waters dipp'd above,
Of this a broad extinguisher he makes,
And hoods the flames that to their quarry strove.
.DE
When he describes the Last Day, and the decisive tribunal,
he intermingles this image:
.DS
When rattling bones together fly,
From the four quarters of the sky.
.DE
It is indeed never in his power to resist the temptation
of a jest.
```

There are two displays in this example. As you can see the **.DS** macro does not fill lines; and by default it indents the displays by 8 n-spaces. The amount of indent is independent of the 'PI' number register.

There are several variations on the **.DS** macro; these are given as an argument to the macro call. The 'I' (for indent) variation is similar to the default. It produces an indented display, but by giving a second argument you can control the amount of indent. For example, **.DS I 5n** will produce a display that is indented 5 n-spaces instead of the usual 8.

The 'C' (for center) variation, **.DS C**, produces a display in which each line is centered on the page:

```
He is sometimes unexpectedly mean.  When he describes
the  Supreme  Being as moved by prayer to stop the Fire
of London, what is his expression?

          A hollow crystal pyramid he takes,
           In firmamental waters dipp'd above,
          Of this a broad extinguisher he makes,
        And hoods the flames that to their quarry strove.

When he describes the Last Day, and the decisive tribu-
nal, he intermingles this image:
```

```
    When rattling bones together fly,
    From the four quarters of the sky.
```

It is indeed never in his power to resist   the   temptation of a jest.

The 'L' (for left) variation, **.DS L** produces a left-aligned display; there is no indentation.

The 'B' (for block) variation, **.DS B** produces a left-aligned block, then centers the block to form the display:

```
    He is sometimes unexpectedly mean.  When he describes
the   Supreme   Being as moved by prayer to stop the Fire
of London, what is his expression?
```

```
    A hollow crystal pyramid he takes,
    In firmamental waters dipp'd above,
    Of this a broad extinguisher he makes,
    And hoods the flames that to their quarry strove.
```

When he describes the Last Day, and the decisive tribunal, he intermingles this image:

```
        When rattling bones together fly,
        From the four quarters of the sky.
```

It is indeed never in his power to resist   the   temptation of a jest.

As you can see the indentation for the two displays is different, because the displays themselves have lines of different lengths.

In all the above macros, the text is kept together as for the **.KS** macro. However, there is no separate provision for floating displays. Beware of using **.KF** in conjunction with **.DS** to achieve a floating display; it doesn't work too well. One possible outcome is that your display doesn't appear in the output text at all! If your display is a figure, your best course is to use **.KF** and the basic **nroff** no fill request, **.nf**, to achieve a floating display. If your display is a table, you should use **.KF** and the **tbl** program **.TS** macro.

There are other macros concerned with displays, but these perform no "keep" function whatsoever:

```
.ID   is the same as .DS or .DS I
.CD   is the same as .DS C
.LD   is the same as .DS L
```

These can be used when there is no requirement to keep the display all on one page. The end of the display is signified by a **.DE** macro call, as usual.

10.1.5 Titles and Cover Sheets

Documents usually have a title and an author, or maybe even several authors. It is usual to show these at the front of the document. Sometimes the place where the authors work or study is also shown. Another common feature found at the front of documents is an abstract, which summarizes the contents of the document. **ms** has macros to define each of these things.

The title of the document is defined with the **.TL** macro; the author or authors are introduced by the **.AU** macro. The **.AI** macro is used to specify the Author's Institutions. The abstract is text appearing between the macros **.AB** and **.AE**. Any of these items may be omitted, but those that do appear must be given in the order we've mentioned them. They should be the first things in the input text, apart from a possible **.DA** or **.ND** macro call to change or suppress the date.

Here is an example of calling the macros:

```
.TL
Courtship Rituals of Old Moldavia
.AU
Horace Postlethwaite
.AI
Anthropological and Sociological Institute
of Narcoville
.AB
The common inhabitants of Moldavia in the Middle
Ages had some complex, and by today's standards
comic, pre-marital practices.
.PP
This treatise details the findings of the author's
research into historical records of these rites,
and traces their devolution into the customs
followed by the young Moldavians of today.
.AE
.NH
Introduction
.PP
Burble bumf boo brag; blurp prog gramph grunge.
Blub blurb blurble burp.
```

We have used all the macros; but we have only one author, and hence only one author's institution (although we have made it occupy two lines because it is so long). We have made the abstract take two paragraphs by calling the **.PP** macro. The paragraph macros are permissible inside an abstract, but you should avoid other macro calls between **.TL** and **.AE**.

The first page of formatted text produced from the above input looks like:

Courtship Rituals of Old Moldavia

Horace Postlethwaite

Anthropological and Sociological Institute
of Narcoville

ABSTRACT

The common inhabitants of Moldavia in the Middle Ages had some complex, and by today's standards comic, pre-marital practices.

This treatise details the findings of the author's research into historical records of these rites, and traces their devolution into the customs followed by the young Moldavians of today.

1.   Introduction

Burble bumf boo brag; blurp prog ramph grunge. Blub blurb blurble burp.

This is rather a lot of material to appear on the first page of a document. It is more usual to have a cover sheet containing the abstract. This is achieved by using what is called "Released Paper" layout, which is done by putting a call on the **.RP** macro as the first thing in the input text. When you do this, the title, author, author's institution, abstract, and the current date all appear on the first output page, thus forming a cover sheet. The title, author, and author's institution are repeated on the top of the next page, which forms the first page of the actual document.

When you use the Released Paper layout, the macro **.ND** has an extra little gimmick. You can give an argument which is a specific date that you want to see on the document, much like that you give to the **.DA** macro. But the date only appears on the cover sheet, it does not appear on each page.

If you have more than one author, you may give each author on a separate line following the **.AU** macro. For instance:

```
.TL
Courtship Rituals of Old Moldavia
.AU
Horace Postlethwaite
John Z. Smith
.NH
```

In the final document, each author will appear on a separate line, centered on the page:

Courtship Rituals of Old Moldavia

Horace Postlethwaite

John Z. Smith

If you wish to show the author's institution for several different authors:

Courtship Rituals of Old Moldavia

Horace Postlethwaite

Anthropological and Sociological Institute of Narcoville

John Z. Smith

Punkville High School

then you can use successive combinations of calls on **.AU** and **.AI**, thus:

```
.TL
Courtship Rituals of Old Moldavia
.AU
Horace Postlethwaite
.AI
Anthropological and Sociological Institute of Narcoville
.AU
John Z. Smith
.AI
Punkville High School
.NH
```

One final macro that falls into this category is the **.SG** macro. This is normally given at the very end of a document. It generates the name of each author over towards the right hand side of the page, and allows above each name a vertical distance which is assumed to be sufficient for the author's signature.

10.2 Multiple Column Documents with 'col'

Using **nroff** and **troff**, it is possible to get documents with multiple columns of text printed side by side on the page, just like a newspaper or magazine is laid out. The **nroff** utility produces the multiple columns by actually generating the individual columns one after the other, with a special codes called "reverse paper-motions" in between each column. A printer which understands reverse paper-motions can move the paper in the reverse direction, so as to get back to the head of the page, or move back a certain number of lines.

Not many printers understand reverse paper-motion codes, and in order to cater for this the **col** utility is used. **col** filters out the reverse paper-motion codes, and builds an image of a complete page, which can then be sent directly to the printer.

Here is a typical use of **col**, when formatting a document called *'magazine'* (magazines usually have multiple-column layout):

```
$ nroff -Tlp magazine | col | lpr
$
```

In the example, we use **nroff** to format the manuscript. The **–Tlp** option indicates that the file is to be formatted for an ordinary line-printer. In order to make this work, we then run the output of **nroff** through **col** to filter out the reverse form-feeds, and finally use **lpr** to print the document.

The **tbl** table layout program also produces reverse paper-motion codes, and **col** is used extensively to handle the output of that utility.

10.3 Laying Out Tables with 'tbl'

There is a frequent need in document processing for laying out material in tabular format. There may be rows and columns of text. Some of the text might be captions, headers, and such. If the material is numeric, the requirements for how the columns are aligned might be different, because columns of figures are usually lined up differently from alphabetic material.

The **tbl** utility is intended to assist with the layout of tabular material. **tbl** is a pre-processor for **troff** (and for **nroff**). The **tbl** command interprets special table layout commands and translates them into streams of detailed commands for **troff** or **nroff**.

In this section, we explore some of **tbl**'s capabilities. In general, those capabilities can only be fully exploited when used in conjunction with **troff**. We can only show some of the simpler aspects of **tbl**, using it with **nroff**. We start off with some very simple examples, then gradually expand on them in order to show **tbl**'s abilities.

10.3.1 Basic Concepts of 'tbl'

Within a document, you must place your **tbl** layout requests between a "table-start" indicator and a "table-end" indicator:

```
.TS
Description of the Table Layout
Data to be Laid Out
.TE
```

In addition to telling **tbl** where the table starts and ends, the .**TS** and .**TE** macros are also used to indicate to **troff** or **nroff** where the streams of table layout commands are.

Do not forget the .**TS** and .**TE** macros in your document file. They are very important, and you get all sorts of weird results if you leave them out.

The **tbl** processor sees a table in terms of three distinct parts:

1.   The overall layout or form of the table. For instance, whether the table is centered on the page, or whether the table is to be enclosed in a box.

2. The layout of each line of data in the table. This part determines how each column in the table is laid out. For instance, whether it is left adjusted, or centered, or numeric data which must be aligned on the decimal point.

3. The actual data (the textual material) of the table itself.

Let us start off with a fairly simple example. Here is a small file of wine information,* with **tbl** requests in it:

```
$ cat cabernet
.TS
tab (/) ;
l l l .
Sterling Vineyards/1974/20.00
Joseph Phelps Vineyard/1975/8.75
Carneros Creek Winery/1976/8.50
Chateau Montelena/1973/8.50
Diamond Creek Vineyards/1976/10.00
Dehlinger/1976/5.00
Chateau Chevalier/1976/10.00
Trefethen/1974/6.50
Mayacamas/1974/9.50
Silver Oak/1973/7.50
.TE
$
```

Let us now explain what these bits mean. Firstly, there is the **.TS** line to tell **tbl** that there is a table to follow.

The line with the

```
tab (/) ;
```

on it is the so called "options" part of the table. This is part (1) from the list above. In this particular case, the only option to **tbl** is to tell it that the "tab" character is to be a slash character. Normally, **tbl** expects to see the columns of *data* in the data part of a table separated by real tab (control-I) characters. It is usually easier to see what is going on if you use a visible character which is not part of the data. In this case we used the slash character, /. The options part of the table is terminated by a semicolon, as shown in the example.

---

* From "A Guide to 110 California Cabernet Sauvignons", reproduced with permission from the Wine Appreciation Guild of San Francisco

The next part of the table header is the description of how the actual columns of data are to be laid out. This is part (2) from the list above. In this case, what we have said is that there are three left adjusted columns, indicated by the l format letters.

As we shall illustrate soon, there can be many lines of format descriptions. Each line of format description in part (2) of the table corresponds to a single data line in part (3), the data part of the table. If, however, there are more lines of data in the data part of the table than there are format description lines, the *last* line of the format description part applies to all the remaining lines of the data.

In this example, the three letter l format letters apply to every line in the data part of the table. The format descriptions are terminated with a period at the end of the last one.

Lastly, there comes the actual data of the table itself. It is the list of wineries, years, and prices. Each of the fields is separated from the next by the / character.

Now we show what happens when this list is formatted by passing it through **tbl** and **nroff**.

The way you use **tbl** is very simple. **tbl** accepts a list of file names as arguments. **tbl** writes its results to the Standard Output, so unless you want the generated **nroff** formatting requests to appear on the screen, you must either redirect the output, or (as is more usual) pipe the output of **tbl** to the formatter.

A list of files may be given to **tbl**, and they are processed one by one in the order in which they are specified on the command line. If you don't give any file names, **tbl** reads the Standard Input. The Standard Input may be read in the middle of a list of files, by typing a minus sign at the desired place.

Let us format the table we showed above:

```
$ tbl cabernet | nroff
Sterling Vineyards          1974    20.00
Joseph Phelps Vineyard      1975    8.75
Carneros Creek Winery       1976    8.50
Chateau Montelena           1973    8.50
Diamond Creek Vineyards     1976    10.00
Dehlinger                   1976    5.00
Chateau Chevalier           1976    10.00
Trefethen                   1974    6.50
Mayacamas                   1974    9.50
Silver Oak                  1973    7.50
$
```

After formatting, the table appears on the left hand side of the page. The chances are, such a table is part of a larger document. Tables which appear in running text usually look better if they are centered on the page. To achieve that, we specify the requirement for centering in part (1), the "options" part of the table, which affects the overall layout:

```
$ cat cabernet
.TS
center tab (/) ;
1 1 1 .
Sterling Vineyards/1974/20.00
Joseph Phelps Vineyard/1975/8.75
            <etc...>
Silver Oak/1973/7.50
.TE
$
```

All we have done here is add a "center" request in the options part of the table. When formatted, this looks much better:

```
$ tbl cabernet | nroff
            Sterling Vineyards        1974    20.00
            Joseph Phelps Vineyard    1975    8.75
            Carneros Creek Winery     1976    8.50
            Chateau Montelena         1973    8.50
            Diamond Creek Vineyards   1976    10.00
            Dehlinger                 1976    5.00
            Chateau Chevalier         1976    10.00
            Trefethen                 1974    6.50
            Mayacamas                 1974    9.50
            Silver Oak                1973    7.50
$
```

There are now 13 spaces at the start of each line. The actual text occupies 38 columns of the page. So **tbl**/**nroff** have placed the table in the middle of a page that is 64 columns wide, and as you can see, the overall appearance of the table has improved somewhat.

10.3.2 Numerically Aligned Columns

There is something wrong with the examples above. The prices are left-aligned. Prices really should appear with the decimal points aligned vertically. The years appear correct because they are all the same size, so their numerical values are not significant here. But they should really be treated as numbers, because that is what they actually are.

Now we show how to make the numeric fields line up properly. We do this by changing the format specification letters for the years and the prices:

```
$ cat cabernet
.TS
center tab (/) ;
l n n .
Sterling Vineyards/1974/20.00
Joseph Phelps Vineyard/1975/8.75
             <etc...>
Mayacamas/1974/9.50
Silver Oak/1973/7.50
.TE
$
```

We have made one important change to the table. The format specification part indicates that the second and third columns are numerically aligned columns. This means that numbers placed in the second and third columns of each line of data will be aligned properly.

If numbers contain decimal points, as in the example, **tbl** lines them up on the decimal points. When numbers do not contain decimal points, **tbl** lines them up on their units digits. Here is how the table looks when we format it:

```
$ tbl cabernet | nroff
            Sterling Vineyards        1974    20.00
            Joseph Phelps Vineyard    1975     8.75
            Carneros Creek Winery     1976     8.50
            Chateau Montelena         1973     8.50
            Diamond Creek Vineyards   1976    10.00
            Dehlinger                 1976     5.00
            Chateau Chevalier         1976    10.00
            Trefethen                 1974     6.50
            Mayacamas                 1974     9.50
            Silver Oak                1973     7.50
$
```

The table looks better when the numerical data is aligned on the decimal point.

10.3.3 Tables with Headings

Now we show how our example can be expanded to include captions for the individual columns. Here is an improved version of our table:

```
$ cat cabernet
.TS
center tab (/) ;
c c c
l n n .
Establishment/Year/Price
.sp 1
Sterling Vineyards/1974/20.00
Joseph Phelps Vineyard/1975/8.75
             <etc...>
Mayacamas/1974/9.50
Silver Oak/1973/7.50
.TE
$
```

The example above now shows an extra line in the format description part, and some extra data in the data part. The first line of the format descriptions indicates that there are to be three columns of data, each one centered within its column. This format applies to the very first line of the data. The second (and last) line of the format description part is the same as before, and it applies to all the remaining data lines in the table.

When we format this new layout, we get something different:

```
$ tbl cabernet | nroff
                 Establishment        Year    Price

            Sterling Vineyards        1974    20.00
            Joseph Phelps Vineyard    1975     8.75
            Carneros Creek Winery     1976     8.50
            Chateau Montelena         1973     8.50
            Diamond Creek Vineyards   1976    10.00
            Dehlinger                 1976     5.00
            Chateau Chevalier         1976    10.00
            Trefethen                 1974     6.50
            Mayacamas                 1974     9.50
            Silver Oak                1973     7.50
$
```

As you can see, we have a table with headers for the specific data columns.

You should note that we used an **nroff** **.sp** request to generate a blank line in the table after the header line. In general, **tbl** ignores **nroff** commands appearing in table layouts. If you were to use a real blank line, **tbl** interprets it as part of the data, and you don't always get the desired results.

10.3.4 Tables with Spanned Headings

Our next example shows a table with a header for the entire table. There is to be an overall heading line, which is only one column, centered across the whole table. When you describe a table, the format description part, part (2) of the table, must always describe the largest number of columns which that table will have. If there are some lines which will have fewer columns of data, you must indicate what to do with those specific lines.

```
$ cat cabernet
.TS
center tab (/) ;
c s s
c c c
l n n .
Selected California Cabernet Sauvignon
.sp 1
Establishment/Year/Price
.sp 1
Sterling Vineyards/1974/20.00
Joseph Phelps Vineyard/1975/8.75
            <etc...>
Mayacamas/1974/9.50
Silver Oak/1973/7.50
.TE
$
```

The first line of the format description part now shows a centered, spanned column. A spanned element can span as many or as few columns as you like.

Here is the results of formatting the above table:

```
$ tbl cabernet | nroff
                Selected California Cabernet Sauvignon

                Establishment          Year    Price

                Sterling Vineyards     1974    20.00
                Joseph Phelps Vineyard 1975     8.75
                Carneros Creek Winery  1976     8.50
                Chateau Montelena      1973     8.50
                Diamond Creek Vineyards 1976   10.00
                Dehlinger              1976     5.00
                Chateau Chevalier      1976    10.00
                Trefethen              1974     6.50
                Mayacamas              1974     9.50
                Silver Oak             1973     7.50
$
```

The table now has an overall header, which is nicely centered over the other columns.

10.3.5 Tables Enclosed in Boxes

tbl also has the capability to enclose a table in a box. There are three choices for boxing in a table:

- The entire table can be enclosed in a box,
- The entire table can be enclosed in a double box,
- The entire table, and every item in it, can be enclosed within box lines.

Here is our wine information table, with specifications for boxing it:

```
$ cat cabernet
.TS
center box tab (/) ;
c s s
c c c
l n n .
Selected California Cabernet Sauvignon
.sp 1
Establishment/Year/Price
.sp 1
Sterling Vineyards/1974/20.00
Joseph Phelps Vineyard/1975/8.75
            <etc...>
Mayacamas/1974/9.50
Silver Oak/1973/7.50
.TE
$
```

In the "options" part, part (1) of the table, we added the "box" keyword, to indicate that the whole table is to be enclosed in a box.

As soon as you start to use boxes, the interface between **tbl** and **nroff** gets somewhat more complicated. When you ask **tbl** to put boxes around tables, it starts generating **nroff** requests which produce reverse paper-motions in the output. As we said previously, most printers cannot handle reverse paper-motions.

To handle this case, we must use **col** as the final filter in the command line. Also, it is necessary to tell **nroff** the specific kind of output device upon which the results will be printed. This means we have to use the **–T** option to **nroff**. In all our examples, we use the regular line printer, so we must use the **–Tlp** option. So the command line for a table with boxes must be expanded as shown in the example, and the results of the process are like this:

```
$ tbl cabernet | nroff -Tlp | col
 ------------------------------------------------
|  Selected California Cabernet Sauvignon|
|                                                |
|     Establishment          Year     Price|
|                                                |
|  Sterling Vineyards        1974     20.00|
|  Joseph Phelps Vineyard    1975      8.75|
|  Carneros Creek Winery     1976      8.50|
|  Chateau Montelena         1973      8.50|
|  Diamond Creek Vineyards   1976     10.00|
|  Dehlinger                 1976      5.00|
|  Chateau Chevalier         1976     10.00|
|  Trefethen                 1974      6.50|
|  Mayacamas                 1974      9.50|
|  Silver Oak                1973      7.50|
|                                                |
 ------------------------------------------------
$
```

The **–Tlp** option to **nroff** indicates that the results are to be printed on the line printer. The output of **nroff** must be piped through the **col** utility in order to filter out the reverse form feeds.

10.3.6 Drawing Lines in Tables

It is also possible to draw horizontal lines in a table. We stick with the same example, but we draw lines after the two headers. Here is how we have to modify the table to do this:

```
$ cat cabernet
.TS
center box tab (/) ;
c s s
c c c
l n n .
Selected California Cabernet Sauvignon
_
Establishment/Year/Price
_
Sterling Vineyards/1974/20.00
Joseph Phelps Vineyard/1975/8.75
             <etc...>
Mayacamas/1974/9.50
Silver Oak/1973/7.50
.TE
$
```

Instead of the **.sp 1** requests, we have placed an underline character _ which indicates to **tbl** that a horizontal line is to be drawn at
this point in the table. When the table is formatted, the results are
like this:

$ tbl cabernet | nroff -Tlp | col

```
---------------------------------------------
| Selected California Cabernet Sauvignon|
|-------------------------------------------|
|     Establishment        Year    Price|
|-------------------------------------------|
| Sterling Vineyards        1974    20.00|
| Joseph Phelps Vineyard    1975     8.75|
| Carneros Creek Winery     1976     8.50|
| Chateau Montelena         1973     8.50|
| Diamond Creek Vineyards   1976    10.00|
| Dehlinger                 1976     5.00|
| Chateau Chevalier         1976    10.00|
| Trefethen                 1974     6.50|
| Mayacamas                 1974     9.50|
| Silver Oak                1973     7.50|
|-------------------------------------------|
$
```

It is possible to draw vertical lines as well, between any selected
columns. It is also possible to draw horizontal lines across parts of a
table. We do not cover these issues here; they are described in the
paper entitled "Tbl — A Program to Format Tables" by M. E. Lesk.

10.3.7 Enclosing Everything in a Table in Boxes

tbl also has the "allbox" capability, which draws lines around every object in the table, as well as drawing a box around the whole table. To get this capability, just change the table header part to include the keyword "allbox" instead of the simple "box" keyword.

```
$ cat cabernet
.TS
center allbox tab (/) ;
c s s
c c c
l n n .
Selected California Cabernet Sauvignon
.sp 1
Establishment/Year/Price
.sp 1
Sterling Vineyards/1974/20.00
Joseph Phelps Vineyard/1975/8.75
              <etc...>
Mayacamas/1974/9.50
Silver Oak/1973/7.50
.TE
$
```

When we format the table, it has the following effects:

```
$ tbl cabernet ¦ nroff -Tlp ¦ col
```

Selected California Cabernet Sauvignon		
Establishment	Year	Price
Sterling Vineyards	1974	20.00
Joseph Phelps Vineyard	1975	8.75
Carneros Creek Winery	1976	8.50
Chateau Montelena	1973	8.50
Diamond Creek Vineyards	1976	10.00
Dehlinger	1976	5.00
Chateau Chevalier	1976	10.00
Trefethen	1974	6.50
Mayacamas	1974	9.50
Silver Oak	1973	7.50

```
$
```

As you can see, **tbl** isn't too clever about drawing boxes on a line printer using **nroff**. The results using **troff** and a phototypesetter are much better.

10.3.8 Flowing Text Blocks in a Column

So far, the data in the columns of the tables have been fixed within certain boundaries. A frequent requirement is to have ordinary flowing text in a specific column of a table. Flowing text is justified between the margins of the specific column in which it appears in the table. In **tbl** parlance, these sections of flowing text are called "text blocks". Each block of text is bracketed with the markers **T{** (at the start), and **T}** (at the end). The **T{** marker must be at the end of a line, and the **T}** marker must be at the start of a line. The example below illustrates this feature. We start the discussion with a small table showing the more popular grape varieties grown in the California wine producing regions. Here is what the source text looks like:

```
$ cat winetypes
.TS
center allbox tab (/) ;
c s
c c
a a .
Guide to California Grapes
Grape Type/Comments
Cabernet Sauvignon/T{
Finest of the red wines. Lots of fruit.
Highly perfumed.  Long lasting wine.
T}
Chardonnay/T{
Finest of the white wines.
Perfumed, grape flavor.  Lasts well.
T}
Johannisberg Riesling/T{
Fruity, flower scented white wine.
Often in late-harvest versions with
high quantities of residual sugar.
T}
.TE
$
```

When we format that file, we get this result:

```
$ tbl winetypes | nroff -Tlp | col
```

Guide to California Grapes	
Grape Type	Comments
Cabernet Sauvignon	Finest of the red wines. Lots of fruit. Highly perfumed. Long lasting wine.
Chardonnay	Finest of the white wines. Perfumed, grape flavor. Lasts well.
Johannisberg Riesling	Fruity, flower scented white wine. Often in late-harvest versions with high quantities of residual sugar.

```
$
```

Although the text in the second column "flows" between the margins of the column, it does not do so very well, because the column is too short. To improve on this, we have to tell **tbl** to make the second column of the table wider.

10.3.9 Modifying the Format of Columns

When you describe the layout of a table, **tbl** makes some decisions as to how wide the columns need to be to accommodate the various pieces of data. It often happens that **tbl**'s decisions are not entirely adequate. For example, you might decide that a particular column should be wider, in order to display some text in a more pleasing way. In the previous example, you can see that the flowing text in the right hand column doesn't really look all that good, because the column is too narrow. It would look better if the column were wider. **tbl** provides the ability to specify the width of a column in the format description part of the table.

When you specify the layout of a column in the format description part of the table, each of the format key letters can be followed by further description items, which modify the column layout in some way. There are a number of these modifiers. Some of them concern changing fonts and altering point sizes, those are not covered in this book.

To change the width of a column, you follow the key letter with a letter **w** (for **w**idth), then enclose the column-width specification in parentheses. The width can be specified as a number, in which case it is taken to be that many n-spaces. Otherwise, you can place a units letter, such as **i** (for inches), after the number. The example below shows a table with the second column defined to be 3.5 inches wide.

```
$ cat winetypes
.TS
center allbox tab (/) ;
c s
c c
a lw(3.5i) .
Guide to California Grapes
Grape Type/Comments
Cabernet Sauvignon;T{
                <etc...>
Fruity, flower scented white wine.
Often in late-harvest versions with
high quantities of residual sugar.
T}
.TE
$
```

We made two changes in the table format. Firstly we defined the second data column to be left adjusted instead of alphanumeric. Then we defined the width of the column to be 3.5 inches wide. Let us format that and see what we get:

```
$ tbl winetypes | nroff -Tlp | col
```

Guide to California Grapes	
Grape Type	Comments
Cabernet Sauvignon	Finest of the red wines. Lots of fruit. Highly perfumed. Long lasting wine.
Chardonnay	Finest of the white wines. Per-fumed, grape flavor. Lasts well.
Johannisberg Riesling	Fruity, flower scented white wine. Often in late-harvest versions with high quantities of residual sugar.

$

The table is now not only formatted somewhat better, with less gaps between the words, but the table is also shorter because of the wider column. Overall, this second table has a more pleasing appearance than does the first example.

10.3.10 Changing the Format of a Table

It is possible to change the layout of the data columns anywhere in a table. The overall layout of the table cannot be changed, but the format specification part can. To do this, the **.T&** request is used, to indicate a temporary end to the current portion of the table, and to introduce a new format specification part for the table.

To illustrate this capability, we add some Chardonnays to our Cabernet file from earlier in this chapter:

```
$ cat cabandchard
.TS
center box tab (/) ;
c s s
c c c
l n n .
Selected California Cabernet Sauvignon
_
Establishment/Year/Price
_
Sterling Vineyards/1974/20.00
Joseph Phelps Vineyard/1975/8.75
            <etc...>
Mayacamas/1974/9.50
Silver Oak/1973/7.50
_
.sp 1
.T&
c s s
c c c
l n n .
Selected California Chardonnay
_
Establishment/Year/Price
_
Caymus Vineyards/1976/12.00
Chateau St. Jean/1976/11.50
Robert Mondavi/1977/9.00
Spring Mountain/1976/10.00
Sterling Vineyards/1976/10.00
Chaparral/1977/8.50
Dry Creek Winery/1977/8.00
St. Clements/1977/10.00
Chateau Montelena/1975/10.00
Mayacamas Vineyards/1976/11.00
.TE
$
```

The **.T&** request states that this is a temporary end to the table, and that a new format specification part is to appear. In this example, we have just inserted a new set of headings for the Chardonnay wines introduced in the latter part of the table. The formatted table produced is shown in figure 10.3.

The **tbl** program has much more capability than we have described above. However, what we have shown should be sufficient to give you an idea of the kinds of things which can be achieved using **tbl**.

10.4 Further Documentation Aids

The UNIX system has other capabilities than those described above. There are other macro packages available, and there is a utility program designed to ease the task of producing documents containing mathematical equations.

The **mm** macro package stands for **m**emorandum **m**acros. This macro package usually appears with the Programmer's Workbench (PWB) versions of the UNIX system. It is intended, not for one-page office memos, but for the kind of documents which many companies call "Internal Technical Memoranda". These documents usually take the form of technical reports. The **mm** macro package is described in the paper called:

> PWB/MM Programmer's Workbench Memorandum Macros
>> by D. W. Smith, and J. R. Mashey
>> Bell Laboratories, New Jersey 07974.

mm is a more sophisticated macro package, providing more capability, than is **ms**. Among other things, **mm** will automatically number items in a list, and will also automatically produce a table of contents.

The **me** macro package, which is available on the Berkeley UNIX system, also provides automatic numbering of lists items, and produces a table of contents. For further reading, consult the paper entitled:

> Writing Papers with NROFF Using -me
>> by Eric P. Allman
>> Electronics Research Laboratory,
>> University of California,
>> Berkeley, California 94720.

One thing to notice about the **me** macro package is that the macro names are lowercase letters, so it is not easy to distinguish between them and basic **nroff** formatting requests.

```
$ tbl cabandchard | nroff -Tlp | col
```

```
---------------------------------------------------------
|              Selected California Cabernet Sauvignon     |
|--------------------------------------------------------|
|        Establishment           Year         Price      |
|--------------------------------------------------------|
| Sterling Vineyards             1974         20.00      |
| Joseph Phelps Vineyard         1975          8.75      |
| Carneros Creek Winery          1976          8.50      |
| Chateau Montelena              1973          8.50      |
| Diamond Creek Vineyards        1976         10.00      |
| Dehlinger                      1976          5.00      |
| Chateau Chevalier              1976         10.00      |
| Trefethen                      1974          6.50      |
| Mayacamas                      1974          9.50      |
| Silver Oak                     1973          7.50      |
|                                                        |
| --------------------------------------------------      |
|                                                        |
|              Selected California Chardonnay            |
|--------------------------------------------------------|
|        Establishment           Year         Price      |
|--------------------------------------------------------|
| Caymus Vineyards               1976         12.00      |
| Chateau St.  Jean             1976         11.50      |
| Robert Mondavi                 1977          9.00      |
| Spring Mountain                1976         10.00      |
| Sterling Vineyards             1976         10.00      |
| Chaparral                      1977          8.50      |
| Dry Creek Winery               1977          8.00      |
| St.  Clements                 1977         10.00      |
| Chateau Montelena              1975         10.00      |
| Mayacamas Vineyards            1976         11.00      |
---------------------------------------------------------
$
```

Figure 10.3   A Table with a Change of Format

The **eqn** and **neqn** packages aid preparation of documents containing mathematical equations. **eqn** is a preprocessor for **troff**; **neqn** is a preprocessor for **nroff**. **eqn** turns an English-like description of an equation into the formatting request necessary to generate the mathematical symbols for that equation. We can only hint at the capabilities of **eqn** here. Because of the limitations of typewriter-like printers, **neqn** does not provide all the capabilities that **eqn** does. We give one very simple example. The description of the equation as shown here:

y = c sub 1 x sup 2 + c sub 2 x + c sub 3

produces the following output when formatted using **neqn** and **nroff**, where the output is directed to a Diablo 1620 printer:

$$y = c_1 x^2 + c_2 x + c_3$$

For a writeup on **eqn**, with many illustrations of the power and flexibility of this remarkable tool, see the paper called:

A System for Typesetting Mathematics,
  by Brian W. Kernighan and Lorinda L. Cherry
  Bell Laboratories, New Jersey 07974.

Other formatting tools available consist of various utilities that check the validity of a document. Bell Laboratories have been working on a suite of packages collectively known as the "Writer's Workbench". This includes a program to check spelling; a utility to compute the reading grade-level of a document; and finally, utilities called **style** and **diction**, which advise the writer of redundant usage, archaic forms, and dubious grammatical constructs.

Finally, on PWB UNIX systems, there is a program called **diffmark**. This program is used, in conjunction with the **diff** command, to generate input to the formatter which will produce revision bars on the final document. It is possible to produce different markings for changes, deletions and additions.

10.5 Summary

By now you should be saturated with the UNIX system's capabilities for handling text and processing documents. It is worth while studying some of the other macro packages available, and comparing their capabilities.

If you have the appropriate output devices, play with **tbl** and **eqn** to see how they function. Experiment with **diffmark** to get revision bars on different versions of your document.

In many ways the UNIX system documentation facilities are somewhat cumbersome. The **nroff** package, after all, is a lineal descendant of a package developed 20 years ago, under entirely different constraints and assumptions. But, the lesson that these documentation packages teach us is clear: do not put all the eggs in one basket. Instead, separate out the functions (equation processing, table layout, revision bar generation, page layout) into independent packages, instead of making one monster utility which does none of those things very well.

Lastly, on-line documentation has the tremendous advantage that once something is typed, it need never be retyped, it only needs correcting and revising. Parts of documents can be replicated at different places in a manuscript without the need to retype it each time. The idea of computer aided documentation is a fairly new idea in most of the computer industry, but is catching on slowly. The tools are there, you just need to use them.

11 Programming the UNIX Shell

We have mentioned the Shell frequently in many of the previous chapters, but just what is the Shell? Consider the diagram representing a computer system as shown in figure 11.1.

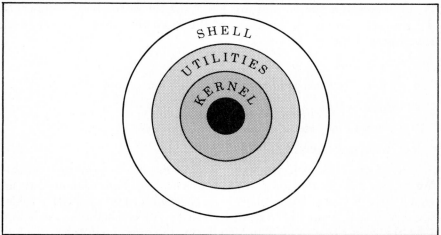

Figure 11.1   Representation of the Computer System

Right in the very center is the computer and associated equipment. This is what is called the hardware of the system.

Surrounding the hardware are some programs that handle details such as talking to disks, managing the computer's resources, organizing the file system, and all sorts of detailed work that users don't really want to know about. This layer of software is the kernel of the UNIX operating system.

The kernel provides a layer of support, independent of the hardware, for the utility programs like **sort**, **grep**, the editors, **nroff**, and various compilers. These utilities are represented by the next layer outside the kernel.

The outermost layer represents the Shell. The Shell forms the interface between users and the rest of the system.

The Shell is a program that runs automatically when you log in to the UNIX system. It reads each command that you type at your terminal, and interprets what you've asked for. We have already seen many of the functions performed by the Shell in earlier chapters. The Shell expands any file-matching wild-card characters you may have used. If you have redirected the Standard Input and Output, or the Diagnostic Output, the Shell deals with that too. Finally, the Shell examines the command you have asked for, calls up the program from the appropriate place (remember that commands can live in more than one place, like */bin* and */usr/bin*), then passes all the arguments to that program and starts it up.

Although we have shown the Shell as a separate outer layer in the diagram above, the Shell is itself just an ordinary program, and can be called up by the command **sh**. The argument that you give to **sh** is the name of a file containing UNIX system commands. When you do this, you can use the features of the Shell that make it very much like a programming language:

- Variables,
- Control structures like "if", "while", and so on,
- Subroutines,
- Parameter passing,
- Interrupt handling.

These features provide you with the capability to design your own tools. We go into this in some detail later in this chapter. Files of commands are called "shell procedures", or "shell files", or "shell scripts", or simply "shells". We distinguish between "a shell", meaning a file of Shell commands, and "the Shell", or even "a Shell", which means the program which runs those commands.

Since the Shell is simply a program called upon to interpret commands which users type, and not an integral part of the kernel, it is easy to have different versions of it. There are several popular Shells. They are all more or less the same in basic essentials, but they vary a lot in detail. In this book we talk about two Shells: the UNIX system version 7 Shell (also called the Bourne Shell)* and the C-Shell which is available on the Berkeley UNIX system and some others.

Some UNIX systems support more than one Shell. For instance, on the Berkeley UNIX system both the Bourne Shell and the C-Shell are available, as the programs **sh** and **csh** respectively. On such systems, the Shell that each user gets when they log in is specified in a field in the password file entry for that user. The field contains the pathname to the Shell to be used, so if you develop your own Shell it is fairly easy to set up to use it.

11.1 Login Profile

When you first log in to the UNIX system, whatever version of the Shell you have is called up to deal with your session. At this point the Shell looks to see if you have a login profile. This is a file, having a specific name, which contains commands that you always want to execute at the beginning of each login session.

Way back in the beginning of the book, we discussed what to do when you make a mistake, and we talked about the erase and kill characters. We showed you how to use **stty** to change the erase and kill characters from their default values. **stty** is a command that could be put in your login profile, since you want to do it each time you log in.

You can put any UNIX system commands you like into your login profile. For instance, when you log on you might like to know who else is logged on, and what the time is. Your profile will look like:

```
stty erase '^H' kill '^U'
who
date
```

Another thing that you might want to do in your profile is change the prompt from the usual $ sign. The prompt is defined by a Shell variable. It is possible to change the value assigned to this variable, which in turn causes the prompt to be different.

---

* After S. R. Bourne of Bell Laboratories

Another Shell variable tells the system where to look for commands. These are usually the system directories */bin* and */usr/bin,* but if you want to set up your own cache of private commands you can tell the system to look in other directories too.

The name that must be given to the login profile file depends on which Shell is being used:

On UNIX system version 7 it must be called *'.profile'.*

For the C Shell it must be called either *'.login'* or *'.cshrc'.*

On some Shells there is a similar action when you log out: commands in a file called *'.logout'* in your home directory are executed.

11.2 Shell Procedures

As we said at the beginning of this chapter, a shell procedure is a file which contains commands. For instance, suppose you have a shell file called *'dothat'* which contains UNIX system commands. There are two ways we can get the system to obey these commands. One is by giving the filename as an argument to the **sh** command (or **csh** if you want to use the C Shell):

```
$ sh dothat
```

The other way is to use the **chmod** command to change the mode of the shell procedure so that it is executable. When you do this you have effectively made your own command. You can then just type the name of the shell file just like a command:

```
$ chmod 755 dothat
$ dothat
```

The **chmod** command makes the file executable (rwxr-xr-x permissions), the shell file can now be called up like any other command.

Be careful how you name your shell files; if you duplicate the name of an existing command (one that lives in */bin* or */usr/bin,* for instance), you lose access to that command and can only use your own version. This is not completely true; you can of course access the original command by giving the full pathname to it, but that's cumbersome.

11.3 Some Simple Shell Procedures

A very simple procedure can be made using the **echo** command. So the very first shell procedure to write is one which just greets you at your terminal:

```
$ cat > greetings
echo  Hi there
^D
$ chmod 755 greetings
$
```

We have created the shell file *'greetings'* and made it executable, now when we type the command **greetings** we get:

```
$ greetings
Hi there
$
```

Let's look at a more useful example. When we discussed the text manipulation utility programs, we took an example of a file containing a list of people and their phone numbers. Suppose we now want to use that file to print out a distribution list, with a heading, and without phone numbers. We can use this pipeline of commands:

```
$ sort +1 -2 people | tr -d 0-9 | pr -h Distribution \
> | lpr
$
```

This is a long command to type, and it is easy to make a mistake. Also, if the distribution list is produced seldom, it is easy to forget what you have to do to get one. The solution to both these problems is to make a shell file:

```
$ cat > makelist
sort +1 -2 people | tr -d 0-9 | pr -h Distribution | lpr
^D
$ chmod 755 makelist
$
```

Now we can make our distribution list by the simple command:

```
$ makelist
$
```

There is no response other than the prompt because we have routed the output to the printer from inside the shell file itself. If we wanted to check the output of **makelist** before it was printed, we would leave off the final **lpr** from the pipeline:

```
$ cat >makelist
sort +1 -2 people ¦ tr -d 0-9 ¦ pr -h Distribution
^D
$ chmod 755 makelist
$
```

The output of this version of *'makelist'* appears on the terminal screen. To send the output to the printer we have to say:

```
$ makelist ¦ lpr
$
```

Let us examine a not-so-simple shell procedure, which illustrates both how to use the Shell effectively, and also demonstrates some of the potential pitfalls. Suppose that whenever you use **ls** you always use the –l option to get a long listing. You get sick of typing **ls –l** all the time, so you make a shell file called *'ll'* (for long ls):

```
$ cat >ll
ls -l
^D
$ chmod 755 ll
$ ll
-r--r--r--  1  maryann     40  Feb 18 10:02 adminpeople
-r--r--r--  1  maryann     60  Feb 18 10:12 hardpeople
-rwxr-xr-x  1  maryann      6  Mar 17 12:00 ll
-r--r--r--  1  maryann     40  Feb 18 10:02 adminpeople
-r--r--r--  1  maryann     60  Feb 19 11:23 managers
-r--r--r--  1  maryann    100  Feb 18 10:19 softpeople
$
```

This looks OK, but suppose you forget and keep using **ls** instead of **ll**. You might be tempted to make a copy of **ll**, and call the new command **ls**:

```
$ cp ll ls
$ ls
```

Now you have your own special version of **ls**, but when you try to use it the system doesn't respond at all! You have to interrupt the command (with BREAK, or RUBOUT, or DEL, or control-C) to get the prompt again. This is because your version of **ls** is trying to call **ls** (that is it is trying to call itself), which is trying to call itself, which is trying to call .... — you see the problem? The way out of this is to use the full pathname to the real **ls**:

```
$ cat >ls
/bin/ls -l
^D
$ chmod 755 ls
$ ls
-r--r--r--   1  maryann     40  Feb 18 10:02 adminpeople
-r--r--r--   1  maryann     60  Feb 18 10:12 hardpeople
-rwxr-xr-x   1  maryann      6  Mar 17 12:00 ll
-rwxr-xr-x   1  maryann     11  Mar 17 12:29 ls
-r--r--r--   1  maryann     40  Feb 18 10:02 adminpeople
-r--r--r--   1  maryann     60  Feb 19 11:23 managers
-r--r--r--   1  maryann    100  Feb 18 10:19 softpeople
$
```

This illustrates that you have to be careful when naming your shell files, especially when you are creating a shell file to produce a modified version of an existing command.

So far we have only used this special version of **ls** to list the current directory, let's see what happens when we try to list some other directory:

```
$ ls /etc
-r--r--r--   1  maryann     40  Feb 18 10:02 adminpeople
-r--r--r--   1  maryann     60  Feb 18 10:12 hardpeople
-rwxr-xr-x   1  maryann      6  Mar 17 12:00 ll
-rwxr-xr-x   1  maryann     11  Mar 17 12:29 ls
-r--r--r--   1  maryann     40  Feb 18 10:02 adminpeople
-r--r--r--   1  maryann     60  Feb 19 11:23 managers
-r--r--r--   1  maryann    100  Feb 18 10:19 softpeople
$
```

We still get a listing of the current directory, because your version of **ls** completely ignores any arguments you give it. In the next few paragraphs we explain how shell procedures can recognize arguments on the calling command line. In the meantime, we can try working around this by changing directory before using your own special variation of **ls**:

```
$ cd /usr
$ ls
bin
dict
games
include
lib
pub
$
```

Now we are back to using the system version of the **ls** command. If we try to use the one you originally made, **ll**, we are even worse off:

```
$ cd /usr
$ ll
ll: not found
$
```

The system doesn't even recognize your command. This is because it looks for commands in various directories in a fixed order, the default order being:

- the current directory,
- the system directory */bin,*
- the system directory */usr/bin.*

If the command isn't in any of those directories, you get the "not found" error message. If a file of the same name as the command lives in one of the directories, but you don't have execute permission on it, you get a different message — "cannot execute". The system executes (or tries to) the first version of the command that it finds, so if a command lives in both */bin* and */usr/bin,* it is the version in */bin* which is usually run. This is why you can have a command of the same name as one of the commands in */bin,* and yours takes precedence.

However, if the name of the command you type contains a / (a pathname rather than a simple command name), the system doesn't search the directories, it uses the command specified by the pathname. So we could have said:

```
$ cd /usr
$ /aa/widget/maryann/ll
drwxr-xr-x 3 bin        256 Jan  7 20:51 bin
drwxr-xr-x 3 bin        128 Feb 14  1981 dict
drwxr-xr-x 5 bin        432 Aug 21 15:15 games
drwxr-xr-x 3 bin        496 Feb 14  1981 include
drwxr-xr-x13 bin        848 Dec 28 16:48 lib
drwxr-xr-x 2 root        80 Feb 14  1981 pub
$
```

The directories that the system looks at to find commands, and the order in which it looks at them is called the "command search path". The search path is set up as a Shell variable, and it can be changed. So you can designate one of your directories to hold all your special commands, then change the command search path by altering the value of the Shell variable that defines it. If you don't want to change this Shell variable every time you log on, you can define it in your login profile. Let's first make a directory containing your special commands:

```
$ mkdir bin
$ mv ll ls bin
$ ls
adminpeople
bin
hardpeople
managers
softpeople
$ ls  bin
ll
ls
$
```

Now that we have moved the files **ll** and **ls** into a different directory, we have reverted to using the real **ls**, because we haven't yet set up your command search path to look in your own private directory.

Notice that you now have an entry called *'bin'* in the **ls** output. This *'bin'* is the directory where you will keep all your own commands. It is normal practice, and consistent with the naming of the system directories, to call the directory containing your private commands *'bin'*. But it doesn't have to be called that, you can call it *'mycmds'*, or whatever you wish.

11.4 Shell Variables

The Shell gives you the capability to define a named variable and assign a value to it. In the version 7 Shell, the simplest way of setting a shell variable is via an assignment statement:

```
variable=value
```

The value assigned to the variable can then be retrieved by preceding the name of the variable with a dollar sign:

```
$variable
```

For example, see what happens when we use these commands:

```
fruit=apple
cheese=cheddar
wine=chardonnay
echo $fruit, $cheese, $wine ....Mmmm!
```

the **echo** command in the example produces the output:

```
apple, cheddar, chardonnay ....Mmmm!
```

The value assigned to a variable can be defined in terms of another shell variable, or even defined in terms of itself:

```
wine=$fruit-jack
fruit=pine$fruit
echo $wine and $fruit
```

This last **echo** command generates the output:

```
apple-jack and pineapple
```

Take note that **wine=$fruitjack** does not give us "applejack", because the Shell is looking for a variable called 'fruitjack' that doesn't exist. The result is that **$wine** is assigned a null (empty) string. If we really want the string "applejack" to be defined in terms of the **$fruit** variable, we must delimit that variable with braces when we use it:

```
$ wine=${fruit}jack
$ echo $wine
applejack
$
```

The curly braces must be used whenever a variable needs to be combined with another string, and there is no other way of distinguishing the end of the variable name and the beginning of the following string.

There are other ways in which a shell variable can be set. For instance, a variable can take the value of the output of a command, or a value taken from a file.

Although Shell variables are mostly used inside shell procedures, they can also be used from the terminal. They are usually used in this way when you want to use a shorthand notation.

For instance, suppose that there is a directory with a long pathname that you are continually accessing. You might set up a shell variable '*d*' to the pathname, then access files in that directory by **$d/file**. This can save a lot of typing, and the frustration of mistyping the pathname again and again.

As another example, if there is a command which you are using frequently, and you have to specify many options, you might want to set it up as a shell variable:

```
$ s="sort +2n +1 -2"
$ $s   tennis | lpr
$ $s   racquetball | lpr
$ $s   squash | lpr
$ $s   pingpong | lpr
$
```

Notice the use of quotes to preserve spaces in the variable definition. If you set up a shell variable as an abbreviation of a command line, the command must not contain pipe symbols (|), redirection (< or >), or the background processing symbol (**&**).

11.4.1 Predefined Shell Variables

There are some variables which are predefined by the Shell. Some of these can be modified, others are read-only (they can be used, but not modified). Some of the more interesting variables which can be modified are:

HOME   is set to be the user's home directory — that is, the default argument to the **cd** command.

PATH   is the set of directories that the system searches in order to find commands.

PS1   is the primary prompt string. That is the system prompt, which on UNIX system version 7 is the dollar sign, $.

From these we can see how we can do two of the things we mentioned might be done in your login profile.

11.4.1.1 Changing the UNIX System Prompt   The system prompt can be changed by redefining the Shell variable which contains the prompt character string.

If you want a reasonably simple prompt, you can include in your login profile the statement:

```
PS1=?
```

Now, instead of the usual $ prompt you will get **?** Be careful with this one, some of the interactive commands also have a prompt **?** (for example **mail**) and you could get confused.

In practice, you will find the system easier to use if there is a space following your prompt. To make sure you get that space, you must use quotes:

```
PS1="? "
```

If you want a more complicated prompt:

```
PS1="whaddya want, OK ?"
```

If you always want to use this prompt, you should put the command that sets the Shell variable in your login profile.

11.4.1.2 Changing the System Command Search Path   The usual order in which the system searches directories to find commands is: the current directory, then the */bin* directory, and finally the */usr/bin* directory (if there is one). On UNIX Version 7, the search path variable is called $PATH:

```
$ echo $PATH
:/bin:/usr/bin
$
```

The full pathnames of the different directories that are searched are separated by colons :, with the current directory implied by the initial :.

If you want to tell the system to look for commands in your own private *'bin'* directory, you simply change the value of the Shell PATH variable:

```
$ echo $HOME
/aa/widget/maryann
$ PATH=:$HOME/bin$PATH
$ echo  $PATH
:/aa/widget/maryann/bin:/bin:/usr/bin
```

this puts your directory in the search path between the current directory and */bin*. This is the usual place, but if you have different requirements you can put them in a different order.

The command to set the search path should be placed in your login profile, otherwise you have to set PATH every time you log in.

11.4.2 Setting a Shell Variable from Command Output

You can set a shell variable to the output of a command by:

```
$ now=`date`
$ echo $now
Sun Feb 14 12:00:01 PST 1982
$
```

The characters surrounding the command in the above example are the grave accent character, not the apostrophe. The grave accent is found in many different places on a terminal keyboard, usually either above the @ sign, or above the tilde ~ sign.

If you want to set a Shell variable equal to a value contained in a file, you can do it by:

```
menu=`cat food`
```

That is the command **cat** with an argument *'food'*, not kitty fodder. If the file *'food'* contains:

```
apples
cheddar
chardonnay
```

The resulting value of "$menu" is:

```
$ echo $menu
apples cheddar chardonnay
$
```

As you can see from the example, newline characters are transformed into spaces.

11.4.3 Arguments to Shell Procedures

A different type of Shell Variable is one which is passed to the shell procedure when it is called. This is an argument to the procedure. These are sometimes called positional parameters, they are accessed by number. For example, if we have a procedure which is called by the command:

```
$ dothis grapes apples pears
```

then *'grapes'*, *'apples'* and *'pears'* are positional parameters, and are accessed by $1, $2, and $3 respectively.

If the command is called:

```
$ dothis gouda brie cheddar
```

then $1 is *'gouda'*, $2 is *'brie'*, and $3 is *'cheddar'*.

A simple example of this is given by the following shell procedure:

```
$ cat reverse
echo  $5 $4 $3 $2 $1
$
```

which takes up to five arguments and echoes them onto the Standard Output in reverse order:

```
$ reverse fee fie fo fum fiddledee
fiddledee fum fo fie fee
$
```

If the procedure is called with fewer than five arguments:

```
$ reverse tic tac toe
toe tac tic
$
```

null strings are substituted for the missing arguments. If it is called with more than five arguments, all except the first five are ignored.

To give an example of where this can be useful, let's go back to our *'makelist'* procedure:

```
$ cat  makelist
sort +1 -2 people ¦ tr -d 0-9 ¦ pr -h Distribution ¦ lpr
$
```

This works on one file, and one file only, namely the *'people'* file. If we put **$1** in place of *'people'*, we can use it on any file we care to name:

```
$ cat makelist
sort +1 -2 $1 ¦ tr -d 0-9 ¦ pr -h Distribution ¦ lpr
$ makelist   adminpeople
$ makelist   hardpeople
$ makelist   softpeople
$
```

There is a limit of nine arguments that can be addressed, **$1** through **$9**. However, there is a "shift" command to the Shell, that discards the first argument, and renumbers the remainder. In this way it is possible to write a shell procedure which can deal with more than nine arguments.

Another way of accessing all the arguments, even if more than nine are given, is by the notation **$∗**. This expands to all the arguments that were given when the shell procedure was invoked. **$∗** is the equivalent of

   $1 $2 $3 ....

for all arguments.

The parameter **$#** is set to the total number of arguments specified when the shell procedure was called up. For example, if we have a procedure "count":

```
$ cat count
echo $# items
$ count grapes apples oranges pears
4 items
$ count belpaese gruyere fontina
3 items
$
```

This is useful when you want to check that the shell procedure has been called with the correct number of arguments.

The name of the shell procedure itself can be addressed by the notation **$0**. The name does not get counted in **$#**, as we saw in the above examples.

11.5 Shell "Programming"

Within shell procedures, you can use several commands which control the action taken by the procedure, depending on some internal or external condition. Programmers will recognize the constructs "if.. else", "while ..do", and other similar statements. In this section, we don't go into all the details of what can be done in shell procedures, but we show some examples of how these flow control commands are used, and some instances of where you might want to use them.

When you are creating a new utility or command, it is often a good idea to write it first as a shell procedure. Then when you are sure that it does what you want, and you have the user interface set up correctly, you can proceed to code it in C, or any other programming language of your choice, if in fact the usage patterns make it necessary to do such a recasting. The advantage to shell procedures is that they are easy to change. You don't have to re-compile, re-link and reload every time you make a change. They are also easy to debug, since there are options to the **sh** command which provide a trace facility.

For non-programmers, writing shell procedures can be a good introduction to the underlying principles of programming.

To illustrate the use of the flow control commands, we take the simple *'makelist'* shell that we introduced in the early paragraphs of this chapter, and refine and expand it. Although the single line:

```
sort +1 -2 people ¦ tr -d 0-9 ¦ pr -h Distribution ¦ lpr
```

is the heart of the procedure, it is largely irrelevant to the point of illustrating the commands, so for the most part we simply show it as "sort ...etc."

This example is not always sufficient to show all the points we want to cover, so occasionally we will also introduce other, unrelated, examples.

11.5.1 Looping with the 'for' statement

Our very first attempt at making our own *'makelist'* command looked like:

```
$ cat makelist
sort +1 -2 people ¦ tr  ...etc
$
```

As we have already pointed out, this deals with only one file, *'people'*. Suppose that we had three files, *'adminpeople'*, *'hardpeople'* and *'softpeople'*. One possibility is that we have three different procedures, one for each file, called *'makalist'*, *'makhlist'* and *'makslist'*, say.

This is rather cumbersome, a better solution is to arrange for the same procedure to deal with all three files. We can do this by using the **for** statement. The general layout of the **for** statement is:

```
for variable in this list of values
do all these following
    commands up until the
    'done' statement.
done
```

The **for** statement defines a variable to take on various values in turn. For each of these values, the sequence of commands between the **do** and **done** keywords is executed. When there are no more values for the variable to take, the commands following **done** are executed. When we use **for** in our *'makelist'* command, we get:

```
for file in adminpeople hardpeople softpeople
do
sort +1 -2 $file | tr  .... etc
done
```

The first line defines a shell variable *'file'*, which takes on the values *'adminpeople'*, *'hardpeople'* and *'softpeople'* in turn. The variable is used in the **sort** command line, the value that it currently has is the name of the file that gets processed. In our case, we only had one command line, the pipeline beginning with **sort** and ending with **lpr**. The output of this version of *'makelist'* is three lists, one for each of the files given following the **in** keyword.

You can use the Shell's metacharacters in the list following the **in** keyword. We could, for example, have written our procedure thus:

```
for file in *people
do
sort +1 -2 $file | tr  .... etc
done
```

This will generate a list for every file in the current directory that ends with the word "people".

We can leave out the keyword **in**; the list then defaults to the arguments that are given when the shell is called up. For example, the shell file:

```
for file
do
sort +1 -2 $file | tr .... etc
done
```

generates three lists if called by the command:

```
$ makelist   adminpeople hardpeople softpeople
$
```

but generates only one list if called by:

```
$ makelist   softpeople
$
```

This is a more general and more useful form of the procedure.

Details of the **for** statement are documented under the entry for the **sh** command in the UNIX Programmer's Manual.

11.5.2 Conditional Execution with 'if'

Let us revisit our original shell file:

```
sort +1 -2 people | tr -d 0-9 | pr -h Distribution | lpr
```

We have already shown that we can make this apply to files generally by putting **$1** in place of the file word "people":

```
sort +1 -2 $1| tr -d 0-9 | pr -h Distribution | lpr
```

Now we generate a list for whichever file we specify when we execute *'makelist'*. However, if we don't specify any filename:

```
$ makelist
```

nothing happens. This is because, when the Shell tries to substitute a value for **$1**, there isn't anything to substitute, so the command we are trying to execute is:

```
sort +1 -2  | tr  .... etc
```

When the **sort** command isn't given any filenames, it expects to sort the Standard Input. The net result is that our own special *'makelist'* command is waiting for us to type in the names that we want to put on the distribution list. This may be a good idea, but if this is what you want, you should arrange to prompt for input in some way.

Let's assume that we only want *'makelist'* to work on files that have been prepared previously. In order to avoid the situation outlined above, we must put into the procedure a check that a filename has been specified:

```
if test $# -eq 0
then echo "you must give a filename"
     exit 1
fi
sort  +1 -2  $1 ¦ tr  .... etc
```

The first line in the example tests whether the number of arguments to *'makelist'* is zero.

We have introduced three new things in the example: an **if** statement, a **test** command, and an **exit** statement. We describe these in a bit more detail in the following paragraphs.

11.5.2.1 The 'if' Statement   The keywords connected with this statement are **if** itself, **then**, and **fi**. The general meaning goes like this:

```
if this command is successful
then execute all
     these commands up to
     the following 'fi'
fi
```

To make the "program" easier to read, it is usual to indent the commands between **then** and **fi**, as we've shown.

When a command is successful, it is said to "return a true value". A true value is the value zero. If the command fails, a non-zero value is returned. In our example, we have used the **test** command to check if the number of arguments is zero. If that is true, obviously no filename was specified when the procedure was called up. The command returns a value of zero if the answer to the test is "yes", otherwise it returns a non-zero value.

Each of the keywords must be the first word on a line to be recognized by the Shell. If you put them anywhere else they cause trouble. For example, if you try to execute this file:

```
if test $# -eq 0 then
    echo "you must give a filename"
    exit 1
fi
sort +1 -2 $1 ¦ tr  .... etc
```

which has the **then** keyword at the end of the line, we get this result:

```
$ makelist people
makelist: syntax error at line 6: 'fi' unexpected
$
```

The **test** command, which we describe below, is probably the most useful one to use with the **if** statement, but you can use any command. For example:

```
if  cd /aa/widget/steve/docs
then echo thingspec
     cat thingspec
fi
```

If the **cd** command is successful, then the file *'thingspec'* is displayed. However, if the attempt to change directory fails for any reason, nothing happens.

11.5.2.2 The 'exit' Statement   In our example, if there is no filename given, we want to print an error message and terminate the procedure without executing the **sort** command. Normally the shell procedure terminates when the end of the file is reached. If you want to finish sooner than that, you must use an **exit** statement.

The statement that we actually used in the example says **exit 1**. This means that the value returned by *'makelist'* is 1 (that is, non-zero) when we have the error condition that no file has been given.

We should properly have put another **exit** statement at the end of the file:

```
if  test $# -eq 0
then echo "you must give a filename" >&2
     exit 1
fi
sort +1 -2 $1 ¦ tr -d 0-9 ¦ pr -h Distribution ¦ lpr
exit 0
```

This ensures that our procedure returns a zero value when it has executed correctly. So we can use *'makelist'* in an **if** statement:

```
if   makelist adminpeople
then echo list made OK
fi
```

We sneaked in another little change above. We changed the **echo** command line to print the error message on the Diagnostic Output, where it belongs, instead of on the Standard Output. In our example it doesn't matter too much that the message goes to the Standard Output. Because we route the required output to the line printer, the only thing that appears on the terminal screen is the error message. However, if we had arranged that *'makelist'* would produce the distribution list on the Standard Output, then when we routed that output to the printer, the error message would get printed too!

For any shell procedure where it is likely that the normal output will be piped to another command, or redirected to a file, it is important that error messages be written on the Diagnostic Output. Incidentally, there is no reason why the error message has to be in quotes, but we feel that it makes the shell file more readable.

The value on the exit statement is optional; you can simply say **exit**. In this case, the value returned by the procedure is the same as the value returned by the last command that was executed, before the procedure was terminated.

Our example command *'makelist'* is unlikely to be called from within another procedure, so we are not really concerned what values it returns. In all the following extensions to the example, we don't bother to set return values.

11.5.2.3 The 'else' Statement This is really part of the **if** statement. The action goes like this:

```
if this command is successful
then execute all
     these commands up to
     the following 'else'.
else execute this
     set of commands up to
     the following 'fi'.
fi
```

So we could have expressed our example:

```
if   test $# -eq 0
then   echo "you must give a filename" >&2
else   sort  +1 -2  $1 ¦ tr  .... etc
fi
```

This time we don't need to use an **exit** statement because the **sort** command follows the **else**, and will only get executed if the number of arguments is greater than zero.

Like the **if**, **then** and **fi** keywords, **else** must appear at the start of a line.

11.5.2.4 The 'elif' Statement   This is a combination of **else** and **if**. To illustrate, let's first see what happens if we call up our shell with the name of a file that doesn't exist:

```
$ makelist   nopeople
sort: can't open nopeople
$
```

If someone was using your *'makelist'* command, and didn't know that **sort** was involved, this message could confuse them. It would be better to check for the existence of the file before calling the **sort** utility.

To do this, we need another **if** to test for presence of the file:

```
if   test $# -eq 0
then    echo "you must give a filename" >&2
elif    test ! -s $1
then    echo "no file $1" >&2
else    sort  +1 -2  $1 ¦ tr  .... etc
fi
```

The second **test** command checks that there is a file of the given name. So now we only execute the **sort** command if a filename is given, and if the file exists.

We could achieve the same thing by using a second **if** statement following the **else**:

```
if test $# -eq 0
then echo "you must give a filename" >&2
else if test ! -s $1
     then echo "no file $1" >&2
     else sort +1 -2 $1 ¦ tr .... etc
     fi
fi
```

This time we have two separate **if** statements, one nested inside the other. Each **if** has its closing **fi** statement. This is different from **elif**, which forms part of the original **if** statement, so there is only one **fi**. There are occasions when you cannot use **elif** to achieve the results you want, and you must use a separate nested **if** statement.

In the above example, the second **if** was not the first thing on the line. This is because the rule is really that the keywords have to be the first in the command. Normally this would mean first on the line, but if a command follows a keyword you will get two keywords one after the other, and that is OK.

The **if**, **elif** and **else** statements, along with the attendant **then** and **fi** are documented under the **sh** command in the UNIX Programmers Manual.

11.5.3 The 'test' Command

The **test** command is not part of the Shell, but it is intended for use inside shell procedures. We have already seen some examples of **test** in action.

Basically, the arguments to **test** form an expression. If the expression is true, **test** returns a zero value (the test was successful). If the test fails, the command returns a non-zero value.

There are three main sorts of test that can be performed:

- tests on numerical values
- tests on file types
- tests on character strings

For each type of test, there are a set of "primitives" which construct the expression that **test** evaluates. These primitives describe the properties to be tested. There are also operators which can be used to invert the meaning of the expression, and to combine expressions.

11.5.3.1 Tests on Numerical Values

These test the relationship between two numbers, which may be represented by shell variables. The general form of the expression tested is:

```
N <primitive> M
```

The primitives that can be used in the expression tested are:

-eq	the values of N and M are equal
-ne	the values of N and M are not equal
-gt	N is greater than M
-lt	N is less than M
-ge	N is greater than or equal to M
-le	N is less than or equal to M

Here are some examples of using these primitives:

```
users='who ¦ wc -l`
if test $users -gt 8
then echo "more than 8 people logged on"
fi
```

The first line of the file sets the shell variable *'users'* equal to the value produced by the pipeline of commands **who | wc –l**. This is in fact a count of the number of users currently logged on to the system. This value is then compared with the number 8, and if it is greater the message is printed.

The following example assumes that the procedure requires one argument, and that the argument is a directory:

```
this='ls ¦ wc -l`
that='ls $1 ¦ wc -l`
if test $this -ne $that
then echo "current directory and $1 do not match"
fi
```

We again use a pipeline involving the **wc** command; this time to count the number of files in the current directory, and again to count the number of files in the given directory. We then compare the two values and print an appropriate message.

The last example:

```
if   test $# -eq 0
then   echo "you must give a filename" >&2
else   sort  +1 -2  $1 ¦ tr  .... etc
fi
```

is one we have already seen. $# is the total number of arguments given when the shell procedure was called up. We check to see if that number is zero, and if it is we print an error message.

In performing the tests, numerical values are taken, so if we define three shell variables:

```
number=1
nombre='    1'
numero=00001
```

they will all compare equal with **–eq**. Any leading zeroes or spaces used in defining the values are ignored.

Negative values are accommodated. Suppose we have a shell file:

```
$ cat  posneg
if test $1 -ge 0
then echo "argument is positive"
else echo "argument is negative"
fi
$ posneg  2300
argument is positive
$ posneg -871
argument is negative
$
```

Negative values are frequently obtained after performing arithmetic on shell variables using the **expr** command, described later in this chapter.

There is a limit to the size of the value that can be held in a shell variable. For example, if we use our *'posneg'* command on a high value:

```
$ posneg  50000
argument is negative
$
```

we get the wrong answer. After the limit is reached, the value of the variable "overflows", or "wraps around", so that the value that the Shell sees is wrong. The limit in a positive direction is 32767. In the negative direction you get one more, the limit is 32768. Those who are familiar with binary arithmetic will realize the origin of these apparently arbitrary numbers.

11.5.3.2 Tests on File Types These tests are concerned with the existence or otherwise of files, and the properties of files. The general layout of the expression to test these things is:

```
<primitive>   filename
```

The most common primitives which are used in this type of test are:

-s   check that the file exists and is not empty
-f   check that the file is an ordinary file
     (not a directory)
-d   check whether the file is really a directory
-w   check that the file is writeable
-r   check that the file is readable

In an example in the previous paragraph, we compared the number of files in the current directory against the number of files in a specified directory. Suppose that the name we were given was not a directory? We would get an incorrect answer, since the output of **wc** would be one line, an error message. But we're only counting lines, not reading them. So we should check that the name we are given is that of a directory:

```
this=`ls | wc -1`
if test -d $1
then that=`ls $1 | wc -1`
else echo "$1: not a directory"
fi
if test $this -ne $that
then echo "current directory and $1 do not match"
fi
```

The check for a name being a directory implies that it exists. If there is nothing existing with the specified name, then it cannot be a directory. Although we have the appropriate test in the procedure, we still go ahead and check the values of the shell variables. Really, we need to reorganize the file:

```
if test -d $1
then that=`ls $1 | wc -1`
     this=`ls | wc -1`
     if test $this -ne $that
     then echo "current directory and $1 do not match"
     fi
else echo "$1: not a directory"
fi
```

This is another example of one **if** statement nested within another **if** statement. Notice that each **if** has its corresponding **fi**.

In practice, it is often easier to deal with all the error (or abnormal) conditions first, then proceed to the details of what to do if all is well. Here, this means testing to see whether the argument given is NOT a directory. This is achieved by using the exclamation mark ! which is the "unary negation operator":

```
if test ! -d $1
then echo "$1: not a directory"
else that=`ls $1 | wc -1`
     this=`ls | wc -1`
     if test $this -ne $that
     then echo "current directory and $1 do not match"
     fi
fi
```

The ! operator inverts the sense of the **–d** primitive; the value returned by the **test** command is zero (true) if the specified name is not a directory. The operator ! and the primitive **–d** are separate arguments to the **test** command, so there are spaces between them.

Perhaps the most useful thing to test about a file is its mere existence. The **–s** primitive checks this, and it even checks that the file has something in it, that it is not a zero-length file. We have used **–s** in our *'makelist'* command:

```
if   test $# -eq 0
then   echo "you must give a filename" >&2
elif test ! -s $1
then   echo "no file $1" >&2
else   sort +1 -2 $1 ¦ tr .... etc
fi
```

We have used **–s** in conjunction with the ! operator. What this means is "NOT(the file exists and has non-zero length)", which translates to "if the file does not exist, or has zero length". We used this rather awkward construct in order to be able to deal with all error conditions first.

11.5.3.3 Tests on Character Strings These tests operate on character strings, they can be subdivided into tests which compare character strings, and tests for the existence of a character string.

For character string comparisons, the form of the expression is:

S <primitive> R

and there are two primitives that can be used:

> =   test that the strings are equal
> !=   test that the strings are not equal

The primitive **!=** is a single argument to the **test** command. In this case there is no space between the ! and the = signs.

Because we are comparing character strings, not numerical values, if we have two variables defined like this:

```
number=1
numero=00001
```

they will not compare equal. If we have another variable defined:

```
nombre='     1 '
```

it will never compare equal with '00001'. Whether or not it compares with '1' depends on how the test is set up. If you just say:

```
test   $number = $nombre
```

the strings will compare equal, because the spaces in the variable 'nombre' get absorbed into the spaces between the arguments of **test**.

If you want to preserve spaces in the strings, you must surround the strings in quotes:

```
test   "$number" = "$nombre"
```

In this case the strings will not be equal.

Here are a couple of examples of using these:

```
if test "$1" = ""
then echo "you must give a filename"
else sort .... etc
fi
```

This is a different way to check for the presence of an argument. We test to see if the argument compares with the null string.

```
if test $LOGNAME != maryann
then echo this command is restricted to maryann
     exit
else ....
fi
```

LOGNAME is one of the special Shell variables. The Shell sets up LOGNAME equal to the user name of the person logged in. This example shows how you can restrict a shell file so that only one particular user can execute it, regardless of whether other people have execute permission on the shell file.

There is another command which has string comparison capabilities, the **expr** command, described later in this chapter.

The **test** command has other expressions to test for the presence or absence of a string. The format of these expressions is:

```
<primitive> S
```

and the primitives available are:

    −z   check if the string S has zero length

    −n   check if the string S has non-zero length

The presence of a string can also be tested by the simple command:

```
test S
```

So now we have several more ways to test for the presence of an argument:

```
if test -z "$1"
then echo "you must give a filename"
else ....
fi
if test ! -n "$1"
then echo "you must give a filename"
else ....
fi
if test ! "$1"
then echo "you must give a filename"
else ....
fi
```

In general, when dealing with character strings, it is best to enclose the strings in quotes. It is especially important to do so in the case where you are using a shell variable which might be a null string. If you leave out the quotes, you get an error message from the Shell:

```
$ cat testarg
if test ! -n $1
then echo no argument
else echo argument is $1
fi
$ testarg
test: argument expected
```

This is because, after the value of the first argument has been substituted for **$1**, the **test** command reads:

```
test ! -n
```

which is an incomplete command.

For the most part, you will probably need double quotes, rather than apostrophes. This is because substitution for shell variables doesn't take place inside single quotes. So if you have two variables:

```
fruit=apple
pie=apple
```

the command

```
test "$fruit" = "$pie"
```

will compare the strings "apple" and "apple", which are equal, whereas

```
test '$fruit' = '$pie'
```

compares the strings "$fruit" and "$pie", which are not equal.

11.5.3.4 Combining tests, the Operators '–a' and '–o' There are two operators, –o and –a, for combining several test expressions on a single **test** command. The –a stand for a logical "and", the result of the test is true only if both expressions are true. The –o stands for logical "or", the result of the test is true if either expression is true.

For example, suppose we have a shell procedure *'append'*, which is invoked:

```
$ append thisfile thatfile
$
```

and has the effect of adding *'thisfile'* onto the end of *'thatfile'*. We can combine suitable checks for read and write permissions in one **if** statement:

```
if test -w $2 -a -r $1
then cat $1 >> $2
else echo cannot append
fi
```

or to turn it around:

```
if test ! -w $2 -o ! -r $1
then echo cannot append
else cat $1 >> $2
fi
```

This is not so good as the original version, we only produce one error message for two different conditions. From the user point of view, explicit reasons why something won't work are better.

11.5.4 Combining 'if' and 'for' Statements

Our *'makelist'* shell procedure, with all the checks for arguments and existence of files, still only copes with a single file. What we really need to do is put these tests into the version that loops around, doing its thing for each given argument.

The check for existence of the file can be put inside the **for** loop:

```
for file
do if test ! -s $file
   then echo "no file $file" >&2
   else sort +1 -2 $file ....
   fi
done
```

This illustrates another exception to the rule that **if** must be the first thing on a line: **if** is recognized following **do**.

Now that we can deal with more than one file, it is important that we are using the **else** statement, and not using **exit** when we find that there is no file of the given name. Consider a shell file that looks like this:

```
for file
do if test !-s $file
   then echo "no file $file" >&2
        exit
   fi
sort $file ....
done
```

If we gave it ten filenames, and the third one was wrong, the remaining seven would be ignored. By using **else** and leaving out the **exit**, we make our command do as much work as it can.

If we call up this shell file without giving it any filenames, it does nothing, and you just get your prompt back straight away. If we had arranged that the output of the command was to the Standard Output, it would be obvious that something was wrong. But we have piped the output to the line printer from within the shell, so we have no indication that anything is amiss. We still need a check for the presence of an argument:

```
if test $# -eq 0
then echo "Usage: $0 file ...." >&2
     exit
fi
for file
do if test !-s $file
   then echo "no file $file" >&2
   else sort $file ....
   fi
done
```

This test goes before the **for** loop, and if there are no arguments, we **exit** the procedure immediately.

Notice that we have changed the error message from what it was when we could only cope with one file. The new message gives a synopsis of how the command should be used, just as it would appear in an entry of the Unix Programmers Manual under the SYNOPSIS heading. Notice too that we have used $0 for the command name. If we decide to call our shell file something else, we don't have to change the text of that message.

11.5.5 Looping with the 'while' Statement

We have used the **for** statement to make our shell procedure *'makelist'* work on more than one file. There is another way we could do this, and that is by using the **while** statement.

while provides another method of looping around, executing various commands. The difference between it and **for** is that whereas you give **for** a list of things that have to have certain actions performed on them, **while** performs certain actions while a specified condition pertains:

```
while this command is successful
do all these
    commands up to
    the following 'done'
done
```

As is the case with the **if** statement, the most common command to use with **while** is **test**, but it could be any command.

Another statement often used in conjunction with **while** is **shift**. Effectively what this does is throw away the first argument $1, and renumber all the following arguments. So what was $2 now becomes $1, what was $3 gets to be $2, and so on down the line. The total number of arguments, $#, is reduced by one.

So we can rewrite our shell file using these two statements:

```
if test $# -eq 0
then echo "Usage: $0 file ...." >&2
    exit
fi
while test $# -gt 0
do  if test ! -s $1
    then echo "no file $1" >&2
    else sort +1 -2 $1 ¦ tr -d  ....
    fi
    shift
done
```

As long as there are some arguments, as tested by $# being greater than zero, the commands between **do** and **done** are executed. One of those commands is **shift**, which renumbers the arguments, and decrements $#. When $# gets down to zero, the loop terminates and we carry on executing the commands after **done**. In this case, there aren't any, and the end of the loop is also the end of the file.

11.5.5.1 The 'until' Statement **until** is very much like **while**, but it inverts the test of loop termination. Whereas **while** keeps going until the test returns a false answer (that is, it loops while the condition is true), **until** finishes looping as soon as it gets a true value.

So we could invert the loop in our *'makelist'* command:

```
if test $# -eq 0
then echo "Usage: $0 file ...." >&2
     exit
fi
until test $# -eq 0
do  if test ! -s $1
    then echo "no file $1" >&2
    else sort +1 -2 $1 ¦ tr -d ....
    fi
    shift
done
```

By using **until** instead of **while** we change the test condition from "still some arguments left" to "no more arguments left".

11.5.6 Selective Execution Using the 'case' Statement

Let's get fancy and expand our command to include some options. Let's introduce one option **–t** (for together), such that if we use this option all the files we specify are sorted and merged together to produce a single distribution list. If we don't use the –t option each file is printed as a separate list. The –t option must be specified before any file names, as is usual on UNIX system commands.

Obviously, we now have to examine the first argument to *'makelist'* to see whether it is "–t" or not. We could do this with an **if** statement, but a more general way to match patterns like this is using the **case** statement:

```
if test $# -eq 0
then echo "Usage: $0 file ...." >&2
     exit
fi
together=no
case $1 in
    -t) together=yes
        shift;;
    -?) echo "$0: no option $1
        exit;;
esac
if test $together = yes
then sort -u +1 -2 $* ¦ tr .....
else while test $# -gt 0
     do    if test ! -s $1
           then echo "no file $1" >&2
           else sort +1 -2 $1 ¦ tr .....
           fi
           shift
     done
fi
```

We start off in the usual fashion, with a test for no arguments. Then we have a shell variable called *'together'*, which is used as a flag to indicate what to do when we get to the **sort**. If the *'together'* variable is set to "yes" all files will be sorted and merged together to produce the list, otherwise they will be listed separately. So we first set the *'together'* variable to its default value of "no".

Then we have the **case** statement. The general layout of a **case** statement is:

```
case string in
string1) if "string" is the same as "string1"
         then execute all these commands up until
         ';;', ignore the rest of the cases ;;
string2) if "string" is the same as "string2"
         then execute all these commands up until
         ';;', ignore the rest of the cases ;;

string3)    .... etc....
esac
```

Basically, we have a list of strings that we want to check against, and a list of actions to be performed if we find a match. The end of each string to be checked is indicated by), and the end of each action to be taken, or set of commands to be executed, is indicated by double semicolons ;;. The end of all the strings is indicated by the keyword **esac**. You can make use of the Shell's pattern-matching capabilities using the metacharacters **?**, *****, and **[–]**.

In our case, we want to check the string that is the first argument to the call on *'makelist'* to see if it matches "–t". If it does we set the shell variable *'together'* to "yes".

If the first argument is a minus sign followed by any single character other than the letter "t", it matches the the "–?" pattern, in which case we give an error message, and exit from the procedure.

The order in which we give the patterns that we want to match is important. The first pattern in the list that matches the string, governs the action to be taken. If we had put the "–?" pattern before the "–t", we would always produce the error message, since "–t" matches the specification of minus sign followed by any other character.

After we have decided whether we have the **–t** option and set the flag accordingly, we then examine that flag. If it is set to "yes", we simply use the notation $* to pass all the remaining arguments to a single **sort** command. We add the **–u** option to **sort** to make sure that the same name doesn't appear on the list twice. If the 'together' flag is set to "no" we process each file separately in the usual fashion.

This may seem a clumsy way of doing things. We could have checked for the first argument being "–t" in the **if** statement, instead of going through all the palaver of setting flags. The reason for using **case** is that we have built a framework in which it is easy to add another options simply by adding another pattern to the list.

Let's add a **–m** (for **multi-column**) option to our shell file. If the **–m** option is used, instead of the names being listed in a single column, they will be listed in three columns. So we have to add an option to **pr** to produce multi-column output. We will define another shell variable, *'cols'* which is set to a null string by default, or is set to "–3" if *'makelist'* is called with the **–m** option.

Actually, going from one option to more than one is not quite so simple. Unless we constrain the options to be in a certain order, which would be very awkward for the user, we have to bring our **case** statement inside the **while** loop:

```
if test $# -eq 0
then echo "Usage: $0 file ...." >&2
     exit
fi
together=no
cols=""
while test $# -gt 0
       ...
```

```
do case $1 in
    -t) together=yes
        shift;;
    -m) cols="-3"
        shift;;
    -?) echo "$0: no option $1"
        exit;;
     *) if test $together = yes
        then sort -u +1 -2 $* | tr -d 0-9 | pr $cols -h ....
             exit
        else if test ! -s $1
             then echo "no file $1" >&2
             else sort +1 -2 $1 | tr -d 0-9 | pr $cols -h ....
             fi
             shift
        fi;;
    esac
done
```

We have four cases. The first two are the options **–t** and **–m**; the next is any other (unknown) option; the last case is anything else (indicated by the * pattern), which is taken to be a filename and treated accordingly.

Because the **sort** command that sorts and merges all files together is inside the while loop now, we have to add an **exit** statement to prevent that command being done over and over again.

11.5.7 Using /tmp Space

The shell file is now arranged such that it is very easy to add more options, simply by adding them to the list of patterns in the **case** statement.

For instance, we could change the command to produce its output on the Standard Output, unless the **–p** (for print) option was given. In order to do this, instead of having the **lpr** command as the last command on our **sort** pipeline, we put the output into a temporary file. If **–p** is specified we route the file to the printer, otherwise we simply display the file on the Standard Output.

We could use a temporary file in the current directory, but there is nothing so far in *'makelist'* that implies the user needs write permission on the current directory. It would be a pity to spoil this state of affairs. There is a special directory, *tmp*, that is available for creating temporary files. The *tmp* directory is writeable by everybody.

The new version of *'makelist'* is shown in figure 11.2. We set up another shell variable, *'print'*, as a flag with a default value of "no". We add another case to change this value to "yes" if *'makelist'* is called with the **–p** option.

The biggest change is in the area of the **sort** command pipeline. Instead of finishing up the pipeline with **lpr**, we leave the **pr** command as the last one in the pipe, and redirect the output of the line to the temporary file *'$0$$'* in the directory */tmp*. There is good reason for this apparently obscure filename. Since the */tmp* directory is open for everybody to create files, it is a good idea if each file has a unique name, otherwise users would overwrite each other's files. The Shell variable $$ translates into the process identity number of the current command, which number is unique to that process. So we could have two different users executing *'makelist'* without them overwriting each other's temporary files, because the filenames are different. Of course, eventually the same process ID number will be allocated to another process, but by that time you will have finished with your files.

To further identify the file we have also used the command name **$0**, so the names of the files that are actually created in */tmp* are something like *'makelist1354'*. It is not really necessary to use the name of the command as part of the name of the temporary file. However, it is sometimes useful to be able to connect */tmp* files with the commands that create them. For example, when debugging the shell procedure, you might want to examine the files created. You don't always know the process ID number, but you do know the name of the command you are debugging, so you can find the relevant files from it.

After executing the **sort** command pipeline we examine the 'print' flag, and either **cat** the temporary file, or route it to the line printer. Then we *remove the temporary file*. This is important. There is usually not much space allocated for */tmp*, and there may be lots of users creating lots of files in the directory. If these files are not removed as soon as they are done with, it is very easy to gobble up the entire */tmp* space allocation, and then commands won't work properly because they can't create the files they want. Although the System Administrator can run a program which removes all old temporary files, and probably does on a regular basis, it is much better to keep */tmp* space clean.

So that we can remove the */tmp* file with impunity, we use the **–c** option on **lpr**. This causes the line printer spooler to make its own copy of the file, which it removes when it has finished.

```
: 'this command takes file(s) containing names and phone numbers'
: 'the numbers are removed and the names are printed with a heading'
: 'Options are:'
: '-t  sort and merge all files together'
: '-p  route file to printer'
: '-m  print names in multi-column (3 columns)'
if test $# -eq 0
then echo "Usage: $0 file ...." >&2
     exit
fi
together=no
cols=""
print=no
while test $# -gt 0
do case $1 in
    -t) together=yes
        shift;;
    -m) cols="-3"
        shift;;
    -p) print=yes
        shift;;
    -?) echo "$0: no option $1
        exit;;
     *) if test $together = yes
        then sort -u +1 -2 $* ¦ tr .... > /tmp/$0$$
             if $print = no
             then cat /tmp/$0$$
             else lpr -c /tmp/$0$$
             fi
             rm /tmp/$0$$
             exit
        else if test ! -s $1
             then echo "no file $1" >&2
             else sort +1 -2 $1 ¦ tr .... > /tmp/$0$$
                  if $print = no
                  then cat /tmp/$0$$
                  else lpr -c /tmp/$0$$
                  fi
                  rm /tmp/$0$$
             fi
             shift
        fi;;
    esac
done
```

Figure 11.2   The Expanded Version of the makelist Procedure

11.5.8 Comments in Shell Programs

In our last example, you will notice that we have added some lines at the front explaining what the command does. This sort of commentary is very useful for someone who has to read the shell file and figure out what it does.

The colon character, :, is interpreted as a null command by the Shell; it does nothing. So it can be used to introduce comments, the comments themselves are the arguments to the null command. To ensure that the Shell doesn't try to interpret any special characters (like $ or *) that may be in your comments, it is wise to surround all your comments in single quotes as we have shown.

11.5.9 Dealing with Interrupts

Suppose you give the *'makelist'* command, then change your mind for some reason, and interrupt it by hitting BREAK or RUBOUT or DEL. An interrupt signal is sent to the process (that is, the *'makelist'* command) and it just stops whatever it was doing and terminates immediately. Now if it had already created some temporary files, but not yet removed them, those temporary files are going to be left lying around forever more (or until the System Administrator cleans up */tmp* space). It would be nice if we could make the procedure tidy up after itself, even if it was interrupted.

There is a **trap** statement which helps you do this. You specify a command that is to be executed when a given signal is received. The layout of the statement is:

```
trap 'command arguments' signal ....
```

The command and its arguments must form a single argument to **trap,** hence the quotes. If you want to execute more than one command, they can be separated by ; characters.

The signal is specified in terms of a number, and more than one can be given. For the most part you are only likely to be concerned with signal number 2, which is what you get when you interrupt a process, or signal number 1, which you get if you hang up (disconnect from the system) while you are in the middle of a process.

To give an example of **trap,** let's arrange that *'makelist'* will clear out any temporary files that it has created, if it gets interrupted:

```
if test $# -eq 0
then echo "Usage: $0 file ...." >&2
     exit
fi
together=no
cols=""
print=no
while test $# -gt 0
do case $1 in
    -t) together=yes
        shift;;
    -m) cols="-3"
        shift;;
    -p) print=yes
        shift;;
    -?) echo "$0: no option $1"
        exit;;
     *) trap 'rm $tmp*; exit' 2 1
        if test ! -s $1
        then echo "no file $1" >&2
        else
              <etc...>
    rm $tmp
fi
```

As soon as we get into the loop where we are creating temporary files, we put in a **trap** statement which catches interrupts and hangups. If either of these occur, we remove all temporary files and exit.

Because there is a possibility that there might not actually be any temporary file in existence at the moment we receive the signal, the **trap** statement should really look like this:

```
trap 'rm $tmp* >/dev/null; exit' 2 1
```

If **rm** produces an error message saying that the file we are trying to remove does not exist, we don't really want to see it. **rm** writes that message to the Standard Output rather than the Diagnostic Output, so we can get rid of it by redirecting the Standard Output to the special device file */dev/null*. */dev/null* is the null device, anything written to it disappears completely.

11.5.10 Doing Arithmetic with 'expr'

The **expr** command evaluates its arguments as an **expr**ession and writes the result on the Standard Output. There are various ways of

using this command, but one of the more interesting ways is to perform arithmetic on shell variables. Here is a very simple example:

```
$ cat sum3
expr $1 + $2 + $3
$ chmod 755  sum3
$ sum3   13 49 2
64
$
```

We have a command which prints the sum of three numbers. If you
give it more than three numbers, all except the last three are
ignored; if you give it fewer than three numbers, that is an error
condition:

```
$ sum3   13 49 2 64 1
64
$ sum3 13 49
syntax error
$
```

This is a pretty useless shell procedure, you would probably be better
off using **expr** directly at your terminal:

```
$ expr 13 + 49 + 2 + 64 + 1
129
$ expr 13 + 49
62
$
```

The arithmetic operators that you can specify to **expr** are:

+	addition
−	subtraction
*	multiplication
/	division
%	remainder

Each operator, and each value to be operated on, forms a separate argument to **expr,** so there are spaces between everything.

Let's look at a more complex example. In an earlier chapter we
showed how to use **awk** to calculate the average score of the players
in the tennis league, from the file *'tennis'*. Here is a shell procedure
that calculates the average using **expr**:

```
$ cat avscore
num=`wc -l < $1`
tot=0
count=$num
while test $count -gt 0
do score=`sed -n ${count}p $1 | tr -dc 0-9`
   tot=`expr $tot + $score`
   count=`expr $count - 1`
done
avint=`expr $tot / $num`
avdec=`expr $tot % $num \* 100`
echo Average score is $avint.$avdec
$ avscore   tennis
Average score is 8.900
$
```

This example uses all the operators. The first thing we do is count
the number of lines in the file, and allocate this number to the variable *'num'*. In counting the lines, we have to use the standard input
to get only a numerical value. If we simply said **wc –l $1** the value
allocated to *'num'* would be the string **10 tennis** because **wc** repeats
the filename. Then we define two more variables: *'tot'* is to hold the
total of all scores, it is initialized to zero; *'count'* will count round the
loop the follows, it starts off equal to the number of lines.

Then we have a loop which, for each line in the file, sets the variable *'score'* equal to the output of the command pipeline:

```
sed -n ${count}p $1 | tr -dc 0-9
```

The output of the stream editor **sed** is the *count*'th line, and only
that line. The **tr** command takes that line and deletes everything
except digits. The value of *'score'* is then added to the total *'tot'*, and
'count' is decremented. The loop is repeated until all lines in the file
have been processed.

The final stage is to divide the total score by the number of lines,
giving *'avint'*. Shell variables can only deal with integers, so the
result is rounded down to the nearest whole number. In order to get
some decimal places, we use the remainder operator, %, and the multiply operator, *.

The important thing about the multiply operator is that the character * has a special meaning to the Shell. So when you use it, you
get an error message:

```
$ expr   2 * 3
syntax error
$
```

When you use ∗ as an argument to **expr** you must escape it, to prevent the Shell trying to expand it to match all file names. There are
several ways we can escape ∗ :

```
$ expr  2 \* 3
6
$ expr  2 "*" 3
6
$ expr  2 '*' 3
6
$
```

In the *'avscore'* shell procedure we used the first of the above
methods.

There are other things you can do with the **expr** command. You
can compare numeric values; you can also compare character strings,
or see if a character string matches a regular expression. All these
things produce output on the Standard Output, so they can be used
to set shell variables which are to be used as flags. If **expr** is used in
conjunction with the **if** statement, you will probably want to throw
away the normal output of **expr**. For example:

```
if expr "$1" : "-."  >/dev/null
then echo argument is an option
else echo argument is not an option
fi
```

finds out whether the first argument is a character preceded with a
minus sign, if it does it is assumed to be an option on the command.
If we didn't have **>/dev/null** in the **expr** command, then 0 or 1 (or
whatever value is returned by **expr**) would appear on the output, as
well as the message.

Note that for matching character strings, **expr** uses regular expressions like **ed**, **grep**, et al, instead of the Shell's pattern-matching
metacharacters.

Details of these expressions are documented under the expr command, in
the UNIX Programmers Manual.

11.5.11 Here Documents

Very early in this chapter we showed a simple shell file, the original
version of *'makelist'*:

```
sort +1 -2 people ¦ tr -d 0-9 ¦ pr -h Distribution ¦ lpr
```

We pointed out that this would only work on one specific file of names. When we have more than one *'people'* file to make lists for, one way of doing it is to have a shell file for each file of names. This doubles the number of files you require because for each file of names (data file), you have an equivalent command file: *'adminpeople'* and *'makealist'*, and so on. An alternative solution is to combine the commands and the data into a single file. If we combine the *'softpeople'* file together with the commands necessary to print it as a distribution list, the resulting file looks like this:

```
sort +1 -2 << ! ¦ tr -d 0-9 ¦ pr -h Distribution ¦ lpr
Sylvia Dawson    110
Sally Smith      113
Steve Daniels    111
Henry Morgan     112
Hank Parker      114
!
```

The notation `<< !` is the important part of the example. The `<<` says "take all the rest of this file, up to a line consisting of the argument following `<<`, to be the input of this command". In our case, the argument following `<<` is the single character !. So all lines, up to the line !, become the input to the **sort** command.

This feature, where the data can be held along with the commands, is called a "here document".

There are several different reasons why you might want to use a "here document". One is that you might have a very long message to give the user, so instead of using several **echo** commands:

```
if test ! -s $1
then cat << end
    You nincompoop !! You have given an invalid filename.
    Check the spelling of the files in your directory.
    Then check that you are in the correct directory.
    When you know what you are doing, try again!!
    end
else cat $1
```

In this case, all of the lines of the shell file, up to the line consisting of the word "end", form the input to the **cat** command, and thus are displayed on the Standard Output.

You could also use a "here document" to use an interactive program from within a shell procedure. Suppose we have a shell file:

```
nroff -ms $1 ¦ lpr
mail $LOGNAME << +
Your format of $1 is complete.
It has been routed to the printer.
+
```

You can put this command in the background to format your file; when it is done you will get mail. Substitution of shell variables takes place normally in the here document. If you don't want values substituted, you can prevent it by putting a reverse slash \ between the << and the following character.

11.6 Debugging Shell Procedures

As we saw in an earlier example of an improper **if** statement, the error messages produced by the **sh** command are very explicit, and are a great help in determining syntactical errors in a shell procedure.

However, there are other aids to help you check out shell procedures. One is a "self-help" technique, where you use the **echo** command to print out messages to trace the path through the procedure. When the procedure is known to be correct, the **echo** commands are removed.

There are also arguments to the **sh** command that are helpful when you are checking out shell procedures.

The **–v** (verbose) option causes the Shell to print the commands before executing them. So if we use it on our shell file to compute the average score, what we see is:

```
$ sh -v avscore tennis
num=`wc -l < $1`
tot=0
count=$num
while test $count -gt 0
do score=`sed -n ${count}p $1 ¦ tr -dc 0-9`
   tot=`expr $tot + $score`
   count=`expr $count - 1`
done
avint=`expr $tot / $num`
avdec=`expr $tot % $num \* 100`
echo Average score is $avint.$avdec
8.900
$
```

```
$ sh -x avscore tennis
+ wc -1
num=        10
tot=0
count=      10
+ test 10 -gt 0
+ tr -dc 0-9
+ sed -n 10p tennis
score=2
+ expr 0 + 2
tot=2
+ expr 10 -1
count=9
+ test 9 -gt 0
        .
        .
<and so on round the loop>
        .
+ test 1 -gt 0
+ tr -dc 0-9
+ sed -n 1p tennis
score=18
+ expr 71 + 18
tot=89
+ expr 1 - 1
count=0
+ test 0 -gt 0
+ expr 89 / 10
avint=8
+ expr 89 % 10 * 100
avdec=900
+ echo 8.900
8.900
$
```

Figure 11.3   Example of Trace Output from the Shell

This is just a listing of the shell file. Everything up until the **done** statement is printed, then there is a pause while the total is computed. Then the remainder of the shell file is printed, followed by the result.

An even better trace facility is the –x (execute) option. When this option is used each command is printed, with all variable substitution shown, as it is executed. The output of the trace through our command is shown in figure 11.3. Each command appears on a line flagged with a + at the beginning. The values of any variables used in the command are shown. After the command has been executed, the values of any variables affected are printed. This feature really lets you see what's going on in your procedure.

11.7 Summary

In this chapter we have shown you most of the features provided by the Version 7 Shell. Try making up your own shell procedures for tasks that you routinely perform. Experiment with the different checks that can be made using the **test** command.

The precise format of the control structures, such as **if**, **for**, and **while**, is slightly different in the C shell, but the basic ideas of what can be achieved are the same. So you should study this chapter even if you are using the C shell.

Most users are unlikely to write shell procedures as complex as the ones we have shown. But you can see that it is possible to design sophisticated tools for specialized tasks. People who are in the position of toolsmiths for particular projects need to be aware of all the Shell's capabilities.

Above all, the important thing when writing shell procedures is to be aware of the power of the UNIX system as a whole. Know what commands are available, and what they can be made to do for you. Make good use of shell variables and pipelines. Build on the work of others.

12 Tools for Software Development

This chapter caters for those who need to write computer programs on the UNIX system. Here we discuss some of the tools that help the task of developing software.

Because the UNIX operating system evolved (and is still evolving) in the environment of computer software development, many of the tools that form part of the system go towards assisting the program development process. The UNIX system provides a particularly rich environment for the development of computer programs and their associated documentation.

This chapter is not intended as a detailed coverage of all available programming tools and languages. But our experience has been that many people have trouble finding out just what is available on the system. So this chapter covers the major available programming tools.

Topics discussed in this chapter are some of the programming languages available, the link-editor facilities for binding many object code files together into an executable program, and the archive utility for building libraries.

12.1 The C Programming Language

When talking about programming on the UNIX system, **C** is the programming language that comes to mind most readily. The history of **C** and that of the UNIX operating system itself are intertwined to such a degree that you might almost say that **C** was invented for the purpose of writing the UNIX system.

There are of course languages other than **C** on the UNIX system. There is a FORTRAN-77 compiler called **f77**. There is also a "Rational FORTRAN" compiler, called **ratfor**.

12.1.1 Running the C Compiler

This is not intended as a tutorial on the **C** programming language. For an excellent introduction to **C**, read "The C Programming Language", by Brian Kernighan and Dennis Ritchie. What we are trying to convey here is the environment in which you must work when using the UNIX system to write programs.

To write a **C** program, you create a file, using your favorite text editor, into which you place the source code of the **C** program which you want to try out. Files containing **C** source text should have a suffix of '*.c*'.

In figure 12.1 we show an example of a small **C** program. It is called '*roman.c*', and its purpose is to convert decimal numbers into Roman numerals. The decimal argument(s) must lie in the range between 1 and 9999. This example is not necessarily representative of optimum **C** programming style.

We don't show the actual process by which the file called '*roman.c*' was created. By now, you should be familiar with at least one of the text editors. We just show the finished result.

To compile this **C** program, use the **cc** (**c** compiler) command:

```
$ cc roman.c
$
```

If there are no errors in your **C** program, the various phases of the compilation proceed without gratuitous chatter from the system.

Eventually, an executable version of this program appears in a file called '*a.out*' (**a**ssembler **out**put).

In general, the executable version of a program always appears in a file called '*a.out*'. If you want the name to be different, you must indicate that fact to the compiler or link-editor.

```
#include   <stdio.h>
                 /*  Roman numeral conversion program  */

#define  ROWS        4
#define  COLS        4

int  pows [ROWS] [COLS] = { {1000, 1000, 1000, 1000},
                           { 900,  500,  400,  100},
                           {  90,   50,   40,   10},
                           {   9,    5,    4,    1} };

char  *roms [ROWS] [COLS] = { { "m",  "m",  "m",  "m"},
                             {"cm", "d",  "cd", "c"},
                             {"xc", "l",  "xl", "x"},
                             {"ix", "v",  "iv", "i"} };

main (argc, argv)
    int  argc;          /*  Number of command line arguments  */
    char  *argv [];     /*  Pointers to command line arguments  */
{
    int  low;           /*  Starting number from command line  */
    int  high;          /*  Ending number from command line  */
    char  roman [25];   /*  Converted Roman number  */

    if (argc < 2)
        fprintf (stderr, "Usage: roman  decimal_number\n");
        exit (0);
    }
    high = low = atoi (argv [1]);
    cheknum (low);
    if (argc > 2)  {
        high = atoi (argv [2]);
        cheknum (high);
        if (low  > high)  {
            fprintf (stderr, "low must be less than high\n");
            exit (0);
        }
    } else
        low = 1;        /*  low side is 1 if only one argument  */
    for (;  low <= high;  low++)  {
        to_roman (low, roman);
        printf ("%d %s\n", low, roman);
    }
}
cheknum (value)
    int  value;
{
    if (value < 1 || value > 9999) {
        fprintf (stderr, "Use numbers in range 1 .. 9999\n");
        exit (0);
    }
}
to_roman (decimal, roman)
  int  decimal;
  char  roman [];
{
    int  rom_pos = 0;   /*  Current character position  */
    int  power;         /*  Current power of 10  */
    int  indx;          /*  Indexes through values to subtract  */
    roman [0] = '\0';
        for (power = 0;  power < ROWS;  power++)
            for (indx = 0;  indx < COLS;  indx++)
                while (decimal >= pows [power] [indx])  {
                    strcat (roman, roms [power], [indx]);
                    decimal -= pows [power] [indx];
                }
}
```

Figure 12.1   An Example C Program

The compilation process makes the *'a.out'* file executable, so to run the program, it is sufficient to just type the *'a.out'* filename:

```
$ a.out
Usage: roman decimal_number
$
```

In the examples to follow, however, we wish to show the runnable version of the program appearing in a file which has the same name as the source file, but minus the suffix.

To get your program into a file other than *'a.out'*, you can do one of two things. You can either change the name of the program from *'a.out'* to *'roman'* (in this case) by using the **mv** command.

```
$ cc roman.c
$ mv a.out roman
$ ls
roman
roman.c
$
```

Alternatively, you can use the **-o** (for output) option to the **C** compiler. Note that the option is a lowercase "o", not an uppercase "O" (the uppercase "O" calls up the Optimizer). This example runs the **C** compiler just as before, but places the executable code in a file called *'roman'*:

```
$ cc -o roman roman.c
$ ls
roman
roman.c
$
```

Now, to run this program, just type the *'roman'* name:

```
$ roman
Usage: roman  decimal_number
$ roman 0
Use numbers in the range 1 .. 9999
$ roman 100 10
low must be less than or equal to high
$ roman 10
1 i
2 ii
3 iii
     . . .
```

```
4 iv
5 v
6 vi
7 vii
8 viii
9 ix
10 x
$ roman   7654   7664
mmmmmmmdcliv
mmmmmmmdclv
mmmmmmmdclvi
mmmmmmmdclvii
mmmmmmmdclviii
mmmmmmmdclix
mmmmmmmdclx
mmmmmmmdclxi
mmmmmmmdclxii
mmmmmmmdclxiii
mmmmmmmdclxiv
$
```

This simple program was self-contained, and so the process of generating an executable version of it was also simple.

In practice things can get more complex than that. If a program is made up of several parts (modules) which are separately compiled, you must know how to use the link-editor to combine those parts into a composite whole.

12.1.2 Linking Multiple Object Files with 'ld'

The example of using the C compiler above really deals with a "toy" program. In practice any reasonably sized project will have many separately compiled modules, each in a separate file. Each of the modules are compiled so as to generate a relocatable object file, and then the final program is generated by linking all the separate bits together.

The **ld** command is the link-editor, sometimes called the linking loader. Its job is to link, or bind, multiple object-code files into a single executable file.

Even though the *'roman'* program above is a small program, and is really better left in one piece, it does have three parts, and can thus serve as a simple example of using the link-editor.

We cut our Roman program into three separate files, called *'roman.c'*, *'cheknum.c'*, and *'toroman.c'*. It is not simply enough to chop the original file into three parts, just containing the three functions. We now have to add declarations to two of them. Here are the three separate files:

```
$ cat roman.c
#include  <stdio.h>
          /*  Roman numeral conversion program  */

#define   ROWS        4
#define   COLS        4
          <etc...>
            <etc...>
              <etc...>
$ cat checknum.c
#include  <stdio.h>
cheknum (value)
     int  value;
   <etc...>
     <etc...>
       <etc...>
$ cat toroman.c
#define   ROWS        4
#define   COLS        4
int  pows [ROWS] [COLS];
char  *roms [ROWS] [COLS];
to_roman (decimal, roman)
     <etc...>
       <etc...>
         <etc...>
$
```

In the *'cheknum.c'* file we had to add an #include statement, because the *'cheknum'* function uses the standard I/O library.

In the *'toroman.c'* file we had to add declarations of the two arrays that are also declared and initialized in the main program.

We can now compile those three programs separately, but first we look at what files we have, so that we can do a before and after comparison:

```
$ ls
cheknum.c
roman.c
toroman.c
```

```
$ cc -c roman.c
$ cc -c cheknum.c
$ cc -c toroman.c
$ ls
cheknum.c
cheknum.o
roman.c
roman.o
toroman.c
toroman.o
$
```

The –c option to the cc command is an instruction that the corresponding '.o' file should be created, and the compilation finish there, instead of going the full course to trying to link the (incomplete) program. At the end of the three compiles, there is a '.o' file corresponding to each '.c' file, as the ls command illustrates.

If you do not use the –c option, the C compiler tries to call up the link-editor after the compilation has completed, and because the program is unfinished, there will be error messages from the loader. For example, if we compile the 'toroman.c' file on its own, without the –c option to the C compiler, we get:

```
$ cc toroman
Undefined:
_main
_pows
_roms
$
```

It is not necessary to compile all the '.c' files separately. They can all be compiled at the same time by typing all the filenames on the cc command line:

```
$ cc -c roman.c cheknum.c toroman.c
$
```

No matter how the object files (the '.o' files) get generated, the next thing is to use the ld command to produce a runnable version of the file:

```
$ ld /lib/crt0.o *.o -lc
$ ls
a.out
cheknum.c
cheknum.o
roman.c
roman.o
toroman.c
toroman.o
$
```

As you can see, the **ld** command generates the file called '*a.out*'. You can now run the resulting file, just as when it was compiled from a single file containing the entire program.

There are a number of points to note about the **ld** command line above.

The first is that we added a filename called *lib/crt0.o* as the first file in the link sequence. *lib/crt0.o* is the run-time startup for **C** programs. The **ld** command uses the first file in the sequence as the entry point for the linked program, and in this case, the run-time startup routines must appear first in the sequence.

Try linking the files in some other order. You get odd results, ranging from a program which doesn't generate any sensible results to one that gives a core dump.

There are different run-time startup files for different applications. For example, the file *lib/fcrt0.o* must be used for FORTRAN programs. The file *lib/mcrt0.o* must be used for programs using the floating point library.

The other point of note is that the last entry on the line is the **–lc** field. This is an abbreviation for

/lib/libc.a

and in general, any field on the **ld** command line of the form

–lx

is an abbreviation for

/lib/lib$x$.a

The **–lx** fields must appear at the correct place in the sequence of files. The reason is that the link-editor searches the libraries for external references after all the external references have been seen. If you were to place the **–lc** field first, for instance, there would have been no unsatisfied external references at that time, and so the library would never get searched. At the end of the link, there would still be a bunch of unsatisfied references, which would give rise to some messages from the link-editor.

If a –*lx* field appears on the **ld** command line, the link-editor first searches the */lib* directory for the files, and then looks in */usr/lib*. The exact location of those files can differ from one UNIX system to another.

The linking loader has various options. As usual on the UNIX system, these options are introduced by a – sign. Beware of confusing the options with the library specifications; the options must precede the names of the programs to be linked, the library specifications follow. A command such as:

```
ld -s -lc program.o
```

will result in an error message, the correct order is:

```
ld -s program.o -lc
```

This is particularly confusing when you are not using the loader as a separate program, but are asking the compiler to call up the loader:

```
cc -o program -O -v -lc program.c
```

has caused grief to many a novice programmer. Remember that the –*l* "options" (they aren't really options, they just look like them) come last:

```
cc -o program -O -v program.c -lc
```

12.2 Maintaining Libraries with 'ar'

In this section we talk about **ar**, the file archive utility. One of **ar**'s major functions (but by no means the only one) is maintaining the libraries which the various compilers and the loader use.

In the previous section, where we showed how to use the **ld** command to link the parts of our roman conversion program, we illustrated that all the '*.o*' filenames must be specified on the **ld** command line. Obviously, if you were working on any substantial project, the number of files required would rapidly get out of hand, and typing them all would be a very tiresome (not to mention error-prone) job.

Using the link-editor's capabilities in conjunction with the **ar** utility, you can keep those subroutine files in a library, and refer to that library on the **ld** command line.

Let us make a library file out of the two subroutines:

```
$ ar rcv roman.a cheknum.o toroman.o
a - cheknum.o
a - toroman.o
$
```

In this example, we assume that this is a new library. The file *'roman.a'* is the name of the new library. Archive files, in general, have a suffix of *'.a'*. The two *'.o'* files are the new files to be placed into the library.

The first argument to **ar** is the options which you want to specify. **ar** basically accepts a *key letter*, which tells it what operation you want to perform. The key letter can then be combined with *options*, which modify the behavior in one way or another.

In this example, the key letter is **r**, which means **r**eplace files in the library. When creating the library for the first time, the replace option simply adds new members to the library.

The options we specified here are **c** (for **c**reate), and **v** (for **v**erbose). **ar** will normally create the library file anyway, if it does not already exist.

We used the **v** option just to show what is going on in library creation. The **ar** utility displays each member as it is added to the archive. Normally, you don't use the **v** option.

You can see what is in the archive by using the **t** (table of contents) key to **ar**:

```
$ ar t roman.a
cheknum.o
toroman.o
$
```

Now, you can link the *'roman'* program with a **ld** command like this:

```
$ ld -o roman /lib/crt0.o roman.o roman.a -lc
$
```

When creating library archives of subroutines, the order of the files in the archive can be important. For instance, if you have a subroutine **jabber** which calls another subroutine **jab**, then *'jabber.o'* must precede *'jab.o'* in the archive. There is a command, **lorder**, which searches a library archive for such dependencies, and prints them.

Although, as we said, these are toy examples, the principles of splitting things into manageable sized pieces applies more strongly as the size of a project increases. Later in this chapter there is a short discussion on the **make** utility, which is intended for automating much of the book-keeping chores associated with complex projects.

12.3 Performance Monitoring Aids

The UNIX system has a number of useful tools to aid the programmer in monitoring the performance of programs. These tools can be used to determine how much time a program takes, enabling comparisons to be made between different programs, and different implementations of the same program.

There are profiling tools which can be used to find out where a program spends its time, and thus suggest areas where algorithms can be improved.

12.3.1 Monitoring Execution Time with 'time'

One of the valuable tools which the UNIX system provides is the facility to find out how much time a program uses. The **time** command accepts the name of a program as its argument, and displays the time taken to run that program.

To time our Roman numerals conversion program, we give it the largest possible number of values to convert. We throw away the results by redirecting them to '*/dev/null*' (the bit-bucket) so as to avoid confusing the time taken with printing the results. **time** produces its output on the error output, so the times show up on the terminal screen, even with the standard output redirected.

```
$ time 9999 roman >/dev/null
real      15.0
user      14.3
sys        0.3
$
```

The three lines of data here indicate the following:

real   is the so-called "wall-clock" time. This is the actual number of seconds that the program takes, and should be the same as if you timed it with a stopwatch. Obviously, in a time-sharing system, the wall-clock time can vary depending on the number of people using the system, and what they are doing.

user   is the amount of time actually spent obeying the instructions in the user's program.

sys   is the time that was spent inside the UNIX system itself, doing work on behalf of the user's program.

This particular example was run on a PDP-11/70, on a Sunday. There were no other users logged on at the time. The results show that the user time and the wall-clock time were very close.

Do not worry if the times don't add up. The UNIX system timing capability has a certain "granularity", so that results of timing tests might vary one way or another.

12.3.2 Finding the Size of a Program with 'size'

The **size** utility displays the size of the different sections of a program. Each program consists of three parts:

1. the executable code (called "text" everywhere).

2. the initialized data portions of the program. In the **roman** program, these are the arrays of numbers and strings that you see defined, plus the strings that occur inside the various **print** statements.

3. the uninitialized data areas.

```
$ size roman
2702+460+1040 = 4202b = 010152b
$
```

In this example, the **size** program displayed the sizes of the *'roman'* file.

If no filename argument is given to **size**, it displays the statistics for the file *'a.out'* by default.

12.3.3 Making a Profile of a Program

The UNIX system provides some tools to generate what is called a profile of a program. A profile generates a list of how much time is spent in various parts of a program. By examining the results of a profile, time-critical or inefficient parts of the program can be identified. The organization of data or the algorithms involved can then be changed to improve the performance, if that is in fact desired.

Let us show the use of the profile capability on the *'roman'* program. First we have to re-compile the program, using the **-p** (for profile) option to the **C** compiler:

```
$ cc -p roman.c
$ mv a.out roman
$
```

This results in a specially modified form of the executable program. Basically, the profile facility inserts code that generates calls to a system routine called *'monitor'*. This routine keeps track of where the running program spends its time. At the end of the program, the profile data is written into a file called *'mon.out'*. The **prof** (**prof**ile) utility is then used to interpret the results found in the *'mon.out'* file.

```
$ roman    9999 >/dev/null
$ ls
mon.out
roman
roman.c
$
$ prof    roman
```

name	%time	cumsecs	#call	ms/call
_to_roma	29.1	4.33	9999	0.43
__doprnt	21.1	7.48		
__strcat	15.4	9.77		
__strout	14.7	11.31		
cret	8.9	13.31		
csv	5.6	14.11		
_write	2.2	14.44		
_main	1.1	14.61	1	166.88
_gtty	0.5	14.69		
_printf	0.5	14.76		
mcount	0.3	14.81		
		<etc...>		
_cheknum	0.0	14.90	1	0.00
_atoi	0.0	14.90		
_malloc	0.0	14.90		

```
$
```

This is a shortened form of the full output of the profile run. Such a tool can tell you a lot of things about your program. For example, the above display indicates that the *'_to_roma'* (truncated form of the *'to_roman'* function) was called 9999 times. This is as it should be, because that is what we typed on the command line when we ran the program. If the number of calls was different, it might indicate something wrong with the logic of the program.

Similarly, the *'cheknum'* function was called once. That is also what we should expect, because only one number was typed on the command line.

The columns in the profile display have these meanings:

name	is the name of the symbol which was monitored.
% time	is the percentage of the total program's run time that was spent in a particular function.
cumsecs	is the cumulative seconds spent in the various parts of the program.
#call	is the number of times that the specific function was called during execution of the program.
ms/call	is the number of milliseconds per call of the specific function.

Only with tools such as profilers can real quantitative measurements be taken, and steps taken to improve things if possible. For example, the **roman** program spends 29% of the time in the function that actually performs the conversion. However, notice that 50% of the time is spent in the C language string routines. If we "improved" the run time of the *'to_roman'* function so that it took no time at all, the overall run time of the program would decrease by 4.33 seconds. This represents a 29% speed up. The remainder of the time is still spent moving strings.

12.3.4 Checking C Programs with 'lint'

Although not strictly a performance tool, the **lint** utility is intended to verify some facets of a C program, such as its potential portability. **lint** derives from the notion of picking the fluff out of a C program. **lint** advises on C constructs and usages which might turn out to be "bugs", portability problems, or dead code.

Let us apply **lint** to the *'roman.c'* program from earlier in this chapter:

```
$ lint roman.c
"roman.c", line 64: warning: rom_pos unused in function to_roma
$
```

If you look at the *'roman.c'* program, sure enough, there is an unused variable. This variable was actually there in an earlier version of the program, and got left in during the evolution to the current state. That was in fact the only thing in our program which **lint** complained about.

12.4 Other Software Development Tools

This section wraps up the discussions on software development tools by providing an overview of some of the other tools which are available to the UNIX system user. It has been our experience that even relatively skilled software people are often unaware of just what is available (probably because there is so much available). Since this book is addressed to the relative newcomer to the system, we supply a rundown of what's there to assist you in your search for the right tools.

12.4.1 Other Programming Languages

In addition to C, the UNIX system also supports the FORTRAN-77 language through the **f77** compiler.

It should be noted that the **f77** supplied by Bell Laboratories was a semi-experimental tool, developed for the purpose of demonstrating the power and effectiveness of the programming tools available on the UNIX system. On some versions of the UNIX system that run on Motorola MC68000-based systems, the FORTRAN language supplied is not the one from from Bell Laboratories, but instead derives from Silicon Valley Software Incorporated.

Had we written the Roman numerals conversion in FORTRAN-77, we would call it *'roman.f'*. FORTRAN-77 programs have a suffix of ".f" in the UNIX system conventions. We do not go into any details of this program, since the mechanics are much the same for all the programming languages. We only show the compilation process. To compile a FORTRAN-77 program, use the **f77** command:

```
$ f77 roman.f
$
```

At the end of the compilation, there is an *'a.out'* file, just as for a C program. While the diagnostics could be improved somewhat, the **f77** language can be valuable for certain types of scientific programming, and can be a useful tool.

The **ratfor** language stands for "**Rat**ional **FORTRAN**", and was developed as a preprocessor for FORTRAN.

ratfor imposes "structured programming" constructs on top of FORTRAN. The constructs emulate the C programming language to a large extent. In addition, **ratfor** supplies some "syntactic sugar", making FORTRAN's syntactic constructs easier to cope with.

To compile a **ratfor** program, use the **ratfor** compiler, **rc**:

```
$ rc roman.r
$
```

On some UNIX systems, you can find a SNOBOL interpreter. SNO-BOL is a world famous language for processing strings. It was originally developed at Bell Laboratories for linguistics research, and has been transported to dozens of different systems.

The Berkeley UNIX system comes with a LISP interpreter called Franz LISP.

There are at least three Pascal systems available for the UNIX system. Berkeley provide a Pascal interpreter and a compiler, plus an execution-time profiler. There is another Pascal compiler from the Vrije Universiteit of Amsterdam. UNIX systems based on the Motorola MC68000 can take advantage of the Pascal compiler from Silicon Valley Software Incorporated.

12.4.2 Maintaining Computer Programs with 'make'

Managing computer software is a task which tends to become overwhelming without some tools to help the process. But this is true of any other process as well. For instance, if you should happen to have the job of looking after a large documentation project, the sheer size of the thing could soon get out of hand.

make is a utility oriented towards easy maintenance of computer programs. **make**'s job is to ease the process of going from the original source text of a computer program to the final executable form of that program. It does this by using built-in rules to decide what commands to run in order to get to the final desired form.

Because **make** was originally designed for maintaining computer programs, we talk about it in that context because it is easier to describe. Bear in mind though, that if your application is, say, managing some huge documentation project such as the Golden Gate Bridge internal guidebook, **make** can certainly ease the burden.

make decides what to do by consulting a file called *'makefile'*, or *'Makefile'* or *'MAKEFILE'*. In *'makefile'* you place a list of source files, object files, and *dependency* information.

In this section, we use our chopped up Roman program as a small example of how **make** can be used to automate the software process. First of all, we create a makefile, containing the following information:

```
$ cat Makefile
FILES=   roman.c cheknum.c toroman.c
OBJECTS=roman.o cheknum.o toroman.o
roman:   ${OBJECTS}
         ld -o roman /lib/crt0.o ${OBJECTS} -lc
$
```

It is common practice to call the file *'Makefile'*, with a capital "M", or *'MAKEFILE'* because it then appears first in a directory listing. Any line of the form:

```
string1 = string2
```

is a macro definition. The name to the left of the = sign is the name of the object, and the stuff to the right is the definition of that object. A macro is referenced by preceding its name with a $ sign. If there is more than one thing in the definition, the reference must be enclosed in parentheses or braces as shown in the example.

In this Makefile, there are two such definitions, namely the FILES (the source files) and the OBJECTS (the .o files). These define the sources and objects for constructing the final *'roman'* program.

Then we have a line which specifies that the executable version of the *'roman'* program depends on the object files listed. Any line with a name followed by a colon : character at the start of the line is a dependency statement.

Under that, there is the **ld** command which must be used to generate the final executable version. A subtlety of **make**'s rules for the makefile is that UNIX system commands must have a tab character in front of them. This is not apparent from the example, so remember those tabs!

Now we can use **make** to do things for us. For example, we can reconstruct the entire *'roman'* program just by typing this command:

```
$ make
cc   -c roman.c
cc   -c cheknum.c
cc   -c toroman.c
ld -o roman /lib/crt0.o roman.o cheknum.o toroman.o -lc
$
```

The **make** process tells you what is going on while it is processing. At the end, there is a runnable version of the *'roman'* program.

It is also possible to just make a part of the program:

```
$ make toroman.o
cc   -c toroman.c
$
```

make is clever enough to know that the file *'toroman.o'* depends upon the file *'toroman.c'*, and if that file is not up to date, **make** calls up the **C** compiler to compile it.

A useful option on **make** is the **−n** option. This does not actually execute the commands in the Makefile, but just shows you what it would do. This is a valuable feature for checking out complex make files.

The **touch** command finds most of its application in connection with the **make** utility just described. **touch** updates the modification date of a file. For example, let us suppose that we want to ensure that the version of *'roman'* program is up to date. If the modification date of the *'.o'* files is the same as or later than that of the *'.c'* files, the following happens when we try to **make** the program:

```
$ make
'xxxxxxx' is up to date
$
```

Often, when dealing with a large project, we want to re-compile everything in sight, just to assuage our feelings of unease that we might have missed something. In this case, we use the **touch** command:

```
$ touch *.c
$
```

Then we can **make** everything in the directory, and it will be up to date.

12.4.3 Language Development Aids

In previous chapters we have made much of the utilities for processing files of text in various ways. These text-processing tools can go a long way towards easing the tiresome jobs usually encountered when writing programs.

Here are a few of the more advanced tools available on the UNIX system for assisting in the program generation process. The philosophy behind many of these tools is one of getting things working quickly so that they may be tried out in a real environment, and most importantly, junking them if they don't work out.

The **lex** utility is one of a family of text-processing tools. **lex** is intended mainly for generating the **lex**ical scan parts of compilers and other language processors.

yacc is a tool for generating language parsers. **yacc** stands for yet another compiler-compiler. **yacc** and **lex** can work together quite happily. The choice of which constructs to place in **lex** and which to handle with **yacc** are purely a matter of the designer's choice.

Technically speaking, **yacc** converts a context-free grammar into a set of tables that drive a LR(1) parsing automaton. It is possible to handle an ambiguous grammar with a **yacc** generated parser, by giving precedence rules which resolve the ambiguous situations.

The **m4** macro processor can be used as a pre-processor for languages such as **f77**, **Ratfor** or **C**. Macro processors can be a valuable aid to mechanizing the generation of things such as tables, where there is a lot of repetitive text with only a few differences between occurrences of distinct items. Macro processors are often used in conjunction with programming languages to define names like EOF (end-of-file), in place of "magic numbers" such as −1.

m4 (and its now obsolete predecessor, **m6**), derive from various efforts to generate "general purpose" macro processors which are not limited to any particular kind of code. They differ from the macros which a typical "macro-assembler" will handle.

12.5 Summary

This then, was a brief "show and tell" of the programming tools available on the UNIX system. If your application is developing new software, the UNIX system is rich in tools to aid this process. In addition, the system is built around the philosophy of sharing information, re-using existing kits of parts, getting things running quickly and trying them out, and rebuilding them if they don't work out.

Although the UNIX system provides a multitude of aids for the software developer, before you decide to rush off and write a program to do a particular job, always ask yourself these questions:

1. Can you avoid doing the job in the first place? Not doing a job is often cheaper.

2. Can the job be done by using existing utilities in a pipeline? The UNIX system's capabilities in this area are often more powerful than you think.

3. Can the job be done using the Shell's capabilities that we described in chapter 11?

If the answer to all these questions is "no", you might then start looking into writing a program to do it. If you do have to write programs, we urge you to write them in the philosophy of so much of the UNIX operating system. Five small programs, that do one job each and can work together, are easier to use and more reliable than one large program that does five functions.

13 The UNIX System at Berkeley

This chapter presents an overview of the Berkeley version of the UNIX system. The Computer Science Department at the University of California at Berkeley has a long and illustrious history of making innovations to the UNIX system. The Berkeley version of the UNIX system has evolved to such a degree that it can be considered as a distinct version in its own right.

At the time of writing* the Berkeley UNIX system is available in two major versions. The version called **2BSD** (**B**erkeley **S**tandard **D**istribution) runs on DEC PDP-11 computers. The other version is called **4BSD**, and is intended for the DEC VAX.

The major features of the Berkeley UNIX system are the **ex** text editor and the **vi** screen editor, already described, the C-Shell, a Pascal program language system, a Lisp interpreter, and a database management system called INGRES. The Berkeley group has developed packages for screen management.

As you read about the C-Shell you will notice many similarities to the **ex** and **vi** editors, both in the command syntax and in the general approach to the use of special characters. This comes about because

---

* Spring of 1982

the two packages were written by the same people. There is thus much commonality and consistency in the user interface.

There are many other features incorporated into the Berkeley UNIX system. Since the system evolves faster than anyone can write about it, we can only skim the surface here. The major topics we cover here are the C-Shell, and some of the more useful commands on the Berkeley UNIX system.

Before we get into the details of the C-Shell and the commands, we should say a little bit about the environment at Berkeley. Many people think that the C-Shell features, and the commands available on the Berkeley UNIX system, are somewhat strange and over-complicated. For the average small system, that is possibly true. However, there are literally hundreds of people with accounts on the different Berkeley systems.

The users are scattered all over creation (or at least all over Berkeley). Many of the people work odd hours. Although many of the Berkeley users work together on similar projects, they are not always in the same physical locations. For those reasons, the facilities for inter-user communications are highly developed.

Because of the user load on the Berkeley systems, the directory structures are complicated. Thus there are many facilities in the C-Shell, and commands in the system, to facilitate moving around and using the system.

13.1 The C Shell

The Berkeley version of the UNIX system has a Shell which is quite different from the version 7 Shell. The Berkeley Shell is called the C-Shell, both because its internal operations are similar to the C programming language, and because the Berkeley group are dedicated punsters.

In this section, we describe the salient features of the C-Shell. The C-Shell departs radically from the regular Version 7 (Bourne) Shell, both in its external features (how you use the system under control of the C-Shell), and in its internal features (the way you use it to write Shell scripts).

We only go into the user interface here. We do not cover programming of the C-Shell. Readers wishing more information are referred to Bill Joy's paper entitled:

An Introduction to the C Shell.

13.1.1 Special Characters in the C Shell

The C-Shell uses even more special characters than does the Version 7 Shell. We summarize them here, and expand upon them in detail in the subsections to follow.

The first thing to note is that the C-Shell uses the percent sign % as its default prompt character, although it can be changed if you wish.

You probably noticed the heavy use of ! in the **ex** editor. The exclamation mark character ! is used heavily in the C-Shell to mean, in general, something that has gone before. For example, !! means repeat the previous command. It is also used to override the "noclobber" facility when redirecting the Standard Output. Again this is similar to its use in **ex** to override conditions, such as using **w**! to force a write over an existing file.

The circumflex character ^ is used to separate strings when correcting a part of the previous command.

The tilde character ~ is used as a prefix to someone's user name, and expands into that user's home directory pathname.

Braces { } group lists of names together for filename expansion.

13.1.2 The C-Shell Startup File

When you log in to the C-Shell, it looks for files called '*.login*' and '*.cshrc*'. If there are such files in your home directory, the C-Shell runs any commands it finds in them.

The '*.login*' file is only executed when the C-Shell is called up as part of the process of logging in to the system. The file '*.cshrc*' is executed any time the C-Shell is invoked; for example, when you fork out of the **ex** editor with the **sh** command.

Two things of special note are the history variable, which we describe next, and the alias feature, which we describe later in this section.

13.1.3 The History Mechanism

The C-Shell has a built-in history mechanism, whereby it will keep track of some number of the commands you typed. The exact number of commands it remembers is determined by a variable called '*history*' that you set in the file called '*.cshrc*'.

It is the history mechanism that provides for being able to type a command or part of a command preceded by an exclamation mark, and have the C-Shell know which command it is you want.

First, here's what you set in the '*.cshrc*' file to get the history mechanism switched on:

```
set history=10
```

We set the history variable to 10 in our example, but you can set it to anything you like (within reason). The C-Shell activates the history mechanism when it sees that the history variable is set to something other than zero.

Having got history turned on, it is possible to get a display of the history buffer by using the **history** command. Here is a typical display from the history buffer:

```
% history
    1   ls -l
    2   mail
    3   history
%
```

We have assumed for the purposes of this and future examples, that the "history" variable is set to 10. So the **history** command displays the last ten commands you typed.

In this example, we assume that Maryann has not long been logged on. There are a couple of commands that are fairly typical of the commands you would use after a log in.

Note that the **history** command you typed appears in the buffer as the last command.

13.1.4 Correcting the Previous Command

The C-Shell provides various means for changing parts of previously typed commands. It is possible to change only the last command typed, or it is possible to repeat a command typed a short while ago, and change parts of it.

The first thing to look at is correcting the previous command. One place that this finds most application is correcting typing mistakes. Supposing that we just typed a **cd** command like this:

```
% cd  /aa/widget/maryann/shels
/aa/widget/maryann/shels: No such file or directory
%
```

The problem here is that we should have typed "shells" instead of "shels". It is easy to correct this on the Berkeley system:

```
% ^shels^shells^
cd /aa/widget/maryann/shells
%
```

The ^ characters act as delimiters to surround the two strings. The first string is the thing you want changed. The second string is the thing you want it changed to. The C-Shell then echoes the corrected command back at you.

We can use the **history** facility to see what happened to the commands:

```
% history
    1  ls -l
    2  mail
    3  history
    4  cd /aa/widget/maryann/shels
    5  cd /aa/widget/maryann/shells
    6  history
%
```

The two **cd** commands from the examples above, the erroneous one and the corrected one, now appear in the history buffer.

13.1.5 Re-Running a Previous Command

If you want to re-run a previous command, you can avoid typing out a long command line all over again by using the C-Shell's history file.

To re-run a command, type an exclamation mark in front of the command name:

```
% !cd
cd /aa/widget/maryann/shells
%
```

The C-Shell searches *backwards* through the history file for a command beginning with the letters "cd". It is not even necessary to type the whole command name. The C-Shell does the name lookup in the history file by a process called "minimum substring recognition". This means that you only need to type the first however many characters of the command name as are needed to make it unique. So the **cd** command could simply be typed like this:

```
%  !c
cd /aa/widget/maryann/shells
%
```

and it will do just as well. Of course this will go awry if there was
another, more recent command which also started with the letter "c",
like **cat** or **cc** or **cp**.

If the C-Shell cannot find a command beginning with the letters
you typed, it displays an error message:

```
%  !xd
xd: Event not found.
%
```

It is also possible to refer directly to a previous command in the
history file, by typing the exclamation mark followed by the number
of the command in the history buffer. For example, we can re-run
command number 1 in the buffer like this:

```
%  !1
ls -1
  .  .  .
        .  .  . output from the ls command . . .
                                                        . . .
%
```

The number must immediately follow the exclamation mark.
There must not be any spaces between the exclamation mark and the
number. Just as with the command recognition, if the number you
type is not in the history buffer, the C-Shell responds with an error
message:

```
%  !234
234: Event not found.
%
```

Another version of "repeat a previous command" is the use of the
dollar sign $ to refer to the last word of the previous command:

```
% mv  /aa/widget/charlie/spacewar.c   space.c
% pr  !$ ¦ lpr
pr space.c ¦ lpr
%
```

13.1.6 Re-Running and Changing Previous Commands

As well as simply repeating a previous command, it is possible to re-run a previous command and make changes to the command at the same time.

This is done by following the command with a substitution request, which looks just like the substitute operation in the **ex** editor that we described in chapter 8.

Let us take a look at the history buffer as it is now, after the last few commands we typed:

```
% history
    2   mail
    3   cd /aa/widget/maryann/shels
    4   cd /aa/widget/maryann/shells
    5   history
    6   cd /aa/widget/maryann/shells
    7   cd /aa/widget/maryann/shells
    8   ls -l
    9   mv /aa/widget/charlie/spacewar.c space.c·
   10   pr space.c ¦ lpr
   11   history
%
```

First of all, you can see that the early commands disappeared from the history buffer. The buffer is said to be "circular" or "cyclic".

Then you can see the substitutions that were made in previous commands.

We assume that the file you want to move from Charlie's directory was actually the Empire game and not Spacewar. To avoid all the tiresome typing of the whole pathname again, you use the substitution capability of the C-Shell:

```
% !9:s/spacewar/empire/
mv /aa/widget/charlie/empire.c space.c
%
```

There are times when this substitution capability is extremely useful, when the set of filenames or pathnames are not regular enough to be expanded using the other Shell metacharacters.

13.1.7 Referring to Another User's Home Directory

The tilde character ~ has a special meaning to the C-Shell. It refers to your own or someone else's home directory. If the tilde appears on its own, it refers to your home directory:

```
% cd   progs/c
% mv   ~/test.c   .
%
```

This example moves the file called *'test.c'* from Maryann's home directory to her subdirectory *progs/c*. We can find out what this example actually did by using the **history** command:

```
% history
     4   cd /aa/widget/maryann/shells
     5   history
     6   cd /aa/widget/maryann/shells
     7   cd /aa/widget/maryann/shells
     8.  ls -l
     9   mv /aa/widget/charlie/spacewar.c space.c
    10   pr space.c | lpr
    11   history
    12   mv /aa/widget/charlie/empire.c space.c
    13   mv /aa/widget/maryann/test.c .
    14   history
%
```

Entry number 13 in the history buffer shows the way that the **mv** command got expanded by using the tilde character on its own. It refers to Maryann's home directory. Then, anything that follows the tilde is just appended as the rest of the pathname.

The other way to use the tilde character is to type it in front of another user's user name. Here, the combination of tilde and user name is expanded to the pathname of that user's home directory:

```
% echo   ~patty
/aa/blivet/patty
%
```

In this example, we used the **echo** command to find out what is the full pathname of Patty in the blivet project.

13.1.8 Expanding Groups of Filenames

The C-Shell uses the braces characters { } to apply a list of names to a common root pathname. This is useful in those circumstances where there are no regularities about the filenames, such that the Shell's wild-card matching capabilities avail you nothing.

Suppose you wish to copy the files *'kettles'*, *'pots'*, and *'pans'* from another directory to your own. These filenames have nothing in common, other than being kitchen equipment. But the C-Shell knows nothing about that subject, so the wild-card matching cannot be used.

The grouping capability can be used in this case, however:

```
% cp /aa/widget/steve/catering/{kettles,pots,pans} .
%
```

To type that pathname for each of the three files would be a painful process, but with the grouping process you only type the root pathname once.

That command line expands to a **cp** command with the first three arguments of:

```
/aa/widget/steve/catering/kettles
/aa/widget/steve/catering/pots
/aa/widget/steve/catering/pans
```

The same effect could be achieved even more easily by using the ~ character to refer to Steve's home directory:

```
% cp ~steve/catering/{kettles,pots,pans} .
%
```

In common with many aspects of the UNIX system, this feature is more subtle than it appears. You can in fact have more than one group of names, and the C-Shell expands them all out like a "matrix product".

For example, if we are not sure where a particular group of files might be, we could type a command like this:

```
% ls  {/bin/,/usr/ucb/}{pi,whereis}
/bin/pi not found
/bin/whereis not found
/usr/ucb/pi
/usr/ucb/whereis
%
```

There is in fact a command called **whereis**, which finds out where a file is. If you were to look at the above **ls** command in the history buffer, you would see that the C-Shell did not expand the command. But you can always determine what the expansion is going to be beforehand, by using the **echo** command:

```
% echo ls  {/bin/,/usr/ucb/}{pi,whereis}
ls /bin/pi /bin/whereis /usr/ucb/pi /usr/ucb/whereis
%
```

The grouping mechanism can be expanded indefinitely, to as many groups as you like, but after two groups as above it is hard to follow what is going on.

13.1.9 The Alias Mechanism

Another feature of the C-Shell is the ability to establish shorthand names for frequently used but long-winded commands. This feature is called an "alias" capability, since you can define a short alias for a long command.

Let us assume that you are working on the manuals which are part of the system. The manuals are all held in separate directories, of the form:

```
/ab/system/documents/manuals/man/man1
```

The last element in the pathname is *'man1'* for section 1 manuals, *'man2'* for section 2, and so on. It is a bore to keep typing these huge pathnames, so we define alias commands in the *'.cshrc'* file, like this:

```
alias cdm1 cd /ab/system/documents/manuals/man/man1
alias cdm2 cd /ab/system/documents/manuals/man/man2
alias cdm3 cd /ab/system/documents/manuals/man/man3
alias cdm4 cd /ab/system/documents/manuals/man/man4
alias cdm5 cd /ab/system/documents/manuals/man/man5
alias cdm6 cd /ab/system/documents/manuals/man/man6
alias cdm7 cd /ab/system/documents/manuals/man/man7
alias cdm8 cd /ab/system/documents/manuals/man/man8
```

What you have done here is to define a bunch of new commands, all called **cdm** *N*, where *N* is the number of the *'man'* directory you want to **cd** into.

Now, all you have to do to change into the *'man5'* directory, for instance, is to issue the **cdm5** command:

```
% cdm5
% pwd
/ab/system/documents/manuals/man/man5
%
```

and as you see, you end up in that directory.

In fact, there is no need to define eight separate **alias** lines for the eight different directories. You can define just one, like this:

```
alias cdm cd /ab/system/documents/manuals/man/man\!$
%
```

The !$ notation, as we saw before, refers to the last word typed on the command line. The \ (escape) character prevents the !$ being expanded until a **cdm** command is actually typed. Now you can change to the *'man8'* directory like this:

```
% cdm 8
% pwd
/ab/system/documents/manuals/man/man8
```

13.1.10 C Shell Variables

Just as in the regular version 7 Shell, the C-Shell has some variables which can be set to influence its behavior. We describe only a few of the more interesting ones here. If you wish to know more, read the C-Shell documentation.

The method of setting a variable in the C-Shell is a little different from the version 7 Shell. The method is:

```
set variable=value
```

The "history" variable we have already described. It defines how many previous commands the C-Shell remembers for you.

The "path" variable is set to the desired search path for commands. The syntax of the path in the Berkeley UNIX system is different from that of the UNIX system version 7. You set the path like this:

```
set path=(/bin /usr/ucb $HOME/bin .)
```

Each separate pathname is separated from the next by a space.

The "prompt" variable is where you can establish what kind of prompt you want to have from the system.

The "shell" variable defines what your initial Shell should be, if in fact you want some Shell other than the C-Shell.

The "noclobber" variable is a safeguard against accidentally clobbering a file. If the "noclobber" variable is set, Shell redirection of the Standard Output will not overwrite the designated file. Here is how it is used.

```
% set noclobber
% fgrep ounds /usr/dict/words >anyfile
anyfile: File exists
%
```

In this example, we try to redirect the Standard Output of the **fgrep** command to a file called *'anyfile'*, which already exists. In such a case, the C-Shell issues the message that you see.

How do you overcome the noclobber capability? One way is to **unset** it, but this then unsets noclobber for all files. The other way is the use the ubiquitous exclamation mark sign ! after the redirection sign:

```
% fgrep ounds /usr/dict/words >! anyfile
%
```

This time, the command is obeyed without question.

You must be aware that the "noclobber" variable *only* applies to redirection. If you just issue a **cp** command, for instance, which names *'anyfile'* as the target, the command is obeyed with no warning.

The remainder of this chapter is devoted to some of the useful commands which are to be found on the Berkeley system.

13.2 Berkeley Variations on the 'ls' Command

Just about every installation changes the way in which the **ls** command works, and Berkeley is no exception. Their version of **ls** lists the filenames in columns, with the names running in alphabetical order down the columns. Here is a typical use of the **ls** command from the Berkeley UNIX system:

```
% ls /usr/lib
Mail.help      ex2.13preserve  libdbm.a      makekey      tmac
Mail.help.     ex2.13recover   libfpsim.a    me           tmac.e
   :              :   <etc...>     :             :            :
atrun          font            libsa.a       px_header    uucp
   :              :   <etc...>     :             :
diff3          lex             llib-lm       struct
diffh          libF77.a        llib-port     tabset
eign           libI77.a        lpd           term
%
```

This variation of the **ls** command arranges the display so that there are as many columns as possible on the screen, and it adjusts the number of columns depending upon the width of the entries in each column. In all cases, it seems to minimize the amount of screen which the display consumes.

A useful option is the **−F** (upper case F) option, which marks which files are executable, and which files are directories:

```
% ls -F /usr/lib
Mail.help       ex2.13strings*  libtermlib.a    spellin*
Mail.help.      font/           lint1*          spellout*
   :               :   <etc...>     :               :
atrun*          how_pix         llib-lc         tabset/
   :               :   <etc...>     :               :
cign            lex/            lpd*            tmac.e
   :               :   <etc...>     :
ex2.13recover*  libsa.a         spell*
%
```

With the **−F** option the files marked with an asterisk sign * after them are executable files, and those marked with a slash character / after them are directories. Because there are these extra characters on the filenames, there may not be as many columns across the screen as with a plain **ls**. In the above example, the number of columns has been reduced from five to four.

13.3 Looking at the Start of Files with 'head'

The Berkeley version of the UNIX system has a command called **head**, which is analogous to the **tail** command, and makes the whole process symmetrical.

In the same way that **tail** normally displays the last ten lines of a file, **head** normally displays the first ten lines. Just as with **tail**, it is possible to display more or less than ten lines, by supplying the number of lines as an option. The **head** command is called up by a command line of the form:

```
% head -4 people
Maryann Clark    101
Sally Smith      113
Jane Bailey      121
Jack Austen      120
%
```

head differs from **tail** in one important way: if you supply **head** with a list of filenames, lines from each file are displayed, with a special header to indicate the filename. So if we had three separate files instead of a single *'people'* file:

```
% head -4 *people
==> adminpeople <==
Bill Williams    100
Maryann Clark    101

==> hardpeople <==
Jack Austen      120
Jane Bailey      121
Charlie Smith    122

==> softpeople <==
Sylvia Dawson    110
Sally Smith      113
Steve Daniels    111
Henry Morgan     112
%
```

Each new file after the first is displayed starting with a blank line, and the filename is enclosed in the ==> and <== signs, as shown above.

13.4 Paging through a File with 'more'

The **more** command ("give me more") reads a text file (or a number of text files) and displays the contents of the file(s) in chunks, a screenful at a time.

more is based upon the terminal handling capabilities that the Berkeley UNIX system uses for the **ex** and **vi** editors, so to use **more**, you must have your terminal type set up correctly in the environment.

At the bottom of the display, **more** places a message informing you what percentage of the current file has been displayed so far. To use **more**, you enter the command:

```
% more somefile
.  .  .  .  .
          .  .  .  .  . Lines of text from "somefile"
       .  .  .  .  .
                  .  .  .  .  .
--More-- (3%)
%
```

Note that the percentage figure which is displayed represents a fraction of the number of characters in the file, not the number of lines. If **more** is part of a pipeline, such that its input is coming from the Standard Output of a previous command, you don't get the percentage display. If the file you are looking at is large, you might see a percentage figure of 0% displayed at the bottom of the screen; this happens because **more**'s internal arithmetic cannot handle large numbers.

When using **more**, there are various keys you can press in order to tell **more** what to do next. The simplest action is pressing the space bar; this tells **more** to go on and display the next screenload. Typing RETURN will cause **more** to display one more line at the bottom of the screen.

more can be terminated at any time by typing the interrupt character (usually RUBOUT or DEL, or BREAK, or sometimes control-C).

There are many more commands to **more**. We refer you to the UNIX Programmer's Manual, if you happen to have **more** on your system.

There are also many options on the **more** command line. The most useful ones are the capability to either start displaying text at a specific line in the file, and to start displaying text at a line containing a specific text pattern. For example, you can get **more** to display text starting at line 194, by typing the command line like this:

```
% more +194 somefile
```

If you want **more** to start displaying text at the first line which contains the string

```
    more than a feeling
```

you type a command line like this:

```
% more  +/'more than a feeling'  somefile
```

The patterns can be specified as regular expressions, as in **ed** and **grep**.

13.5 Scanning the Manuals with 'apropos'

The **apropos** command is used to determine if there is anything relevant to a particular keyword in the online version of the manuals. Here are a couple of examples of how **apropos** can be used. The first one looks for anything apropos *'sort'*:

```
% apropos sort
ddsort (3/21/80) - sort DDBS files
look (1)         - find lines in a sorted list
asort (3)        - quicker sort
sort (1)         - sort or merge files
tsort (1)        - topological sort
%
```

Having found everything relevant to the *'sort'* keyword by using **apropos** as shown above, you can then go on to look in the relevant section of the manual.

   The search is not on a specific command, but is actually on the string you supply as an argument to **apropos**. This example illustrates how to get a load of irrelevant stuff:

```
% apropos rm
access (2)        - determine accessibility of file
alarm (2)         - schedule signal after specified time
ar (5)            - archive (library) file format
                  <etc...>
dump, ddate (5)   - incremental dump format
                  <etc...>
ttys (5)          - terminal initialization data
unstr (1)         - undo strfile formatted file.
wait (2)          - wait for process to terminate
%
```

As you can see, the search for something relevant to *'rm'* also finds words like "terminal", "formatted", and "determine". We did not show all the lines which this particular example generated, since there were lots of them. It is entirely up to you to make the selection process as wide open or as selective as you wish.

13.6 Viewing the Manual Titles with 'whatis'

Closely associated with the **apropos** command is the **whatis** command. **whatis** simply displays the title lines from the on-line manuals. For example:

```
% whatis mv ln cp
cp (1)                  - copy
ln (1)                  - make links
mv (1)                  - move or rename files
%
```

These are the title lines for the **cp, ln,** and the **mv** manual pages. The entries are displayed in alphabetical order, regardless of the order in which you typed them on the command line.

13.7 Finding Files with 'whereis'

The **whereis** command performs a restricted search for the specific files relating to commands. To find out where the manual page for the **rm** command is, you type:

```
% whereis -m rm
rm: /usr/man/man1/rm.1
%
```

The **–m** option restricts the search to the **m**anual pages only. Similarly, the **–b** option restricts the search to the binary of the command:

```
% whereis -b rm
rm: /bin/rm
%
```

The **whereis** command without any options tries to locate the source, binary, and manual pages for the specified file.

13.8 Finding a User with 'finger'

The **finger** command is used to find out more about a given user.
The Berkeley system uses the so-called "GCOS" field in the password
file to record information about the users on the system. In that
field is kept the users' real names, telephone numbers, and room
numbers.

The **finger** command also looks in the user's home directory for files called
'project' and *'plan'*. If either of those files exists **finger** displays information
about the current projects and plans of that user.

The **finger** command is said to be undergoing a major overhaul at
Berkeley, to keep a database of users instead of updating the password file. For that reason, the information here is not necessarily
accurate, but exists to give you an idea of what is available.

```
% finger hank
Login name: hank          In real life: Hank Parker
Directory: /aa/widget/hank
Last login Wed Jul  7 16:00 on tty04
No unread mail.
No Plan.
%
```

Hank does not have a file called *'.plan'*, so there is no information
about what he is doing.
   Here is another example of **finger**:

```
% finger patty
Login name: patty         In real life: Patricia Cadwallader
Directory: /aa/blivet/patty
On since Jul 2 08:14:56 on tty09 3 minutes 17 seconds idle time
Unread mail since Tue Jul  6 20:20:14 1982
Project: A computer controlled combine-harvester.
Plan:
Finish up on the hay-baling controller.
%
```

13.9 Looking for Character Strings
with 'strings'

The **strings** command looks in an executable file for any string of
characters which looks like an ASCII text string. Instead of trying to
explain the whys and wherefores of **strings**, we show by example how
to use it.

Consider the Roman numerals conversion program that we developed in chapter 12. Here is how you would run **strings** on that program:

```
$ strings progs/c/roman
Usage: roman  decimal_number
low must be less than high
%d %s
Use numbers in range 1 .. 9999
(null)
$
```

As you can see, there are the character strings that appeared in the various "printf" statements in the program.

13.10 Summary

This was only intended as a short overview of the Berkeley UNIX system. We would like to tell you more, but that would be another whole book, and by the time we'd written it, the Berkeley system would have changed out of all recognition.

We hope you have a good idea of what the C-Shell can do. Read the documentation for the C-Shell, and experiment with the features it provides for you.

There are many more commands and facilities available. If you happen to be a user on a Berkeley based UNIX system, it is worth sitting at a terminal and scanning through the manuals for some of the other goodies that are there. Talk to the other users on your system — there is always something new in the works.

14 UNIX System Management Guide

System administration is concerned with the day-to-day aspects of looking after the UNIX system, assigning new login names, managing the file system, and a host of other duties.

Under normal circumstances, system administration is an area with which the average user doesn't need to be concerned. However, with the spread of the UNIX operating system to small computers such as the Motorola MC68000, a given UNIX system is no longer a large installation in a company or a laboratory, but may exist in a small business office or even in the home. In these latter cases, the owner of the system will also have to be the system administrator. This chapter covers the major aspects of caring for and feeding your UNIX system. It is impossible to cover every detail. It is hoped that your particular supplier will have provided adequate documentation — if they haven't, go beat on them until they do.

In this chapter we describe a number of commands which are specially oriented towards system administration. These commands (such as **fsck**, **mount**, **chown**, and so on) are usually found in the /etc directory. They are placed in /etc instead of /bin so that users other than the administrator won't inadvertently use them. The placement of those commands in /etc or /bin or anywhere else is dependent upon the particular administration at your site. If you have any control over where those commands live, it is recommended that they be placed in the */etc* directory.

Just about all of the discussions in this chapter assume that you are the super-user. In fact, only the super-user can issue some of these commands. The super-user gets a different system prompt, namely a # sign instead of a $ sign or a % sign. Throughout the examples in this chapter, we show the prompt as the # sign, to remind you that you are the super-user.

14.1 Special Users

On any given UNIX system, in addition to the hordes of "normal" users, there are a number of "special" users who can use commands, and do things on the system, which are unavailable to the normal user.

In this section, we only talk in detail about the so-called "super-user", who also may be called "root". The other special users are given an honorable mention, but not discussed further, because every UNIX system has a different complement of these special users.

"root" is the "super-user", who has Olympian powers over the running (and the possible destruction) of the system. The super-user is unconstrained by any protections that the system has, can get at any file, and kill any process.

There are some system operations which only the super-user can do. Setting the date with the **date** command is one example. Mounting a file system with the **mount** command, and making special files with the **mknod** command are others.

There are a number of ways in which you can become the super-user. The first of these is to bring the system up in single-user state. This situation occurs when the system is booted up (see the discussion below on booting the system). At boot-up time, the initial Shell runs with all the super-user privileges. On a multi-user system, you can either log out and log in again as the super-user, or you can use the **su** command to gain access as the super-user.

Another of the special users is "bin". "bin" is in charge of commands which live in the */bin* and */usr/bin* directories, and is also responsible for libraries which live in the various *'lib'* directories.

Whenever possible, you should log in as "bin" if your duties do not require you to be "root". There are valid reasons for this. Apart from the ability to kill the system, the super-user's powers override all permissions in the system. Thus many times you can set up files and assign permissions, only to find that as a regular user you cannot access these things, nor do anything useful. Those who are drunk with power can ignore this advice.

14.2 Starting Up and Shutting Down the System

"Booting" is the process you must apply to get the system running when the computer is initially switched on, or when the computer is restarted after a halt.

"Booting" derives from the notion of "lifting yourself by your bootstraps". A small stupid program loads in a medium sized smart program which knows enough to load, configure, and start entire wizard systems such as the UNIX system.

Now it may turn out that you are running your UNIX system on a small (cabinet-sized, or table-top) computer, in which case the boot process might very well turn out to involve floppy disks. Such systems require some form of "stand-alone restoration" capability, such that the entire system can be regenerated on a blank slate.

We cannot, obviously, tell you exactly how to boot the particular UNIX system that you happen to have. We don't know whose UNIX system it is. If you are on a PDP-11, for example, booting involves setting console switches, and loading a particular disk. On other systems, you might just insert a floppy disk, then press some reset switch. You will have to consult the documentation for your UNIX system (if there is any) for details of how to boot up.

The initial boot program often lives in the magical "block zero" of the device (most likely a disk) which must be located on the boot device. When the boot program runs, you usually have a dialog which might look something like this:

```
boot device ? dw(0,0)unix
Loading at 0x1000: 68492+3820+3616
Welcome to Wonderful Widgets Co. UNIX System
#
```

In the example, the 'dw(0,0)' refers to the device called 'dw'. The (0,0) refers to the device number and block offset to use. The name 'unix' is the name of the file in which you can find the kernel. The first '0' in this case, refers to device 'dw0', that is, major device 'dw' and minor device '0' (we discuss these topics later on in this chapter). The second '0' in the parentheses above refers to the block offset where the root file system is to be found on that device. It is possible to start a file system at some block other than the very first, in which case, the dialog might look like this:

```
boot device ? dw(0,60)unix
Loading at 0x1000: 68492+3820+3616
Welcome to Wonderful Widgets Co. UNIX System
#
```

The numbers displayed indicate the sizes of the various parts of the UNIX system, namely, the text (executable code), the initialized data area, and the uninitialized data area.

The initial program does not have to be called *'unix'*. The boot program understands the structure of the file system. It might be that you wish to load up some form of stand-alone diagnostic. For example, all the diagnostics might live in the */tests* directory under the root. In that case, the boot up sequence might well look like this:

```
boot device ? dw(0,0)/tests/memory
. . . . . messages from the memory test program . . .
```

In this example, we are loading up a memory test program called *'memory'* from the */tests* directory.

On many UNIX systems, you will find a directory called */stand*. This usually contains stand-alone programs for checking the system before you proceed further. Typical utilities which live in */stand* might be a stand-alone **ls** command, a stand-alone **icheck**, to check the integrity of the file system, and stand-alone **dump** and **restor** programs.

When the system first boots up, you are up in "single-user" state. This means that the system is only running one user at this time, and the multi-user capability (if any) is not yet enabled. When a single-user system is running, there are only a Shell and the system initialization processes active. The person at the console (who should be the super-user) is the only person who can do anything.

After an initial boot-up, one of the first things you must do is set the date.

14.2.1 Setting the Date with 'date'

The **date**, when typed without arguments, displays the date. The other variation on **date**, namely setting the date, is only available to the super-user.

```
# date   8202140834
#
```

The argument you give to the **date** command is in the form

```
yymmddhhmm
```

where 'yy' is a two-digit year, 'mm' is a two-digit month, 'dd' is the two-digit day of the month, 'hh' is the two-digit hour of the day (24-hour clock), and 'mm' is the two-digit minutes in the hour field. Each of the fields must be two digits in length, so you might have to pad out a field with a zero to make it two digits long.

The example above sets the time and date to 8:34 in the morning of 14th February, 1982.

It is possible to omit leading fields in the date. If (say) the year and month are the same as they were the last time you set the date, you don't have to type them:

```
# date   140834
#
```

sets the date the same as in the previous example.

Having set the date you are now ready to bring up the system in multi-user state. To start the system multi-user you essentially "log-out" from the single-user state by typing a control-D. The system then asks you to log in just as it would on a regular terminal:

```
# ^D
;login: maryann
Password: wizard
$
```

Usually, you would log in as a normal user unless you absolutely must be the super-user. The dialog here shows Maryann, having booted the system, bringing it up in multi-user state, and then logging in as her normal unprivileged self.

There are other things you might have to do to make the system fully operational, such as mounting file systems. We cover this topic later, under the **mount** command.

14.2.2 The System Initialization Script

Upon startup, the system initialization process looks for a file called */etc/rc*. This file is simply a Shell script, and can contain any commands you like. It typically contains commands to clean out the */tmp* directories and others, and to start up some of the daemons. Here is a typical */etc/rc* file:

```
# cat /etc/rc
PATH=/bin:/usr/bin
rm   /etc/mtab
cat   /dev/null  >/etc/utmp
/etc/mount   /dev/rm1   /usr
rm   -rf   /usr/tmp/*
rm   -rf   /tmp/*
/etc/update
/etc/cron
date   >/dev/console
#
```

The steps that this script goes through are:

- remove the /etc/mtab file, used later by **mount**,
- empty out the record of logged in users,
- mount the /usr directory,
- clean out the temporary space directories,
- start up the **update** and **cron** processes,
- display the date on the console.

14.2.3 Shutting Down the System

In a large multi-user system it might be necessary to shut down the machine now and again. The exact procedure will differ depending on the configuration. A typical procedure might be something like this:

- Send out warning messages to everyone logged in that the system is coming off the air in five minutes, four minutes, ... right now! This can be done using the **wall** command, which is similar to **write**, but **w**rites to **all** users.
- **kill** all running processes except the console process,
- Use the **sync** command to make sure that all file system input-output activity has stopped,
- Demount file systems as required,
- Perform any backup dump procedures which might be required,
- Power down the system, if required.

14.3 Accounts, Users, and Groups

Every user who has an account on the UNIX system has an entry in the password file. In addition, it is possible that there is a *'group'* file, where the information about which users live in what groups is recorded.

The password file is called *'passwd'*, and lives in the */etc* directory. Similarly, the group file is called *'group'* and also lives in the */etc* directory.

14.3.1 The Password File

There is nothing magic about the password file. It is just a regular old ASCII text file which you can change with a text editor. If you look in the password file you see something like this:

```
# cat  /etc/passwd
root:kWFpmBP9vvKr2:0:1::/:
daemon:1fOk6tjt9Wn5a:1:1::/:
sys:8VMat0UUSkz41:2:2::/:
bin:Par19UAYok4R1:3:3::/bin:
maryann:KmHuRTfMVK1hE:201:10::/aa/widget/maryann:
sally:rDG6OoXq32m17:202:10::/aa/widget/sally:
jane:GXkGUFA1NofyM:203:10::/aa/widget/jane:
jack:Koris34zpim3m:204:10::/aa/widget/jack:
steve:oPUUJ3YLgN2Zc:204:10::/aa/widget/steve:
sylvia:kxUUskz41mqu5:206:10::/aa/widget/sylvia:
henry:Nz1gLj157en8c:207:10::/aa/widget/henry:
hank:79NiJVTuyF3ts:208:10::/aa/widget/hank:
charlie:yLKXK5936GyIw:209:10::/aa/widget/charlie:
bill:86mZodBsaCk4d:210:10::/aa/widget/bill:
joe:jRXtm96jotPc7:210:20::/aa/blivet/joe:
fred:tBnFQs45kph99:210:20::/aa/blivet/fred:
patty:H0eay7ZfOxfTg:210:20::/aa/blivet/patty:
#
```

This is not the most lucid display in the world, but each of the fields on each line in the password file does in fact have some rational meaning. The entries in the password file are mostly intelligible, but the second field on each line is the encrypted form of the user's password. The entries from a typical line in the password file are pointed out in figure 14.1.

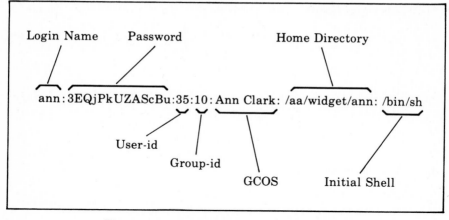

Figure 14.1   A Line from the Password File

The fields in the line have these meanings:

Login name
: login name for that user. Note that *'root'* and *'bin'* are not special in any way.

Encrypted password
: this field is set when the user's password is assigned via the **passwd** command.

User Identity
: numerical user id. This is a unique number given to a user.

Group Identity
: numerical group id. You can see that we have two main groups. The people in the "widget" project have all been placed in group 10, and the members of the "blivet" project are all in group 20. The numbers are purely arbitrary. Choose something that is easy to deal with.

GCOS field
: this has different uses on different UNIX systems. Some version 6 UNIX systems use this field for accounting purposes. Bell Laboratories uses the GCOS field on the GE (GCOS) timesharing system. The Berkeley UNIX system uses the GCOS field to hold the user's real name, telephone number, room number, and so on. The information stored therein is then used by the **finger** command which we described in chapter 13.

Home Directory
: this is the directory in which users find themselves when they log in.

Initial Shell
: name of the program to use as a Shell, for use on those UNIX systems where there is a choice of Shells available. For example, on the Berkeley UNIX system you can choose to use the C-Shell, in which case this entry in the password file reads */bin/csh.*

At this point we wish to highlight some of the features of the way in which user numbers and such are allocated in the system.

You will notice that all the regular users in the above password file start at number 101 or 201. This choice of numbers to allocate to users is entirely arbitrary.

Also note that all the users are in the two main groups. Again, the choice of group number is arbitrary.

There are, however, some gotchas in this scheme. The "root" must always have user-id zero. Many of the system utilities depend on this. In addition, many of the system utilities also depend on the root actually being called "root". It might seem reasonable to call yourself by any name you want, even if you are the super-user. Unfortunately, if you do that you will find you have shut yourself out of the system.

14.3.2 The Group File

As stated previously, the group file lives in */etc/group*. Here is a typical group file for our system:

```
# cat  /etc/group
root::1:root,shutup,daemon
sys::2:bin,sys
widget::10:maryann,sally,jane,jack,steve,sylvia,\
henry,hank,charlie,bill
blivet::20:joe,fred,patty
#
```

The first field in a group entry is the group name.

The second field is the group password. All our groups here are without a password.

The third field is the group ID. This number is what the utilities look for when any work has to be done on groups.

The last field in a group entry is a comma-separated list of the people who belong in that group. In our case all the "widget" project are in group 10, and all the "blivet" project in group 20.

14.3.3 Adding a New User to the System

If you have to add new users to the system there are three things which must be done:

1. The new user's name and other information must be placed in the password file.

2. The new user must have a home directory allocated for them. The ownership of that directory must reflect that user's ID.

3. That user must be placed in the group file if necessary.

On some systems there is a specially built Shell script, usually called **adduser**, which allocates new users. In fact, some systems have a special "adduser" administrator whose sole duties are to add new users, and that is all that can be done from the "adduser" account.

In this discussion, we go the simple route of adding a new user by hacking the password file with the editor. This seems to be the way most administrators do the job. The easiest way to do it is simply to replicate a line in the password file, then change the user-id, name, home directory, and initial Shell as required.

Here, we have to add a new account to the system for Roxanne. She is going to work in the 'blivet' project, and she wants the C-Shell as her initial Shell. Here is how we add a new user called "roxanne" to the password file:

```
# cd   /etc
# ed   passwd
705
* $
patty:H0eay7ZfOxfTg:210:20::/aa/blivet/patty:
* t.
* s/patty/roxanne/g
* s/H0.*Tg//
* s/210/211/p
roxanne::211:20::/aa/blivet/roxanne:
* s/$/\/bin\/csh/p
roxanne::211:20::/aa/blivet/roxanne:/bin/csh
* w
742
* q
#
```

What we did here was to replicate the last line of the password file, whose entry is for Patty, then change "patty" to "roxanne", change the user-id from 210 to 211, and wipe out the encrypted password field. Roxanne now has no password until she decides to create one for herself.

Now we have to create a home directory for Roxanne, with the appropriate ownership:

```
# cd /aa/blivet
# mkdir roxanne
# ls -ld roxanne
drwxrwxrwx  2 root          32 Apr 24 09:28 roxanne
# /etc/chown roxanne roxanne
# /etc/chgrp blivet roxanne
# ls -ld roxanne
drwxrwxrwx  2 roxanne       32 Apr 24 09:28 roxanne
#
```

The only other thing left to do is to add Roxanne to the list of people in the "blivet" project in the group file.

14.3.4 Changing Ownership with 'chown' and 'chgrp'

The **chown** (change **own**er) command is used to change the ownership of a directory or file, that is, to "give" the directory or file to someone else. We saw one use of **chown**, above, when we created a new account for Roxanne. The directory that we created as her home directory must belong to her, else she will find it hard to work on the system.

The **chgrp** (change **gro**up) command changes the group ownership of directories or files. In other words, those directories or files are assigned to a different group in the system.

Only the super-user can change the ownership or the group ownership.

14.3.5 Changing a User's Password with 'passwd'

As you know, you can change your own password with the **passwd** command. If you are the super-user, you can change anybody's password. Newcomers to a site often forget their password. In that case, they will come to the super-user with their tale of woe. What you do as a super-user is to assign them a known password, usually "stoopid" or something like that, with the **passwd** command.

Let us assume that Roxanne has forgotten whatever password she chose. You log in as the super-user, and use **passwd** like this:

```
# passwd  roxanne
New password: stoopid
Retype new password: stoopid
#
```

We showed the actual password as you typed it here. In reality, the password is not echoed as you type it.

14.3.6 Setting Special File Modes
with 'chmod'

In addition to the nine protection modes that a file or directory normally has, there are three more special modes that affect the way that the file is used as an executable program.

Only the super-user can set these modes. They only apply to executable files. These extra modes correspond to octal values 4000, 2000, and 1000, and have the following meanings in the system:

mode 4000   is called the "set user ID" bit, and indicates that when the program executes the user-ID is set to that of the owner of the actual file.

mode 2000   is called the "set group ID" bit, and indicates that when the program executes the group-ID is set to that of the group ownership of the actual file.

Both the set user ID and the set group ID bits are there for the purposes of programs such as **mail**, which must create files in directories not necessarily owned by the person running the program. Under normal circumstances, a person running **mail** could not create the mail information file in the */usr/spool/mail* directory, because they don't own that directory. The owner of the **mail** program, however, is usually "root", and so the set user ID bit for **mail** means that for the duration of its execution, the effective owner is "root", who can create files anywhere.

mode 1000   is called the "sticky-bit", and applies to programs whose executable text is sharable by many users. The sticky-bit implies that the swap-space for that program is not abandoned even when there is no-one using it. The sticky bit is usually only set for heavily used programs. It improves overall response time for use of that program.

14.4 Becoming the Super-User with 'su'

Frequently, you will find that you are logged in as a regular (non-super) user, and you suddenly have to do something that requires your super-user powers. Instead of logging out and logging in again, you simply use the **su** (for **s**witch **u**ser) command:

```
$ su
Password: genghis
#
```

Now you can do whatever it is that is required. When you have finished, you revert to your old user status by typing a control-D, just as if you were logging out.

In fact, you can use **su** to switch to be any other user, providing you know the password. For instance, if Joe Mugg is logged in as "joe", and wishes to do something under the "payroll" account, he can change over by:

```
$ su payroll
Password: sheckels
$
```

To revert to being "joe" he must type control-D.

14.5 File Systems

In the UNIX system, a file system is a complete directory structure, including a root directory, and all the directories which live under the root.

We cannot talk about file systems in any constructive way without also discussing devices. A device (on which you put a file system) is usually some form of magnetic disk.

A file system can correspond to a physical device, or more than one file system can live on a device. If a disk is a small one (in the region of 5000 blocks), the entire disk can be devoted to a single file system. It is in fact possible to place a file system on a floppy disk, which might have a capacity of between 500 and 1000 blocks. If a disk is large, it is possible to split it into several "logical" disks, each of which occupies some portion of the physical disk. It is then possible to put several file systems on it. Each file system then occupies one of the logical disks.

When a file system is first brought on-line, it must be "mounted" so that the kernel is aware of its existence. The notion of mounting a file system corresponds very well to the idea of mounting a physical disk pack. This notion is carried over even to the situation where there are several file systems on the same disk. Each one of the file systems still must be mounted separately.

On the UNIX system version 7, a file system is limited to a maximum of 65536 files. Of course, a file system can be smaller than this.

Every file system has the same basic layout, as shown in figure 14.2. Every file system has four fundamental parts:

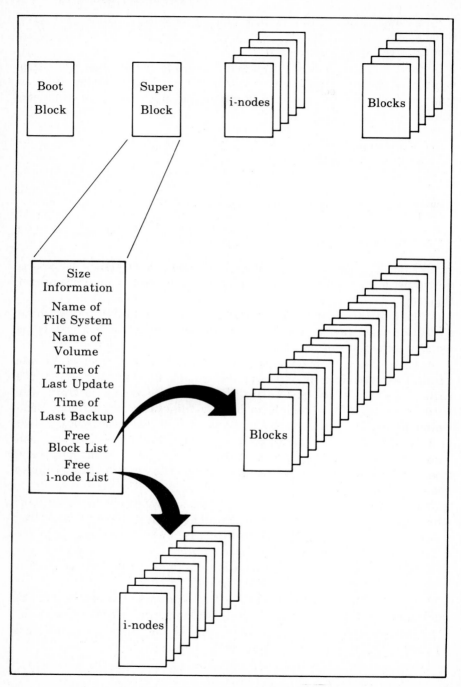

Figure 14.2   Layout of a Version 7 File System

The boot block   The very first block (block zero) on every file system, is reserved for a bootstrap program. It can, of course, contain anything you want to place there. Block zero does not have any meaning in the file system. All file system information really starts in block one of the device.

The Super-block   The first block (block one) of every file system is called the "super-block". It contains the major pieces of information about the file system, such as its size in blocks, the file system name, number of blocks reserved for i-nodes, the free i-node list, and the start of the chain of free blocks. All these topics are expanded upon in the sections to follow.

i-nodes   Following the super-block come a number of blocks containing i-nodes. The number of blocks of i-nodes varies depending on the number of blocks in the file system. The number of i-nodes is specified in the super-block. There is one i-node for every directory and file in the file system. If an i-node is allocated, it contains a description of a directory or file somewhere in the file system.

Data Blocks   The rest of the logical device is full of data blocks. Data blocks contain the actual data stored in the directories and files. There are also data blocks which serve as indirect blocks, containing block-numbers of large files.

A file in the UNIX system is described by an object called an "i-node". We think that the name means "interior node", since the UNIX file-system is (in principle at least) a directed graph. For every file there is a single i-node that describes that file, and contains pointers to the blocks that comprise that file.

The structure of a file, its i-node, and its blocks, are shown in figure 14.3. The i-node contains information about the access rights (permissions) on the file, number of links, and some other information. Then there appear the block numbers. The first ten block number entries directly refer to blocks containing the actual data in the file. So the direct blocks can handle a file up to

```
512 . 10 = 5,120 bytes
```

If the file is larger than ten blocks, the eleventh pointer refers to a block that contains 128 pointers to blocks. This is called an "indirect block". Using one indirect block means that the file can be up to

```
512 . (10 + 128) = 70,656 bytes
```

If there are more than 138 blocks in the file, the twelfth pointer refers to a block that contains pointers to 128 indirect blocks. This second level of blocks is known as "double-indirect blocks". Such a

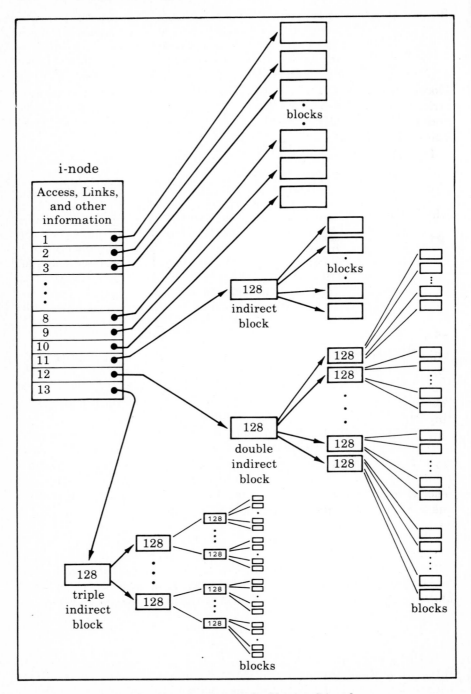

Figure 14.3   Layout of a Version 7 i-node

file, using double-indirect blocks, can now contain up to

$$512 \ . \ (10 + 128 + 128^2) = 8,459,264 \text{ bytes}$$

If the file is still bigger than can be accommodated in 16,522 blocks, the thirteenth and last pointer in the i-node refers to a "triple-indirect block". This is a block that contains pointers to 128 double-indirect blocks. This block extends the size of the file by another 2,097,152 blocks.

Thus the maximum size of a file in the UNIX system is

$$512 \ . \ (10 + 128 + 128^2 + 128^3) \text{ bytes}$$

which is equivalent to 1,082,201,088 bytes.

 It should be clearly understood that the previous discussion on file layout applies to UNIX system version 7. The UNIX system at Berkeley is quite different, with a different layout for the i-node, and different block sizes. Earlier versions of the UNIX system had more limited file sizes.

14.5.1 The Root File System

When the system is booted up there is always one predetermined file system on a well-known device, which is the root file system. In the root file system can be found all the important directories such as /dev, /etc, /bin, and so on. It is from this root file system that all the important system programs, such as the Shell, and the system initialization program, can be found.

14.5.2 Making a File System with 'mkfs'

The **mkfs** command creates a new file system. The basic form of the **mkfs** command is like this:

```
# /etc/mkfs name size
#
```

Notice that the **mkfs** command lives in the /etc directory. It is there so that users won't inadvertently start creating file systems all over the place by executing the command out of /bin or /usr/bin.

When you make a new file system, you must specify the number of blocks that the file system contains. The **mkfs** command uses that number to determine, by some rules of thumb, the number of blocks it will set aside for i-nodes.

Let us assume that there is a device out there on a floppy disk, and it is called */dev/fl0*. Let us further assume that a maximum of 2000 blocks can fit on this floppy. You make a file system on this device like this:

```
# /etc/mkfs /dev/fl0 2000
isize = 230
m/n = 3 500
#
```

The **mkfs** command responds with two messages. The first is the number of blocks it has reserved for i-nodes.

The second is an interleave factor and a cycle number. Only those who are deep into the theory of rotating disks need bother with that second message.

As it stands, all you have now is a file system created on a device. There still remains the need to make this file system known to the rest of the UNIX system. This is done with the **mount** command, described next.

14.5.3 Mounting a File System with 'mount'

Having made a file system on a device, it is just sitting out there, and only you know it is there. The UNIX system is quite indifferent to all the work you just did to create the file system.

The way to get a file system on a device attached to the rest of the file system is to create a directory entry in the root of the file system, then mount the device under that directory.

The **mount** command is what actually mounts a file system so that the kernel is aware that the file system is there. Even if the device which contains the specified file system also contains other file systems, each file system must be mounted separately. This associates a file system with a logical device, quite independently of other file systems on the same physical device. Therefore any given file system can be moved to a different logical device with no trouble.

The **mount** command is used like this:

```
# /etc/mount device dirname
#
```

device   is the name of the device on which the file system is to be mounted.

dirname   is the name of the directory under which that file system is to be mounted. *'dirname'* must already exist — it is usually created by a prior **mkdir** command.

Let us use as an example the file system we just created on the floppy disk. We will create a new directory under the root, and mount the file system on the floppy under that directory.

```
# cd /
# mkdir /supergiz
# /etc/mount /dev/fl0 /supergiz
#
```

Now you have a file system, which is just another directory under the root file system. You can now change directory into the new file system, make directories, create files, and so on. There is no special magic about it.

At any time, you can find out what file systems are mounted by just giving a **mount** command on its own, without arguments:

```
# /etc/mount
/dev/fl0 on /supergiz
#
```

The information as to what is mounted is kept in a file called */etc/mtab*. Every time you mount a file system, the **mount** command updates that file to reflect the new mounted file system. Every time you unmount a file system, the specific entry in the */etc/mtab* file is removed. You should be aware, however, that the **mount** and **umount** commands update the */etc/mtab* file purely for the convenience of the users. This file is not used in any other way. In particular, the table is not used as any form of validity check as to what is already mounted, since the system keeps its own mount table in memory.

☛ Make sure that the permissions on the root directory of a mounted file system match those of the directory under which it is mounted. Strange and wonderful things happen when the permissions don't match, especially when the underlying file system is less privileged than the directory under which it is mounted.

Eventually, you will probably want to take the removable device off the system, and store it away somewhere safe, perhaps in the cellar with your champagne. Demounting (or "unmounting") a device is our next topic of discussion.

14.5.4 Demounting a File System
with 'umount'

Given that you have one or more file systems on a removable device, you cannot just simply walk up and remove it. After all, there might be people using it. Even if there is nobody using that particular file system at the moment, someone might decide to use it later, and if the operating system couldn't find it, there could be problems.

The **umount** command is used to "unmount" (demount) a file system or device. Note that the command is spelled "**umount**". There is only one "n" in the word.

The **umount** command is used like this:

```
# /etc/umount device
#
```

'*device*' is the name of the file system which is to be demounted. Let us assume that the file system on the */dev/fl0* floppy disk is to be removed. You would go through the following sequence of commands:

```
# cd /
# /etc/umount /dev/fl0
#
```

First of all, we changed our current working directory to the root of the file system.

Then we gave the **umount** command, as shown. This now results in a disassociation of the specific device with the directory it was attached to. The device can now be removed safely, and stored away somewhere.

Note that the */supergiz* directory is still there. It has not gone away, but an **ls** command issued on */supergiz* would not show anything — there is nobody home. It is perfectly feasible now, to mount an entirely different file system under the */supergiz* directory, or to use */supergiz* as a normal directory and create subdirectories under it.

What kinds of problems and responses can you get from **umount**? Well, one very common problem is that you are not back at the root of the file system when you try to unmount the device, but instead you are (or someone else is) positioned in a directory somewhere in the file system you are trying to unmount. In this case, you get this response:

```
# /etc/umount /dev/fl0
umount: device busy
# pwd
/supergiz/frammis
# cd /
# /etc/umount /dev/fl0
#
```

A "device busy" response gives you a clue that your working directory is somewhere in the file system you are trying to unmount. In this example, we used the **pwd** command to discover that we are positioned somewhere down the */supergiz* hierarchy. We then changed directory back up to the root, and issued the **umount** command again, and this time, all went well.

Another fairly common mistake is to try to unmount the directory which the device was associated with:

```
# cd /
# /etc/umount /supergiz
umount: Block device required
#
```

This is a fairly easy mistake to make. Remember, you unmount the device containing the file system, not the directory which is associated with that file system.

Lastly, if you try to unmount a non existent device (that is, one which has no entry in */dev*) you get the following rather cryptic results:

```
# /etc/umount /dev/f10
umount: Invalid argument
#
```

14.5.5 Synchronizing Input Output with 'sync'

The UNIX system is a multi-tasking system. Because of this, you cannot just shut down the system at any old time — data which is destined to be written to the disk devices might still be lying around in memory.

In particular, the system maintains an in-memory cache of free blocks, i-nodes, and most important of all, the super-block.

If you were to just walk up and shut down the system, the state of the file systems would be horribly corrupted.

During normal operation, the system sweeps through all the disk buffers on a periodic basis and "flushes" the buffers (ensures they are written to the disk devices). This regular visitation is called "synchronization".

Therefore, if at any time you wish to shut the system down or, as we described above in the discussion on the **umount** command, you want to remove a device which has a file system on it, you must ensure that all the disk buffers have been flushed. To do this you use the **sync** command:

```
# /etc/sync
#
```

sync does not display any messages when operating.

You should also be aware that when you see the system prompt **#** after the **sync** command is complete, that does not mean that the buffers have all been written out; it means that the flushing process has started. For this reason, you often see people typing two **sync** commands, one after the other, because of superstition.

14.6 Devices and Special Files

Any given UNIX system knows about certain kinds of peripheral devices on the system. These take the form of magnetic disks, magnetic tapes, terminals, communication lines, and all sorts of other things. Every different kind of device has a piece of the UNIX system called a "driver" which is responsible for communicating with that device. Somewhere deep inside the system there is a table that points to the different device drivers. All devices are treated just like files. The physical bridge between the device name (filename) and the table of drivers is to be found in the /dev directory, that lives just under the root of the file system.

14.6.1 Adding a Device to the System with 'mknod'

When a new device is added to the system, it is necessary to add a new device name in the /dev directory. This is called "making a node", and is done with the **mknod** (**make nod**e) command.

Let us look in the /dev directory of a typical UNIX system. We only show parts of /dev, since a lot of it is repetitive:

```
# ls -l /dev
Total 3
crw--w--w- 1 root     0,   0 Mar  9 21:00 console
               <etc...>
crw--w--w- 1 root     1,   0 Mar  8 14:33 lp
brw-rw-rw- 1 root     2,   2 Mar  9 08:24 null
brw-rw-rw- 1 root     5,   0 Dec 21 21:17 rm0
               <etc...>
crw-r--r-- 1 root     5,   8 Feb 11 20:44 rrm0
brw-rw-rw- 1 root     5,   5 Dec 21 21:16 mt0
               <etc...>
crw--w--w- 1 root    18,   0 Mar  4 16:11 tty00
crw--w--w- 1 maryann 18,   1 Mar  9 08:15 tty01
crw--w--w- 1 root    18,   2 Mar  4 20:44 tty02
crw--w--w- 1 jack    18,   3 Mar  4 13:55 tty03
               <etc...>
#
```

This list of a */dev* directory is taken from a fairly typical large UNIX timesharing system.

When you want to create an entry for a new device, say 'tty16', you do it with **mknod**:

```
# /etc/mknod /dev/tty16 c 18 16
#
```

The first argument is the name of the device you are making, in this case it is */dev/tty16*.

The second argument (the **c** here) indicates whether this device is a character (**c**) oriented device such as a terminal, or a block (**b**) oriented device like a disk.

The third and fourth arguments are the major and minor device numbers for that device. Each device in the UNIX system has some "driver" software buried deep in the system, which handles the interactions of that device. In general, the major device number indicates a class of devices that can all be handled by the same driver. The driver uses the minor device number to determine which actual device it is that it is talking to.

The list of devices is something which varies the most from one system to another, so your supplier had better have that information for you.

14.7 System Backups and Restores

Whether your UNIX system is a huge overloaded installation with 100 users, or just a table-top system with only one user (yourself), it is important to "back up" the files on a regular basis, to ensure that if anything happens (a "crash") only a small amount of work needs to be redone.

There are various ways to perform backup operations in a system. The most useful is to take a full dump once a week, then do an incremental dump daily. This means that every day you dump, to some backup device, those files which have changed since the last dump, and every week you dump the entire file system whether it has changed or not.

Backup devices are usually magnetic tape, but in small systems, floppy disks can serve just as well.

The **dump** program described below knows about dump "levels". Level 0 is the highest level, and level 9 is the lowest. For any given level, **dump** dumps all files which have been modified since the last dump of the same or lower level. Thus a level 0 dump dumps the whole file system, and is called the "epoch".

14.7.1 Dumping a File System with 'dump'

The **dump** and **restor** utilities are the main method of getting back-ups of the system. On larger systems which come equipped with magnetic tapes, **dump** and **restor** move directories and files to and from the tapes. But in fact, they can work with any kind of blocked device, so if you have a small system, you can use floppy disks or tape cartridges to dump and restore files. The important thing is to make regular backups. That way you will rarely have any problems.

Let us assume that you have a floppy disk called *|dev|fl0* on the system. You can use **dump** to dump an entire file system to that disk with a command like this:

```
# /etc/dump 0uf /dev/fl0   /dev/dw0
     date = Mon May 17 10:15:58 1982
dump date = the epoch
dumping /dev/dw0 to /dev/fl0
I
II
estimated 5905 blocks on 9 volume(s)
III
IV
change volumes and type return:
        .  .  .  .  .
DONE
6002 blocks on 9 volume(s)
#
```

Let us discuss what some of these things mean in the example above. This **dump** command dumps the entire *|dev|dw0* file system to *|dev|fl0*.

The digit 0 means to perform a level 0 dump, which dumps the entire file system. The letter **u** means to update the file *|etc|ddate*. This file can then be used in subsequent **dump** operations of a lower level, to determine what files to dump. The letter **f** indicates that the next argument on the command line is the name of the file on which the files are to be dumped. The default filename varies from one installation to another, so look in your particular documentation for what is appropriate.

The **dump** command does its job in four distinct phases, as labelled in the example:

Phase I   determines the structure of the directories that will be dumped.

Phase II	guesses the number of blocks to dump, and makes sure that the files are readable. The estimate of the number of blocks is usually low, but the number of volumes is usually correct.
Phase III	writes out the directory structure to the dump device.
Phase IV	writes out the blocks from the files.

14.7.2 Restoring Files with 'restor'

Restoring files is easier. Usually, you are only restoring one or two files. It is rare that an entire file system must be restored. To restore a single file called *'comeback'* off the tape we dumped it on before, use a command like this:

```
# /etc/restor xf /dev/fl0 comeback
#
```

If you have to restore a whole file system, you should ensure that it is a new and clear file system. The **r** option of **restor** is used to do this. Restoring a whole file system is often used to change the size of the file system. You do a complete **dump** of the file system, remake it with a different number of blocks, then **restor** it again.

When restoring a whole file system, **restor** asks you for confirmation:

```
# /etc/restor rf /dev/fl0  /dev/dw0
Last chance before scribbling on /dev/dw0.
#
```

A "y" response to this prompt tells **restor** to go ahead and restore the file system.

If you are restoring one file from a multi-volume dump, it is quicker to start at the last volume in the set first, then work back towards the first.

14.7.3 Notes on 'dump' and 'restor'

Here are some notes to help you with the **dump** and **restor** programs.

Regrettably, **dump** and **restor** are two of the dumber programs on the UNIX system. **dump** tends to ignore device errors when it is dumping, and just goes merrily on its way. For example, if you try to dump a file system to a 600 foot tape, and there are too many blocks to fit, **dump** just ignores the fact that it gets to the end of the tape, so you have to ensure that the tape (or whatever) is long enough.

When **restor**ing, always do an **fsck** or an **icheck –s** afterwards, because **restor** doesn't do anything sensible with the free block lists. It doesn't update any of the counts.

When you **restore** a file system, there had better be a file system on the target device, otherwise **restor** just writes for ever.

14.7.4 Dumping Files to Tape with 'tar'

On the UNIX system version 7, a useful command for dumping files to tape is the **tar** (for **tape ar**chive) command. At first sight, **tar** looks like the **ar** archive program, but **tar** knows about directories and links and so on. **tar** dumps files onto a specified device in a special format, with headers and checksums and all. **tar** writes out a faithful representation of directory structures, files, permissions and all that, such that a subsequent **tar** run can recover all or part of the dumped files. It is not necessary to place files on a tape with **tar**. You can if you wish just make a tape archive on another disk.

Although we have included **tar** in this appendix on system administration, any user can in fact use **tar** at any time.

You use **tar** with a command line that looks like this:

```
# tar options files
#
```

In common with most other commands on the UNIX system, **tar** does its work quietly with no extraneous chatter, unless you use the **v** (for verbose) option.

Let us assume that you have a floppy disk device called */dev/fl0* out there. Here is a typical **tar** run to dump all the files in a directory to */dev/fl0.*

```
# tar cf /dev/fl0 *
#
```

Here we have given two options to **tar**. The **c** (for **c**reate) option tells **tar** that this is a new archive. In the absence of the **c** option, **tar** assumes that you are adding to an existing archive.

The **f** (for **f**ile) option tells **tar** that the very next argument on the command line is the name of a file on which the archive is to be placed. In the absence of the **f** option, **tar** places the archive on a magnetic tape device called */dev/rm0.*

Now, if you want to, you can look at what we placed in the archive, using the **t** (for **t**able of contents) option:

```
# tar tf /dev/fl0
Blocksize = 40
<list
      of
        files
              on
                 the
                     tape>
```

Having made a tape archive, how do you get stuff back off the archive? This is easy, you just use the **x** (for extract) option to **tar**:

```
# tar xf /dev/fl0 *people
#
```

The **x** option tells **tar** to extract the specified files from the archive. Again, **tar** does this work silently.

There is a hidden flaw in the use of the extract option to **tar**, that is not evident from the above example. It is the Shell that expands the shorthand notation of '*people*', and not the **tar** command. So, in order for **tar** to get a correct list of *'people'* files, they must already exist in the directory in which you want them. If the files do not already exist in the directory, the Shell will not supply the list of filenames to **tar** (because no names were matched), and **tar** will (silently) do nothing. In such a case, you have to spell out the list of names explicitly.

There are a few subtleties in the use of **tar** which can help overcome the problems noted just above. One way to get **tar** to restore everything is to tell it a directory name:

```
# tar xf /dev/fl0 maryann
#
```

where *'maryann'* is the name of a directory. Now **tar** will restore all files from *⁄dev⁄fl0* to that directory.

Another feature is that files placed implicitly on a **tar** archive from a directory, just go on the archive with their names; the pathname is not included. Such files can be restored to any other directory. But, if you explicitly spell out a pathname, such as *⁄aa⁄widget⁄maryann⁄myfile,* that file goes on the archive with the full pathname included, and must be extracted with that name.

14.8 Maintaining File Systems

The file systems are wonderfully organized things. Unfortunately, there are many non-wonderful things that can go wrong with a file system if the wrong things happen at the wrong time. This section is a guide to the sorts of things that can go wrong in a file system. In here, we introduce the UNIX commands which can tell you what problems have arisen, and what you can do to repair those problem areas.

Back in the main discussion on file systems, earlier, we described the layout of a file system, with its i-nodes, blocks, indirect-blocks, the super-block, and so on.

This elegant structure is, unfortunately, subject to disruption due to many causes. For example, consider what happens to a large file if the triple-indirect block gets clobbered in some way. Some of the more prevalent problems that arise are these:

- A given block might be missing from the system. That is, it is not part of a file, nor is it in the free list.

- There might be duplicate i-nodes. That is, i-nodes that seem to describe the same thing twice.

- A block might appear both in a file, and in the free list. This is one of the more serious problems that can arise. If, for example, the block in question is an indirect block, its erroneous presence in the free list might cause it to be reallocated to another file, and so two entirely different files will end up as a badly formed amalgam.

- A file can exist, but is not linked to any directory anywhere.

In the midst of all this gloom, it is fortunate that the organization of the file system brings with it a certain degree of redundancy. Some of the redundant information comes from these situations:

- a data-block which happens to be a directory contains file-names (and/or directory names) and i-numbers. But somewhere, there is an i-node which corresponds to that directory, and that i-node should be marked as a directory, not an ordinary file.

- a block which is part of the free-list should not, in theory, be part of a file anywhere. It is easy to scan through all the i-nodes looking for blocks which are allocated to files as well as the free-list.

- similarly, a block which belongs to a file should belong only to one file. It is easy to check for this.

There are many other redundancies which enable a cleverly constructed program to verify the correctness of the file system, and to make a creditable attempt at fixing up any problems which are found. The next few sections cover the various tools available for inspecting and cleaning up the file system.

The serious user or administrator should read the paper:

> FSCK - The UNIX File System Check Program
> by T. J. Kowalski,
>   Bell Laboratories,
>   Murray Hill, New Jersey 07974

This paper contains an excellent discussion of the UNIX file system, the things that can go wrong with it, and the things that a clever program (such as **fsck**) can do to help.

14.8.1 Checking the Integrity of a File System with 'fsck'

The **fsck** command is used to perform a file system check. There are other commands, namely **icheck**, **dcheck**, **ncheck**, and so on, which we describe below. These commands have been more or less overtaken by **fsck**. If you have **fsck** on your system, use it in preference to any of the others. It is more thorough, and can do a better job of recovering things if they are garbled.

Here is a typical **fsck** run:

```
# /etc/fsck
** Phase 1 - Check Blocks and Sizes
** Phase 2 - Check Pathnames
** Phase 3 - Check Connectivity
** Phase 4 - Check Reference Counts
** Phase 5 - Check Free List
#
```

As you can see from the example run above, **fsck** does its work in several phases. Contrary to most commands on the UNIX system, **fsck** is chatty and tells you what it is doing, so that you can respond intelligently. The separate phases do the following work:

1. this phase checks the consistency of i-nodes, such as link counts, i-node types, and i-node formats.

2. this phase checks for directories which point to i-nodes previously found to be in error.

3. this part of **fsck** determines errors resulting from unreferenced directories.

4. this part checks the consistency of the link counts in directories and files.

5. this phase checks for bad blocks in the free list, duplicate blocks in the free list, unused blocks which should be in the free list but aren't, and the total free block count.

In addition to the phases described above, there are some subsidiary phases (phase 1b for example) that are only called into play when a prior phase finds some error.

The **fsck** command checks several file systems by default. It always checks the root file system. You can tell it which other file systems to check by placing their names in the file */etc/checklist*.

In the example above, we showed a perfect **fsck** run, where it did not discover any problems. Now we are about to show the kinds of things that **fsck** can discover, what you can do about them, and what they mean.

```
# /etc/fsck
** Phase 1 - Check Blocks and Sizes
528627 BAD I=66
** Phase 2 - Check Pathnames
DUP/BAD  I=66   OWNER=root MODE=100755
SIZE=78409 MTIME=Feb 24 16:45 1982
FILE=/usr/src/sys/unix
REMOVE? y
** Phase 3 - Check Connectivity
** Phase 4 - Check Reference Counts
BAD/DUP  I=66   OWNER=root MODE=100755
SIZE=78409 MTIME=Feb 24 16:45 1982
FILE=/usr/src/sys/unix
CLEAR? y
UNREF FILE  I=361   OWNER=root MODE=100600
SIZE=0 MTIME=Feb 25 09:40 1982
RECONNECT? y
** Phase 5 - Check Free List
157 BLK(S) MISSING
BAD FREE LIST
SALVAGE? y
** Phase 6 - Salvage Free List
302 files 5833 blocks 371 free
#
```

This example was taken from a real UNIX system under development, where there were often "bugs" (mistakes) introduced, which mangled the file system.

In the above example, **fsck** has discovered a duplicate i-node for a file called *'unix'* in the directory */usr/src/sys.* This happened to be where the development work was being done. In this case, the super-user decided that that copy of *'unix'* was of no use, and told **fsck** to go ahead and clear the problem (the **"y"** responses in the dialog).

At the end of the run **fsck** decides that there are blocks missing from the free-list. It asks if the free-list is to be salvaged. Upon a positive response to this question, **fsck** goes ahead and salvages the free list. Note that there is then a Phase 6, which did not appear in a normal run of **fsck**.

At the end of an **fsck** run, there may be some messages which indicate the state of things. After a successful run (in which no errors were found), **fsck** prints a message to the effect:

```
N files B blocks F free
```

meaning that there were **N** files in a file system of **B** blocks, leaving **F** blocks free.

After a run of **fsck** where the file system had major surgery done, the message

```
***** BOOT UNIX (NO SYNC!) *****
```

may appear. This message means that the root file system or a mounted file system has been modified in some way. If the UNIX system is not immediately rebooted, the salvage job just done will be undone because of the in-memory copies of tables that the system keeps. In that case, you must reboot the system, *without* doing a **sync** command first (else the **sync** causes all the salvaged information to be overwritten).

14.8.2 The 'lost+found' Directory

The *'lost+found'* directory is an integral part of using the **fsck** program. There must be a *'lost+found'* directory in the root directory of each file system.

'lost+found' contains null file entries for use in recovery. When **fsck** finds directories which are not linked into the file system in a sane way, it links them into the *'lost+found'* directory instead.

On some systems there is a command called **mklost+found**, which creates this directory and its null entries.

14.8.3 Checking Integrity of a File
System with 'icheck'

The **icheck** command searches through a file system to verify the goodness or otherwise of that file system. In general, you won't have to run **icheck** if there is an **fsck** command on the system, but sometimes, you might have to run a stand-alone **icheck**. Be aware that the stand alone check programs are not as clever as **fsck**. For example, **icheck** believes silly block numbers.

Here is a typical **icheck** run on a device:

```
# /etc/icheck /dev/rrm0
/dev/rrm0:
files    345 (r=294, d=12, b=8, c=32)
used     6475 (i=172 ii=4, iii=0, d=6295)
free     3127
missing 0
#
```

icheck displays the following pieces of information:

1. The total number of files in that file system, plus the number of regular files, directories, block-special files, and character-special files.

2. The total number of blocks in use, plus the number of single-indirect blocks (i), double-indirect blocks (ii), triple-indirect blocks (iii), and directory blocks (d).

3. The number of free blocks.

4. The number of missing blocks.

14.8.4 Checking a Directory with 'dcheck'

The **dcheck** command checks the integrity of a directory. Here is a **dcheck** command in action:

```
# /etc/dcheck /dev/rrm2
/dev/rrm2:
         entries    link cnt
5211        1          0
#
```

What this display tells us is that i-node number 5211 has one entry, but zero links to it. As you will recall, an i-node represents a file in the system. Every file must have at least one link, which refers to the parent directory.

If an i-node is found with zero links, it may mean that there is something amiss in the file system. In that case you use the **ncheck** command to determine what file is supposed to be claiming that i-node.

14.8.5 Relating i-numbers to Filenames
with 'ncheck'

As we saw above, the **dcheck** command indicated that there is an i-node with a zero link count. This indicates that there is something potentially wrong, because every i-node should have at least one link.

We use **ncheck** here to find out what file is claiming that i-node.

```
# /etc/ncheck -i 5211 /dev/rrm2
/dev/rrm2:
5211      /aa/widget/hank/progs/old.roman.p
#
```

If you do not give any arguments to **ncheck**, it checks a predetermined set of file systems. In this case we only want one i-node, so we use the **-i** (for i-node) option to restrict the search to that specific i-node.

Here, **ncheck** informs us that the i-node in question belongs to the file *file /aa/widget/hank/progs/old.roman.p*

Since that i-node was seen to have zero links, we should get rid of that i-node. We do that job with the **clri** command, discussed next.

14.8.6 Clearing i-nodes with 'clri'

The **clri** command is a dangerous command which should be used with trepidation and care. **clri** writes zeros throughout the indicated i-nodes. The i-nodes are unallocatable for other purposes, and they are labelled as missing if you do an **icheck** of that file system, which is why programs like **fsck** exist.

In the case of our i-node with zero links from above, we must get rid of that i-node, like this:

```
# /etc/clri 5211
#
```

14.9 Other Administrative Topics

This section covers a few topics which do not fit in anywhere else.

14.9.1 Changing Terminal Characteristics

All the terminals which can log in to a UNIX system are described in a file called *letc/ttys*. Here is a typical *letc/ttys* file from a UNIX system which can handle a maximum of eight users:

```
# cat /etc/ttys
14console
13tty00
13tty01
13tty02
13tty03
13tty04
13tty05
12tty06
12tty07
12tty08
#
```

Ignoring the two digits at the start of each line for now, the names, "console" or "tty04", are the names of the actual devices as seen in the *ldev* directory.

The first digit on the line indicates whether the device is enabled. A 1 in this position enables the terminal, so that the **init** process watches that device. A 0 in this position disables that device.

The second digit refers to the way the system determines the baud rate for that device. Baud rates are assigned according to the following correspondence table:

   0   Hunt through 300-1200-150-110 Baud.

   —   On-line Teletype 33, usually an operator's console.

   1   150-Baud Teletype model 37.

   2   On-line 9600-Baud terminal.

   3   Hunts from 1200-Baud to 300-Baud and back.

   4   On-line DECWriter (LA36), usually an operator's console.

   5   Hunts from 300-Baud to 1200-Baud and back.

Your particular installation might do things differently, so you will have to check the installation information.

14.9.2 Running Periodic Jobs with 'cron'

The UNIX system provides for running tasks on a periodic basis. Way back in the start of this chapter, we showed a typical *letc/rc* file which the **init** process executes. One of the commands started at that time was **/etc/cron**. It is **cron** which performs tasks on a periodic basis.

The **cron** utility is a permanent process that wakes up once every minute. **cron** consults a file called */usr/lib/crontab* to find out what tasks are to be done, and when those tasks are to be done. If the time is right, as specified in the */usr/lib/crontab* file, **cron** starts the indicated task.

Here is a typical *'crontab'* file for a system:

```
# cat  /usr/lib/crontab
0     *   *   *   *   /bin/date > /dev/console
20    1   *   *   *   /bin/calendar -
0,10,20,30,40,50 * * * * /usr/lib/atrun
#
```

Each line in the *'crontab'* file consists of six fields. The last field is simple, being the command which is to be run. In the example above, you can see that the **date** command displays the date on the system console every now and again. The **calendar** command is run periodically, and the **atrun** command is also run on a periodic basis.

The other five fields on each line indicate when the jobs are to be done. All of the fields are separated by spaces or tabs, this is standard practice on the UNIX system.

The first field is a minutes field. It can take on values in the range 0 through 59.

The second field is an hours field, which can have values in the range 0 through 23.

The third field is a day of the month, in the range 1 through 31.

The fourth field is the month of the year, in the range 1 through 12.

The fifth field is a day of the week, in the range 1 through 7. Monday is day 1 in this scheme of things.

Any one of those fields can be a whole list of values, as shown in line 3 of the *'crontab'* file above. If the field contains an asterisk character * it means that the job is done for all possible values of the field. Finally, a value in a field can be a pair of numbers separated by a hyphen, which indicates that the job is to be done for all the times in the specified range.

Let us interpret the *'crontab'* file from the example above. The first line says that the **date** command displays the current date and time on the console at minute 0 of every hour of every day of every month. In other words, once every hour, on the hour, the date is printed on the console.

The second line runs the **calendar** command on behalf of the users at 20 minutes past one o'clock in the morning, on every day.

The third line says that the **atrun** command (which processes shell scripts which users have set up with **at**) is to be run every ten minutes. This is why the **at** command has a certain granularity in a given system.

If your system has any monitoring processes to do on a periodic basis, it is in */usr/lib/crontab* that the relevant conditions are set up. For example, you might have a program which runs once a day to find out how much storage all the users are using, so you can publish a "hog" list. You might place an entry in */usr/lib/crontab* that looks like this:

```
0       18      *       *       *       /admin/hogs
```

14.10 Looking After the UNIX System Manuals

As a system administrator, one of your duties might well be to keep the manuals up to date, and to add new entries as users add new tools and facilities to the system. This is a very important part of the administrator's job, since a system without documentation is a poor system indeed.

In general, all the UNIX Programmer's Manual lives on-line. Only on very small systems do the manuals have to be off-line on some backup storage device.

The *source* text for the manuals live on-line in various subdirectories of the */usr/man* directory. If you list the directory contents, here is what you see:

```
$ ls /usr/man
man0   man1   man2   man3   man4   man5   man6   man7   man8
$
```

We have assumed, for the purpose of the discussion, that the **ls** command displays many filenames on a line.

If you look further, you will find that the entries in */usr/man* are themselves directories. Each one of those directories corresponds to one section in the UNIX Programmer's Manual. In each of the directories is to be found the source text for the individual manual entries. Let us take a look at */usr/man/man1,* for example:

```
$ ls /usr/man/man1
ac.1m     cu.1c        intro.1      mv.1          roff.1     tk.1
adb.1     cwrite.1     iostat.1m    ncheck.1m     rtpip.1    touch.1
                       <etc...>
cpio.1    grep.1       mknod.1m     rev.1         test.1
crypt.1   icheck.1m    mount.1m     rm.1          time.1
$
```

We have not shown all the entries, just enough to give the flavor of things.

Each entry in the directory of */usr/man/man1* corresponds to the specific entry in the manual. Entries labelled '*whatever.1m*' are the entries for maintenance commands, such as **icheck**.

Some UNIX systems keep the formatted, ready-to-print, form of the manuals on-line as well as the source. If the formatted versions are on-line, they are usually found in the various subdirectories of the */usr/cat* directory. Again, there is a specific '*catx*' subdirectory for section "x" of the manual.

When a user calls up the **man** command, **man** first looks in the appropriate */usr/cat* subdirectory for the required manual entry. If it is not found there, **man** then looks in the appropriate */usr/man* subdirectory for the source. Having found the source of the manual entry, **man** then calls up **nroff** to format the manual on the fly.

The manual entries for the UNIX Programmer's Manual are, with very few exceptions, formatted in conjunction with the '*man*' macro package. To format one of the manual pages (for the **adb** command, say) you issue the following command:

```
$ nroff -man /usr/man/man1/adb.1 ¦ lpr
$
```

This example assumes that the formatted copy is to be sent straight to the line printer, hence the **lpr** command in the pipeline.

The '*man*' macro package is described (tersely) in section 7 of the UNIX Programmer's Manual. When you have to add new manual entries to the system, it is much easier to make a copy of an existing entry and hack it about, rather than trying to understand the '*man*' macro package from a cold start.

The exception to the use of the '*man*' macro package is that the sources in */usr/man/man0* require the **ms** macro package (described in chapter 10) in order to format.

14.11 Concluding Remarks on Administration

This chapter was intended to give you a feel for the kinds of things you need to know about managing a UNIX system installation. You should at least be aware that even when the system is running on a computer which fits on a desktop, it is not a simple system where you can just remove the floppy disks and turn off the power.

Obviously, we could not be specific in this chapter. We have given you enough information to be a menace to yourself and to others. If you have the job of system management, we recommend that you read the relevant sections of the UNIX Programmer's Manual. There is lots of helpful information in there. Make a special effort to absorb the sections called "boot" (how to boot the system), "crash" (what to do after a crash), and "init" (the system initialization process). Although these sections are often written for DEC PDP-11's, the generic information is useful.

Above all, have lots of fun with your UNIX system (we do!).

A Selected UNIX Bibliography

This appendix is a selected bibliography of literature relating to the UNIX system and its many utilities. This field is now so vast that a thorough bibliography would be a book in its own right, therefore this bibliography is intended to provide a bird's-eye view of the more relevant topics. Most of the documents noted here contain signposts to the rest of the available literature.

For a general overview of the UNIX system, the Bell System Technical Journal of July-August 1978 (volume 57, number 6, part 2) is almost entirely devoted to the system. Many of the papers mentioned in the sections to follow are from that book. In addition to the twenty or so good papers, the bibliographical entries in the book alone are worth the price ($2.00 last time we looked).

A.1 General UNIX System Literature

The UNIX Time-Sharing System by D.M. Ritchie and K. Thompson, Bell System Technical Journal, July-August 1978, Volume 57, Number 6, Part 2
A technical guide to major features of the UNIX system.

A User Guide to the UNIX System Jean Yates and Rebecca Thomas, Published by Osborne/McGraw Hill
A tutorial introduction to the 40 most-used UNIX system commands. Contains an extensive bibliography and list of vendors.

A Retrospective by D. M. Ritchie, Bell System Technical Journal, July-August 1978, Volume 57, Number 6, Part 2

UNIX For Beginners (Second Edition) by Brian W. Kernighan, Bell Laboratories, Murray Hill, New Jersey 07974.

Communicating with UNIX (A Tutorial in 5 sessions) by Ricki Blau, Computing Services, University of California, Berkeley, California 94720.

UNIX on a Microprocessor by H. Lycklama, Bell System Technical Journal, July-August 1978, Volume 57, Number 6, Part 2

A description of a UNIX system for a PDP LSI/11 with Floppy Disks

A.2 Editors and Text Manipulation

Edit: A Tutorial by Ricki Blau and James Joyce, Computing Services, University of California, Berkeley, California 94720.

Ex Reference Manual by William Joy, Computer Science Division, Department of Computer Science and Electrical Engineering, University of California, Berkeley, California 94720.

An Introduction to Display Editing with Vi by William N. Joy, Berkeley UNIX Programmers' Manual

A Tutorial Introduction to the UNIX Text Editor by Brian W. Kernighan, Bell Laboratories, Murray Hill, New Jersey 07974.

Advanced editing on UNIX by Brian W. Kernighan, Bell Laboratories, Murray Hill, New Jersey 07974.

Awk — A Pattern Scanning and Text Processing Language (Second Edition) by Alfred V. Aho, Brian W. Kernighan, and Peter J. Weinberger, Bell Laboratories, Murray Hill, New Jersey 07974.

The first edition of this paper appeared in Software — Practice and Experience, Volume 9, 1979.

SED — A Non-interactive Text Editor by Lee E. McMahon, Bell Laboratories, Murray Hill, New Jersey 07974.

A.3 Document Preparation and Writing Aids

Document Preparation by B. W. Kernighan, M. E. Lesk and J. F. Ossanna, Jr., Bell System Technical Journal, July-August 1978, Volume 57, Number 6, Part 2

NROFF/TROFF User's Manual by Joseph F. Ossanna, Bell Laboratories, Murray Hill, New Jersey 07974.

A TROFF Tutorial by Brian W. Kernighan, Bell Laboratories, Murray Hill, New Jersey 07974.

Typing Documents on the UNIX System: Using the −ms Macros with Troff and Nroff by M. E. Lesk, Bell Laboratories, Murray Hill, New Jersey 07974.

Document Formatting on UNIX Using the −ms Macros by Joel Kies, Computing Services, University of California, Berkeley, California 94720.

Writing Papers with NROFF Using −me by Eric P. Allman, Electronics Research Laboratory, University of California, Berkeley, California 94720.

A System for Typesetting Mathematics by Brian W. Kernighan and Lorinda L. Cherry, Bell Laboratories, Murray Hill, New Jersey 07974.

Tbl − A Program to Format Tables by M. E. Lesk, Bell Laboratories, Murray Hill, New Jersey 07974.

A.4 Programming the Shell

The UNIX Shell by S. R. Bourne, Bell System Technical Journal, July-August 1978, Volume 57, Number 6, Part 2
Introduces the "Bourne Shell" and how to program it.

An Introduction to the C shell by William N. Joy Computer Science Division, Department of Electrical Engineering and Computer Science University of California at Berkeley

PWB/UNIX Shell Tutorial by John R. Mashey, Bell Laboratories, Murray Hill, New Jersey 07974.

A.5 Software Development Tools

The UNIX Programming Environment Brian W. Kernighan and John R. Mashey, Software − Practice and Experience, Volume 9, 1979.

The Programmer's Workbench − A Machine for Software Development by Evan L. Ivie, Communications of the ACM, Volume 20, number 10, October 1977.

Language Development Tools by S. C. Johnson and M. E. Lesk, Bell System Technical Journal, July-August 1978, Volume 57, Number 6, Part 2

The Programmer's Workbench by T. A. Dolotta, R. C. Haight and J. R. Mashey, Bell System Technical Journal, July-August 1978, Volume 57, Number 6, Part 2

UNIX Programming − Second Edition by Brian W. Kernighan and Dennis M. Ritchie, Bell Laboratories, Murray Hill, New Jersey 07974.

The C Programming Language by Brian W. Kernighan and Dennis M. Ritchie, Prentice-Hall Incorporated, Englewood Cliffs, New Jersey 07632.
Also see: The C Programming Language − Reference Manual, by Dennis M. Ritchie, Bell Laboratories, Murray Hill, New Jersey 07974.

Lint, a C Program Checker by S. C. Johnson, Bell Laboratories, Murray Hill, New Jersey 07974.

Make − A Program for Maintaining Computer Programs by Stuart I. Feldman, Bell Laboratories, Murray Hill, New Jersey 07974.
This article also appeared in Software − Practice and Experience, Volume 9, 1979

A Tutorial Introduction to ADB by J.F. Maranzano and S.R. Bourne, Bell Laboratories, Murray Hill, New Jersey 07974.

The Source Code Control System by Marc J. Rochkind, IEEE Transactions on Software Engineering Volume SE-1, Number 4, December 1975, pp364-370

Berkeley Pascal PX Implementation Notes by William N. Joy and M. Kirk McKusick, Computer Science Division, Department of Electrical Engineering and Computer Science University of California at Berkeley

Lex — A Lexical Analyzer Generator by M.E. Lesk and E. Schmidt, Bell Laboratories, Murray Hill, New Jersey 07974.

Yacc: Yet Another Compiler-Compiler by Stephen C. Johnson, Bell Laboratories, Murray Hill, New Jersey 07974.

The M4 Macro Processor by Brian W. Kernighan and Dennis M. Ritchie, Bell Laboratories, Murray Hill, New Jersey 07974.

A Portable Fortran 77 Compiler by S.I. Feldman and P.J. Weinberger, Bell Laboratories, Murray Hill, New Jersey 07974.

RATFOR — A Preprocessor for a Rational Fortran by Brian W. Kernighan, Bell Laboratories, Murray Hill, New Jersey 07974.

A.6 UNIX System Maintenance

Setting Up UNIX — Seventh Edition by Charles B. Haley and Dennis M. Ritchie, Bell Laboratories, Murray Hill, New Jersey 07974.

Regenerating System Software by Charles B. Haley and Dennis M. Ritchie, Bell Laboratories, Murray Hill, New Jersey 07974.

FSCK — The UNIX File System Check Program by T.J. Kowalski Bell Laboratories, Murray Hill, New Jersey 07974.

Recommended for anyone using the **fsck** utility.

A.7 Miscellaneous Literature

The UNIX Programming Environment by Brian W. Kernighan and John R. Mashey, Computer Magazine, Volume 14, number 4, April 1981.

Document Formatting Systems: Surveys, Concepts and Issues by Richard Furuta, Jeffrey Scofield, and Alan Shaw, Department of Computer Science, University of Washington, Seattle, Washington 98195.

A general survey of formatters, with much comment on the UNIX system formatting tools.

The Elements of Programming Style by Brian W. Kernighan and P.J. Plauger, McGraw-Hill Book Company.

Special attention should be given to the chapter entitled "Efficiency and Instrumentation"

Index